International Equity Exchange-Traded Funds

Tomasz Miziołek · Ewa Feder-Sempach · Adam Zaremba

International Equity Exchange-Traded Funds

Navigating Global ETF Market Opportunities and Risks

palgrave
macmillan

Tomasz Miziołek
Department of International Finance and Investments
University of Lodz
Lodz, Poland

Ewa Feder-Sempach
Department of International Finance and Investments
University of Lodz
Lodz, Poland

Adam Zaremba
Montpellier Business School
Montpellier, France

Poznan University of Economics and Business
Poznan, Poland

ISBN 978-3-030-53863-7 ISBN 978-3-030-53864-4 (eBook)
https://doi.org/10.1007/978-3-030-53864-4

This Palgrave Macmillan imprint is published by the registered company Springer Nature Switzerland AG
The registered company address is: Gewerbestrasse 11, 6330 Cham, Switzerland

Preface

"There is no place like home". We say these words when we return home after a long absence. This usually happens when we come back from shorter or longer trips, often abroad.

"My home is my castle". This is what we say when we want to express the conviction that we feel most secure in the place we know well—it is usually our home.

Our home, neighborhood, city, region, and finally our country is therefore our "comfort zone". It is because we are familiar with this place, we feel confident and it provides emotional comfort.

From time to time, some forces make us leave our "nest" and—in a more or less risky manner—embark on a journey. Why? Certainly, there are many reasons, yet they can be reduced to the following statement: we wish to experience something new, unknown, which (more or less consciously) will bring us satisfaction, joy, provide emotional benefits, enrich us spiritually and sometimes materially. Although we are usually aware of existing threats or dangers even, we take this challenge, believing that such a journey will contribute to our self-development, turn us into more valuable people.

It is no different when it comes to investing. Most of us usually invest exclusively "at home", i.e. on the domestic market. This is confirmed by many studies on the phenomenon of "home bias", which is a consequence of the availability heuristics known from behavioral finances. This simplified inference method, consisting in assigning greater probability to the events that are easier to bring to mind and are more charged emotionally, prompts investors to invest excessively in domestic assets at the expense of foreign assets. This is part of a wider phenomenon known as "familiarity bias", i.e. a tendency to invest in well-known assets and aversion to acquiring stocks with foreign exposure.

This behavior is perfectly understandable. We invest in companies that are familiar to us—though this is not necessarily always the case—because of the fact that they originate from our country, their shares are listed on the domestic stock exchange, and their products or services are most accessible to us. On the other hand, we avoid investing in foreign assets, which in our opinion are less attractive than domestic ones. Paradoxically, we resign from investing capital on foreign markets as we are apprehensive about the unknown, while simultaneously we often buy products derived from abroad.

Let us emphasize again: although from the behavioral finance perspective our conduct in this regard is justified, it is noteworthy that by limiting investments only to the domestic market, we actually deprive ourselves of the opportunities related to the advantages offered by other markets. This compels us to be more involved, leave the current "comfort zone", and even take a risk—just like when we decide to explore other countries or regions of the world on our own. However, as experience shows, such an effort is usually rewarded. When investing, the main reward is a more diversified investment portfolio, more resistant to all sorts of shocks or market turbulences. Furthermore, diversifying the portfolio by investing a portion of capital in foreign markets reduces the risk associated with business cycles. By investing in shares of companies from various markets with different business cycles, we avoid exposure to those countries whose economies are currently entering a slowdown phase or even recession. In addition, by expanding the spectrum of investment in international stocks, we gain the opportunity to benefit from very profitable industries that are not represented on our local market.

Although the awareness of potential benefits offered by international investments has been developing in investors for some time, their capitalizing posed many problems. Both legal restrictions on capital flows, technical and institutional obstacles stood in the way. On the other hand conditions for making financial transactions on the global capital market have improved significantly over the past few decades. This results mainly from the liberalization of capital flows (though it does not apply to all countries yet) as well as revolutionary and disruptive technological changes that enabled relatively quick, simple and cheap foreign investments and facilitated access to information from various markets.

All these factors have undoubtedly played a very important role; still they would be insufficient, were it not for the financial innovations that have appeared on the financial market in recent decades. For the first time, many of those innovations allowed to disseminate international investing, even though they had a fairly limited range as they were addressed mainly to wealthy individuals with investment experience and to professional financial institutions. Stock market lacked a financial instrument that would be available to a wide range of people, easy to use, understandable in its functioning, liquid and cheap.

A breakthrough in this respect was made in the 1990s. First on the North American stock exchanges (in Canada and the USA), then in Asia-Pacific region, and in the early 2000s in Europe and other regions of the world, a financial instrument fulfilling the above expectations appeared. Currently, from the perspective of 30 years since the launch of the first exchange-traded fund, it can be said with complete confidence that it has become the most significant financial innovation of the last decades, the one that has revolutionized the world of investments.

There are many reasons why ETFs are widely recognized as a breakthrough investment solution. First of all, they combine the best features of index funds (passively managed diversified investment portfolio, relatively low costs and often better performance—especially in the long-term—in comparison with actively managed funds) and stocks listed on the stock exchange (intraday trading, price transparency and multiple applications). Among many advantages, the most important one might be the fact that the ETF—like probably no other financial instrument recently—has democratized investing. It is available both to large, professional investors, for whom it can be an alternative or complement to existing investment solutions, as well as to retail investors, who often have limited possibilities of using some potentially attractive financial instruments. Meanwhile, ETFs provide both groups of investors—from various parts of the world and on similar conditions—with access to a variety of asset classes (equities, fixed income, commodities, alternatives) and investment themes, offer versatile applications (tactical and strategic) and enable international investing. Thus, equity portfolio diversification from international perspective has become as easy as never before.

Through one simple transaction, made either by using one's own brokerage account or by financial institutions, investors can buy a diversified basket of stocks and equity-like instruments from a specific country, region or the ones with the global exposure. In the case of the most developed ETF markets, this can be done domestically, while in the case of other countries it is possible by investing in foreign stock exchanges. What is more, we are often offered diverse investment strategies at our disposal, especially when we want to achieve exposure to the largest country markets or developed markets. We can invest in plain vanilla ETFs, tracking the indexes weighted by market capitalization, funds using other weighing methods or in the ETFs replicating the smart beta indexes, being an intermediate link between passive and active investing. Finally, we can invest in shares of large, medium or small companies, value or growth stocks, or we can target investments sectorally by choosing equities from a specific industry or representing a given investment theme.

International equity ETFs allow to choose a particular geographical exposure desired by an investor. They provide access to a given country, to group of countries being part of a specific geographical region, to group of countries with a similar level of economic and financial market development, or to a global opportunity set. Investors may also buy international ETFs that are hedged against the risk of currency fluctuations.

The versatile and diverse possibilities offered by international equity ETFs have fostered their use by individual investors, financial advisors as well as various types of institutional investors, including mutual funds, pension funds, sovereign wealth funds, even hedge funds. They are typically used as a supplement to the international investment portfolio ("satellite"), though they can also be an essential part of it ("core"). For financial institutions, they are applied to achieve long-term allocation, but more often for short-term portfolio management (e.g. cash equitization, manager transitions, portfolio rebalancing, portfolio completion, liquidity sleeves). Financial institutions can also use international equity ETFs to generate an extra return, and thus mitigate tracking difference, by lending out their shares. Regardless of the motives behind and purposes of ETFs' use, they are now an inseparable part of the portfolios of numerous investors seeking investment opportunities outside their own backyard.

Exchange-traded funds, including international equity ETFs, are obviously not free from drawbacks. When investing, we must be aware of the various risks associated with their use, especially those resulting from their international exposure. Therefore, the basic objective of our book is both to present the advantages that result from investing in these financial instruments, and to provide a deep insight into different types of risk that accompany them and present some rules of thumb to navigate among them. Practical tips that can be found in the book include those related to strictly technical aspects of investing in ETFs (e.g. regarding order placing), as well as those resulting from specificity of funds with international exposure (including their valuation, liquidity, and currency risk hedging). Through profound knowledge and better understanding of the nuances (often intricate and difficult) regarding the functioning and trading of international equity ETFs, investors can not only mitigate the risk, but also the total cost of investing. Those who are already using ETFs in practice, will be able to take full advantage of the opportunities offered by these instruments. For those, in turn, who have not used them so far or have done it occasionally, getting acquainted with their merits may prove to be an impulse, at least, to consider including them in their own portfolio or their clients' portfolios.

Although our book provides arguments to both groups, we would like to emphasize the fact that the final investment decision belongs to the investors themselves. The diversification of the equity portfolio through international ETFs—like any other financial investment—should be an informed decision, based on one's own detailed analysis of potential pros and cons.

The book consists of four parts divided into nine chapters.

The first part is devoted to international investments and diversification.

Chapter 1 presents the economic foundation of international equity investments. First, foreign investment opportunities and then international parity and inflation relationships, as well as exchange rate issues—mostly currency exposure and hedging against exchange rate movements—are discussed. All of them are crucial for cross-border investments. This chapter also provides monetary variables and their impact on investments, international asset pricing, and the global investment structure to help the reader understand the complex international environment. It also describes the home bias issue and market segmentation theory. It is devoted to the practical problem of the international investment strategy, and it attempts to apply psychological concepts to avoid suboptimal asset allocation.

Chapter 2 presents the modern portfolio theory from the theoretical perspective. It is demonstrated how investors may choose the optimal portfolio out of different sets of portfolios, considering risk and return characteristics. This chapter introduces the primary relationship between the rate of return and risk with the first well-known model of market equilibrium: the capital asset pricing model (CAPM). Furthermore, the chapter discusses potential benefits derived from international diversification and the idea of regional diversification. The main aim of the chapter is to provide knowledge of the portfolio theory to help investors cope with this demanding task.

The second part of the book focuses on exchange-traded funds' fundamentals, including special features of those funds that are exposed to international equities.

Chapter 3 outlines the most important formal and investment characteristics of ETFs. It discusses legal aspects regarding these financial instruments, in relation both to the U.S. market and to other highly developed financial markets. This is followed by the issues that are in the spotlight of the investors and advisors using ETFs, related mainly to index-tracking. Among them, there are presented the two basic methods of index replication—physical (direct) and synthetic (swap-based), as well as securities lending. Additionally, there is also thorough characteristics of various types of risk faced by investors, resulting from index tracking and securities lending, as well as the presentation of costs associated with these practices.

Chapter 4 describes microstructure and mechanics of ETFs. First, the launch of an ETF, creation and redemption of ETF shares, and ETF share pricing and valuation are shown. Next, we thoroughly explain and discuss the most important issues related to the primary and secondary ETF markets. They are focused chiefly on the liquidity of these financial instruments, and various risks and costs arising from it. Since investing in ETFs requires also in-depth knowledge in the field of best practices concerning execution and trading, many practical rules are also discussed, including those regarding investing in international markets.

The subject matter of the third part of the book comprises various forms of investing via international equity ETFs.

Chapter 5 is devoted to global equity ETFs, permitting investors to obtain the broadest and often the most diverse possible exposure to the global stock market through listed passive instruments. It provides rationales for global geographical portfolio diversification, based on the results of numerous studies, but also outlines the potential threats arising from this approach. This chapter also describes selected broad global equity indexes offering the highest degree of portfolio diversification—in terms of countries, sectors, and individual holdings. Finally, there are presented some investment opportunities related to global equity ETFs, mostly tracking broad global indexes comprising stocks from both developed and emerging countries.

Chapter 6 focuses on regional equity ETFs that are an indirect investment solution between global and single-country funds. We discuss pros and cons of regional diversification, paying particular attention to benefits and drawbacks of this form of investment, characterized by a huge variety. As it is investing in countries according to their economic and financial status that constitutes the most popular and widespread form of regional ETFs, the characteristics of investing on developed, emerging and frontier markets is described in detail. Furthermore, the chapter discusses major indexes and ETFs investing within a given geographical region (or its part), as well as within a specified group of countries (e.g. EMU, ASEAN, BRIC).

Chapter 7 aims to provide a deep insight into single-country ETFs. As investing in stocks from a particular country via ETFs seems to be the most convenient and the simplest way of targeted international diversification of the equity portfolio, it is widespread in almost every latitude. This is also the case because of the easiest access to these funds and their immense selection. The chapter starts with the characteristics of the most significant practical aspects and nuances that should be considered when realizing this type of international exposure. Moreover, there is a description of selected investment opportunities within this category, available to investors worldwide, broken down into funds enabling exposure to country equity markets in Americas, EMEA and Asia-Pacific regions.

Chapter 8 presents two narrow-focused investment solutions available on international equity markets—sector ETFs and thematic ETFs. Despite the geographical diversification of their portfolios, investors usually bear higher risk when investing in these funds than when applying other forms of international investing. This happens due to high concentration on a specific sector or investment theme. In return, however, one may expect a reward in the form of a higher rate of return. The chapter outlines the most important types of sector ETFs, based on commonly used sector classifications (GICS and ICB), and thematic ETFs employing the most popular investment ideas.

The last part of the book discusses the ETFs' investment strategies.

Chapter 9 of the book focuses on the crafting of effective capital allocation strategies in the ETF universe. The last three decades saw an enormous proliferation of investment opportunities in ETF markets. This was followed by the mounting evidence regarding the cross-sectional predictability of country equity returns. The studies not only documented country-level counterparts of well-established stock-level anomalies, such as size, value, or momentum, but also demonstrated some unique return-predicting signals such as fund flows or political regimes. Nonetheless, different studies vary remarkably in terms of their dataset and methods employed. Hence, Chapter 9 aims to provide a comprehensive review of the current literature on the cross-section of country equity returns. We focus on three particular aspects of the asset pricing literature. First, we study the choice of the dataset and sample preparation methods. Next, we survey different aspects of methodological approaches. Last but not least, we review the country-level equity anomalies discovered so far. The discussed cross-sectional return patterns not only provide new insights into international asset pricing but they can also be potentially translated into effective country allocation strategies.

When writing this book, not only did we strive to include a lot of information useful to the people interested in investing in international equity ETFs, but we also wanted our considerations and analyzes to be evidence-based, thus making them reliable. Therefore, we used the most recognized sources—both academic and professional literature. Among them, one can find books on international investments and exchange-traded funds, valued financial academic journals, as well as studies, reports and commentaries from many different entities, including leading ETF sponsors and index providers, companies monitoring ETF market, major international financial institutions, financial watchdogs, associations representing regulated funds, stock exchanges, and other market participants.

In each case, we have made every effort to ensure that each information, analysis and research represents the highest substantive level and reliability at present. However, we are aware that the timeliness of some data presented in the book may already be disputable at the moment of the book's publication. This is a natural consequence of every publishing process and it cannot be avoided. Therefore, we encourage you to reach for the primary sources indicated in the book. With regard to ETFs, we have tried to present the analyzed issues from a long-term, historical perspective.

While preparing the book, we also tried to make it interesting, inspiring, as well as understandable and easy to read for different groups of readers. Therefore, the publication is addressed to those who have been using ETFs (including international equity ETFs) in their investment practice for many years. We hope that they will find many aspects of investing in these financial instruments, rarely described so far. Still, we also address it to the people who have not invested in ETFs up to now, or who have done it rarely, mostly in relation to domestic equity ETFs. We believe that thanks to our book they will find convincing arguments both for international portfolio diversification and for the use of ETFs for this purpose.

The addressees of the book also comprise the people who professionally deal with international equity ETFs. This applies, though not limited, to employees of ETF sponsors, index suppliers, analytical companies, data providers, authorized participants, market makers, liquidity providers and other ETF market participants. We hope that this book will prove useful to financial advisors providing services for their clients, robo-advisors, and all entities who want to effectively manage their clients' funds. Finally, we want it to be used by researchers and academics dealing with international investments.

In the end, we want to stress that the international dimension of the book is not limited only to its investment exposure. We believe that the book will meet expectations of the readers from different corners of the world. Although, the perspective of American and European investor dominated the book, but the reader can also find many references to all ETF markets worldwide. We wanted the publication to be as universal as possible so that it could be used by all investors regardless of their country of origin. This was not always possible, concerning the diversity of legal, institutional and even terminological solutions applied in individual regions of the world.

We hope that our book will bridge a gap in the publishing market and meet with a favorable reception from readers. Against the background of the fast-growing literature on exchange-traded funds, usually focusing on domestic investing, our book provides a profound insight into theoretical and practical aspects of investing in international equity ETFs. We are aware that it does not exhaust all possible issues related to this segment of the ETF market. We will therefore be grateful for all constructive comments on the content, which will allow us to improve it in the future perspective.

This publication is a result of the authors' combined efforts and continuous exchange of ideas over the course of years. Naturally, any possible errors are entirely our own. Likewise, all views and opinions presented in the book are ours.

Lodz, Poland — Tomasz Miziołek
Lodz, Poland — Ewa Feder-Sempach
Montpellier, France — Adam Zaremba

Acknowledgments

So many people have helped us to write this book. We would like to begin with Tula Weis, Senior Editor and Lucy Kidwell, Assistant Editor, and all the staff at Palgrave Macmillan for their assistance and commitment. Thank you sincerely for your continuous support, feedback, and professional management of the publishing process. It was a great pleasure to work with you.

Special thanks should be given to the peer reviewers, Michael C. Thomsett and David Abner, and the proofreaders. The quality of the final version would be significantly lower without their assistance.

We would like to thank our Dean, Professor Rafał Matera, from the University of Lodz for his positive attitude and endorsement. We are also extremely grateful to Mark Muirhead for helping us to improve our English writing skills and style.

We also give the credit to our colleagues in academia, and the exchange-traded fund industry for their insights and mentorship.

As it has been, and always will be, our heartfelt gratitude to our families for their love, support, patience and understanding during the book writing process.

Contents

List of Figures

List of Tables

Part I

International Investments

1

The Economics of the International Market

1.1 Introduction

International investing has exploded in popularity in recent years. There have been several major trends in global markets that have made foreign financial markets more welcome. The first one is growing global integration, which has created new opportunities both for investors and issuers who want to raise capital across national borders. The second one is the increasing importance of multinational financial corporations as facilitators of international investment products in host countries in different parts of the world. The third and final trend is the integration of the money and capital markets in European Union (EU) countries to remove market imperfections that impede the flow of international capital worldwide.

Every international investor should be aware of all the benefits and constraints that come from the international marketplace. Investing in an international financial market is not easy due to culture shock, which is mostly caused by different institutions, procedures, and traditions. However, many barriers to international investment exist besides the lack of knowledge investors may have, like psychological, political, or legal restrictions. The main aim of this chapter is to familiarize the reader with the international financial markets and the economic rules that could potentially help to achieve expected rates of return.

T. Miziołek et al., *International Equity Exchange-Traded Funds*,
https://doi.org/10.1007/978-3-030-53864-4_1

1.2 Foreign Investment Opportunities

International portfolio investments are an everyday practice for institutional investors all over the world. Many individual and institutional investors have more than half of their portfolio assets abroad. The mere size of foreign capital markets justifies international diversification, even for American or European investors. If the world's capital market were fully efficient, buying internationally diversified portfolios would be a suitable behavior. However, we are aware that no fully integrated international capital market exists, even in the EU, and that some constraints may be present. International investments offer expected additional profit because investors may reduce portfolio risk, and risk-adjusted performance may be enhanced. Every domestic security tends to behave in the same way because it is affected by the country's economic conditions—interest rates, money supply, unemployment, budget deficit, and GDP growth. This causes a strong positive correlation between the different equity types traded in one market and is why many investors have tried to diversify this risk using international financial markets.

International capital markets should be independent; otherwise, diversification opportunities would not exist. An example of the impression of the independence of international capital markets could be the performance of major stock indices from different parts of the world, from 1989 to 2019, and the **correlation coefficients** between them (see Fig. 1.1 and Table 1.1).

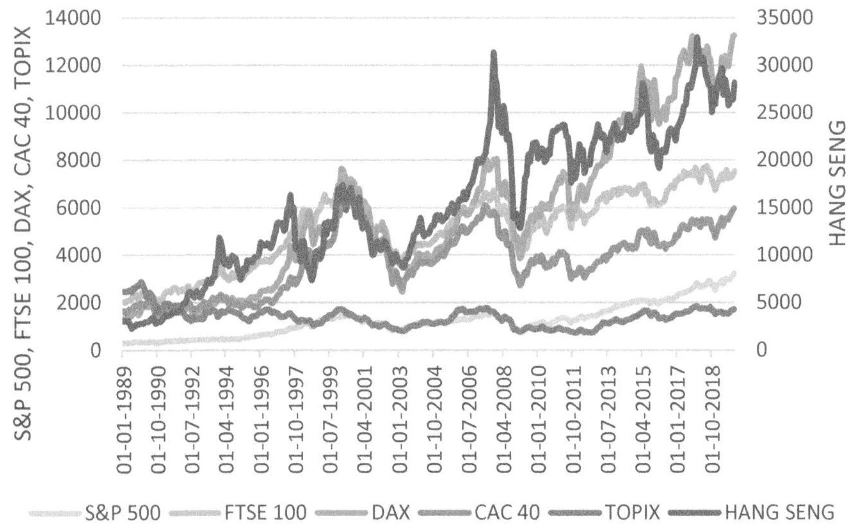

Fig. 1.1 Major stock markets indices, 1989–2019 (points) (*Source* Thomson Reuters EIKON)

Table 1.1 Correlation matrix: major stock market indices between 1989 and 2019 (monthly logarithmic returns)

	S&P 500 USA	FTSE 100 UK	DAX DE	CAC 40 FR	TOPIX JP	HANG SENG CN
S&P 500 USA	1.00	0.77	0.73	0.73	0.50	0.61
FTSE 100 UK	0.77	1.00	0.74	0.79	0.46	0.59
DAX DE	0.73	0.74	1.00	0.87	0.48	0.54
CAC 40 FR	0.73	0.79	0.87	1.00	0.51	0.53
TOPIX JP	0.50	0.46	0.48	0.51	1.00	0.40
HANG SENG CN	0.61	0.59	0.54	0.53	0.40	1.00

Source Own calculations based on Thomson Reuters EIKON data

According to Table 1.1, the correlation coefficients between major international stock market returns in the last thirty-one years may have changed over the period, but still they are far from unity. The correlation between American and European stock returns is quite strong but when considering American or European and Asian stock returns it is much weaker. Interestingly, the correlation coefficient between the Japanese TOPIX and the Chinese HANG SENG is 0.40, and it is the lowest value. Not surprisingly, the strongest correlation coefficient is between the German DAX and the French CAC40, which is 0.87, and these countries are closely linked. This is caused by strong economic integration and collaboration. This table shows that international portfolio managers have many diversification opportunities throughout the different stock markets. Low correlation across different stock markets is the main idea of international portfolio diversification and global stock exposure. The results of many studies show that, compared to the domestic portfolio approach, international diversification has potential benefits.

The independence level of a country's stock market is closely related to government policies and the independence of the economy. To some extent, global factors could influence national companies and their stock prices, but purely national factors seem to play a major role in asset pricing. In particular, it depends on the company's size and level of internationalization. Constraints and legal regulations imposed by the government, fiscal and monetary policy, the stage of technological advancement, and cultural and sociological inequalities all contribute to the independence of the country's stock market.

By contrast, we should consider globalization processes and international economic integration, mostly in European countries. The harmonization of economic policy within the EU has had a considerable impact on the economies of member countries, and economic integration among euro area countries has important consequences for the factors driving asset returns in financial markets. Some recent research even showed that diversification over industries yields more efficient portfolios than diversification over Eurozone countries (Moerman 2004).

Many studies have been carried out to assess the level of international correlation coefficients between single-country stock markets at the European and American levels. One was conducted by Gilmore and McManus (2002), who compared the US stock market and three Central European markets. They revealed that US investors could obtain benefits from international diversification into these markets, apart from the Polish and Hungarian markets, in which stock returns were positively correlated.

There are also studies that tried to find leads or lags between single-country stock markets. The relationship between emerging and emerged markets was analyzed by Ullah and Ullah (2016), who stated that an emerging market's volatility could be explained by an emerged market's volatility. Thus, their overall results support the existence of a lead-lag relationship between selected emerging and emerged stock market indices. Another study was carried out by Wong et al. (2004), who used the concept of cointegration to investigate the existence of co-movement between stock markets in major developed countries and in Asian emerging economies. They found increasing interdependence between the majority of developed and emerging markets after the Stock Market Crash in 1987, and this interdependence intensified after the Asian Financial Crisis in 1997. Because this increasing co-movement between developed and emerging stock markets was observed, it could mean that the benefits of international diversification become smaller. However, no evidence of continued delayed[1] of one national stock market to another has been revealed so far.

In general, one can establish the following stylized facts regarding **international stock return movements** based on the work of Bekaert et al. (2005), who studied weekly portfolio returns from 23 developed markets:

[1]Continued delayed—lasting delayed, the same pattern of co-movement.

- There is no evidence for an overall upward trend in return correlations, except for European stock market returns. They stressed that correlation coefficients are not the perfect measure, and they could rise because of changes in many financial determinants.
- They recognized that there was something like an excessive correlation period, which they referred to as the contagion effect. It means that correlations in times of crisis may be problematic and over-exaggerated.
- They recognized that globalization and integration processes would lead to increased correlations across the stock returns of different countries, reducing potential diversification benefits.
- They recognized that globalization processes increase country stock return correlations while causing more distinct pricing of industry-specific factors, lowering the correlations between industry portfolios. Many investors have observed the increasing importance of industry factors relative to country factors, but it was a transient, temporary phenomenon.
- They recognized that globalization has led correlations of large-company stocks to be increasingly higher across countries while correlations for small-company stocks remain relatively low. It could be explained by the fact that international investors buy large stocks of well-known companies.
- There is no evidence for a trend in idiosyncratic (specific) risk in any of the countries they examined.
- There is no evidence of lasting delayed of one national stock market to another.

1.3 International Parity Conditions

Any investor who is attracted by international investment benefits, as well as better performance, has to convert the prices of foreign assets into the home currency using exchange rates. Returns on foreign financial markets are directly affected by international currency movements and indirectly by the reaction of asset values to exchange rate adjustments. It means that asset prices, exchange rates, and interest rates are complex and mutually related. Indeed, to invest across national borders, investors have to be familiar with the simple model of the international environment, which is useful for analyzing relationships between global financial variables. The international parity relationships are:

- Purchasing Power Parity,
- The International Fisher Relation,

- Foreign Exchange Expectations,
- Interest Rate Parity (Solnik 1988).

Purchasing Power Parity (PPP) is a widely used and very well-known relationship based on the law of one price. If there are identical products or services in different markets without any restrictions, the price of the product or service should be the same. If the products or services are traded in two different countries, the price may be stated in different currency terms, but the price should be the same. Price comparison requires conversion from one currency to another using the exchange rate.

PPP theory has two versions—Absolute PPP and Relative PPP. The former states that the equilibrium exchange rate between two currencies is equal to the ratio of price levels in two different countries (Salvatore 2007). In other words, it means that the spot exchange rate is determined by the relative prices of similar products or services. If one compares two identical goods denominated in different currencies, one could determine the real—PPP exchange rate, on condition that both markets are efficient. It means that, according to the law of one price, any goods or services should have the same price in both currencies expressed in terms of one of the currencies so that the purchasing power parity of two currencies is at parity.

The latter, Relative PPP, states that the change in exchange rates over a specific period should be proportional to the relative change in the price levels in two countries over the same period (Salvatore 2007). It is important to remember that if absolute PPP holds, relative PPP also holds; however, even if relative PPP holds, the absolute PPP does not always hold. What is more, not all goods and services can be traded on international markets. There are nontraded goods whose transportation costs are too high to take part in international cooperation, as well as nontraded services, like family doctors or advisors.

In general, PPP states that spot exchange rates adjust to inflation differentials. If prices rise in one country in relation to another, then the country's exchange rate has to depreciate to make the level of prices in the two countries similar for the same goods or services. If trade between nations was instant, at no cost, and with no barriers, one might expect the exchange rate to offset any inflation differential. This relationship could be written as follows (Solnik 1988):

$$\frac{S_1}{S_0} = \frac{1 + I_f}{1 + I_d};$$

where:

S_1—spot exchange rate at the end of the period,
S_0—spot exchange rate at the beginning of the period,
I_f—inflation rate in the foreign country over the period,
I_d—inflation rate in the domestic country over the period.

This is why inflation differentials could explain the movements in exchange rates in the long run.[2] Many extensive tests of PPP have been carried out, but most of them did not prove the PPP theory in predicting futures exchange rates. In general, it works over the very long run but poorly for shorter time horizons, and better for countries with relatively high rates of inflation and underdeveloped financial markets (Eiteman et al. 2016).

PPP theory is of major importance for international portfolio management because it states that the real rate of the return on assets is identical for any investor from any country worldwide. It explains how the prices of goods in different countries should be related through exchange rates. Now, we have to examine how interest rates are linked with exchange rates. The **International Fisher Relation** or International Fisher Effect[3] explains the percentage change in the spot exchange rate over a time period and the differential between comparable interest rates in different national financial markets. The International Fisher Relation states that the spot exchange rate should change in an equal amount but in the opposite direction to the difference in interest rates in two different countries (Eiteman et al. 2016). This relationship could be written as follows:

$$\frac{S_1}{S_0} = \frac{1 + r_d}{1 + r_f};$$

$$\frac{S_1 - S_0}{S_0} = \frac{r_d - r_f}{1 + r_f} = r_d - r_f;$$

where:

S_1—spot exchange rate at the end of the period,
S_0—spot exchange rate at the beginning of the period,
r_f—interest rate in the foreign country over the period,
r_d—interest rate in the domestic country over the period.

[2]Clark et al. (1994) showed that it can take from three to twelve years for exchange rates to convert to purchasing power parity.

[3]Sometimes called the Fisher-open.

One explanation for the International Fisher Relation is that international investors should be rewarded or punished to offset the expected change in the exchange rate.

International Fisher Effect theory is of major importance for international portfolio management because it states that real interest rates are stable and equal across countries, so interest rate differentials are caused by the different expectations of national inflation rates. Differences in real interest rates could motivate international capital flows to take advantage of the differentials.

Many empirical tests of the International Fisher Effect have shown some short-term deviations, which could be explained by speculation motives. Thus, the expected change in exchange rates might be greater than the difference in exchange rates.

Foreign Exchange Expectations, or forward rates, are exchange rates quoted today for settlement at a future date, i.e., they are a forward exchange agreement. This agreement between currencies states a rate of exchange at which a foreign currency will be bought or sold forward at a specific date in the future. Forward rates are usually used by portfolio managers as a forecast.

The Foreign Exchange Expectations relationship states that the forward exchange rate at time zero for delivery at time one is equal to the expected value of the spot exchange rate at time one (Solnik 1988). This relationship could be written as follows:

$$F = E(S_1);$$

where:

F—the forward exchange rate.

This formula for Foreign Exchange Expectations could be stated relative to the current spot exchange rate; the current spot exchange rate is known with certainty. If we subtract S_0 on both sides of our equitation and then divide by S_0, we get:

$$\frac{F - S_0}{S_0} = E\frac{S_1 - S_0}{S_0};$$

$$\frac{F}{S_0} - 1 = \frac{E(S_1)}{S_0} - 1.$$

The left-hand side of the equitation is known as the forward discount or premium. It is defined as the percentage deviation of the forward rate from the current spot rate, so it means that the forward discount (premium) is equal to the expected exchange rate movement. Overall, the premium or discount is a percentage difference between the spot and forward exchange rates.

This relationship states that there is no reward for bearing foreign exchange risk. If a risk premium were to be added to the relationship, the symmetry means that it would be paid by some investors and received by others. From the international portfolio management perspective, a zero-risk premium means that the use of forward currency contracts to hedge the exchange rate risk is costless in terms of expected returns (Solnik 1988).

Interest Rate Parity explains how the foreign exchange market and international money market are linked. The theory states that the difference to national interest rates of financial instruments with the same risk and maturity should be equal—but opposite in sign—to the forward rate discount or premium for the foreign currency (Eiteman et al. 2016). In other words, the interest rate differential should equal the forward discount or premium, and the relationship could be written as follows:

$$\frac{F}{S_1} - 1 = \frac{F - S_0}{S_0} = \frac{r_d - r_f}{1 + r_f} = r_d - r_f;$$

To sum up, Fig. 1.2 illustrates the relationships between the parity conditions.

The various parity relationships illustrated in Fig. 1.2 provide a very helpful basis to understand the relationship between exchange rates, inflation rates,

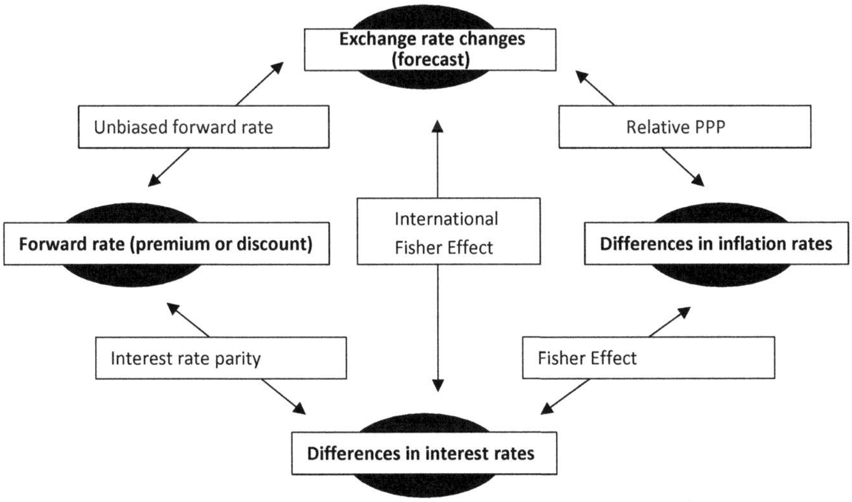

Fig. 1.2 Diagram of international parity conditions (Approximate form) (*Source* Eiteman et al. 2016, p. 186)

and interest rates. This diagram provides many practical implications for international investors. Firstly, interest rate differentials reflect expectations about currency changes. Secondly, exchange risk is reduced to inflation risk, so international investors should not be affected by exchange rate uncertainty. Thirdly, the Fisher-open states that the spot exchange rate should change in an equal amount, though opposite direction, to the difference in interest rates. Fourthly, the spot exchange rate, inflation, interest, and forward discount or premium are all directly proportional to each other and mutually determined.

This theory is a useful framework to analyze international interconnections between monetary variables. In the real economy, future exchange rates and inflation are uncertain, goods cannot be instantly transferred, shipping costs are usually high, and there are many international trade restrictions. Research shows that the international investor should remember that short-term movements of exchange rates tend to follow random patterns, mostly because of different consumption habits and that many other factors can influence exchange rates, not only inflation. The International Fisher Relation could be applied to major currencies, so any arbitrage strategy that takes advantage of the real interest rates or different currency movements has an unpredicted outcome. This means that each international institution or single investor who wants to enhance their portfolio return has to forecast exchange rates correctly and develop an international asset pricing model that incorporates exchange risk (Solnik 1988).

1.4 Monetary Variables and Security Prices

Security prices are influenced by changes in inflation, interest rates, and exchange rates, which are classified as **monetary variables**. According to the Fisher hypothesis—that the monetary and real sectors of the economy are independent—expected asset returns should move one-to-one with expected inflation. This relationship applies mostly to those assets that represent physical capital, such as stocks or real estate. These assets should be hedged against inflation. Usually, stocks prevent their owners from unexpected inflation, but not all empirical studies have proved this. There are many well-documented studies showing the negative correlation between returns on equity investments and inflation. It is known that equity prices are very good indicators of future changes in real economic activity. Stock market returns could successfully forecast economic growth, industrial output, earnings, and unemployment.

One of the first studies concerning the relationship between common stock returns and inflation was presented by Fama (1981). This rule contradicted the accepted wisdom that stocks, which represent ownership of the income generated by the real assets, should be hedged against inflation. The negative relationship between stock market returns and inflation is caused by the negative relationship between real economic activity and inflation. This relationship was explained by the money demand theory and the quantity theory of money. Fama states that lower anticipated growth rates of real activity are associated with higher inflation because lower activity means a decrease in demand; with a fixed supply of money, it results in inflation. In other words, higher inflation causes lower future output, the impact of which is negative for current stock market returns. This study was also used by Mandelker and Tandom (1985) as a proxy for the positive relationship between stock returns and real activity variables in some major industrial countries between 1966 and 1979.

Subsequent research has questioned some of the presented assumptions. Benderly and Zwick (1985) agreed with the negative relationship between stock returns and inflation, but they stated that the effect goes from inflation to output, not the other way around.

Another explanation of the negative relationship between stock returns and inflation was proposed by Geske and Roll (1983), using US data. They stated that economic slowdowns mean smaller tax revenues; with fixed government expenditures, it leads to a budget deficit. When the government finances the deficit, it borrows money, and the real interest rate may increase. This is called debt demonetization, and it means that the government finances the deficit by borrowing on future taxes. An increase in treasury bills rates is observed with the decrease in equity prices; therefore, both the expected inflation rate and real interest rate are seen as rising.

Security prices and inflation rates have been examined over short and long periods in different countries. The relationship can be influenced by the time frame and the monetary policy, which, in many countries, is determined by political goals. Additionally, Grande et al. (1998) showed that the relationship between stock returns and inflation is not limited to monetary policy but also to fiscal and income policies, and changes in the institutional environment. By contrast, Boudoukh and Richardson (1993) found that stock returns and inflation are positively correlated for USA and UK data. They explained that in long periods, the relationship could be different due to exchange rate regimes and the degree of capital mobility.

It also has to be stressed that a negative correlation between stock returns and interest rates has been empirically proved, mostly for the USA, although this relationship has also been observed in other major stock markets. According to Assefa et al. (2017), economic growth has been substantially lower and interest rates have fallen in developed economies, so they stated that the effects of interest rates on stock returns in developed countries do exist. It could be explained by the different monetary policies and more mature capital markets inherent in developed countries compared to developing countries, where the relationship was not observed.

The international investor should remember that not all companies are equally sensitive to changes in interest rates and inflation. An expected inflation rise will affect the company's future cash flow, increasing the cost of financing, and the required rate of return of equity. Some financial institutions, such as banks, might be more sensitive to interest rate movements. If they have fixed interest loans, their value will change as the interest rate level changes, which may cause a variation in the bank's security prices.

Now let us move on to exchange rates and how they can affect domestic equity prices. International investors usually are concerned about exchange rate movements and their impact on the domestic capital market. Investors who would like to use their domestic currency to value the return of the portfolio have to bear both market and exchange rate risks. The most important thing is the reaction of security prices to currency movements. The prime concern is whether stocks provide a hedge against exchange rate changes. It depends on the correlation between stock returns and exchange rate movements, which could be positive, negative, or there might be no correlation. The majority of empirical studies show very low correlation coefficients between stock returns and exchange rate movements—even weaker than expected. The overall stock market reacts poorly to currency movements, but investors should remember the cost structure, foreign trade amounts, and that this reaction is company specific.

Following the macroeconomic approach, economic activity is one of the main stock market return determinants. We can explain the relationship between exchange rate movements and stock returns through economic activity. The traditional explanation states that a decline in a currency's real exchange rate enhances competitiveness, but a deterioration in terms of trade increases the cost of imports, which creates domestic inflation, thereby reducing real income and demand. A downturn in the real Gross National Product could be offset by international competitiveness and exports until purchasing power parity is restored. We can assume that real exchange rate appreciation reduces the competitiveness of the domestic economy and, therefore, domestic activity.

There is also another approach, called the money demand model, where real growth in the domestic economy increases demand for the domestic currency through the traditional money equation. The increase in currency demand induces a rise in the relative value of the domestic currency. When stock prices are strongly influenced by real economic growth, this model can prove the positive relationship between stock market returns and domestic currency appreciation. This theory leads to the opposite effect—an increase in domestic economic growth leads to real currency appreciation (Solnik 1988).

To conclude, the influence of international variables is rather weak in comparison with domestic variables, but it is still important for international investors. Generally, equity prices and currency movements result from changes in domestic interest rates. It implies that international monetary changes influence domestic economic activity to a small extent when isolated from domestic monetary variables.

1.5 Global Financial Marketplace, Financial Globalization, and Risk

The global financial marketplace is a collection of institutions such as central banks, investment banks, commercial banks, the International Monetary Fund, and the World Bank, and securities such as stocks, bonds, and derivatives, which are linked by global networks and infrastructure (see Fig. 1.3). The exchange of any type of securities is connected with capital movement in the **global financial system**, and this all takes place through a vehicle called currencies. The links between institutions are interbank networks, which use different currencies. The exchange of currencies is itself the largest part of the international financial marketplace (Eiteman et al. 2016).

The global financial system is understood as an integrated system of national financial markets and institutions, and it is inevitably linked with the process of economic integration and financial globalization. **Financial globalization** is one of the most discussed topics in contemporary economic debate. Differences in the approach to financial globalization have been driven as much by social philosophy, fads, and different political circumstances as by economic factors. Usually, it is thought to increase capital account liberalization and unfettered capital flows. In general, it can be treated as an increased openness to capital flows, which could be a serious impediment to global financial stability. Financial globalization involves the increasingly greater integration of national financial markets within the international financial market. This results in a growth in financial relations and

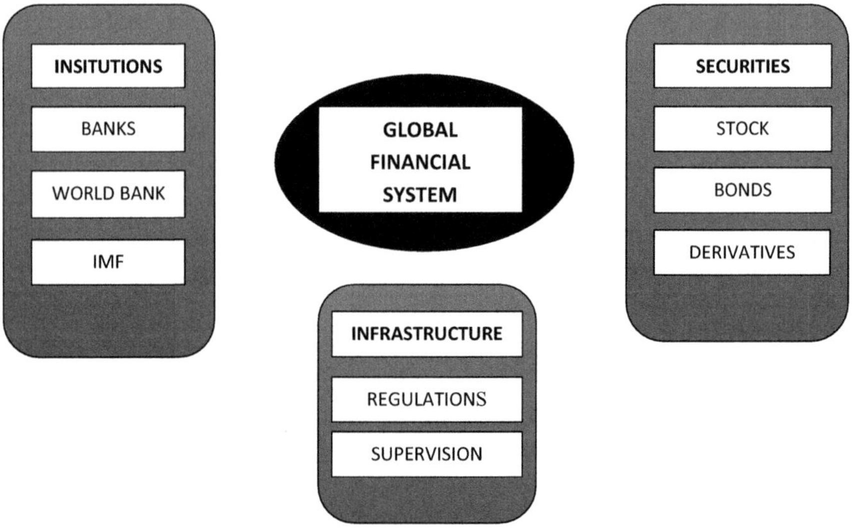

Fig. 1.3 Diagram of the global financial system (*Source* Author's own elaboration based on the cited literature)

transnational flows of capital at a global level. The global financial market has always been in the vanguard of globalization, driven by declining costs of communication and the desire of investors to diversify investment risks. The dominant problem is the complexity of risk associated with financial globalization. Financial globalization is a matter of policy relevance, with major world economies and developing countries aiming to upgrade their income. By prompting deregulation of capital too hastily, financial globalization is often blamed for economic crises and the resulting bankruptcies—leaving developing countries vulnerable to international capital movements and market herd effects.

The complexity of potential risk factors connected with financial globalization is as follows (Eiteman et al. 2016):

- The financial market is being transformed by technology, which itself has contributed to the intensification of competition and threats, e.g., FinTech risk.
- The contemporary international monetary system is a mix of floating and managed fixed exchange rates, but the role of the dollar and euro has changed, witnessing the growing role of the Chinese renminbi and the new phenomenon of cryptocurrencies.
- Large fiscal deficits plague most of the major trading countries, changing their fiscal and monetary policies, interest rates, and exchange rates.

- The continuing balance of payment imbalances. In some countries there are large deficits, in others there are surpluses. What is worse, there are twin surpluses in China and a current account surplus in Germany, while there is a continuing current account deficit in the USA. All of this inevitably alters exchange rates.
- Ownership, control, and governance vary worldwide. Publicly traded companies no longer dominate global business organizations; rather, it is privately or family-owned businesses. It means that the aims and economic goals are different in those two business models.
- Global capital markets, which usually lower a company's cost of capital, have, in many cases, become less open and smaller. Some may also question the excessive concentration of financial power in selected geographic markets like the USA.
- Financial product innovations, which are mostly in credit derivatives with the growing sophistication of mathematical models to use them.
- The growing number of "mega" institutions of international origin poses a risk that the regulatory authorities will be forced to bail them out, no matter the economic conditions, to prevent a crisis.
- The vision of business has become more short term, and the approach to investments has changed; it depends more on short-term results and the evolution of share prices. Therefore, companies concentrate on short-term stock market revaluations rather than investments that would bear fruit in the longer term (Azkunaga et al. 2013).
- This process poses new challenges for policymakers. They have to manage financial globalization in a way that countries can take as much as possible with fewer affordable policy instruments that they have in globalizing world.
- International financial market imperfections can generate bubbles or lead to a crisis, herding behavior, speculative attacks, and crashes, even in countries with sound economies. There is the problem of contagion and financial shocks transmitted across countries by the panic behavior of investors.
- Financial globalization has resulted in the ebb and flow of capital in both advanced and emerging markets, so it has made financial management more confusing and complex.

Financial globalization can also be very worthwhile and beneficial to its participants. It could help the national financial system to improve by increasing the availability of funds and reducing the problem of information asymmetry. The greater the capital, the better the bonds and stock market development. Market participants can use international financial intermediaries, broaden the local financial services, and improve the whole financial market infrastructure. The entry of foreign banks enhances financial development because they manage funds from all over the world, adopt best practices, and are less likely to bail out witnessing solvency problems. It usually leads to greater competition and potentially generates profits. Usually, it is also mentioned that financial globalization improves corporate governance by adopting international accounting standards, and it helps to monitor managers and increase transparency. The potential gain from financial globalization leads to more financially interconnected markets and higher integration of local financial markets in developing countries with the global financial market. The main benefit of financial globalization for developing countries is the development of their financial system, making it more efficient, stable, and better-regulated. In other words, funds can flow freely from countries with excess funds to countries where they think it might grow faster than in advanced economies. As a result, developing countries can smooth consumption and provide financing through foreign capital (Schmukler 2004).

Nowadays, the perception of increasing financial globalization is very strong, but the international financial system is far from perfectly integrated. There is evidence of persistent capital market segmentation, home bias, and the correlation between domestic savings and investment. The main challenge to all international market participants is to build strong international financial architecture and work out integration patterns with the global financial system to prevent a crisis.

1.6 Global Stock Market Structure

The role of the selected countries and regions in the global financial market is different. The three main markets—the USA, Japanese, and European markets—account for more than 80% of the world's financial stock market, and they play a dominant role in last twenty years (Fig. 1.4).'

The US financial market takes up about 40–50% of the global financial stock market structure. The European financial markets are integrating and gaining share after the creation of the euro and the economic integration processes in Central and Eastern European countries. By contrast, Japan's financial market is becoming less important in the global financial system, while Asia's—mainly China's—are growing very fast (Fig. 1.5).'

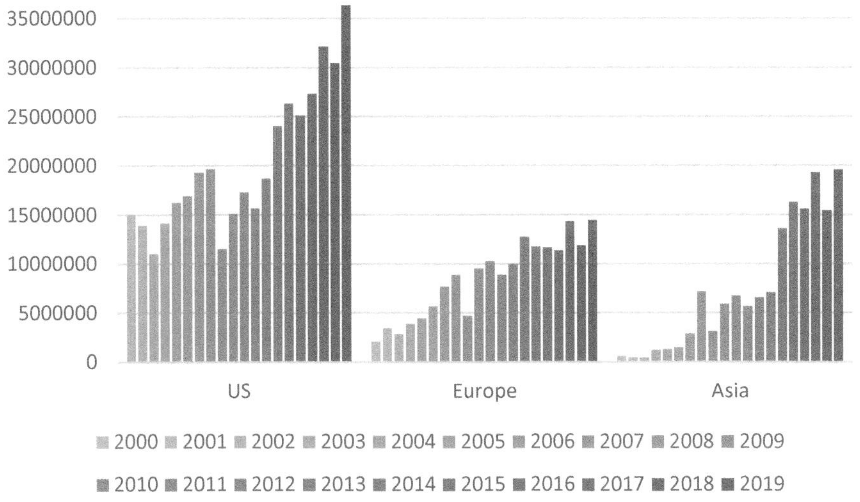

Fig. 1.4 Stock market capitalization of major stock exchanges in 2000–2019 (USD m). *USA is the sum of the NYSE and Nasdaq—USA; Europe is the sum of the LSE Group, Euronext, Deutsche Boerse, SIX Swiss Exchange, and Nasdaq Nordic and Baltics; Asia is the sum of the Japan Exchange Group, Hong Kong Exchanges and Clearing, the Shanghai Stock Exchange and the Shenzhen Stock Exchange (*Source* https://statistics.world-exchanges.org)

The USA plays a unique role in the global financial sector, not only as the largest financial market but also as a global capital hub. The New York Stock exchange is the largest stock exchange in the world. The US stock market is the largest; it is very liquid, deep, developed, and still growing. This is caused by the US dollar's unique position as the world's reserve currency. Europe is the second-largest region and is gaining strength through economic integration, although it still perceived as a combination of single capital markets. European stock markets are large, growing, developed markets that were shaped by the processes of economic integration and by the dynamism of Central and Eastern European economies. The Eurozone constitutes two-thirds of Europe's stock markets due to the monetary integration process. The UK acts as the European financial hub, while Switzerland is treated as a global private bank. Asia is a region made up of markets that are relatively isolated, with Japan in a dominating role. Asian emerging markets are on the rise but in terms of the overall market capitalization Japanese market is still leading. Chinese markets are driving the region's financial stock growth, and China has emerged as an important player in the global capital marketplace (McKinsey 2010). In China, there are two stock exchanges on the mainland the Shanghai Stock Exchange and the Shenzhen Stock Exchange, and

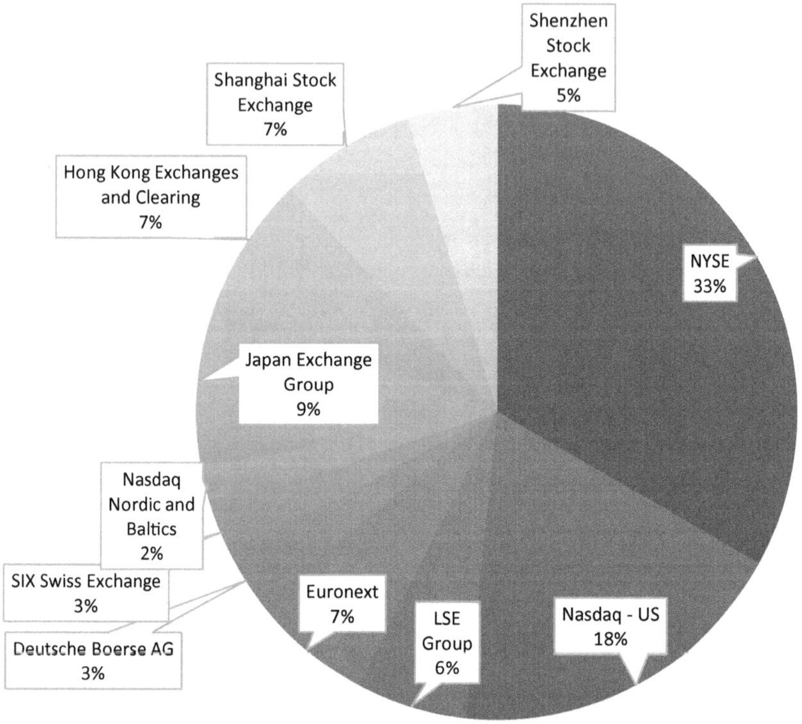

Fig. 1.5 Stock market capitalization of major stock exchanges in 2019 in USD (%) (*Source* https://statistics.world-exchanges.org)

there are two others located in Hong Kong and Taiwan. Chinese government has recently reformed the issuance system of new shares and lessened the investment and listing regulations for international issuers to enhance China's capital market development. It was very significant for the growth and improvement of the capital markets and could result in China becoming a future world leader.

It is important to stress that there are significant differences among these stock markets. The US stock market is dominated by private debt and equity markets, with the US government playing a limited role. Government debt is relatively small in the American market in comparison with Europe or Asia. The US stock market is regarded as the most efficient, with the prominent role of the New York Stock Exchange and NASDAQ. Initial public offerings of small and medium-size companies are a significant source of equity in the USA. In Europe, the banking sector plays a major role in the financial system, although the European debt capital market is growing very fast. Equity growth also comes from newly floated shares from the privatizations of state-owned companies. Meanwhile, Asian financial markets are relatively isolated from each other and hard to compare and characterize. Japan has the region's largest financial stock market, the Japan Stock Exchange, but it is growing slowly. The huge expansion of government debt is the only meaningful source of financial stock growth in the country, and its debt is the largest in relation to GDP all over the world. China's financial stock market is among the fastest growing in the world but remains heavily oriented on the banking sector, which is dominated by the government. Bank deposits account for two-thirds of the financial stock market, and debt instruments show the fastest growth (McKinsey 2010). The Chinese economy and its financial market are unique, barely resembling its American and European counterparts. As far as the Asian markets are concerned, we have to stress the role of public institutions and policies that affect the quality and quantity of all investments.

Significant differences in stock market structure and different trading practices could be explained by the historical and cultural background rather than a detailed analysis of each national market. Although each stock market has its own unique characteristics and legal organization, all stock exchanges are one of three main market structures:

- a public stock exchange,
- a private stock exchange,
- a banker stock exchange.

A **public stock exchange** is a public institution where brokers are appointed by the government. This kind of stock exchange is organized under the authority of the state, and one can find them in Belgium, Spain, Italy, Greece, and some Latin American Countries. Nowadays, deregulation is progressively affecting all public bourses, and the majority of stock exchanges are private even if they were state-owned at the beginning.

Private stock exchanges are usually founded by independent members of a securities trading association, and they can compete within the same country, like in the USA. In countries such as the UK, there is one leading bourse, and it emerged by absorbing its competitors. Private stock exchanges are not free from public regulation, but they are a mix of self-regulation and government supervision. Commissions are set by the exchange or imposed by the public authorities, but they can be negotiable. One can find them in countries like Canada, the UK, and Australia, where the Anglo-American model of the financial market exists.

Banker stock exchanges can be either private or semipublic, but their main function is to provide a convenient place for banks to carry out transactions. Usually, regulations are imposed by the bourse itself or the government, and trading might take place directly between banks without a stock exchange. Some regional banker stock exchanges were founded by chambers of commerce and not incorporated. Banker stock exchanges are located in countries with a German sphere of influence, like Austria and Switzerland, or Scandinavian countries, where banks are the major securities traders (Solnik 1988).

Global stock exchanges have experienced major changes in recent years. Large international stock exchanges operate as private exchanges by demutualization[4] or privatization. Privately owned and self-listed exchanges are now widespread across America, Europe, and some Asian countries. Both processes have initiated an intense debate on the role and ownership of stock exchanges as the guardian of public goods facilitated by capital markets. The transformation of many exchanges from member-owned mutual companies to stock companies was a major determinant in the world's market structure. There are numerous benefits of privatization for stock exchanges, as it may lead to financial profitability and improve decision-making compared to government-owned exchanges. Private stock exchanges can easily raise capital, in contrast to state-owned or mutually organized markets, and in state-owned exchanges, the government can interfere in the operation and management of the exchange, creating additional political risk factors. From another perspective, when an exchange transforms into a for-profit, its owners and management may put less emphasis on regulation in order to increase profits without caring about protecting the public interest (OECD 2014).

The most important measure of the financial market development is the depth of the financial market or the ratio of the stock market to the size of the underlying economy. Financial deepening is likely to continue as long as the whole market becomes increasingly liquid. The global financial stock market has grown faster than the whole economy in recent years. What is more, there are no apparent limits to the financial market's deepening. Countries like the USA or UK continue to grow deeper, while many emerging economies, like India and Eastern European countries, have the potential to deepen much faster as their financial systems develop.

This process of financial deepening is quite complex because it is hard to estimate what the best level of the financial system's development is to provide the best possible GDP performance. It is thought that if the financial market is more extensively developed, the transformation of savings into investments

[4]Demutualization is the process of converting a non-profit, mutually owned stock exchange into a for-profit, investor-owned corporation.

will be better, thereby promoting economic growth. As a result, the financial deepening process is usually regarded as beneficial. It gives households and companies more opportunities to invest and raise capital and to facilitate the more efficient allocation of assets. However, financial depth alone does not indicate the strength of an economy, and financial depth does not always mean a healthier financial system (McKinsey 2010). One has to remember that an increase in financial depth may pose threats, like market bubbles, the underestimation of risks, the fragility of the financial system, and vulnerability to shocks. In consequence, the price instability of financial assets may have a substantial adverse effect on economic activity.

In recent years, stock markets have experienced multiple financial crises and a great deal of turmoil, such as those situations connected with derivatives, corporate governance, and insider trading. The last financial crisis of 2007–2009 is regarded as a great depression that reduced the supply of capital to the real economy and showed the systemic failure of many financial markets all over the world. This crisis originated in the USA, but it had a profound influence on the global financial system as a whole. It reinforced concerns about the global financial market's structure and raised questions about government scrutiny. As a result, some investors were unsure about the composition of many financial institutions' portfolios and the true economic value of their financial assets.

1.7 Market Segmentation

In the last few decades, the global financial markets have been characterized by numerous barriers and constraints to the free flow of capital. It is sometimes claimed that international markets are not integrated but segmented. Even though a single capital market could be efficient, numerous factors might prevent international capital flows from taking advantage of relative mispricing among national financial markets. Some impediments may occur and hold back investors, e.g., taxation and transaction costs, explicit restrictions on foreign ownership or capital mobility, and foreign exchange transactions. To be more specific, one can divide the barriers into the following categories:

- Psychological—unfamiliarity with foreign markets,
- Legal—foreign investment regulations, avoiding loss of national control, etc.
- Transactional—the high cost of foreign transactions, management fees, etc.

- Discriminatory taxation—more heavily taxed than domestic investments,
- Political—political changes and instability in the country. Those barriers may dampen the enthusiasm for international allocation due to high uncertainty (e.g. nepotism, corruption, protectionism),
- Exchange risk—foreign exchange risk—the investment value may change due to currency fluctuations (Solnik 1988).

In the mid-twentieth century, many financial markets were generally not equally developed and less liquid, insufficiently regulated, and had lax disclosure requirements. It resulted in portfolio suppression, and there were many consequences, e.g., the bank was the primary source of funding, foreign financial markets were accessible only to the government, their agencies, or large firms, and the national capital markets were smaller and segmented, with domestic investors holding most of the local instruments. All these factors tend to reduce international capital flows, and they led to **segmented national markets**. After the 1970s and 1980s of twentieth century, many countries reformed and liberalized their economies allowing the possibility of foreign portfolio investments. As a consequence local equity markets developed resulting in large portfolio capital flows (Errunza and Miller 2000).

If **market segmentation** still exists, we would be able to observe differential rates of return for the financial instruments listed on different stock markets, which are equally risky. In turn, capital markets segmentation means the reduction in foreign investors' profits from international diversification discouraging international capital movements. Barriers to enter foreign markets and differentials in values, if they exist, impact the amount of risk undertaken by the investor. It means that when traded financial assets are not spread across countries, factor price heterogeneity will result in market segmentation, for example, in China, where the A-share market is only open to local investors and the B-share to foreign investors. What can be observed is that China's B-shares trade at a discount relative to the A-shares (Sun and Tong 2000, pp. 1875–1902).

Many national capital markets could be described as partially segmented and partially integrated rather than a polar case of complete segmentation or integration (Choi and Rajan 1997). The nature of segmentation is not clearly defined. The market reforms, international integration, and liberalization led to the removal of many of the mentioned barriers. The deregulation and the development of many local stock markets, especially in Asia and Central and Eastern Europe, allowed foreign portfolio investments. In many countries, investors invest extensively abroad, all major corporations have multinational operations, and their stocks are listed on several international stock exchanges.

Institutional investors, corporations, as well as governments borrow internationally, taking advantage of relative mispricing and making the market more efficient. Those changes provide a new source of capital and internationalize domestic stock markets all over the world; however, the problem of financial market segmentation is still visible. The growing flow of foreign investments over the years has resulted in international markets not being fully segmented, and consequently, many firms may face the high cost of capital problems (Errunza and Miller 2000). If markets are segmented, a company has an incentive to adopt policies to mitigate the negative effects of investment barriers and undertake the dual-listing of their shares.

1.8 Familiarity and Home Bias

Experimental evidence on judgment and decision-making shows that individuals prefer familiar goods and investments. These effects are most visible in both the goods and the financial markets. Investors favor investments that they are more familiar with and that are geographically and linguistically proximate over those that are unknown, and that potentially could be more prolific. Geographical proximity drives many economic processes, such as trade or investments. A change in the investment pattern is often risky, so there can be a reason to be more afraid. However, too much fear could mean bad economic choices. Unfamiliarity or fear of the unknown induces anomalies related to the unwillingness to invest internationally or to change the investment policy. If investors prefer what they know, they will build portfolios with limited diversification across stocks and asset classes. Many inefficient portfolios can be explained by many different puzzles: the home bias puzzle, the local stock investment puzzle (investing in one's own company), the under-diversification puzzle, and attachment to well-known investing styles, among others.

Furthermore, investors are reluctant to take risky decisions compared to bearing the risks associated with remaining passive. It has been observed that individuals hold relatively few asset classes in their portfolios and have a home bias incomparable to the institutional ones. Beyond the purely decision-making context, investors, like all people, tend to like characteristics, incentives that they are familiar with, for example, being loyal to local sports teams or organizations, or preferring friendships with those whom they are located close to, and many other biased everyday behaviors. Home bias is closely linked with familiarity bias, and it is mostly explained by this phenomenon.

Home bias, or the home bias puzzle, is defined as concentrating on domestic equities to a much greater degree than is justified by portfolio theory. In other words, there is a strong preference for domestic equities, i.e., investors who prefer geographically proximate targets are home biased. Portfolio theory suggests that investors hold diversified portfolios in order to reduce risk, and international diversification would reduce the risk significantly without affecting the expected rate of return. According to international portfolio theory, domestic investors can build a less risky portfolio. When there are no barriers to international portfolio investments, and all investors are the same: They hold the same portfolio of risky assets—a global market portfolio. Each investor should build a portfolio in which its country shares are equal to its shares in world market capitalization (French and Poterba 1991). For example, a US investor's portfolio should contain 30–40% US equity, where the US market represents approximately 30–40% of the world market capitalization.

What is important is that the home bias puzzle is not only about comparable patterns of investor behaviors, it is also about calibrating the mechanisms that generate different rates of return in different locations to offset the gains from international diversification. The majority of studies take the world equity-market portfolio as the standard according to international portfolio theory, in the sense that any deviation between observed portfolio weights and the world market weights is regarded as inefficient and needs explanation. The idea is that the world market portfolio is the investor's best choice (Cooper et al. 2012).

The existing literature provides four main explanations of the home bias conundrum:

- familiarity,
- information asymmetries,
- strategy,
- location effects.

Familiarity is explained by investors' cognitive bias toward their own local environment (Huberman 2001). It is related to the neighborhood effect, which states that investors—and people in general—tend to overvalue their own region. Familiarity can be regarded as an irrational or unconscious factor. The point at which an investor stops diversifying is defined as familiarity bias, and in reality, many investors hold poorly diversified portfolios. It has also been observed that stocks that receive greater publicity, or whose name is often mentioned in the news, tend to be purchased more, even if the news is, on average, neutral. Those financial instruments become more and more familiar, and this implies that investors feel greater comfort for such instruments and assess them more favorably. One could describe those stocks as having a positive buzz or positive hype (Cao et al. 2011).

This familiarity is often observed in companies that consider cross-listing in foreign markets. They may find it problematic when they are faced with an unfamiliar situation, e.g., investors who are nearby and who live in countries that share a common culture or language, or where the legal system is less strict. In consequence, the cost of capital could be lower for firms that cross-list in countries that are proximate in these respects. On the other hand, equity investors who hold foreign shares do so disproportionately in countries that are close to their home country; close here means the same culture, language, and sometimes distance. By and large, it is hard to reconcile portfolio theory with the size, pervasiveness, and persistence of the home bias puzzle.

Information asymmetries refer to unevenly distributed information, which limits an investor's choices. All investors in geographical proximity have easily accessible and better information than non-locals and, therefore, they have a different search context (Ellwanger and Boschma 2015). They prefer to hold a local company's stocks rather than a distant one's because they have a relative information advantage. Local investors can easily talk to the managers and employees of the company, and they can also easily get important information from the local media and have close personal ties to the local executives. All those factors may result in an information advantage in local equities. The favorability of geographically close investments could be explained by many different factors coming from different sources. Some investors may feel more comfortable about local firms or firms they know and hear a lot about. Some may have a strong desire to invest in the local community to gain mutual benefits with the local executives (Coval and Moskowitz 1999).

Strategy, which is understood as strategic reasoning, occurs when an investor is willing to choose a proximate target for easy price competition and the capacity to monitor the company's financial performance. This behavior could be related to a misperception of the risks in foreign markets, while a perceived competence in local stocks may lead to an underestimation of local risks and an overestimation of foreign risks. This means that home bias is motivated by a particularly high expected risk abroad.

The last explanation is the **location effect**, which refers to the spatial distribution of potential investments that satisfy the favored profile. If certain investments are clustered in terms of industry or country, they are automatically home biased. The main reason to buy stocks from the same or a similar industry is the possibility to realize synergy effects, such as similar products, technologies, distribution. However, international investors, who might strategically opt for distant targets in order to generate returns in new geographic markets, are expected to be home biased as well.

To sum up, there is a wide body of research that offers a variety of explanations for the home country bias conundrum. The initial explanation focused on barriers to international investments, such as high transaction costs, governmental restrictions, foreign taxes. Although many of these obstacles have substantially diminished, the tendency to invest in the home country remains strong, and most investors still invest largely at home. The vast majority of different explanations could be grouped into two categories: those associated with national boundaries or those with a preference for geographic proximity. With the first explanation, obstacles arise when capital crosses political and monetary boundaries, and it faces exchange rate fluctuations, different regulations, and sovereign risk. These obstacles may be the main factor that discourages investment abroad. The second explanation is that geographic proximity causes information asymmetries. Some investors may still have easier access to information about companies located near them. There are two possible psychological explanations for this home biased behavior, i.e., strong risk aversion and wishful thinking. Investors are afraid to incur relative losses, and they rely more than others on analytical instruments that make them behave in accordance with the herd. Their reliance on home assets could fit into this picture, as it may reveal a false perception of risk reduction. Wishful thinking in their discussion of relative optimism could also help to explain the perceived informational advantage of companies located in the same country. The home bias of investors appears to be driven by more forces than previously assumed, and they all play a useful role in improving our understanding of this phenomenon (Lütje and Menkhoff 2007).

If we can assume that international portfolio home bias is mostly influenced by distance, then distance can play an identifiable role in domestic investments as well, and it is called **home bias at home**. This highly inefficient behavior is mostly observed in the USA, where the average US fund manager buys stocks of companies that are closer than the average stock he could hold. One in ten companies in a fund manager's portfolio is chosen because it is located in the same city. Local equity preference could also be explained by three company characteristics: size, leverage, and output. Stocks of locally held companies are issued by small and highly leveraged entities, and they do not produce internationally traded goods. Furthermore, size and leverage are associated with higher returns. Applying this idea to the European context, one might expect that investors who show a home bias prefer European issuers over others in the world. This shows that the home bias puzzle need not be linked to the international market but with distance, and it may account for about one-third of the whole home bias puzzle. It means that the most important factor is the preference for geographic proximity and the relative scale of the world economy, rather than national borders (Coval and Moskowitz 1999).

According to some international studies (Bellalah 2010), the home bias is different in different parts of the world, and it depends on the country's economic development. Home bias is large for developed countries, but at different levels. Developed Asian markets have the highest home bias. The lowest home bias level is in Great Britain and the USA. Investors from emerging countries, as a whole, concentrate on domestic equities to a great extent. For the emerging American markets, the highest home bias is in Brazil and Chile. The same is true for emerging European and Asian countries, where investors invest mostly in domestic stock markets. According to Cooper et al. (2018), one can distinguish between home bias (the overweighting of home stocks) and foreign bias (the relative underweighting of more "distant" countries), and find pure home bias only in emerging markets. Countries classified as emerging usually have high tax rates and low credit standing, which results in higher pure home bias, while more developed countries come with lower distance aversion. Thus, portfolios are distant from the optimal diversification level as recommended by international portfolio theory. Despite the liberalization of the capital market, economic integration processes, and mostly the gains provided by international diversification, many investors still underweight their portfolios with foreign assets.

References

Assefa, T., Esqueda, O., & Mollick, A. (2017, January–February). Stock Returns and Interest Rates Around the World: A Panel Data Approach. *Journal of Economics and Business, 89,* 20–35.

Azkunaga, J., San-Jose, L., & Urionabarrenetxea, S. (2013). The Impact of Financial Globalization and Financialization on the Economy in the Current Crisis Through Banking Corporate Governance. *Contemporary Economics, 7*(3), 79–94.

Bekaert, G., Hodrick, R., & Zhang, X. (2005). *International Stock Return Comovements.* National Bureau of Economic Research. https://www.nber.org/papers/w11906.pdf. Accessed 30 Oct 2019.

Bellalah, M. (2010). The Equity Home Bias: Explanations and Financial Anomalies. *International Journal of Economics and Finance, 2*(2), 78–96. https://doi.org/10.5539/IJEF.V2N2P78.

Benderly, J., & Zwick, B. (1985). Inflation, Real Balances, Output, and Real Stock Returns. *American Economic Review, 75*(5), 1115–1123.

Boudoukh, J., & Richardson, M. (1993). Stock Returns and Inflation: A Long-Horizon Perspective. *American Economic Review, 83*(5), 1346–1355.

Cao, H., Han, B., Hirshleifer, D., & Zhang, H. (2011). Fear of the Unknown: Familiarity and Economic Decisions. *Review of Finance, 15*(1), 173–206. https://doi.org/10.1093/rof/rfp023.

Clark, P., Bartolini, L., Bayoumi, T., & Symansky, S. (1994, December). *Exchange Rates and Economic Fundamentals: A Framework for Analysis*. Washington, DC: International Monetary Fund.

Cooper, I., Sercu, P., & Vanpée, R. (2012). The Equity Home Bias Puzzle: A Survey. *Foundations and Trends in Finance, 7*(4), 289–416.

Cooper, I., Sercu, P., & Vanpée, R. (2018). A Measure of Pure Home Bias. *Review of Finance, 22*(4), 1469–1514.

Coval, J., & Moskowitz, T. (1999). Home Bias at Home: Local Equity Preference in Domestic Portfolios. *Journal of Finance, LIV*(6), 2045–2073.

Choi, J., & Rajan, M. (1997). A Joint Test of Market Segmentation and Exchange Risk Factor in International Capital Market. *Journal of International Business Studies, 28*(1), 29–49.

Eiteman, D., Stonehill, A., & Moffett, M. (2016). *Multinational Business Finance* (14th ed.). England: PEARSON.

Ellwanger, N., & Boschma, R. (2015). Who Acquires Whom? The Role of Geographical Proximity and Industrial Relatedness in Dutch Domestic M&As Between 2002 and 2008. *Journal of Economic & Social Geography, 106*(5), 608–624.

Errunza, V., & Miller, D. (2000). Market Segmentation and the Cost of Capital in International Equity Markets. *The Journal of Financial and Quantitative Analysis, 35*(4), 577–600.

Fama, E. (1981). Stock Returns, Real Activity, Inflation, and Money. *The American Economic Review, 71*(4), 545–565.

French, K., & Poterba, J. (1991). Investor Diversification and International Equity Markets. *American Economic Review, 81*, 222–226.

Geske, R., & Roll, R. (1983). The Fiscal and Monetary Linkage Between Stock Returns and Inflation. *The Journal of Finance, 38*(1), 1–33.

Gilmore, C., & McManus, G. (2002). International Portfolio Diversification: US and Central European Equity Markets. *Emerging Markets Review, 3*(1), 69–83.

Grande, G., Locarno, A., & Massa, M. (1998). *Stock Market Returns, Inflation and Monetary Regimes*. https://www.bis.org/publ/confp05f.pdf. Accessed 15 Oct 2019.

Huberman, G. (2001). Familiarity Breeds Investment. *The Review of Financial Studies, 14*, 659–680.

Lütje, T., & Menkhoff, L. (2007). What Drives Home Bias? Evidence from Fund Managers' Views. *International Journal of Finance and Economics, 12*(1), 21–35.

Mandelker, G., & Tandom, K. (1985). Common Stock Returns, Real Activity, Money, and Inflation: Some International Evidence. *Journal of International Money and Finance, 4*(2), 267–286.

McKinsey Global Institute. (2010). *$118 Trillion and Counting: Taking Stock of the World's Capital Markets.* https://www.mckinsey.com/-/media/McKinsey/Featured%20Insights/Global%20Capital%20Markets/118%20trillion%20and%20counting/MGI_118_trillion_and_counting_Taking_stock_of_capital_markets_Full_Report.ashx. Accessed 30 Oct 2019.

Moerman, G. (2004, April). *Diversification in Euro Area Stock Markets: Country Versus Industry* (Working Paper Series No. 327). European Central Bank. file:///C:/Users/admin/Downloads/SSRN-id526990.pdf. Accessed 5 Dec 2019.

OECD. (2014). Privatisation and Demutualisation of MENA Stock Exchanges: To Be or Not to Be? https://www.oecd.org/corporate/PrivatisationDemutualisationMENAStockExchanges.pdf. Accessed 10 Sept 2019.

Salvatore, D. (2007). *International Economics* (9th ed.). Hoboken, NJ: Wiley.

Schmukler, S. (2004). Benefits and Risks of Financial Globalization: Challenges for Developing Countries. World Bank Group, Open Repository. http://citeseerx.ist.psu.edu/viewdoc/download?doi=10.1.1.511.9274&rep=rep1&type=pdf. Accessed 27 Sept 2019.

Solnik, B. (1988). *International Investments.* Reading, MA: Addison-Wesley Publishing Company Inc.

Sun, Q., & Tong, W. (2000). The Effect of Market Segmentation on Stock Prices: The China Syndrome. *Journal of Banking & Finance, 24*(12), 1875–1902.

Symansky, S., Clark, P., Bartolini, L., & Bayoumi, T. (1994). *Exchange Rates and Economic Fundamentals: A Framework for Analysis* (IMF Occasional Papers, No 115). International Monetary Fund. http://www.imf.org/external/pubs/cat/longres.aspx?sk=436, 24 Oct 2019.

Thomson Reuters EIKON database available at the University of Lodz. Accessed 24 Apr 2020.

Ullah, H., & Ullah, S. (2016). Lead-Lag Relationship Between the Emerging and Emerged Markets. *Journal of Administrative & Business Studies, 1*(2), 1–15.

Wong, W., Penm, J., Terrell, R., & Yann Ching Lim, K. (2004). The Relationship Between Stock Markets of Major Developed Countries and Asian Emerging Markets. *Journal of Applied Mathematics and Decision Sciences, 8*(4), 201–218.

World Federation of Exchanges, Statistical Portal. https://statistics.world-exchanges.org. Accessed 22 Apr 2020.

2

Portfolio Theory and International Diversification

2.1 Introduction

Modern portfolio theory is concerned with the characteristics and analysis of individual securities as well as portfolios whose characteristics are significantly different from the individual assets from which they are built. Every investor should be aware of the basics of portfolio theory, from the relationship of portfolio characteristics to security characteristics and a desirable set of portfolios. It is crucial to understand how investors might choose the optimal portfolio from among a set of different portfolios meeting his objectives. According to Markowitz, an optimal portfolio minimizes the risk for a given level of return or maximizes return at a given level of risk. Implementing the above portfolio risk-return formula, any investor would find the capital market theory and capital asset pricing model (CAPM) useful, as it focuses on the appropriate measure of risk, which is the beta coefficient. Portfolio theory generates a number of benefits, i.e., proper asset selection and risk reduction for a properly selected set of investments. One possible way to achieve above-average returns is international diversification, which gives significant benefits, including market risk reduction far beyond the national level.

The main aim of this chapter is to familiarize the reader with portfolio theory and international diversification, which, in fully integrated and efficient capital markets, are the best and most natural strategy. A proper understanding of the risk-return characteristics of an investment portfolio will provide investors with future support for international investments.

T. Miziołek et al., *International Equity Exchange-Traded Funds*,
https://doi.org/10.1007/978-3-030-53864-4_2

2.2 Risk and Rate of Return

An investment could be defined as the current commitment of funds for a certain period to derive a future flow of funds that will compensate the investing unit for the time the funds are committed, for the expected rate of inflation, and the uncertainty involved in the future flow of funds (Reilly 1986). The primary purpose of investing is to consume more in the future, so the increase in wealth results from the investment. It means that an investment generates a return, and this return is influenced by many different factors. Return is measured in terms of the relationship between the amount invested and the amount returned. This relation is expressed as the **rate of return** and can be written as follows:

$$R_{i,t} = \frac{\text{Ending value} - \text{Begining value}}{\text{Begining value}} = \frac{P_{i,t} - P_{i,t-1}}{P_{i,t-1}} = \frac{P_{i,t}}{P_{i,t-1}} - 1;$$

where:

$R_{i,t}$—The rate of return of the *i*-th asset at time *t*,
$P_{i,t}$—The price of the *i*-th asset at the end of the period,
P_{it-1}—The price of the *i*-th asset at the beginning of the period.

Many investments provide a cash flow (income received) in addition to changing value while the funds are invested. If we consider a stock investment, it could be a dividend. If we consider bonds, it could be interests. If cash flow is considered, the above relation can be written as follows:

$$R_{i,t} = \frac{(P_{i,t} - P_{i,t-1}) + C_{i,t}}{P_{i,t-1}};$$

where:

$C_{i,t}$—Cash flow of the *i*-th asset at time *t*.

This formula indicates the rate of increase in wealth, and it could be split into two parts: capital appreciation or capital gain (the change in price) and cash flow (income received). When the rate of return is positive, it is considered a gain; when it is negative, it reflects a loss. The rate of return is a relative measure usually expressed in the form of a percentage.

The second factor is **risk**. Investment risk is defined as uncertainty regarding the expected rate of return from an investment. The terms risk and uncertainty are usually used interchangeably, but formally, there is a difference between them. The distinction was explained by Knight (1921), who used *risk* to mean that there is a situation in which the decision-maker assigns probabilities to events based on "known chances." By contrast, *uncertainty* means there are situations in which the decision-maker is unable to assign probabilities to events because it is not possible to calculate chances.

From the investor's perspective, the expected return can be defined under certain economic conditions. The return could be high or low, negative or positive. The most important thing is that the wider the range of possible returns, the more uncertain the actual return is, and the greater the risk. To determine the investor's level of certainty, the probability distribution of expected returns must be analyzed. The probability distribution indicates the possible returns and assigns probabilities to each of them. The probabilities of return range from zero (no chance of this particular return) to one (complete certainty of this particular return). Those probabilities could be subjective estimates or based on past frequencies. The expected rate of return is calculated by multiplying the potential outcomes by the chances of them occurring, and it could be written as follows:

$$E(R_i) = \sum (Probability\, of\, return)(Possible\, return)$$
$$= \sum_{t=1}^{T} P_{i,t} R_{i,t} = P_1 R_{i,1} + P_2 R_{i,2} + \ldots + P_T R_{i,T};$$

where:

$E(R_i)$—The expected return of the *i*-th asset,

P_{it}—The probability of the *i*-th asset (chances),

R_{it}—The particular rate of return of the *i*-th asset (potential outcomes),

T—The number of events.

The expected rate of return is usually based on historical data, and it cannot be guaranteed. Making an investment decision on expected rates of return could be dangerous because it does not contain risk. Thus, investors need one more characteristic, a measure of the dispersion of returns. Of the many different measures of risk, the most important one is the variance of the estimated distribution of expected returns, or the square root of variance standard deviation. The investor must know how much the outcomes differ from the average. In a literal meaning, variance is a measure of dispersion, and it shows how far from the expected return the actual outcome might be. The variance of return can be written as follows:

$$\sigma^2(R_i) = \sum_{t=1}^{T} P_{i,t}[R_{i,t} - E(R_i)]^2 = P_{i,1}[R_{i,1} - E(R_i)]^2 + P_{i,2}[R_{i,2} - E(R_i)]^2$$
$$+ \ldots + P_{i,T}[R_{i,T} - E(R_i)]^2;$$

where:

$\sigma^2(R_i)$—Variance.

The larger the variance, while everything else remains constant, the greater the dispersion and risk. In the event of perfect certainty, there is no variance and no risk.

The standard deviation is calculated by taking the square root of the variance.

$$\sigma(R_i) = \sqrt{\sigma^2(R_i)};$$

where:

$\sigma(R_i)$—The standard deviation.

Generally, it is assumed that investors are risk-averse. It means that if they are given an investment with a smaller standard deviation, i.e., a smaller risk, they will choose it.

To better illustrate the previous discussion, it is crucial to explain the relationship between risk and return and emphasize what causes changes in the required returns over the investment period. This basic relationship between risk and return is positive and linear, as can be seen in Fig. 2.1.

Looking at Fig. 2.1, we can see that investors select investments that are consistent with their risk preferences. Some will consider low-risk investments, whereas others will consider high-risk ones. Figure 2.5 also indicates the risk-free rate (RFR) point. This basic rate indicates no uncertainty of

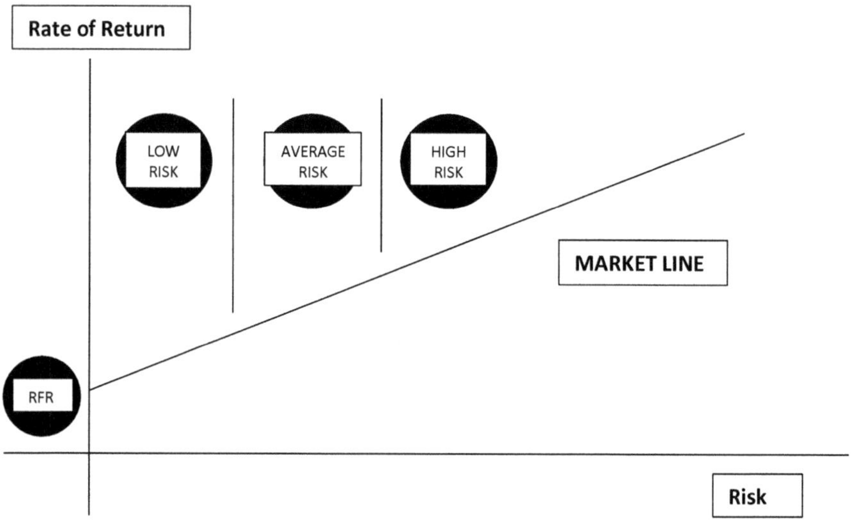

Fig. 2.1 Relationship between risk and rate of the return (*Source* Reilly 1986, p. 18)

future flows, meaning that investors know what cash flow they will receive and when. Additionally, there is no probability of default. The graph shows that investors want the risk-free rate on riskless investments and that they increase the required rate of return as perceived uncertainty increases. A crucial issue is also the slope of the market line, which indicates the composite return per unit of risk required by all market participants (Reilly 1986, pp. 17–18).

2.3 Markowitz's Portfolio Theory

After the comprehensive discussion of all issues connected with the rate of return and risk, it is time to combine individual assets into a portfolio that reflects risk and return preferences. The basic portfolio theory was developed by Harry Markowitz (1952). He was pondering how investors should combine assets into a portfolio that would provide the best possible combination of risk and return, i.e., the highest potential rate of return for a given level of risk or that would minimize the amount of risk for a given level of return.

Firstly, investors should consider the relationship between different investment opportunities, including all types of assets and liabilities, not only stocks. It is vital to consider the whole spectrum of investments because the returns from all these investments interact, and this relationship is important. Secondly, portfolio theory assumes that investors are **risk-averse**, meaning that given a choice between two assets with equal rates of the return, they will choose the one with the lower level of risk. Therefore, it is expected that the relationship between the return and risk is positive. Hence, investors require a higher rate of return to accept the higher risk (Reilly and Brown 1997).

As previously stated, the basic portfolio model was proposed by Markowitz, who showed that the variance of the rate of the return was a significant measure of portfolio risk. He derived the formula for the portfolio risk using the variance of the portfolio, and this formula indicates the importance of diversification in reducing the total portfolio's risk. This model is based on assumptions regarding investor behavior:

- Investors consider each investment alternative to be represented by a probability distribution of expected returns over the holding period.
- Investors maximize one-period expected utility, and the utility curves show a declining marginal utility of wealth.

- Investors estimate the risk of the portfolio on the basis of the variability of expected returns.
- Investors make decisions regarding expected return and risk alone.
- For a given risk level, investors prefer higher returns to lower returns, and for the given level of expected return, less risk to more risk (Reilly and Brown 1997, p. 253).

The first most important factor for each investment is the rate of return. The expected rate of return for the portfolio of assets is simply the weighted average of the expected rates of return for the individual assets in the portfolio. The weights are the proportion of the total value of the assets. This relation can be written as follows:

$$E\left(R_{\text{portfolio}}\right) = \sum_{i=1}^{n} W_i R_i;$$

where:

$E_{\text{portfolio}}$—The expected return of the portfolio,
W_i—The percent of the portfolio in asset i,
R_i—The expected rate of return for asset i.

The second important characteristic is risk. As previously stated, the variance and standard deviation of the return are used as the measure of risk. To present the formula for the standard deviation of the portfolio, we must recall two basic concepts in statistics: covariance and correlation. Covariance is a measure of how returns of assets move together, as they have positive and negative deviations at similar times or dissimilar times, or if they are unrelated (Elton and Gruber 1995, p. 56). A positive covariance means that the rates of return for two investments move in the same direction relative to their individual means during the same period. In contrast, negative covariance means that the rates of return for two investments move in different directions relative to their individual means during the same period (Reilly and Brown 1997, p. 256).

In order to simplify the whole concept, it is useful to standardize the covariance. Dividing the covariance between two investments by the product of the standard deviation of each one, the formula produces a measure called the correlation coefficient with a range of -1 to 1. This formula can be written as follows:

$$r_{i,j} = \frac{\text{Cov}_{i,j}}{\sigma_i \sigma_j};$$

where:

$r_{i,j}$—The correlation coefficient of returns,
σ_i—The standard deviation of $R_{i,t}$,
σ_j—The standard deviation of $R_{j,t}$.

A value of 1 indicates a perfect positive linear relationship, meaning that two returns of investments move together in a completely linear manner. A value of −1 indicates that there is a perfect negative linear relationship between two return series; when one investment rate of return is above its mean, the other is below by a comparable amount. A value of 0 indicates that the returns have no linear relationship, and they are uncorrelated statistically, but it does not indicate that they are independent.

According to portfolio risk, it is now possible to present the basic formula of the standard deviation of returns for a portfolio of assets. Markowitz derived the general formula for portfolio risk using the standard deviation. This formula can be written as follows:

$$\sigma_{\text{portfolio}} = \sqrt{\sum_{i=1}^{n} w_i^2 \sigma_i^2 + \sum_{i=1}^{n} \sum_{j=1}^{n} w_i w_j \text{Cov}_{i,j}};$$

where:

$\sigma_{\text{portfolio}}$—The standard deviation of the portfolio,
w_i—The weights of the individual assets in the portfolio, where weights are determined by the proportion of value in the portfolio,
σ_i^2—The variance of rates of return asset for i,
$\text{Cov}_{i,j}$—Covariance between the rates of return for assets i and j.

The above formula shows that the standard deviation for a portfolio is a function of the weighted average of the individual variances plus the weighted covariances between all assets. What is also shown is that the standard deviation for a portfolio indicates not only the variance but also the covariance between pairs of individual securities in the portfolio. Further, it can be proved that in a portfolio with a large number of assets, this formula reduces to the sum of weighted covariances (Reilly and Brown 1997, p. 261).

Now it is time to consider what happens to the portfolio risk when you add a new security to such a combination. According to the above formula, there are two effects. The first is the assets' variance of returns, and the second is the covariance between the new asset and every other asset that is already in the portfolio. The relative weight of these covariances is substantially greater than the asset's variance; hence, the more securities in the portfolio, the more this is true (Reilly and Brown 1997, p. 262). This means that the contribution to the portfolio variance of the variance of the individual assets goes to zero as the number of securities in a portfolio gets very large. It means that the individual risk of an asset can be fully diversified, but the contribution to the total risk caused by the covariance terms cannot be diversified (Elton and Gruber 1995, p. 60). So, the bottom line is that the most critical factor is not a single security's own variance, but the average covariance with all the other securities in the portfolio. Still, what is important is that in most international markets, the correlation coefficient and the covariance between assets are positive; therefore, the risk of the portfolio cannot be made to go to zero, but it can be much less than the variance of individual assets in a portfolio.

Markowitz showed that the variance (standard deviation) of a portfolio is a function not only of the variance (standard deviation) for the individual assets but also of the covariance between the return for all pairs of assets that are part of the portfolio (Reilly and Brown 1997, p. 272).

To visualize all conceivable combinations of risky assets in the return standard deviation space, it is possible to derive different curves that assume different possibilities. In theory, it is also possible to plot an infinite number of possibilities that group risky and non-risky assets in all possible percentage comparisons. However, we must remember that investors are risk-averse, and they would prefer more return to less, and less risk to more. Thus, it is desirable to find a portfolio that offers a greater return for the same risk, or a lower risk for the same return. That is why there is an efficient set that consists of an envelope curve of all portfolios that lie between the global minimum variance portfolio and the maximum return portfolio. This specific set of portfolios is called the **efficient frontier** (Elton and Gruber 1995, pp. 82–83). The efficient frontier contains the best of all possible combinations. It represents the set of portfolios that has the maximum rate of return for every given level of risk or the minimum risk for every level of return. Figure 2.2 depicts the graph of the efficient frontier.

As can be seen in Fig. 2.2, each portfolio that lies on the efficient frontier has either a higher rate of return for an equal risk or a lower risk for an equal rate of return. We can observe that portfolio A is better than portfolio C because it has an equal return but substantially less risk. The same rule is adjustable to portfolio B, which is better than C because it has equal risk but a higher expected return. The slope of the efficient frontier curve

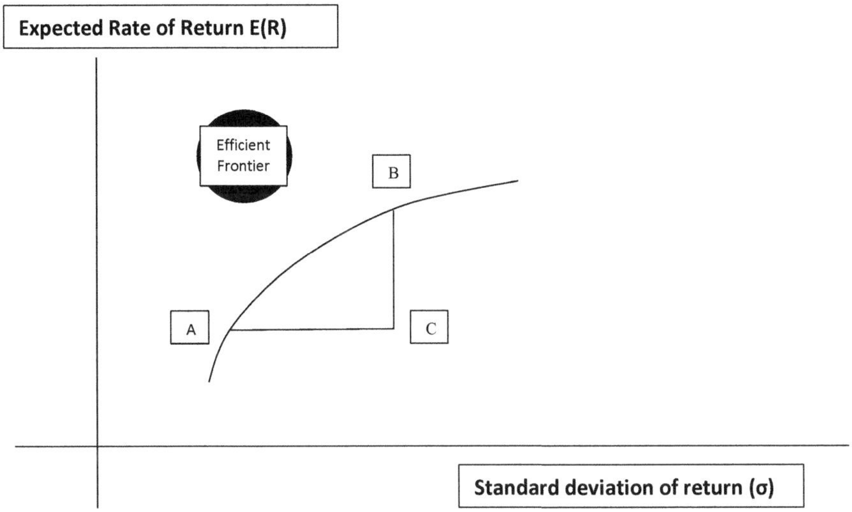

Fig. 2.2 The efficient frontier for alternative portfolios (*Source* Reilly and Brown 1997, p. 271)

steadily decreases as you move upward. This shows that adding equal increments of risk as the investor moves up the curve gives diminishing increments of expected return. It means that the efficient frontier is a concave function in the expected return standard deviation space that extends from the minimum variance portfolio to the maximum return one (Elton and Gruber 1995, p. 84).

Every investor can choose a point along the efficient frontier based on his or her utility function and risk awareness. What is important is that no portfolio on the efficient frontier can dominate any other portfolio on the efficient frontier; thus, all of them have different rates of return and risk characteristics. Because each investor's risk-return utility function differs, an individual investor's portfolio choice will be different from others.

2.4 The Single-Index Model

After outlining the basis of Markowitz's portfolio theory, it is important to keep in mind that the results of asset allocation entirely depend on the data being implemented. The first problem is the simplification of the amount and type of input data required to perform the portfolio analysis. The second problem is the simplification of the computational procedure because, for each security, the expected return and standard deviation have to be estimated, not to mention the correlation coefficients among the entire set of assets. The most widely used simplification of portfolio theory is the **single-index model**[1] proposed by William Sharpe (1963).

Sharpe invented a practical application of Markowitz's portfolio analysis technique after casually observing stock prices. He noticed that when the market goes up (as measured by the stock market index), most stocks tend to increase in price, and when the market goes down, most stocks decrease in price. Those movements reveal that one reason asset returns might be correlated is the common response to market changes, which could be shown by the return of the stock market index. Consequently, it is possible to reduce the number of correlation coefficients by assuming that stock returns can be described by a single-index market model. According to this model, returns on a security can be represented by the performance of a single-factor-market index. The formula of the model can be written as follows (Elton and Gruber 1995, pp. 130–131):

$$R_i = \alpha_i + \beta_i R_m + \varepsilon_i;$$

where:

R_i—The rate of return for asset i.

α_i—The component of the i-th security return that is independent of the market index,

β_i—The slope coefficient that relates the return of the i-th security to the return of the market index,

R_m—The rate of return for the aggregate stock market index,

$\mathcal{E}_i$—Random variable, $E(\mathcal{E}_i) = 0$.

The new, crucial measure is **beta**, and it is a measure of the sensitivity of a stock to market movements. The use of a single-index market model calls for estimates of the beta parameter for individual stocks that could potentially be included in a portfolio. The single-index market model is mostly used to estimate historical beta parameters, which can be used as an estimate of a future beta. There is evidence that historical betas provide useful information for future investments. To estimate the risk measured by beta, investors use the regression model. The procedure is to plot R_i versus R_m to obtain a scatter of points; each one represents the return on a particular stock and the return on the market. The next step is to fit the straight line to the data that minimized the sum of the squared deviation from the line in the vertical direction. The slope of the line is the best estimate of beta over the period to which the line was fit, and the intercept is the estimate of alpha. This regression line is called

[1]There is a distinction between the single-index model and the market model. The market model is identical to the single-index model except the assumption that $\text{cov}(e_i,e_j) = 0$ is not made.

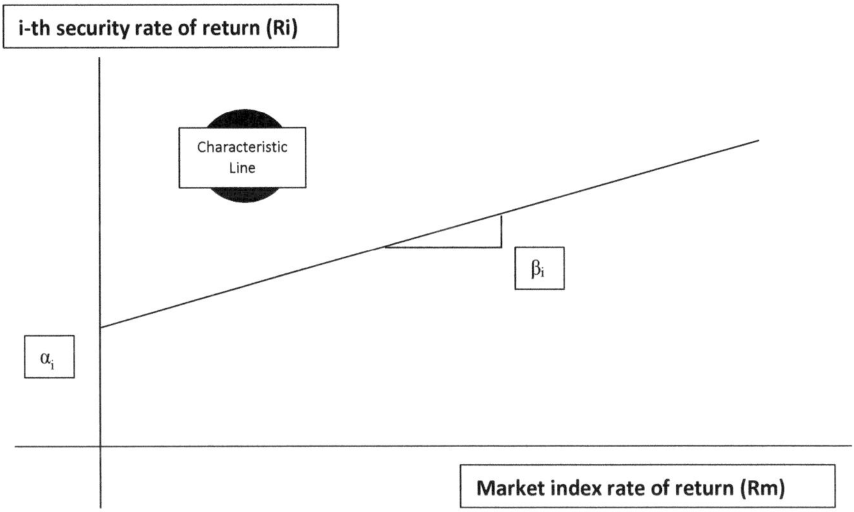

Fig. 2.3 Security characteristic line (*Source* Elton and Gruber 1995, p. 138)

the **security characteristic line**. It is defined as the regression line of best fit through a scatter plot of rates of return for individual risky stock and for the market portfolio over a designated period (see Fig. 2.3).

As can be seen from Fig. 2.3, beta is a measure of a stock's volatility relative to the overall market. The beta parameter is treated as an indicator of risk, and the value of the beta could be interpreted as a measure of single stock risk:

$0 < \beta < 1$—a beta of less than one indicates that the stock return moves less than the market return; there is a lower systematic risk than the market. Defensive stocks have a beta of less than one.

$B = 1$—a beta equal to one indicates that the stock return is the same as the market return.

$B > 1$—a beta greater than one indicates stock return moves larger than the market return; there is a higher systematic risk than the market. Aggressive stocks have a beta greater than one.

Beta is a measure of risk because it relates the covariance of any asset with the variance of the market portfolio. Another basic formula to calculate the beta parameter can be given as (Periasamy 2009, p. 7.33):

$$\beta_i = \frac{\mathrm{cov}_{i,m}}{\sigma_m^2};$$

where:

β_i—The i-th stock beta parameter,

$cov_{i,m}$—Covariance of the i-th stock with the market,

σ_m^2—Variance of the market returns.

The beta that measures relative risk in finance, which most investors estimate, is subject to errors. Furthermore, the entire process of estimation is complicated by the fact that betas are not perfectly stationary over time. Numerous studies have examined the stability of beta and reached similar conclusions; beta is not stable for individual stocks, but for portfolios, its stability increases dramatically (Levy 1971). Marshall Blume (1971) similarly indicated that beta coefficients were highly stable for portfolios containing a large number of securities but unstable for individual stocks. The beta parameter is made to measure the stock's risk, which is related to many economic factors that vary over the cycle, so it is vulnerable to change. Blume proposed a scheme to correct the estimated beta parameters by directly measuring the adjustment toward one and assuming that adjustment in one period is a good estimate for the adjacent one.

In practice, there are several issues that can influence the beta estimates, and each investor should be aware that they exist.[2] The first problem is the selection of a market index. In fact, there are no indices that measure the market portfolio. Many equity market indices measure domestic or international stock market performance, but they are not comprehensive. The most widely used indices for beta estimation are the S&P500 or EURO STOXX, but they include only a subset of stocks that are traded in the USA or European stock exchanges.

The second problem is the choice of period. In choosing a period for beta estimation, it is vital to be aware of the trade-off effect. By going further back in time, an investor gets more observations, but this might be offset by changes in the company's characteristics. The best solution is to select a period that is relatively stable in terms of a firm's business and financial development.

The third problem is the choice of the return interval, which can affect the beta estimates. Stock returns can be measured daily, weekly, monthly, quarterly, or even annually, depending on data availability. Using short time intervals increases the number of observations, but when there is non-trading, the beta estimates could be affected. By contrast, longer return intervals result in few observations, and the information from the market is incomplete. A consequence of different choices in the above-mentioned market index, period, and return interval is that the individual investors can obtain different

---

[2]Read more: Dębski et al. (2018, pp. 5–16).

beta coefficient estimates for the same companies and make other investment choices (Damodaran 1999).

Many attempts have been made to incorporate more data than only returns to estimate beta coefficients. One idea is to relate the beta parameter to fundamental company variables, such as dividend payout, asset growth, liquidity, and many more (Beaver et al. 1970). In addition, another idea was to combine the historical beta and the fundamental beta (Rosenberg and Guy 1976), and implement a dummy variable in the regression model to capture differences in the beta parameters in different industries (Rosenberg and Marathe 1975).

2.5 The Capital Asset Pricing Model (CAPM)

Earlier, we explained how an individual investor should act to select the optimum portfolio following Markowitz's theory. If we assume that all investors behave according to portfolio theory rules, it is possible to determine how the aggregate of investors will behave and how the prices of securities are set. One major theory that explains the valuation of risky assets is capital market theory, which extends portfolio theory and proposes a model for pricing all risky assets. The main idea of this theory is the **Capital Asset Pricing Model (CAPM)**, which enables investors to determine the required rate of return for any risky asset in efficient markets (Sharpe 1964; Lintner 1965; Mossin 1966).[3]

The CAPM is built under a set of assumptions to better explain the valuation of risky securities. It is also built on the Markowitz portfolio model, so it requires the same assumptions and some additional ones (Elton and Gruber 1995, p. 295):

- There are no transaction costs.
- Assets are infinitely divisible.
- There are no taxes.
- Individual investors cannot affect the price of a stock through their buying or selling actions.
- Investors make decisions solely in terms of expected values and standard deviation on their returns on their portfolio.
- Unlimited short sales are allowed.
- Investors can lend or borrow any amount of funds at a risk-free rate.

[3]CAPM was invented by William Sharpe (1964), John Lintner (1965), and Jan Mossin (1966) independently.

- Investors have homogeneous expectations regarding necessary inputs—expected returns and standard deviation of returns.
- There is no inflation, or inflation is fully anticipated.
- All assets are markable.

Some of these assumptions may be considered unrealistic, but relaxing many of them would have only a minor impact on the model and its conclusions. This theory is regarded as very useful in explaining the rates of return on a wide variety of risky assets.

One of the above-mentioned factors that is very important, and that allowed portfolio theory to develop, is the concept of risk-free rate (see Fig. 2.5). Following to Markowitz's model, several authors considered the assumption of a risk-free asset with no variance. This asset provides a risk-free rate of return, which lies on the vertical axis of the portfolio graph. We assume that the risk-free asset expected return is entirely certain, so the variance or standard deviation of return is zero. This return is a risk-free rate of return, and it should be equal to the expected long-run growth of the economy (Reilly and Brown 1997, p. 280).

Combining a risk-free asset with the Markowitz portfolio model has important implications for the whole capital market theory. Because the return of a risk-free asset is certain, the covariance of a risk-free asset with any risky asset will always equal zero, like the correlation (see equation on page 39). At this point, it is essential to consider what happens to the average rate of the return and risk (the variance or standard deviation of return) when you join a risk-free asset to a risky asset portfolio. Like the expected return of two risky assets, the expected rate of return for a portfolio is the weighted average of two returns, written as follows:

$$E\left(R_{\text{portfolio}}\right) = w_{\text{RF}}(\text{RFR}) + (1 - w_{\text{RF}})E(R_i);$$

where:

W_{RF}—The proportion of the portfolio invested in the risk-free asset,
$E(R_i)$—The expected rate of return on risky portfolio i.

Risk for a two-asset portfolio, expressed by variance according to the formula present on page 39, is:

$$E\left(\sigma^2_{\text{portfolio}}\right) = w_1^2\sigma_1^2 + w_2^2\sigma_2^2 + w_1 w_2 \text{cov}_{1,2};$$

Substituting the risk-free rate for the first security and the risky asset portfolio for the second, the formula is as follows:

$$E\left(\sigma^2_{\mathrm{portfolio}}\right) = w^2_{\mathrm{RF}}\sigma^2_{\mathrm{RF}} + (1 - w_{\mathrm{RF}})^2\sigma^2_2 + 2w_{\mathrm{RF}}(1 - w_{\mathrm{RF}})\mathrm{cov}_{\mathrm{RF},2};$$

As stated before, the variance of the risk-free asset is zero. The correlation between the risk-free asset and the risky portfolio is also zero, and the covariance is also zero. After the adjustments, the formula for variance is:

$$E\left(\sigma^2_{\mathrm{portfolio}}\right) = (1 - w_{\mathrm{RF}})^2\sigma^2_2;$$

The standard deviation is:

$$E\left(\sigma_{\mathrm{portfolio}}\right) = (1 - w_{\mathrm{RF}})\sigma_2;$$

Therefore, the standard deviation of such a portfolio with risk-free assets and risky assets is the linear proportion of the standard deviation of the risky asset portfolio (Reilly and Brown 1997, p. 281). Because the expected return and the standard deviation of return are linear combinations, the graph of possible returns and risk looks like a straight line (see Fig. 2.4).

Figure 2.4 shows a graph with portfolio possibilities when a risk-free asset is combined with risky portfolios on the Markowitz efficient frontier. An

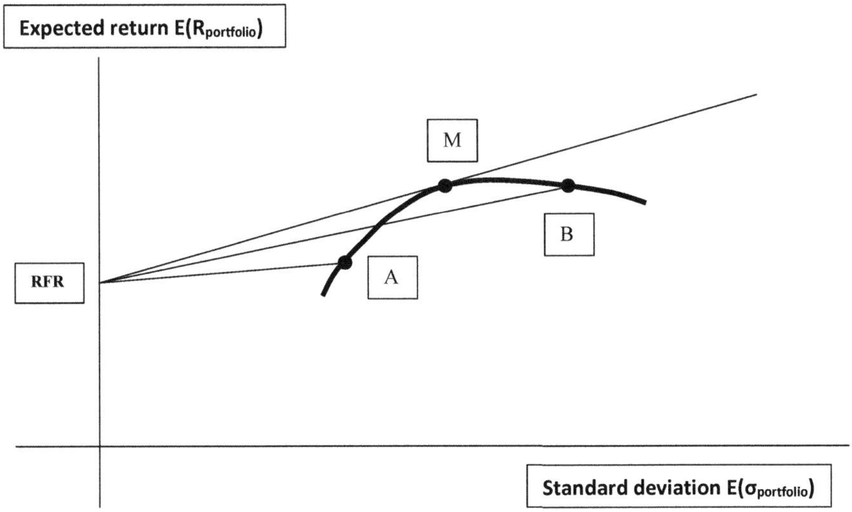

Fig. 2.4 Portfolio possibilities combining a risk-free asset and risky portfolios on the efficient frontier (*Source* Reilly and Brown 1997, p. 282)

investor may attain any point along the straight line between RFR and A by investing money in the risk-free asset W_{RF} and the risky asset portfolio $(1-W_{RF})$ at point A on the efficient frontier. This portfolio set dominates all the risky asset portfolios on the efficient frontier below point A because some portfolios along the line have equal variance with a higher rate of return than the portfolio on the original efficient frontier. Similarly, an investor can attain any point along RFR and B, and again this combination dominates all portfolio possibilities on the original efficient frontier below point B. The investor can draw a line from the RFR point to the efficient frontier until he reaches the point where the line is a tangent to the frontier at point M. The set of portfolio possibilities along the RFR and M line dominates all portfolios below point M (Reilly and Brown 1997, p. 282).

We can imagine that an investor would like to attain a higher expected return than that available at point M, while accepting a higher risk. One possible way to do it is to add (leverage) to the portfolio by borrowing money at the risk-free rate and investing it in a risky assets portfolio. Consequently, both risk and return increase in a linear fashion along the RFR and M line. This means that an investor can have a new efficient frontier—from the RFR tangent to point M—and it is known as the **capital market line (CML)** (see Fig. 2.5).

As can be seen from Fig. 2.5, the capital market line is straight, implying that all portfolios lying on the CML are perfectly positively correlated. All of

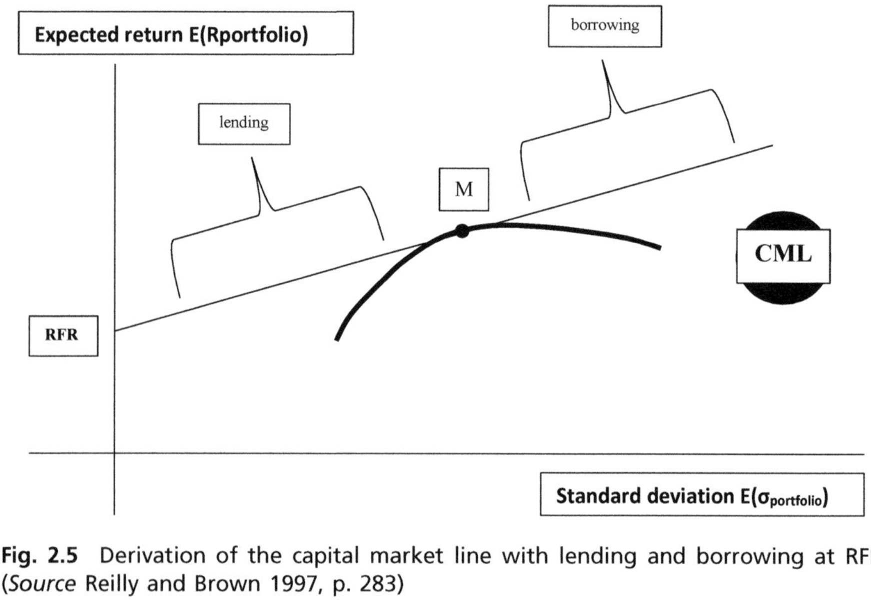

Fig. 2.5 Derivation of the capital market line with lending and borrowing at RFR (*Source* Reilly and Brown 1997, p. 283)

them consist of the risky asset portfolio M and a risk-free asset. Investors have a portfolio partly built on the risk-free rate asset and the risky portfolio M, or they borrow at a risk-free rate and invest those funds in the risky portfolio (Reilly and Brown 1997, p. 283).

Portfolio M lies on the tangent point, and it means that it has the highest portfolio possibility line. Thus, all investors would like to invest their money in portfolio M, borrow, or lend to be somewhere on the capital market line. We can assume that this M portfolio contains all risky assets in proportion to their market value because the whole market is in equilibrium. If all investors hold the same risky portfolio, then, in equilibrium, it must be the **market portfolio**. The market portfolio includes not only stocks but also bonds, derivatives, commodities, and real estate. Each asset is held in the proportion that the market value of that asset represents of the total market value of all assets. The market portfolio contains all risky assets, which may imply that it is completely diversified; each unique risk of any asset is offset by the unique variability of other assets that are part of this portfolio. This unique risk is called an **unsystematic risk** (it is specific to a particular security, sometimes called idiosyncratic risk),[4] and it is fully diversifiable. For every well-diversified portfolio, the unsystematic risk tends toward zero. This means that only **systematic risk**, which is caused by macroeconomic variables, remains in the market portfolio and it is not diversifiable. Systematic risk arises from changes in macro-level factors, like national income, or monetary and fiscal policy, which affect the overall market. This systematic risk, measured by the standard deviation of the returns of the market portfolio, changes over time with macroeconomic variables that affect the valuation of all risk assets. To sum up, the total risk of each security can be broken down into two parts: market risk (systematic), which is proportional to the risk of the market portfolio, and specific risk (unsystematic), which is uncorrelated with the market risk, which is fully diversifiable (see Fig. 2.6).

The capital market line concept leads all investors to build the same risky asset portfolio, called the market portfolio. With different risk preferences, individual investors have a different position on the CML based on financing decisions. If the investor is relatively risk-averse, he will lend part of the portfolio at the RFR by buying some risk-free assets and investing the rest in the market portfolio. In contrast, if the investor is less risk-averse, he can borrow funds at the RFR and invest everything in the market portfolio. As proven earlier, portfolios on the CML dominate other portfolios, and the CML is

---

[4]For example, labor strike or technological breakthrough.

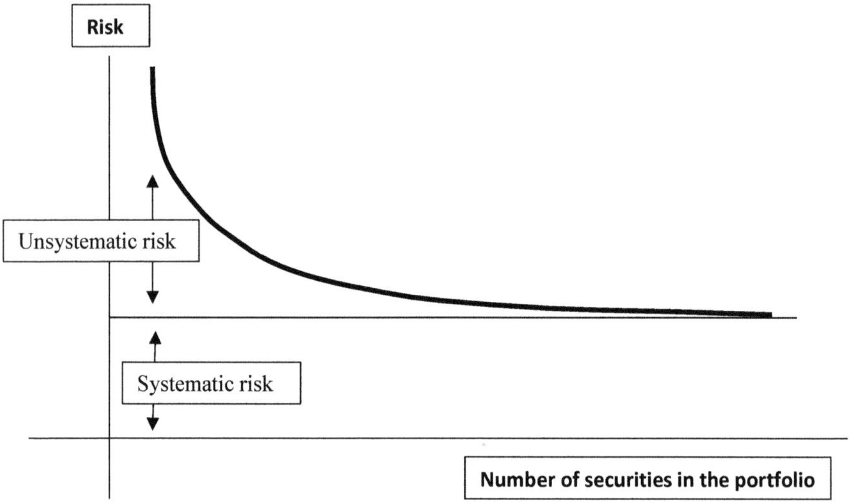

Fig. 2.6 Systematic and unsystematic risk (*Source* Siddaiah 2009, p. 392)

the efficient frontier. James Tobin (1958) defined this division of the investment decision as the **separation theorem**. The separation theorem claims that everyone should hold a portfolio of risky assets—the market portfolio—made up of all the assets traded, and adjust their risk preferences by putting some of the funds in risk-free assets (Solnik 1988).

Now it is time to consider what the measure of risk is for the capital market line. As stated earlier, the relevant risk measure for a risky asset is the covariance with the market portfolio. It was first discussed in Markowitz's portfolio model, where it was noted that the relevant risk for an investor who adds securities to a portfolio is their average covariance with all other assets in the portfolio. Later, it was proven that the only relevant portfolio is the market portfolio. Consequently, these two findings show that the only consideration for an individual risky asset is its average covariance with all the risky assets in the market portfolio or the asset's covariance with the market portfolio (Reilly and Brown 1997, p. 286).

As previously stated, an asset's covariance with the market portfolio emerged as a relevant risk measure; therefore, now it is time to determine an appropriate expected rate of return on a risky asset. This measure is critical because it enables you to value an asset and compare this estimated rate of return to the required rate of return implied by the Capital Asset Pricing Model and stipulate whether it is undervalued or overvalued. The visual representation of the relation between risk and the required rate of return of an asset is the **security market line (SML)** (see Fig. 2.7).

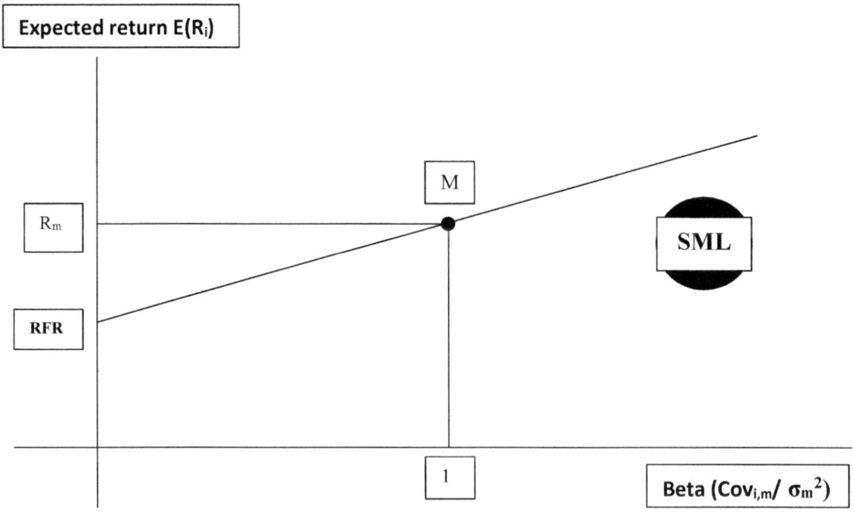

Fig. 2.7 Security market line (*Source* Reilly and Brown 1997, p. 283)

We already know that the relevant measure of risk for an individual risky asset is its covariance with the market portfolio ($\text{Cov}_{i,m}$). The return for the market portfolio should be consistent with its own risk (R_m), which is the covariance of the market with itself, the covariance for any asset with itself its variance σ_m^2. In turn, the equation for the risk-return line is as follows:

$$E(R_i) = \text{RFR} + \frac{R_m - \text{RFR}}{\sigma_m^2}\left(\text{cov}_{i,m}\right) = \text{RFR} + \frac{\text{cov}_{i,m}}{\sigma_m^2}(R_m - \text{RFR});$$

If we define $\text{Cov}_{i,m}/\sigma_m^2$ as the beta parameter, the equation can be written as:

$$E(R_i) = \text{RFR} + \beta_i(R_m - \text{RFR});$$

The equation of SML explains that the expected rate of return for a risky asset is determined by the RFR plus a risk premium for the individual asset. The risk premium is defined as a product of the systematic risk of an asset (beta) and the prevailing market risk premium (Reilly and Brown 1997, p. 288).

In market equilibrium, all assets and portfolios should be plotted on the security market line (SML). This means that their estimated rates of return are consistent with their level of systematic risk. If an asset with an estimated rate of return that plots above the SML is perceived as **underpriced**, it means that an investor would receive a rate of return that is above its required rate of return based on its systematic risk. In contrast, if an asset with an estimated rate of return that plots below the SML is perceived as **overpriced**, it means that an investor would receive a rate of return that is below its required rate of return based on its systematic risk. In an efficient market in equilibrium, an investor cannot expect any asset to plot off the SML because all securities should provide returns that are equal to their required rates of return (Reilly and Brown 1997, p. 290). A direct implication of CAPM is that the equilibrium expected return of an asset should be equal to the risk-free rate plus a risk premium that is proportional to the covariance of the asset return with the return on the market portfolio, which is the famous measure of the systematic risk beta coefficient (Solnik 1988).

2.6 International Diversification and the Reduction of Risk

Earlier, we showed that the risk of a portfolio is measured by the ratio of the variance of the portfolio's return relative to the variance of the market return.[5] This ratio is the beta coefficient. When the number of securities in a portfolio increases, the portfolio risk declines rapidly and then asymptotically approaches the level of systematic risk. As a result, the total risk of the portfolio is composed of a systematic risk and an unsystematic risk, which could be fully diversifiable. A fully diversified domestic portfolio has a beta parameter equal to one, which is the market risk.

Now, it is time to explain what happens when we attempt to reduce risk by investing in more than one country. The opportunity set of possible investments is growing extensively. Internationally, more assets and more kinds of financial products are available. The indication of the gain of including foreign stocks in a portfolio was presented by Bruno Solnik (1974a). He computed the risk of randomly selected international portfolios and showed that an international portfolio of stocks has about half of as much risk as a portfolio of the same size containing only US stocks (see Fig. 2.8).

As we can see from Fig. 2.8, there are incremental gains from diversifying both domestically and internationally. The risk of a US portfolio is 27% of the risk of a typical security; the risk of an internationally diversified portfolio (the lower line) is 12% of the risk of a typical security. This means that, for an American investor, the international portfolio's risk is lower than the domestic one. This relation arises because the returns from international markets are

[5]More formally, the covariance between portfolio's return and the variance of market portfolio return.

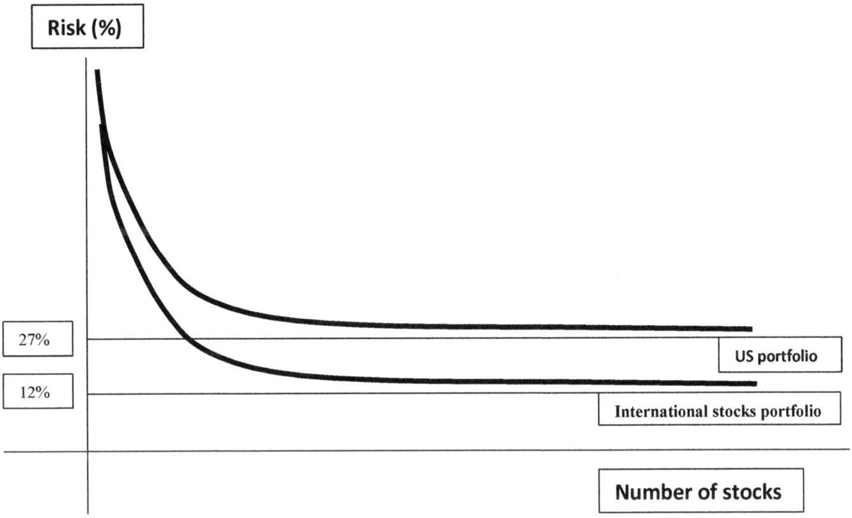

Fig. 2.8 International diversification gain (*Source* Solnik 1974a, pp. 45–54)

not perfectly correlated. Internationally diversified portfolios are the same in principle because the idea is to find stocks that are not perfectly correlated in order to reduce the portfolio's risk (Eiteman et al. 2016, pp. 381–382).

While there is a gain from **international diversification** because of the independent returns between domestic and international assets, there is a possibility of added risk from unanticipated changes in exchange rates. The investor has to acquire an additional asset: currency. In principle, it is one asset, but it is two in the expected return and risk. The risk associated with international diversification, including currency risk, is more complex than domestic diversification. However, when measured in terms of the local currency, it is crucial to decide whether the gains from imperfect correlations between stock returns more than compensate for the exchange rate risk. This additional risk factor depends on both the volatility of exchange rates and the correlation of exchange rates and security prices. It is also important whether the stocks come from one foreign country or more (Levi 2009).

Some investors may observe that, due to international economic integration and the globalization of the financial markets, the benefits of international diversification have declined in recent years. Nowadays, national economies are closely linked due to transnational companies and organizations, informational technology, cross-border investments, and the convertibility of major currencies. This closeness of the world's economies is strengthened by their interdependence, and the benefits of international diversification may decrease. This observation was verified by Kevin Chang and Christian Leonhard (2007), who showed that the benefits of international diversification have remained stable in recent years. This interesting implication was explained by the fact that the globalization process has a mainly regional effect, like the EU, and when the variance composition is examined at a global scale, the gain still exists. It is more likely that much closer economic links within an economic region reduce the gains of international diversification, and it has been proven that regional diversification within the EU has become less effective.

Consequently, the high degree of independence between regions, not countries, is the source of diversification opportunities for internationally oriented investors. However, we have to remember that even closely linked countries may not be closely correlated because of different business cycles and levels of economic development, e.g., advanced, emerging, or frontier. Nowadays, international diversification is still effective at the regional level. To conclude, it is vital to identify international stock markets or correlation coefficients of economic regions to determine the countries and regions whose stock prices move together and those who move in opposite and unrelated directions.

2.7 The Efficient Frontier for the International Investor

Based on the above, international investors can possibly obtain a better risk-return trade-off in comparison with domestic investors. Expanding the universe of assets should lead to higher returns for the same level of risk or less risk for the same level of expected return. For the presentation of the international portfolio's diversification, the efficient frontier has to be mentioned to explain the gains from building the portfolio on the global marketplace.

Herbert Grubel (1968) was one of the first to propose a model consisting of two countries that can both interchangeably invest in their bonds, showing gains on the international efficient frontier. Further studies have extended this research, showing a positive diversification impact on a portfolio's risk (Levy and Sarnat 1970).

We already know that the efficient frontier represents portfolios that have a minimum expected risk for each level of expected return. However, with the international environment, the efficient frontier shifts to the left of the purely domestic environment (see Fig. 2.9).

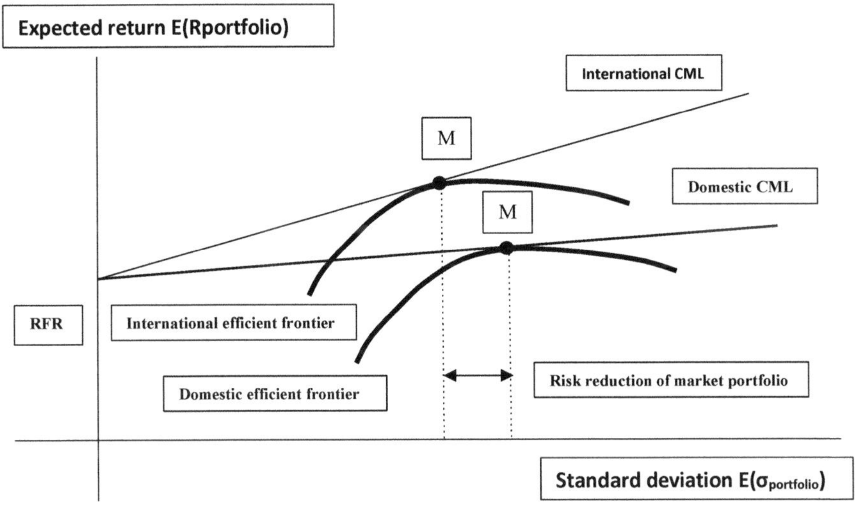

Fig. 2.9 International and domestic efficient frontiers (*Source* Siddaiah 2009, p. 395)

As can be seen from Fig. 2.9, the curvature of the international efficient frontier increases; the greater the curvature, the greater the risk reduction for the given level of return. We can assume that an internationally diversified portfolio provides a lower risk for each level of the expected return. The new CML with the steeper slope starts from the same risk-free rate and goes through the tangent point along the internationally diversified efficient frontier. So, we can assume that the international market portfolio is superior to the domestic market portfolio, giving a higher expected return and lower risk (Siddaiah 2009, p. 395).

From an application perspective, it is useful to know which countries' portfolios lie on the efficient frontier and provide better diversification alternatives, and if such relationships are time-invariant. This research question was explicitly explained by Abuaf et al. (2019). Their study was made from the US perspective, so they stated that countries that are more economically independent from the USA provide better diversification for American investors. Securities issued by Mexican and Chinese companies appeared to be the best diversifiers of US portfolios.

2.8 International Capital Asset Pricing Model (ICAPM)

The traditional CAPM discussed earlier proposes a clear theory of asset pricing in the domestic environment. This analysis is related to the return and risk of the market and portfolio under a single currency. The theoretical framework of the CAPM can be easily extended to the international market. Recently, investors have witnessed the extension of investments in foreign countries, and they are aware that they need explanations for factors that affect expected returns. At present, investors build portfolios in different financial markets all over the world. It is important to assume that the assets are priced in an internationally integrated capital market because the expected returns on foreign stock are appropriate for the risk of these stocks in an internationally diversified portfolio. The **International CAPM** could be a single-factor ICAPM or a multiple-factor ICAPM (Solnik 1974b). The equation of a single-factor ICAPM for the risk-return line is as follows:

$$E(R_w) = RFR_w + \beta_w(R_{\text{wm}} - RFR_w);$$

where:

$E(R_w)$—Expected return for the risky asset as part of the international portfolio,

RFR_w—World risk-free interest rate,

β_w—International or global beta parameter,

R_{wm}—World market index.

The first problem is to define the risk-free element in the model, which is usually the risk-free rate in the currency in which the overall returns are being measured. The next step is to evaluate the beta parameter, in which case it is advisable to use the world index. There is a whole range of world indices calculated by MSCI, S&P, the FTSE, and EURO STOXX. The beta parameter for this particular model indicates the world risk premium regarding the world index (Madura and Fox 2017, p. 589).

The single-factor International Capital Pricing Model is based on the following assumptions:

- The world market portfolio is stable.
- Purchasing Power Parity holds all over the whole period.
- All investors have the same consumption basket.
- Investors hold a portfolio of risk-free assets in their own currency and the unchanged world market portfolio,

- All investors are homogeneous, and they hold every security in the market portfolio (Siddaiah 2009, p. 396).

The above single-factor CAPM variation does not capture foreign exchange risk and it is called the global CAPM applied by Stulz (1995a, b). If Purchasing Power Parity holds, a percentage depreciation of the domestic currency is offset by the same increase in domestic prices. In that case, the return of foreign assets is not exposed to exchange risk, meaning that the returns are subject only to the global market factor, and all assets are priced correctly (Siddaiah 2009, p. 396). Single-factor ICAPM has the same structure that domestic CAPM with the global market index and it is simpler to use than the multi-factor model.

The next step is the violation of the Purchasing Power Parity. It means that investors in different countries realize different real returns for a given asset when PPP does not hold and it is connected with exchange rate risk exposure. International CAPM implies that investing in foreign assets, measured in the home currency, is exposed to two different kinds of risk: the sensitivity of the domestic country index to a global market portfolio and the performance of a domestic currency against foreign currency. When the domestic market portfolio does not move in line with the world market, the beta coefficient evaluated on the domestic CAPM will be different from the beta evaluated on the International CAPM. It means that the International CAPM established the condition under which integrated financial markets are in equilibrium. If the world's financial markets were not integrated, the world market portfolio would not exist. The markets are considered integrated if all assets with the same risk are priced equally; if not, those world's markets are segmented.

The second issue is currency risk. If an investor holds foreign assets, the return in domestic currency is influenced by the exchange rate. From the investor's perspective when the Purchasing Power Parity does not hold, it means that investors from different countries expect different returns for the same assets.[6] If the market is in equilibrium, the expected return on any security, denominated in the domestic currency, is equal to the risk-free domestic return plus the risk premium for the exposure to the global market and the exchange rate risk. The formula can be written as follows:

$$E(R_w) = RFR_w + \beta_w(R_{\text{wm}} - RFR_w) + \beta_w(FCRP);$$

FCRP—Foreign currency risk premium.

[6]The offset mechanism does not work.

This formula depicts a simple multi-factor international CAPM but this model could be relatively complex in terms of estimating risk coefficients and risk premium, see Dumas and Solnik (1995).

Another solution, if Purchasing Power Parity does not hold, is to hedge foreign assets against exchange the rate risk using available derivatives. When an investor cannot hedge against the currency risk, the return on international investments is influenced by changes in exchange rates. Foreign currencies might be used for financing investments and investments per se.[7] If the foreign currency depreciates against the domestic currency, the cost of financing the investment will be low, and if the foreign currency appreciates, the cost will be high. The same rule applies to foreign investments. Appreciation of the foreign currency would yield high effective returns for the investor, and depreciation would yield low effective returns.

As previously stated, investors can use a portfolio of currencies to reduce exchange rate risk aimed at financing or investments. Foreign financing with a highly diversified portfolio of currencies could be less costly than financing with one or a few currencies. If foreign interest rates are lower, it is unlikely that all currencies appreciate enough to offset the benefits of lower interest rates. Exchange rates do not usually move in the same direction if they are not highly correlated. The same is true with investments in a diversified portfolio of many currencies; it may be more rewarding than investing in a single currency (Siddaiah 2009, p. 398).

To summarize, rather than considering only the domestic market, the International CAPM takes the single global market concept as a market. That idea of the International CAPM was extended by explaining international relations between the prices of securities through a multiple-factor specification that takes into account both national and international factors (Solnik 1974b). The multiple-factor International Asset Pricing Model assumes that investors differ not only regarding risk aversion but also consumption patterns. Regarding the multi-country model, each stock is influenced by the domestic market factor, which in turn is influenced by the single world market factor. This means that all stocks are indirectly influenced by the global factor through the national factor. Hence, a stock risk could be divided into risks caused by the global factor and the internal, country factor. The sensitivity of the stock to the world factor results in many economic relations, like the degree of international trade and investments, monetary policy, and capital flows. Therefore, these led to multiple-factor solutions like the International Capital Asset Pricing Model for the pricing of single assets that are

[7] Investment per se means buying and selling currencies.

Table 2.1 Comparison between the international and domestic capital asset pricing models

International CAPM	Domestic CAPM
Risk and return are influenced by different currencies	Risk and return are influenced by one country's currency
Investors have homogeneous expectations toward return and risk	Investors have different expectations toward return and risk
Portfolio efficiency is influenced by different currencies	Portfolio efficiency is influenced by one currency
The market is considered a whole, and it has linked with other countries	The market has segments within a country

Source Naderi et al. (2012, p. 5)

part of international portfolios, and which take into consideration inflation, exchange rates, and forward premiums.

In theory, the primary distinction between the standard CAPM and the ICAPM is the definition of the market (the global portfolio index) and the calculation of the beta parameter. There are also numerous model variations that take into account different factors. To compare the standard CAPM model and International CAPM, it is possible to point out four major differences (see Table 2.1).

Another problem could be the practical application of the International multiple-factor CAPM. It requires defining the world's risk-free rate and making assumptions about the preferences of investors from different countries. Many studies have been made, and the empirical results of international portfolio diversification can be concluded in three propositions: (1) country (region) selection is better than security selection; (2) do not hedge against currency risk when investing in emerging markets; and (3) the degree of segmentation of international markets is still considerable. Presently, the degree of national market integration with the global market is difficult and subjective. To use those solutions in practical investing, the best option is to select the most segmented country markets and not hedge against currency risk (Thalassinos and Kiriazidis 2003).

References

Abuaf, N., Ayala, T., & Sinclair, D. (2019). Global Equity Investing: An Efficient Frontier Approach. *International Finance, 22*(1), 70–85.

Beaver, W., Kettler, P., & Scholes, M. (1970). The Association Between Market Determined and Accounting Determined Risk Measures. *The Accounting Review, 45*(4), 654–682.

Blume, M. (1971). On the Assessment of Risk. *The Journal of Finance, 26*(1), 1–10.
Chang, K., & Leonhard, C. (2007). International Diversification: The Within- and Between-Region Effects. *The Journal of Investing, 16,* 51–68.
Damodaran, A. (1999). *Estimating Risk Parameters.* Stern School of Business. https://archive.nyu.edu/bitstream/2451/26789/2/S-CDM-99-02.pdf. Accessed 17 Mar 2020.
Dębski, W., Feder-Sempach, E., & Wójcik, S. (2018). Statistical Properties of Rates of Return on Shares Listed on the German, French, and Polish Markets—A Comparative Study. *Contemporary Economics, 12*(1), 5–16. https://doi.org/10.5709/ce.1897-9254.248.
Dumas, B., & Solnik, B. (1995). The World Price of Foreign Exchange Risk. *Journal of Finance, 50*(2), 445–479. https://doi.org/10.1111/j.1540-6261.1995.tb04791.x.
Eiteman, D., Stonehill, A., & Moffett, M. (2016). *Multinational Business Finance* (14th ed.). Boston: Pearson.
Elton, E., & Gruber, M. (1995). *Modern Portfolio Theory and Investment Analysis.* New York: Wiley.
Grubel, H. (1968). Internationally Diversified Portfolios: Welfare Gains and Capital Flows. *American Economic Review, 58*(5), 1299–1314.
Knight, F. (1921). *Risk, Uncertainty, and Profit*. Boston: Houghton Mifflin.
Levi M. (2009). *International Finance* (1st ed.). London: Routledge. https://books.google.pl/books?id=J7J4LO72I0IC&pg=PA327&lpg=PA327&dq=Why+Not+Diversify+Internationally+Rather+than+Domestically?&source=bl&ots=YMFxW8HF5Z&sig=ACfU3U0meU1G4Wnu3X6RJG0EU1u75qTp7Q&hl=pl&sa=X&ved=2ahUKEwiNm4-w0bDoAhVnlosKHd0cB6oQ6AEwCXoECAkQAQ#v=onepage&q=Why%20Not%20Diversify%20Internationally%20Rather%20than%20Domestically%3F&f=false. Accessed 23 Mar 2020.
Levy, H., & Sarnat, M. (1970). International Diversification of Investment Portfolios. *The American Economic Review, 60*(4), 668–675.
Levy, R. (1971). On the Short-Term Stationarity of Beta Coefficients. *Financial Analysts Journal, 27*(6), 55–62.
Lintner, J. (1965). The Valuation of Risk Assets and the Selection of Risky Investments in Stock Portfolios and Capital Budgets. *Review of Economics and Statistics, 47*(1), 13–37.
Madura, J., & Fox, R. (2017). *International Financial Management* (4th ed.). Boston: Cengage Learning EMEA. https://books.google.pl/books?id=5cBqxUwGtvkC&pg=PA589&lpg=PA589&dq=world+risk+free+rate+international+capm&source=bl&ots=v6yK7UnxMm&sig=ACfU3U1_6Oivpd-yZDJL2WIewCkFEdScrg&hl=pl&sa=X&ved=2ahUKEwj8ktiX9LDoAhXJ-ioKHbTFDoc4ChDoATADegQICRAB#v=onepage&q=world%20risk%20free%20rate%20international%20capm&f=false. Accessed 23 Mar 2020.
Markowitz, H. (1952). Portfolio Selection. *The Journal of Finance, 7*(1), 77–91.
Mossin, J. (1966). Equilibrium in a Capital Asset Market. *Econometrica, 34*(4), 768–783.

Naderi, M., Amirhosseni, Z., & Ahmadinia, H. (2012). A Comprehensive Review on International Capital Asset Pricing Models. *Science Series Data Report, 4*(8), 4–19.

Periasamy, P. (2009). *Financial Management*. New Delhi: Tata McGraw-Hill Education. https://books.google.pl/books?id=ZAtjZwZN5pcC&printsec=frontcover&redir_esc=y#v=onepage&q&f=false. Accessed 16 Mar 2020.

Reilly, F. (1986). *Investments* (2nd ed.). Chicago, IL: The Dryden Press.

Reilly, F., & Brown, K. (1997). *Investment Analysis and Portfolio Management* (5th ed.). Fort Worth, TX: The Dryden Press.

Rosenberg, B., & Guy, J. (1976). Prediction of Beta from Investment Fundamentals: Part Two. Alternative Prediction Methods. *Financial Analysts Journal, 32*(4), 62–70.

Rosenberg, B., & Marathe, V. (1975). *The Prediction of Investment Risk: Systematic and Residual Risk*. Reprint 21 (Berkley Working Paper Series).

Sharpe, W. (1963). A Simplified Model for Portfolio Analysis. *Management Science, 9*(2), 277–293.

Sharpe, W. (1964). Capital Asset Prices: A Theory of Market Equilibrium Under Conditions of Risk. *The Journal of Finance, 19*(3), 425–442.

Solnik, B. (1988). *International Investments*. Reading, MA: Addison-Wesley.

Solnik, B. (1974a). Why Not Diversify Internationally Rather Than Domestically? *Financial Analysts Journal, 30*(4), 48–52.

Solnik, B. (1974b). The International Pricing of Risk: An Empirical Investigation of the World Capital Market Structure. *Journal of Finance, 29*(2), 365–378.

Siddaiah, T. (2009). *International Financial Management*. https://books.google.pl/books?id=0XllKAoOES8C&pg=PR1&hl=pl&source=gbs_selected_pages&cad=3#v=onepage&q&f=false. New Delhi, India: Publisher Pearson Education.

Stulz, R. (1995a). The Cost of Capital in Internationally Integrated Markets: The Case of Nestlé. *European Financial Management, 1*, 11–22.

Stulz, R. (1995b). Globalization of Capital Markets and the Cost of Capital: The Case of Nestlé. *Journal of Applied Corporate Finance, 8*, 30–38.

Thalassinos, E., & Kiriazidis, T. (2003). Degrees of Integration in International Portfolio Diversification: Effective Systemic Risk. *European Research Studies, VI*(1–2), 111–122.

Tobin, J. (1958). Liquidity Preference as Behavior Towards Risk. *The Review of Economic Studies, 25*(2), 65–86.

Part II

Fundamentals of Exchange-Traded Funds

3

The Basics of Exchange-Traded Funds

3.1 Introduction

The history of exchange-traded funds (ETFs) dates back to the late 1980s and early 1990s. The first financial instrument of this kind[1]—Toronto 35 Index Participation Units (then known as TIPs or TIPs35)—made their debut on the Toronto Stock Exchange (TSE) on March 9, 1990. It was a warehouse receipt-based stock portfolio instrument that allowed investors to participate in the performance of the TSX 35 Index. Over the last 30 years, exchange-traded funds have become not only one of the largest financial innovations in the asset management industry but also one of the most recognizable financial instruments available to both individual investors and various types of institutional investors.

The first ETFs created in the early 1990s were aimed at imitating the performance of the main benchmarks of domestic stock markets. They included the above-mentioned TIPs, which replicated the performance of the TSX 35 Index, Standard & Poor's Depositary Receipts (currently known as SPDR S&P 500 ETF Trust) launched in January 1993 and which mirrored the performance of the S&P 500 Index—the first ETF listed on the US

[1]According to some authors (e.g., Kupiec [1990], Gastineau [2010], and Seddik Meziani [2016]), the first financial products with features similar to exchange-traded funds as we know them today were Index Participation Shares (IPS). Two types—Equity Index Participations (EIPs) and Cash Index Participations (CIPs)—were briefly traded in 1989, respectively, on the American Stock Exchange and on the Philadelphia Stock Exchange. These "basket" financial instruments were meant to be a relatively simple proxy for the S&P 500 Index and were simultaneously traded on stock exchanges, like stocks. IPS were hybrid instruments that had some characteristics similar to those of existing index-futures contracts, index options contracts, and index mutual funds (Kupiec 1990).

T. Miziołek et al., *International Equity Exchange-Traded Funds*,
https://doi.org/10.1007/978-3-030-53864-4_3

market, the ETF tracking performance of the Nikkei 300 Index (currently known as the Nomura Nikkei 300 Stock Index Listed Fund), which launched in May 1995—the first ETF listed in Japan (Osaki 2001), and the NZ Top 10 Fund (currently known as the NZ Top 10 ETF), which launched in June 1996—the first ETF listed on the Pacific exchange.

However, as far back as the second half of the 1990s, ETFs that offered exposure to international equity markets started to be introduced to stock exchanges—mainly in the USA. The first country-specific ETFs debuted on the AMEX in March 1996 as Morgan Stanley launched 17 World Equity Benchmark Shares (WEBS), which replicated the performance of the MSCI country equity indexes, mainly developed ones (they were managed by Barclays Global Investors [BGI]) as well as 9 Country Baskets that imitated the performance of the Financial Times (now FTSE Russell) country stock indexes (Wiandt and McClatchy 2002). A year later—in August 1997—the first global equity ETF was launched in New Zealand (BlackRock 2011).[2]

Since then, exchange-traded funds, including international equity ETFs, have experienced unprecedented growth, not encountered in the history of collective investment institutions. In the 2010s, these financial instruments became an integral part of many investment portfolios, especially for institutional investors who operate in developed markets. International equity ETFs have also become increasingly popular as tools that enable the effective diversification of investments on a regional or global scale. In many cases, they replaced financial instruments used thus far, including stocks, equity derivatives (single stock and index futures, index equity options), or structured products.

In the following parts of this chapter, we will outline the most important formal and investment characteristics of exchange-traded funds. We will start by discussing the legal aspects related to these financial instruments, both in relation to the US market and other highly developed financial markets. Then, attention will be paid to issues that are in the spotlight of investors and advisors who use ETFs, i.e., issues related to index-tracking, including methods of index replication and securities-lending practices. When discussing the above, various types of risk faced by investors owning ETFs' shares, as well as the costs associated with investing in them will also be thoroughly characterized. All of the above topics will be presented, especially with regard to international equity ETFs. Importantly, this analysis will be made—where it is possible and justified—from the point of view of entities that invest in ETFs in various parts of the world, so that analysis

[2]More information about the history of global, regional, and single-country equity ETFs will be presented in Chapters 5, 6, and 7.

will be as universal as possible. However, most references will apply to US and European markets since they are the most developed, matured, and best examined.

3.2 Legal Structures

An exchange-traded fund is a pooled investment vehicle with shares (units) that are listed and traded on registered secondary markets—stock exchanges or other trading platforms—or over-the-counter (OTC). They can be bought or sold on exchanges throughout the day, at any time during the trading session, through broker-dealers on a commission basis at a market-determined price, much like publicly traded stocks[3] or other financial instruments listed on exchanges (Fang and Heinrichs 2017). Sometimes they can be traded at their net asset value (NAV) based on the closing prices of the ETF's underlying assets. Large, usually institutional investors also buy and sell ETFs' shares on the OTC market through liquidity providers, and on the primary market through authorized participants.

Like the majority of other investment funds, ETFs offer access to multiple financial instruments, various asset classes, and domestic and international markets in one transaction. Thus, they help investors to spread risk through portfolio diversification and lower the cost of investing. Simultaneously, they enable investors to realize the idea of passive investing, i.e., mirroring the performance (return) and thus investment risk of a selected benchmark, usually a financial index. Finally, ETFs, probably like no other financial instrument in the modern history of financial markets, democratized investing. They enabled not only large institutional investors but also not very wealthy and non-professional individual market participants from different parts of the world to access markets, assets, and sectors/themes previously out of their reach. In turn, mainly due to the growing competition among ETF providers—and the value of their assets and trading volumes that are increasing enormously—the total costs of investing have dropped considerably, regarding both total expense ratios as well as transaction costs (e.g., trading spreads). This allows investors to keep more of the returns they earn.

Exchange-traded funds are commonly structured in most countries as open-end investment funds (investment companies) (OEFs), so they are governed by the regulations as traditional mutual funds. For example, in the USA, the vast majority of ETFs are structured as OEFs and regulated by

[3] In fact, ETF trading is—in many aspects—different from stock trading. More information on these differences and various aspects of ETF trading will be presented in the next chapter.

the Investment Company Act of 1940 (1940 Act),[4,5] while in the European Union, they are mostly structured as UCITS funds (Undertakings for Collective Investments in Transferable Securities) and regulated by the UCITS Directive.[6,7] The open-end fund structure is generally used by ETFs whose primary objective is to provide exposure to stock and bond asset classes. Other advantages of this type of structure include the ability to immediately reinvest dividends and interest, and the possibility to use derivatives, portfolio sampling, and securities lending. Such funds are, however, subject to significant restrictions in the investment policy, e.g., they have quite strict rules for investment portfolio diversification and limited access to some financial instruments and alternative assets (such as commodities and currencies).

Some ETFs are structured differently. For example, in the USA, they are unit investment trusts (UITs)[8] or grantor trusts.[9] A unit investment trust is a type of fund that mixes the basic characteristics of mutual funds (issuing redeemable shares) and closed-end funds (CEFs) (typically issuing only a specific, fixed number of shares). Additionally, a UIT does not actively trade its investment portfolio. Instead, it buys and holds a fixed portfolio of securities until the UIT's set termination date, at which time the trust is dissolved, and the proceeds are paid to shareholders (Investment Company Institute 2019). Since UITs have no boards of directors or investment advisors who

[4]However, ETFs must receive exemptive relief from the Securities and Exchange Commission (SEC) from certain provisions of the 1940 Act. This structure, like the other structures in the USA, is subject to the Securities Act of 1933 (Securities Act) and the Securities Exchange Act of 1934 (Exchange Act). In September 2019, the Securities and Exchange Commission adopted a new rule (Rule 6c-11) and formed amendments that are designed to modernize the regulation of ETFs, by establishing a clear and consistent framework for the vast majority of ETFs in the USA. The rule provides several exemptions from the 1940 Act to permit ETFs to form and operate without the need to obtain individual exemptive relief from the SEC.

[5]According to Morningstar calculations, as of June 30, 2018, as many as 98% of US ETFs (considering their assets) are organized and regulated as registered investment companies (RICs) under the US Investment Company Act of 1940 (Vanguard 2019).

[6]Directive 2009/65/EC of the European Parliament and of the Council of July 13, 2009, on the coordination of laws, regulations, and administrative provisions relating to undertakings for collective investment in transferable securities (UCITS) (with amendments). UCITS funds may be constituted in accordance with contract law (as common funds managed by management companies), trust law (as unit trusts), or statute (as investment companies).

[7]According to Morningstar estimates, 91% of European-domiciled ETFs, considering their assets, are organized and regulated as registered investment companies under the UCITS Directive (as of September 30, 2015) (Vanguard 2016). European ETFs that are not regulated by this Directive operate in countries outside the European Union (mainly in Switzerland) as well as in some other EU member states where they are regulated by national law (e.g., in Poland).

[8]In such a legal form first and biggest ETF in the USA operates—the SPDR S&P 500 ETF Trust.

[9]More information about different ETF structures in the USA—with regard to legal and tax considerations—can be found in Vanguard (2015).

manage the portfolio, they have less investment flexibility than open-end ETFs.

Moreover, UITs are not permitted to lend securities in their portfolios or use derivatives, and they must fully replicate the indexes they track, which means they cannot use sampling. Like open-end funds, UITs are registered investment companies (RICs) that are regulated under the 1940 Act, and therefore, they offer the same level of investor protections as OEFs. In turn, grantor trusts are required to hold a fixed portfolio, which makes the structure ideally suited for ETFs that invest solely in physical commodities or currencies. Because the nature of the underlying investments prevents grantor trusts from being classified as investment companies under the 1940 Act, grantor trust ETFs are regulated only by the Securities Act and Exchange Act.

Interestingly, in some countries, exchange-traded funds do not act in the legal form of open-end funds. For example, in Poland, ETFs can act untypically as closed-end funds (called portfolio funds). However, their units—called investment certificates—can be created and canceled, like in OEFs, on an ongoing (daily) basis. In addition to ETFs structured as various types of investment funds, there are—especially in Europe—many similar investment vehicles that aim to track the performance of the financial index that have a completely different legal form.[10] For example, in many countries, exchange-traded notes (ETNs) are listed on stock exchanges. These are debt securities that have a pre-set maturity date, but they usually do not pay out an annual coupon or dividend. They provide access to niche markets, sectors, or strategies that could be difficult to track with traditional ETFs. ETNs represent a promise by the issuer (usually a bank) to pay a specified return of a given index. In this context, it is worth bearing in mind that investors in ETNs become unsecured creditors of the issuing bank and therefore need to take into account an additional risk—credit risk. Exchange-traded commodities (ETCs) have quite a similar nature. They are also debt securities that mainly track the performance of a single commodity or a basket of commodities (sometimes a currency or a basket of currencies). Both ETNs and ETCs, together with ETFs, are often classified as exchange-traded products (ETPs).

In most countries, ETNs and ETCs constitute a small part of the ETP market, which is usually dominated by ETFs that are often the only passive instruments listed on the exchange in a given country. However, in some countries, index-tracking exchange-traded products are structured—or until recently have been listed—as debt instruments. For example, in Mexico, ETPs are regulated as a specific type of security, i.e., indexed trust notes

[10] A review of various structures of such financial instrument is presented by Stevenson (2010).

(certificados bursátiles indizados). They are securities issued by Mexican trusts whose purpose is to track the performance of an underlying index, asset, or parameter. They are listed on the stock exchange and treated similarly to corporate issuers (Vanguard Mexico 2019). Some ETFs in Japan, with exposure to foreign markets, are listed on the Japan Exchange Group (JPX) as Japanese Depositary Receipts (JDRs). In Israel, until 2018, passively managed financial instruments listed on the Tel Aviv Stock Exchange (TASE) were structured as ETNs.[11]

The type of legal structure of exchange-traded passive instruments is essential for investors looking for exposure to international equity markets. This is valid primarily due to the different investment opportunities or restrictions that are provided by individual structures, various potential types of risk associated with a given legal form, and—last but not least—for tax reasons. When investing in ETFs in foreign stock exchanges, it should be necessary to thoroughly know the legal form of these instruments in order to avoid unexpected and unpleasant consequences. However, it should also be remembered that in many cases, ETFs registered in one country are distributed in other countries outside their country of origin and listed on other exchanges. Cross-border sales of ETFs and conventional open-end funds mainly refer to UCITS funds (i.e., OEFs that comply with the UCITS Directive) domiciled in Luxembourg and Ireland that are sold to investors not only in EU countries, but worldwide.[12] However, US ETFs also are cross-listed, for example, on many Latin America exchanges (e.g., on the Mexican Bolsa, the B3—Brasil Bolsa Balcão [formerly known as BM&F Bovespa], and the Santiago Stock Exchange), as well as on Asia-Pacific exchanges (e.g., on the Australian Securities Exchange [ASX], the Singapore Exchange [SGX] and the Hong Kong Exchanges [HKEX]). Additionally, many ETFs registered in developed and emerging countries are cross-listed on trading platforms in various countries. This applies especially to those countries whose markets are relatively small or underdeveloped; hence, ETF providers are forced to look for customers through distribution abroad.

Cross-listing gives both institutional and retail investors the chance to buy and sell financial instruments, including ETFs, that might not otherwise be available to them (especially to individual investors) on a home exchange. It often increases liquidity and enhances the tracking quality of cross-listed

[11]The Israeli ETF reform known as the "28th amendment" was completed in the last quarter of 2018. As a result, most of the 714 ETNs listed on the TASE in August 2018 were turned into ETFs.

[12]According to PricewaterhouseCoopers (2019), European domiciled ETFs have been registered for distribution in 24 European countries, 4 Asia-Pacific countries, 4 countries in the Americas, 2 Middle Eastern countries, and one African country (as of end June 2019).

ETFs, especially in the case of trading domestic ETFs in their own time zone (Atkinson and Green 2005).[13]

For more sophisticated investors, the type of ETF structure may be important for one more reason. Namely shares of ETFs or securities of other exchange-traded products can be used in the case of ETF of ETFs (fund of funds)—instead of, e.g., stocks or bonds—as a tool that makes it possible to achieve exposure to a specific market or asset class. Therefore, even when investing in an ETF on the domestic market, we should pay attention to whether there are ETFs or other ETPs in its portfolio, and if so, whether—and to what extent—their legal form may impact our investment.

3.3 Indexing

The history of passively managed investment products goes back to the early 1970s when the first indexed funds hit the US market.[14] Despite launching successive index funds to the market in subsequent years, it turned out later that it was only the first step in fundamental changes in the financial markets worldwide. They gained pace in the 90s, when the first exchange-traded funds began to be listed on stock exchanges. However, it was not until after the financial crisis of 2008–2009 that there was a seismic shift toward passive investing.

Although traditional index funds—both institutional and retail—and ETFs differ in many aspects,[15] they were all (except actively managed ETFs) designed, created, and introduced to the market for one main purpose—to track the performance of a specific financial index.[16] During the last 50 years, the evolution of index investing has led to a wide range of investment vehicles, as described earlier. However, it was ETFs that became

---

[13]More information about trading ETFs in international markets will be presented in the next chapter.

[14]The first indexed mutual fund (the Qualidex Fund) was launched in 1972. The first institutional indexed funds were created by Wells Fargo (Wells Fargo Stagecoach Fund) and American National Bank together with Batterymarch in 1973. The first retail index fund commenced in 1975 (the Vanguard 500 Index Fund).

[15]Differences and similarities between index funds and exchange-traded funds are widely described, e.g., in Ferri (2009) and Stevenson (2010).

[16]It is worth noting that, although ETFs were invented as strictly passive investment vehicles, in the following years they were used as a financial instrument that enabled the seamless combination of a passive and active investment approach (the first ETF smart beta was launched in 2000) and as a tool for active management (the first active ETFs appeared in 2008). What is more, recent momentous changes on the US ETF market, i.e., the creation at the beginning of 2020 of the first so-called non-transparent (or semi-transparent) ETFs, means that these instruments are, in practice, becoming a "wrapper" that will find a number of new, not just standard, passive applications.

the financial instrument that most successfully implemented the idea of passive investing.[17] Currently, not all ETFs pursue this investment concept,[18] although they are still unambiguously and commonly associated with this investment approach.

The main objective of a passively managed exchange-traded fund is to closely track the performance of a selected financial index. Index replication is, therefore, a key tool for portfolio managers seeking returns of indexes. This investment goal is fundamentally different from what we are dealing with for two other most recognized ways of investing in the asset management industry. The main aim of actively managed funds is typically to beat the benchmark (i.e., generating alpha), while hedge fund managers strive to achieve an absolute return, regardless of market conditions. An ETF's aim is, therefore, quite simple and clear, although it does not mean that it is easy to achieve.

Tracking the performance of a given index as closely as possible is—contrary to appearances—a very complex and demanding task. The investment policy of passive asset managers seems only seemingly trivially simple and easy to apply, but in fact, it often demands no less skill, commitment, and effort than in the case of an actively managed fund or hedge fund. This is a consequence of the fact that financial indexes themselves are not directly investable—they are synthetic, statistical indicators. There are many factors connected both with indexes (e.g., their heterogeneity, complexity, and variability of index portfolio constituents) as well as with different financial market circumstances that cause deviations of the fund's return from the benchmark. This is particularly evident in international equity ETFs, where—apart from the standard actions taken by domestic equity ETF managers—additional activities are necessary. They arise from the specifics of these funds, for example, from investing in securities denominated in various currencies and listed in stock exchanges in different time zones.

Thus, the management of an ETF equity portfolio does not mean that it is in any way passive, i.e., only a simple, mechanical approach to the investment process. "Passivity" should be understood only as a lack of active bets

---

[17]The genesis of the theoretical idea of passive investing can be traced to the 1960s, when famed Chicago economist and Nobel laureate Eugene Fama created the foundations for the Efficient Market Hypothesis (EMH). However, the precise description of the academic issues related to passive investing goes beyond the scope of this book (some of them were discussed in Chapters 1 and 2). They have been described in, e.g., Ferri (2011), Stevenson (2010), and Seddik Meziani (2006).

[18]According to ETFGI (2019), assets of actively managed ETFs and ETPs amounted to USD 151.2 billion, which at the end of November 2019 accounted for nearly 2.5% of total assets invested globally in ETFs and ETPs.

on the market,[19] as managers who use (or only declare) an active approach to investing do (or should do).[20] In such cases, it translates essentially to overweighting or underweighting specific markets or regions (in global investing), sectors or themes (in sector or thematic investing) and stocks (in different types of investing) in the scope of asset selection, and to the right timing within asset allocation. Passive investing—in plain vanilla equity ETFs that replicate market capitalization-weighted indexes—also requires taking various investment activities. However, since the purpose of these funds is different—i.e., to mirror the return of a given market, not to beat it—these activities must be of a different nature. For example, in equity ETFs, this refers to actions related to a change in the composition of the investment portfolio at the time of index reconstitution[21] and rebalancing,[22] cash management during inflows/outflows of capital to/from the fund, managing capital from

[19]It is worth emphasizing, that this issue looks different in the case of ETFs that replicate so-called smart beta (or strategic beta or enhanced) indexes. The term "smart beta" (often considered to be a strictly marketing term) refers broadly to a group of indexes (and indirectly also to ETFs and other financial products tracking them), which are created—often on the orders of financial institutions who intend to offer products based on them—to deliver enhanced returns or minimize risk relative to traditional (capitalization-weighted) benchmarks. These indexes may aim to capture a specific factor or set of factors such as value, momentum, small size, low volatility, quality, etc.

[20]Some managers of equity funds—contrary to the declarations and promises given to investors—rarely take bets on the market in practice. It means that the composition of the fund's investment portfolio largely overlaps the benchmark portfolio—taking into account both stocks in the portfolio and their weights. When such an investment approach is accompanied by the simultaneous charging of a relatively high management fee (at the level close to the actively managed funds) this is referred to as closet indexing (closet tracking). This unethical practice, which seriously harms investment fund clients, has been the subject of interest and studies for researchers, supervisory authorities, and institutions that represent the interests of financial services users for several years in many countries (especially in European). More information on closet indexing in Europe can be found in, e.g., SCM Direct (2015), ESMA (2016), and Better Finance (2017).

[21]Reconstituting an index is the practice of adding or deleting securities to/from the index. Decisions are based on whether these securities (e.g., stocks in equity indexes) meet the index criteria or not. In rules-based indexes, it refers to, e.g., free-float market capitalization and liquidity. Reconstitution is also required to reflect the changes in the securities value (driven, for example, by mergers or acquisitions, delisting, or bankruptcy). In turn, in discretionary indexes, these decisions are the result of the subjective view of members of the index committee. The frequency of reconstitution can be different—the more often it is carried out and the more shares it deals with, generally, the more difficult it is to achieve high quality of index replication (in physical replication) due to possible problems with the purchase or sale of shares in a short time (especially on low-liquid markets or segments) and due to the increase in transaction costs.

[22]Rebalancing an index is the practice of adjusting the weight of securities in an index portfolio according to the methodology used in creating the index on a regularly scheduled basis (usually quarterly). The change in the market price of securities (index constituents) in a specific period necessitates rebalancing and leads to buying and selling securities by index investors, including ETFs. This, in turn, may (as in reconstitution) cause problems with the accuracy of the index replication. That is why index providers must balance the desire to achieve index accuracy and its representativeness with the requirement to avoid unnecessary index turnover. In capitalization-weighted indexes, turnover that results from changes in relative company size can be reduced by applying "buffer zones" to capitalization bands that define eligibility for particular sizes of segments.

dividends paid by companies, and activities made during other types of corporate actions and events[23] (mandatory corporate actions including stock splits, bonus issues and spin-offs [demergers], as well as voluntary corporate actions including tender offers, rights issues, and buybacks). Major index providers publish comprehensive guides that comprise policies regarding the treatment of corporate actions and events and their implementation in indexes, for example, "MSCI Corporate Events Methodology" (MSCI) or "Corporate Actions and Events Guide for Market Capitalisation Weighted Indexes" (FTSE Russell).

It should be emphasized that portfolio modifications resulting from the construction principles of the replicated index (i.e., the majority of which are carried out by ETF managers[24]) are not really autonomous actions but are conditioned by the decisions of the index provider. Because ETF managers strive for the best quality of index replication, both on a daily basis and in the long term, they must adapt investment activities to the index methodology. Otherwise, the accuracy of imitating index performance will deteriorate, which in turn may result in an outflow of capital from the fund.

Limited flexibility is undoubtedly one of the most important challenges in managing equity ETFs. It applies even more to funds with international exposure, whose specific features compel the manager to take into account other aspects when making investment decisions. As part of the process of creating and then maintaining international equity indexes, their providers mostly decide to include (or exclude) stocks from a given country to (from) the developed markets universe or the emerging markets universe as a result of country reclassification (in addition to the standard procedures used in all types of equity indexes). Similar decisions may also include (or weight increase) or exclude (or weight decrease) in an index specific share classes (e.g., in Chinese equity indexes), types of shares (e.g., non-voting shares or limited voting shares—as in the case of the social media company Snap), shares denominated in a specific currency (e.g., yuan-denominated shares), shares listed on a particular exchange (e.g., shares listed on Shenzhen's ChiNext market) or other equity instruments (e.g., depositary receipts).

---

[23]There are different definitions of this kind of event. For example, FTSE Russell defines a corporate action as an action on shareholders with a prescribed ex-date (e.g., rights issue, special dividend and share split), while a corporate event as a reaction to company news that might impact the index, depending on the index ground rules (e.g., a large sale of shares by a strategic shareholder which impacts a company's free float) (FTSE Russell 2015).

[24]Among the relatively few investment decisions that are exclusively the responsibility of ETF manager (not an index provider), the most significant seems to be the choice of the index replication method. Others are, for example, decisions on lending securities held by the fund and level of cash in the portfolio. They will be described later in this chapter.

Moreover, during index construction and review processes, constituents' weightings can be adjusted not only for a free float but also for Foreign Ownership Limit (FOL) and/or foreign (head)room limit.[25] This applies, in particular, to emerging and frontier markets. Therefore, changes to foreign equity ownership rules can be critical during passive investing on these markets because investors may face an additional type of investment risk involved with government intervention. For example, under Chinese rules, combined foreign ownership in a China-listed company must not exceed 30%, while the ownership cap for an individual overseas investor is 10%.[26] Thailand's stock exchange caps foreign ownership on most shares at around 49%, or 25% for banks. Brazil limits overseas holdings of banks, media, and transportation companies (Bloomberg 2019), and the UAE caps foreign ownership of businesses at 49%, except in economic free zones (The Business Times 2019). These restrictions have been totally abolished or gradually reduced in recent years (e.g., in Qatar, in 2014, foreign ownership caps were raised from 25 to 49%), which has contributed to a surge in inflows of international capital. Sometimes, however, they are only eliminated in relation to some sectors (e.g., it concerned only consumer goods and industrial companies in Vietnam in 2015), which results in a significant re-allocation of sector weightings within the index. This is all the more important in passive investing, where benchmarks that track equity markets that are subject to restrictions on foreign ownership typically employ a free-floating market capitalization methodology. It means that individual stock and sector weightings are calculated on the basis of their theoretical availability to international investors (Lamont 2015).

Sometimes, such restrictions can also be found in some developed countries, e.g., in Europe and the USA, such limits are applied to shares in airline companies. However, these measures are usually enforced for political rather than economic reasons. Detailed rules for considering foreign ownership restrictions in the design and calculation of international indexes are available in documents published by major providers, e.g., in FTSE Russell's "Foreign Ownership Restrictions and Minimum Foreign Headroom Requirement."

Even in the case of company dividends—the commonest type of corporate action—the differences in their treatment in some countries force index

[25]According to MSCI, "foreign room" is calculated as the proportion of shares still available to foreign investors relative to the maximum allowed. Similarly, FTSE Russell defines "foreign headroom" as the percentage of shares available to foreign investors as a proportion of the company's FOL.

[26]Interestingly, MSCI removed and reduced the weights of two Chinese companies listed on the Shenzhen Stock Exchange (SZSE) from its China indexes in March 2019 when Chinese regulators blocked foreign purchases of their shares as offshore ownership of the firms neared the 30% cap (Reuters 2019).

providers to adjust them accordingly. Sometimes corporate events may also have a cross-border element, which requires suitable adaptations in many index series.[27]

3.4 Index Replication Methods

As can be seen from the above, one of the key decisions in index-tracking ETF management is the choice of benchmark—which will be analyzed in detail in the next four chapters relating to global, regional, country, and sector (thematic) investing—and it is also vital to choose an appropriate method to replicate its performance.

The financial index replication method specifies how the ETF pursues its primary investment objective, which is to track as accurately as possible the performance (return) of the index (before fees and expenses). For example, it states which financial instruments and transactions, and sometimes which quantitative methods are used.

Generally,[28] two basic methods of index replication are distinguished:

- physical (direct, in-specie) replication,
- synthetic (indirect, swap-based) replication.

3.4.1 Physical Replication

Physical replication makes it possible to track an index[29] as a result of buying financial instruments, which makes it possible to precisely gain a specific investment exposure. Holding physical securities or other assets, in addition to the benefits of following the index itself, may also offer other opportunities, such as securities lending, to boost returns (or to reduce tracking difference),

[27]For example, in September 2013 Vodafone, which has had a primary listing on the London Stock Exchange (LSE), announced that it would sell its 45% stake in Verizon Wireless to US-listed Verizon Communications, in return for cash and Verizon Communications shares, which it would distribute to its own shareholders. This corporate event required different treatment in different FTSE Russell indexes (FTSE Russell 2015).

[28]In practice, some entities analyzing the ETF market sometimes distinguish also hybrid replication. Hybrid ETFs, launched in 2010, are structures that combine both replication techniques purely as a means to mitigate their downsides or special events such as the occasional impact of market closings (i.e., long public holiday periods in certain jurisdictions) or the temporary unavailability of certain securities (IOSCO 2013).

[29]In this book, as well as in many professional ETF publications, the shorthand term "index replication" is often used. However, it does not mean that it refers to mimicking the index composition, rather tracking its return (only in the case of full physical replication does it usually mean the same).

which will be discussed separately.[30] Exchange-traded funds that use this kind of replication (sometimes called physical-based ETFs or simply physical ETFs) buy different types of securities, depending on the type of exposure offered. Equity ETFs invest mostly in common, publicly traded stocks, but sometimes they buy other financial instruments with exposure on equity markets when it is more convenient, or they are forced to when there is no other option. Their portfolios may consist of shares (units) of different types of collective investment institutions, e.g., closed-end funds, other exchange-traded funds, Real Estate Investment Trusts (REITs), or preferred stocks.[31] The specificity of international equity ETFs means that you can also find other equity-like financial instruments quite often, which broaden investment opportunities for investors interested in portfolio diversification overseas, in particular, depositary receipts.

A depositary receipt (DR) is a negotiable certificate issued to investors by an authorized depositary (usually a bank), which represents ownership of a foreign company's shares (McLeavey and Solnik 2009). The depositary is empowered to transfer ownership of the depositary receipts between investors but continues to be the registered holder of the underlying securities. Depositary receipt programs (first established by JPMorgan in 1927) can be structured in a variety of ways, but two are by far the most popular: American Depositary Receipts (ADRs) and Global Depositary Receipts (GDRs). Other popular types of depositary receipts include European Depositary Receipts (EDRs), Chinese Depositary Receipts (CDR), Japanese Depositary Receipts (JDRs), Indian Depositary Receipts (IDRs), and Brazilian Depositary Receipts (BDRs). These are depositary receipts issued by (respectively) European (Chinese, Japanese, Indian, or Brazilian) banks representing the security of a non-European (non-Chinese, non-Japanese, non-Indian, or non-Brazilian) company, denominated in the local currency and traded on the European (Chinese, Japanese, Indian, or Brazilian) exchange.

American Depositary Receipts are negotiable instruments that represent ownership of shares in a non-US company; typically, they represent a multiple or a fraction of the underlying securities because of the convenience in

[30]It is noteworthy (also in the context of the synthetic replication in which counterparty risk occurs) that the portfolio securities of physical ETFs are held in a segregated custody account; therefore, the investor has direct recourse to those assets in the event that the fund sponsor fails.

[31]Preferred stocks (securities) are hybrid instruments that exhibit the characteristics of both equity and debt securities. The main issuers of these securities are banks and other financial institutions because they can help satisfy regulatory requirements to support their liabilities (it is reflected in major indexes comprising preferred stocks—e.g., more than 80% of the sector composition of the S&P US Preferred Stock Index is about financials and real estate [Dhanraj 2018]). ETFs investing in preferred stocks are popular, especially in the USA—total assets managed by 12 US-listed funds amounted to nearly USD 30 bn in mid-2019 (ETFdb.com 2019).

trading. They are quoted in USD and are traded (on stock exchanges or OTC), cleared, and settled like any other security. ADRs offer companies that are domiciled outside the US access to the world's largest and most active capital market (JPMorgan Chase 2005). That is why they are the preferred vehicle for non-US issuers entering the US securities market in most countries.[32] Additionally, they ensure that investors have the same rights and voting privileges as the owners of the underlying securities. Simultaneously, investors may return ADRs to the authorized depositary at any time for cancellation and take delivery of the actual securities. Other significant advantages of investing in a foreign company's ADRs include convenience in trading and gaining information. Regarding the first advantage, because ADRs are traded and settled like other US securities, they simplify the buying and selling of foreign securities. In terms of gaining information, the depositary provides US investors with a local liaison with the foreign company, through which they receive annual and interim reports and other information.[33] Moreover, the depositary receives dividends directly from the issuing company in its local currency and issues dividend checks in USD (PricewaterhouseCoopers 2004).

Unlike ADRs and other national depositary receipts, Global Depositary Receipts are cross-listed on two or more markets. On the one hand, this increases the investor base, and on the other, it improves their liquidity. A typical GDR structure combines a depositary receipt offered in Europe under Regulation S with a depositary receipt offered in the US under Rule 144A. GDRs are most commonly used to raise capital in Europe and sometimes in the USA (provided that they are placed with qualified US buyers). They are most often denominated in USD or euros.

Depositary receipts are generally used by ETFs and other investment funds when investing in emerging and frontier markets. This seems to be the easiest and cheapest way to invest in the securities of companies from these countries as they are listed on recognized exchanges. However, it should not be forgotten that investing in these instruments may also expose investors to special types of risk (usually inherent to all foreign investments), namely currency (exchange rate) risk, inflation risk, liquidity risk, political risk, and

---

[32]There are three different levels of ADR programs which differ mainly in terms of listing exposure and reporting requirements: Level 1 (ADRs can only be traded on the OTC market, and the issuing company has minimal reporting requirements with the SEC), Level 2 (ADRs can be listed on a US stock exchange, but they must be registered with the SEC, and the company is required to file an annual financial report that conforms to US GAAP standards), and Level 3 (it requires the issuing company to meet even stricter reporting rules that are similar to those followed by US companies, but companies can issue shares to raise capital rather than just list existing shares on a US exchange).

[33]However, depending on the level of the ADR program, investors may not have access to all the information available on domestic companies.

transparency risk. Currency risk is caused by the fact that depositary receipts and their underlying securities are predominantly denominated in different currencies. Therefore, investors may be affected by currency fluctuations (especially in the case of relatively volatile emerging and frontier currencies), which might even erase any gains made by investing in the foreign company's DRs. Inflation risk means that relatively high inflation in the issuing company's country may erode the value of that currency.

Liquidity risk depends mostly on:

- the type of DR program (e.g., ADRs of Levels II and III are the most liquid because they are traded on US exchanges—mostly on the NYSE and NASDAQ),
- the exchange where the depositary receipt is traded (the more mature the market, generally the higher the trading volume and liquidity, but even there they are sometimes delisted),
- and its level of volatility (the higher volatility, the less the liquidity).

The manifestation of political risk is when politics or regime changes in the ADR issuing company's country may undermine exchange rates or destabilize the company and its earnings. Transparency risk is a consequence of the fact that some DR issuers do not need to provide sufficient information about their activity or financial data, and they may not be required to comply with the generally accepted accounting principles (GAAP).

Interestingly, in some countries, depositary receipts represent exchange-traded funds. For example, in Japan, some foreign ETFs are tradable on the Japan Exchange Group (JPX) as JDRs (Japanese Depositary Receipts), i.e., negotiable securities which indicate ownership of shares issued by foreign entities. JDRs are also used to distribute foreign stocks or ETNs.[34] ETF-JDRs have been developed as a convenient way to invest in foreign ETFs in a structure that trades and settles like a Japanese security (Hill et al. 2015). Additionally, some ETF providers create ETF-JDRs for cross-border listings; for example, China Asset Management and China Southern Asset Management were the first ETF providers to create ETF-JDRs for Hong Kong-listed ETFs in February 2013 (Fuhr 2014). In turn, in December 2018, the Stock Exchange of Thailand (SET) commenced listing depositary receipts issued by Bualuang Securities. It represents the VFMVN30 ETF, which tracks the VN30 Index—the top 30 large-cap stocks listed on the Ho Chi Minh Stock Exchange (HOSE) in Vietnam (SET 2018).

---

[34]ETF-JDRs are issued by a trust bank. They are backed by ETFs bought by a securities house on the foreign stock exchange.

International statistics on the ETF market structure—in terms of the type of replication applied—clearly show that physical replication is used much more often than synthetic replication. In the USA, almost all ETFs use this kind of replication, except for leveraged and inverse ETFs, where swaps and other derivatives are applied. One of the reasons for this is that, starting in 2010, the US Securities and Exchange Commission not longer allows the launch of new synthetic ETFs unless an asset manager was already sponsoring synthetic ETFs before 2010 (Aramonte et al. 2017). The situation is similar in Canada, for example, where physical ETFs represent most ETFs (Investment Industry Association of Canada 2019). In Europe, direct replication accounts for 82% of the market, although in 2010, its share was only 55% (Lyxor 2019). In the current decade, a significant shift in the distribution of ETF assets by synthetic replication in favor of physically replicated funds in Europe, both in equity and fixed-income ETFs, has been driven by investors' preference for the simplicity and lower perceived risk of the physical approach, especially after the financial crisis. Many European ETF providers, which earlier offered only (or mainly) a synthetic product line-up, have transitioned to a hybrid offering, converting many ETFs to physical replication and/or launching new physical ETFs (Bioy et al. 2019). The drift away from synthetic replication was partially attributable to the release of a Consultative Document by the Financial Stability Board (FSB) (2011), which emphasized potential financial stability issues arising from synthetic ETFs. In the same period, reports of a similar nature have also been published by other recognized international financial institutions, e.g., the International Monetary Fund (IMF) (2011), the International Organization of Securities Commissions (IOSCO) (2012), the Bank for International Settlements (BIS) (Ramaswamy 2011), the European Securities and Markets Authority (ESMA) (2011), and the European Systemic Risk Board (ESRB) (2011). Subsequent publications published in recent years by the ESRB (Pagano et al. 2019), the Federal Reserve Bank of Boston (Anadu et al. 2018), the IMF (2015), the BIS (Sushko and Turner 2018), the European Central Bank (ECB) (Grill et al. 2018), and CFA Institute (Bhattacharya and O'Hara 2020) also pointed out the potential impact of ETFs on financial stability.

Physical replication is applied in ETFs and other index-linked investment products in two basic forms: full replication or incomplete (partial) replication. Full (complete) replication involves buying all (or nearly all) the securities that make up an underlying benchmark or index in exactly the same or very approximate proportions as in the benchmark (index) (i.e., the index's composition is replicated, as a rule, 1:1). This basic and original ETF replication method was widely used in the initial phase of ETF market development and is still very popular among many ETF providers, particularly in Europe (according to Deutsche Bundesbank [2018], it was applied by about 1000 European ETFs in 2018). This is because full replication is not only the simplest and most convenient replication technique, but it is also the most understandable (and thus acceptable and "user-friendly") for "the average investor" (he/she knows exactly what the fund invests in and in what proportions). As most underlying indexes replicated by ETFs are very transparent, it also results in the greatest possible degree of transparency of the ETFs' portfolios. Full information on the composition of assets is often updated (most asset managers do it daily), which helps to mitigate the transparency risk (especially in comparison with synthetic ETFs and non-transparent active ETFs). It can, therefore, be assumed that fully replicated ETFs are the most desirable investment solution within index-tracking ETFs because of the usually high tracking quality (relatively low tracking errors[35] and tracking differences[36]), relatively low costs, and high clarity.

Among international equity ETFs, this kind of replication is used most often by funds tracking large-cap indexes, and thus, ordinarily, relatively liquid ones. It is therefore used to replicate the most popular and recognizable benchmark indexes that group the shares of companies with the largest free-float market capitalization and the highest liquidity in a given market (in single-country equity ETFs), e.g., the S&P 500, the S&P/TSX, the FTSE 100, the Nikkei 225, or the S&P/ASX 200 indexes, or on many markets (in regional and global equity ETFs), e.g., the EuroStoxx 50, the S&P Developed BMI, the MSCI Emerging Markets, or the FTSE All-World indexes. Because developed markets usually have higher liquidity, particularly among blue chips, full replication is applied relatively more often in ETFs with exposure in these countries than in funds that invest in emerging and especially frontier markets. This is particularly significant when the fund manager needs to quickly (in practice, on a going basis) and effectively (i.e., to limit the costs of market impact) adjust the portfolio composition to the index during reconstitution and rebalancing.

However, it should be remembered that full replication restricts the flexibility of the manager's actions, leaving virtually no room for discretionary decisions. Because ETFs seek to provide investment results that as closely as possible correspond to the index return (before fees and expenses), the manager should periodically map the changing index very precisely; otherwise, the quality of replication and the fund's reputation will suffer. Another significant disadvantage of this method of replication is the increase in costs

[35]Tracking error is a measure of how consistently a fund is tracking its benchmark.

[36]Tracking difference measures the under- or outperformance of a fund relative to its benchmark.

resulting from the necessity to accurately match relatively broad indexes, especially in the case of stocks with the smallest weights and liquidity (both transaction costs and spread costs) (Beasley et al. 2003).

Although full replication has many advantages, it is not always possible for an ETF to invest in every constituent from the index portfolio. In certain cases, it is not economically justified for the managers of equity index-tracking funds to buy exactly all shares from a given index. This applies especially to securities, whose impact on the index value is negligible, and, simultaneously, the cost of their acquisition outweighs the tracking benefit of owning them. Therefore, for ETFs striving to mirror indexes in more complex and/or less liquid segments of the financial market, full replication might not be the best way to deliver the returns of the index. In particular, this concerns situations where the replicated index includes a very large number of constituents (i.e., mostly major broad market indexes), where some of its components are illiquid (in some niche segments of financial market—e.g., small-cap stocks on equity markets), and where an index's market capitalization weighting would violate regulatory requirements for fund diversification. This prohibits funds, including ETFs, from concentrating more than a given percentage of their total assets in one security.[37] This latter issue makes full replication impossible for ETFs that track even narrow indexes, e.g., some sector/industry indexes or country-specific indexes from some emerging and frontier markets, which are dominated by one particular company or a small handful of companies. Moreover, applying full replication can also be infeasible due to the country-specific tax laws for foreign holdings (JPMorgan 2009). All of the above cases refer to investing on international equity markets, for example, global, regional, or even single-country indexes that consist of a few thousand stocks. As of June 28, 2019, the MSCI World Index had more than 1600 constituents, the FTSE Emerging Index had more than 1700 constituents, the CRSP US Total Market Index had more than 3500 constituents, and the S&P Developed BMI Index had more than 8100 constituents.[38]

[37] In the latter case, full replication can be used provided that the index itself is adapted to the legal requirements concerning portfolio diversification in force in a given country—as a rule capped indexes are created (they will be described later in the book).

[38] Such numerous indexes are over-diversified, which—as shown by many studies—is costly and does not give significant advantages in terms of lower firm-specific (idiosyncratic) risk. Most researchers indicate that an optimally diversified investment portfolio should cover approximately 20–40 securities; only a few show that it should be even more than 100 (e.g., Meir Statman (2004) claims that it should be at least 300 stocks). Although the issue of the optimum level of diversification has been extensively debated in the financial literature for over 50 years (the first paper devoted to this topic was authored by Evans and Archer [1968]), the definitive answer to that question remains elusive.

Where full replication of the index is either difficult to implement or is deliberately not employed, the best solution for an ETF manager is to use one of two methods of incomplete index replication: representative (stratified) sampling or optimization.[39] In both cases, and based on certain criteria, the fund invests in only a portion of the securities included in the index and in slightly different proportions than those in the benchmark. Sometimes, it also invests in instruments that are not included in the corresponding index, but that are useful to improve replication efficiency. Thus, the manager decides not to purchase some financial instruments that constitute the index—usually the least liquid and with a relatively low share in the index—because any attempt to accurately replicate the performance of the index with the above-mentioned characteristics is usually doomed to failure. The ETF performance is affected by many types of costs (e.g., brokerage fees, costs of bid/ask spread, market impact cost), which do not occur for the theoretical portfolio, i.e., the index portfolio. The skillful use of incomplete index replication, therefore, may be the most cost-effective and, as a result, it may allow the ETF to achieve results very similar to funds applying full replication method. This can happen even if the ETF's purpose is to reflect returns of a broad market index that includes a large number of often low-liquid securities.[40]

Incomplete index replication methods are used to attempt to build a smaller but representative portfolio that mimics the performance and risk characteristics of the broader benchmark. The most common method (especially in the USA[41]), and one which is relatively simple, is representative sampling (stratified sampling). When used, an ETF holds only a subset of securities that make up the index portfolio. There are several variants of this method that differ primarily in the dimensions of risk employed and the technique used to match the exposures of the index and the tracking fund. Generally, a fund manager divides all index constituents into small groups (cells) across a variety of key characteristics, e.g., market capitalization, sector (industry), weighting, return variability, liquidity, fundamental ratios, etc.,

---

[39]In practice, optimized sampling is also used, which combines both methods.

[40]It should be noted that, regardless of the replication method used, almost all index-tracking ETFs benefit from a liquidity screen in the index methodology, which serves to avoid highly illiquid assets. The problem of asset liquidity in the fund's portfolio, however, is important for the investor not only with regard to the quality of index replication, but also—and perhaps even more so—in the event of liquidity mismatch. This emerges when liquid ETFs hold relatively illiquid securities, and although they offer daily dealing, they are unable to meet that promise because of the hard-to-sell nature of their underlying holdings. Additionally, liquidity mismatch can reduce market efficiency and increase the fragility of ETFs (Pan and Zeng 2017).

[41]According to Deutsche Bundesbank (2018), representative sampling is dominant method of replication in the USA—in 2018 it has been using by ca. 1600 ETFs. In Europe it is applied by ca. 600 ETFs.

and then assigns each company (in the case of equity indexes) to a specific category. Then the weight of each category in the index is determined, i.e., the share of companies with a certain trait in the index. When creating a portfolio, a fund acquires only a selected group of shares from each category (e.g., excluding less liquid assets), but in such a way that the weights of the shares of a given category strictly correspond to the weight of that category in the index. In this way, a sample of securities can be selected that best embody the investment characteristics and fundamentals of the underlying index as a whole. Sometimes, the remaining assets are invested in securities not included in the underlying index as well as derivative instruments (futures, options, or swap contracts). This is done when the fund manager feels these instruments can create a more efficient replica of the original index.

Selecting and weighting portfolio constituents according to the corresponding weight in the index may adversely affect the quality of index replication (in comparison to full replication), because in this method, only selected criteria (dimensions of risk) are taken into account; besides, it does not take into account the specific risk. Sampling may also not work very effectively in a turbulent market environment, when historical statistical attributes (correlations, volatility measures, etc.) are less likely to align with the index. Then it can result in the higher-than-expected tracking error and tracking difference of the fund (Bioy et al. 2019).

However, this approach also has many significant advantages. First of all, it makes it possible to create an investment portfolio based on a limited number of securities (see Table 3.1), which can significantly reduce costs while maintaining the basic properties of the replicated index (the degree of matching depends on how many criteria have been used in this method). Accordingly, stratified sampling is widely used in mirroring global equity indexes, in broad regional equity indexes, and in some single-country and sector indexes that are comprised of a large number of financial instruments. However, it also applies in the case of replicating indexes with a relatively small number of securities, in which one or several companies have a very significant share in the index. The use of full replication is then not possible due to legal restrictions regarding the participation of one company in the index (Rey and Seiler 2001).

Optimization is a more advanced replication method, wherein advanced mathematical models are used to select securities for a fund's portfolio (sometimes it is referred to as a "black box" approach). There are many different sophisticated optimization techniques. One of the most commonly implemented involves the use of highly quantitative multifactor risk models, in which the exposure to index risk and individual securities is measured. These

Table 3.1 The number of ETF holdings in selected exchange-traded funds that replicate the performance of international equity indexes (as of 31 July 2019)

Index name	Number of index holdings	ETF name (ticker)	Number of ETF holdings[a]	Percentage share (%)
MSCI ACWI ex USA Index	2205	iShares MSCI ACWI ex U.S. ETF (ACWX US)	1341[b]	61
		SPDR MSCI ACWI ex-US ETF (CWI US)	990[b]	45
MSCI ACWI Index	2844	iShares MSCI ACWI ETF (ACWI US)	1420[b]	50
		SPDR MSCI ACWI UCITS ETF (SPYY GR)	2463	87
		Xtrackers MSCI AC World UCITS ETF (XMAW GR)	1642[c]	58
MSCI Emerging Markets Index	1193	BMO MSCI Emerging Markets Index ETF (ZEM CN)	672	56
		HSBC MSCI Emerging Markets UCITS ETF (HMEM LN)	771	65
		iShares MSCI Emerging Markets ETF (EEM US)	1027[b]	86
		NEXT FUNDS Emerging Market Equity MSCI-EM Unhedged ETF (2520 JP)	939	79
		SPDR MSCI Emerging Markets UCITS ETF (SPYM GR)	1038	87
MSCI Emerging Markets Asia Index	903	iShares MSCI EM Asia UCITS ETF USD (Acc) (CEMA LN)	658	73

(continued)

Table 3.1 (continued)

Index name	Number of index holdings	ETF name (ticker)	Number of ETF holdings[a]	Percentage share (%)
		SPDR MSCI EM Asia UCITS ETF (SPYA GR)	743	82

[a]Portfolio components may include, in addition to shares, cash positions, and derivatives
[b]As of 30.06.2019
[c]As of 14.08.2019
Source Factsheets of MSCI indexes and exchange-traded funds

factors may include both typical market factors (e.g., market capitalization, beta) and macroeconomic ones (e.g., interest rates). These models aim at minimizing tracking error through an understanding of the covariance between factors that drive asset returns. In order to determine the optimal portfolio composition, both historical data on price changes and the correlation of securities are input into such models. Another optimization technique is to use an objective function that makes it possible to determine which securities should be in the ETF portfolio and in which weights. The ultimate aim is, therefore, to find a portfolio with a minimum expected tracking error at a minimum cost.[42] Optimization methods are entirely model-driven, with a computer system making the buy and sell decisions.

Optimization has similar pros and cons to stratified sampling. As the technique is fully dependent on complex mathematical models, which themselves rely on historical statistical relationships, the economic outcome for the investor is subject to "model risk" (Deutsche Bank 2012). In this case, the main problems may result from possible misspecifying risk models or overfitting the data, for example.[43] While optimization can be a cost-effective index approximation, and it can improve the trading characteristics of the ETF itself, it also inherently increases the chances of tracking error. Potentially higher tracking errors arise from the performance of excluded securities, which comprise the underlying index. However, as studies have proven (e.g., Kilbert and Subramanian 2010), passive investors looking to track international equity indexes, including a very large number of constituents—e.g.,

[42]More detailed information on optimizing the investment portfolio can be found in, e.g., Liu et al. (2001) and Olma (2001).

[43]Overfitting is the modeling error which can happen when a function is too closely fit to a limited set of data points. It occurs when a model describes noise rather than signal and, as a result, it finds patterns that aren't actually there. An illustration of the problems created by overfitting (and collinearity) in the case of ETFs was described in, e.g., Lee (2014).

global, broad small-cap indexes[44]—should employ optimization techniques coupled with an appropriate risk model. This makes it possible to build a portfolio that overcomes the challenge of the high number of index constituents with reasonable tracking error and transaction costs. In addition to the methods mentioned above, there are also those related to the limited liquidity of many portfolio components.

Although the selection of a subset of securities present in the benchmark index is undoubtedly the most common approach to incomplete index replication, it is not the only possible approach. Interestingly, high-quality replication can also be achieved using partly or completely non-overlapping portfolios. A passively managed portfolio can be created by selecting a group of assets that jointly match specified characteristics (e.g., factors such as beta, size, industry, growth/value, or momentum) without regard to whether the selected financial instruments are actually present in the original benchmark. It can happen because, in practice, the key determinants of whether an asset should be included in a replicating portfolio are the characteristics that it has in common with the index. To replicate the return and risk of a selected benchmark, an index-tracking fund should try to mimic the systematic component of return (driven by factors that are common to other securities). However, it is not necessary to replicate specific (idiosyncratic) return components particular to a single security (such as company's competitive position, management capabilities), which tend to cancel each other out, as winners and losers are both embedded in the index. There are many methods of replicating an index with a non-overlapping portfolio, depending on the characteristics of the benchmark and the factors that are replicated, some of which are more complicated than others. In the case of traditional equity indexes, it is enough to match a few characteristics (e.g., beta or sector exposure), while in more complex benchmarks, more sophisticated methods and data are required to achieve the best quality tracking (Jagannathan et al. 2015). This applies to private equity or venture capital indexes, for example, which can be developed using public shares that match the PE or VC risk-and-return profile (The Economist 2017).

Managing a portfolio of physical ETFs is not only limited to choosing the most efficient replication method. As signaled earlier, managers also undertake other activities in portfolio management, sometimes typical for active funds, in order to minimize the fund's costs and thus enhance its return and improve the quality of index replication. Among the most popular active

[44]For example, the MSCI ACWI Small Cap Index has 6002 constituents, the S&P Global SmallCap Index has 8330 constituents and the FTSE Global Small Cap Index has 4972 constituents (as of 31 July 2019). More on global passive equity investing in small-caps can be found in Chapter 4.

management techniques applied by ETFs and index funds are managing cash, trading around index reconstitutions/rebalancing, using derivatives, optimizing tax and dividends, and engaging in securities lending[45] (Bioy et al. 2019), the last of which will be discussed in detail later in this chapter. A major challenge for physical ETFs is cash drag, when a fund's assets are not fully invested in the index. The exception is a small amount of cash necessary to meet the requests of investors looking to redeem shares. The main source of temporarily uninvested capital is usually ongoing cash inflow from investors acquiring ETF shares. However, there are also many other instances when fund managers are faced with cash flows. For example, they are unable to immediately reinvest dividends or coupon payments received, or distribute that income to shareholders. It is also difficult when the index composition changes because there may be a time lag between the liquidation of the index's old constituents and the addition of new constituents. Whenever there is uninvested cash in the fund's portfolio, this results in increased tracking error and a worsening of the replication quality. The commonest way to overcome or at least reduce the detrimental effects of cash drag is equitizing cash holdings. It is done usually by reinvesting cash through the use of futures contracts or other derivatives. However, this is possible provided that applicable index futures are available, which unfortunately is not obvious on some international equity markets. In such events, ETF managers may use proxy and correlation techniques.

3.4.2 Synthetic Replication

Synthetic (indirect) replication, unlike physical replication, derives specific market exposure through derivatives—mostly swap contracts.[46] Therefore, it is often referred to as swap-based or derivative replication. Sometimes, credit

[45]In the European Union, the use of efficient portfolio management techniques (EPM) by UCITS funds (including ETFs) is regulated by ESMA guidelines (ESMA 2014). A number of various activities fall under EPM, including securities lending, engaging in (reverse) repurchase agreements, and employing financial derivatives. UCITS funds are permitted to engage in EPM in order to reduce risk and costs, or generate additional capital or income. However, such an activity should be in line with the funds' risk profiles and respect the rules laid down in ESMA's guidelines.

[46]A swap is an agreement between two parties whereby they promise to exchange the return from a particular asset in lieu of actually transferring ownership. They are often non-standardized arrangements, tailored to the specific needs of the parties involved. The terms of the swap, such as what is actually being exchanged and for what time period, are set out in a contract usually based on a template that has been created by the International Swaps and Derivatives Association (ISDA) (Johnson et al. 2012a).

(equity) linked notes (CLNs), futures, or options are also employed. Generally, this replication method involves using a total return swap (TRS)[47]—also called a performance swap—agreement concluded between an ETF and a counterparty, which assumes that it delivers ETF return of the index (called the "reference index") in exchange for the total return of the portfolio of securities bought by the fund. The counterparty is usually an investment bank, often the parent or an affiliated bank, although sometimes it may also be a securities dealer or other financial institution.

There are two main ways for ETFs to use derivative instruments or transactions to gain exposure to a specific benchmark: the unfunded swap model and the funded swap model. In both structures, swap counterparties are responsible for providing the index's return to the ETF investors.

In the unfunded swap model, an ETF acquires a basket of securities from a swap counterparty (e.g., a bank) using the cash received from the authorized participant in exchange for newly created shares. This procedure is in contrast to the typical in-kind process for the physical ETF. On the basis of the total return swap agreement, the bank commits to delivering the performance of a selected index to the ETF (sometimes minus swap fees), in exchange for the return delivered by this basket of securities (plus the additional income resulting from owning them). In addition to the index performance, there is a swap spread, which can be either positive—i.e., the ETF receives additional performance from the swap counterparty, or negative—i.e., the ETF pays a cost to the counterparty.

It is worth noting that the basket of securities bought by the fund—often referred to in an ETF's documents, financial statements, or on its website as "substitute basket," "reference basket," "collateral basket" or simply "fund holdings"—usually do not include the index constituents. In the case of equity ETFs, they are usually blue chips with superior liquidity. Additionally, they can be characterized by a high degree of correlation with the shares that create the index, but in some cases, they may be completely unrelated to them. The substitute basket often consists of securities that the investment bank, which acts as the swap counterparty, may have within its inventory. It is also important to emphasize that the fund remains the owner of these assets and enjoys direct access to them. If the swap counterparty defaults, the ETF provider should be able to swiftly liquidate the assets. The unfunded swap model, introduced in 2001, was the first method to be used in Europe to synthetically track the performance of an index. This model is also employed by some Asian and Australian ETF providers (Johnson et al. 2012a; Dickson

[47]A total return swap is a bilateral financial transaction where the counterparties swap the total return of a single asset or basket of assets for periodic cash flows, typically a floating rate such as LIBOR.

et al. 2013; Lyxor 2019). According to the data collected in 2017 by Federal Reserve (FED), in a sample consisting of 899 ETFs using synthetic replication, 54% of funds with managed 78% of all assets employed the unfunded model (Aramonte et al. 2017).

In a funded swap model, ETF delivers cash directly to the counterparty, which posts a collateral basket into a segregated account with an independent (third party) custodian. The account can be held either in the name of the fund, in the case of a transfer of title, or in the name of the counterparty and pledged in favor of the fund, in the case of a pledge arrangement. In exchange for the receipt of the cash, the counterparty is obliged to deliver to the ETF the index performance (less swap fees) plus the principal at a future date. Using the term swap in relation to this model seems to be a misnomer since a swap-type payment is technically made in only one direction (only the counterparty delivers a return to the ETF). Ramaswamy (2011) describes this transaction as the purchase of a structured note by the ETF that is secured by a collateral pledge. As in the previously described model, the collateral basket is usually composed of securities that come from the swap counterparty's inventory and should meet certain conditions in terms of asset type, liquidity, or diversification.[48] In the case of equity ETFs, it usually consists of stocks included in well-recognized indexes (Johnson et al. 2012a; Dickson et al. 2013). The funded swap model was introduced in Europe in 2009. In the sample analyzed in 2017 by FED, 46% of ETFs, which managed 22% of all assets, used the funded model (Aramonte et al. 2017).

In practice, appropriate haircuts apply to the assets posted as collateral to account for the risk of value fluctuations and the imperfect correlation between the index and the collateral value. The level of haircuts or margins applied depends on the type of securities and the relevant home domicile law. In Europe, because there is no harmonized pan-European policy on haircuts, practices vary significantly from one ETF provider to another. Haircuts can vary between 0 and 30% depending on the type, liquidity, volatility, correlation, and creditworthiness of the securities delivered as collateral. Riskier asset types, like equities, typically require larger haircuts than bonds and cash (Johnson et al. 2012a). According to ESMA guidelines (ESMA 2014), UCITS funds should have in place a clear haircut policy described in prospectus adapted for each class of assets received as collateral. Additionally, when devising this policy, UCITS should take into account the characteristics of the assets, such as the credit standing or the price volatility, as well as the outcome of the stress tests.

[48] In the European Union, these securities should be consistent with CESR guidelines (CESR 2010) and ESMA guidelines (ESMA 2014).

Synthetic replication is employed by ETF providers (sponsors)[49] for two main reasons. The first one is the best quality of index replication measured by tracking difference, tracking error, or other measures; this has been confirmed by most studies—both academic and professional.[50] It is because a synthetic ETF's return is guaranteed by the counterparty, while in physical ETFs, especially in the case of representative sampling or optimization, inexact replication may occur. Besides, ETFs which apply synthetic replication can experience lower tracking error because of two aspects related to dividends. The first one concerns the assumption that in the case of swap-based ETFs, dividends are paid and reinvested as soon as the stock goes ex-dividend. The second one refers to the fact that some physical ETFs may have dividend tax withholdings at the fund level, so they produce a lower after-tax return relative to synthetic ETFs. On the other hand, changing either swap terms or costs over time, especially the costs of transactions, is likely to increase tracking errors (Dickson et al. 2013). Turnover ratios in synthetic ETFs tend to be much higher than those of physical ETFs, which reflects the resets of the swap agreements as well as the higher turnover in the substitute/collateral baskets. Additionally, some physical ETFs can mitigate tracking errors by employing securities lending.

Another benefit of using this replication method is the greater opportunity for cost reduction, which then usually translates to lower tracking error. This applies in particular to equity and bond ETFs, which are designed to mirror indexes that cover a large number of components and have a relatively large share of illiquid instruments when tracking is complex and expensive. For this reason, it is very often employed by funds aiming at mimicking emerging and frontier market indexes,[51] especially niche equity markets in small and less developed countries and those to which access is difficult, e.g., in countries with foreign equity ownership restrictions.[52] According to Lyxor (2019),

---

[49]The analysis of the advantages and disadvantages of ETFs using synthetic replication is conducted from their providers' and investors' point of view. We have omitted the potential impact of these kinds of financial instruments on financial market stability on a global scale—which is the subject of many studies listed earlier—as well as the point of view of other entities (e.g., a bank operating as a swap counterpart).

[50]See, for example, Deutsche Bank (2010), Johnson et al. (2012b), Elia (2012), Dickson et al. (2013), and Meinhardt et al. (2015). Different results are presented in, e.g., Naumenko and Chystiakova (2015) and Mateus and Rahmani (2017). Similar tracking efficiency was observed by Maurer and Williams (2014).

[51]According to data collected by Vanguard (Dickson et al. 2013), emerging markets equity is the only asset class category in which synthetic ETFs has outstandingly higher share in European ETF market in comparison with physical ETFs (13% vs. 6%).

[52]Apart from ETFs with exposure to major asset classes, i.e., equity and fixed income, synthetic replication is widely employed—using oftentimes futures and option contracts—by leveraged, inverse, and leveraged inverse ETFs, as well as commodity ETFs and ETCs (exchange-traded commodities).

European-listed, synthetically replicated ETFs that track emerging market indexes, e.g., the MSCI Emerging Market Index, offer a tracking error that is, on average, two to three times lower, though sometimes it can be as much as ten times lower, simultaneously giving a much smoother performance. Also, research from Elia (2012) indicated that synthetic emerging market ETFs had exhibited markedly lower tracking errors than physical emerging market ETFs.

Despite the benefits, synthetic replication has been retreating for years, especially from the European market, where it was still very eagerly used only a decade ago. Unfortunately, after the financial crisis of the last decade, it turned out that there is a price to pay for its biggest advantages—protection against tracking error risk and relatively high tracking quality. This price is primarily the counterparty risk (also generally known as default risk)[53] and the associated collateral risk. The trade-off relies on the fact that the lower tracking error risk comes at the cost of increased counterparty risk to the swap provider.

Currently, the share of synthetic ETFs in Europe, taking into account the value of assets, is 18% (as of 29 March 2019), while in 2010, it was as much as 45% (Lyxor 2019). They have a much larger share in terms of the number of funds.[54] The synthetic and futures-based ETFs also have relatively high importance in some Asian countries, e.g., in Hong Kong (18 and 20%, respectively, as of 30 June 2017). However, the number of local synthetic ETFs has experienced a significant decrease in recent years, largely due to the recent introduction of initiatives such as the RQFII scheme and Stock Connect, which allows ETF managers to launch physical ETFs by investing directly in the mainland securities market. As a result, a number of synthetic ETFs were either deauthorized and delisted or transformed into physical ETFs (SFC 2018). In the USA, synthetic replication is hardly used at all, except for leveraged and inverse ETFs, because the affiliated transactions employed in it are generally not permitted under US securities laws, notably the Investment Company Act of 1940 (though such transactions are permitted under the Securities Act of 1933).[55] In Australia, synthetic ETFs

[53]It should be added that also investors in physical ETFs that lend securities are exposed to counterparty risk, which will be discussed later in this chapter.

[54]The number of synthetic ETFs amounts to 912 funds, which is about 32% of all European-domiciled ETFs (as at the end of June 2018). There are 1025 ETFs in total, including also derivative-based ETFs (36% of all European-domiciled ETFs) (Pagano et al. 2019).

[55]In November 2019, Securities and Exchange Commission proposed new regulations for the use of derivatives by investment funds, especially inverse and leveraged ETFs, to introduce some safeguards for more risky products and increase competition. New proposals are aimed to standardize the framework for funds' derivatives risk management.

are limited to only three commodity ETFs and account for less than 1% of total AUM (Cunningham 2017).

Counterparty risk refers to the possibility that the entity providing the swap, usually an affiliated bank or third party, will fail to fulfill its obligation to deliver the performance of the index being tracked.[56] Net counterparty exposure is measured as the difference between the net asset value (NAV) of the ETF and the value of the substitute basket. The swap is marked-to-market at the end of each day and is reset whenever the counterparty exposure approaches a specified limit defined by general regulations[57] or is set at the discretion of the ETF provider, provided it is lower than the legal limit. In the event of a reset, the fund demands that the counterparty pay the swap mark-to-market by delivering additional securities to top up the collateral basket. In practice, swap reset policies vary across ETF sponsors and funds. The majority of ETF providers who use the unfunded swap model apply stricter reset triggers than the UCITS threshold. Consequently, resets are more frequent, and counterparty risk is generally lower (Johnson et al. 2012a). In practice, many ETF issuers implement resets on time-based intervals, i.e., monthly or quarterly, even if the counterparty exposure fails to reach a stated riffle; interestingly, some ETFs reset swaps even daily (Dickson et al. 2013). ETF managers may also minimize counterparty risk by overcollateralizing the swap agreements[58] and by engaging multiple swap counterparties in order to mitigate exposure to any one of them.

To sum up, the higher the level of collateralization, the more frequent the swap resets; and the more swap counterparties there are, the more investors would be protected from losses following a counterparty default. This is usually at the expense of a slightly higher swap spread. According to the BlackRock classification, taking the above aspects into account, the least favorable variant of synthetic replication from the point of view of the investor's security level is single swap counterparty replication with uncollateralized swap exposure. The most favorable variant is replication

[56]The Commission Directive 2010/43/EU defines counterparty risk as "the risk of loss for the UCITS resulting from the fact that the counterparty to a transaction may default on its obligations prior to the final settlement of the transaction's cash flow" (Commission Directive 2010/43/EU of 1 July 2010 implementing Directive 2009/65/EC of the European Parliament and of the Council as regards organizational requirements, conflicts of interest, conduct of business, risk management, and content of the agreement between a depositary and a management company—article 3, point 7).

[57]For instance, under Europe's UCITS Directive, a fund's exposure to counterparties may not exceed a total of 10% of its net asset value. This means that the daily NAV of the substitute basket should amount to at least 90% of the ETF's NAV. For swap counterparties which are not credit institutions, this limit is reduced to 5%.

[58]According to research conducted by Hurlin et al. (2019), average collateralization amounts to 101.3% in the unfunded swap model, 114.6% in the funded swap model, and 108.4% in all synthetic ETFs. Similar results were obtained by Aramonte et al. (2017).

with multiple swap counterparties and overcollateralized swap exposure (BlackRock 2010).

Collateral risk is closely related to the counterparty risk. Collateral is held in a segregated account with the fund custodian; it should be monitored to ensure it provides sufficient protection and—in the case of UCITS ETFs—it should meet ESMA and CESR guidelines.[59] However, a risk may arise from the inadequate quality of assets in the substitute (collateral) basket. These securities could be completely different from those in the benchmark index that the ETF tries to replicate, e.g., stocks as collateral for government bond ETFs, or even emerging market stocks as collateral for US Treasuries ETFs.[60] Another type of risk associated with collateral could be interest rate risk that occurs when the return on collateral is insufficient to cover the funding costs of the swap. Additionally, attention is drawn to the potential conflict of interest arising from the dual role of some banks as the ETF provider and swap counterparty.[61] This kind of risk can trigger a run on ETFs in periods of heightened counterparty risk.

However, it seems that from the average ETF investor's point of view, synthetic replication is, above all, very complicated, difficult to understand, and, therefore, opaque. This is true, even if the ETF provider publishes all information necessary to assess counterparty risk or collateral risk in the required documents and on its website.[62] This method often raises doubts, even from the simple fact that ETF uses derivative instruments and/or swap

[59]According to EMSA guidelines (2014), all collateral used to reduce counterparty risk exposure should comply with the following criteria: liquidity (any collateral other than cash should be highly liquid and traded on a regulated market or MTF with transparent pricing in order that it can be sold quickly at a price that is close to pre-sale valuation), valuation (collateral should be valued on at least a daily basis and assets that exhibit high price volatility should not be accepted as collateral unless suitably conservative haircuts are in place), high quality, independence and correlation (collateral should be issued by an entity that is independent from the counterparty and is expected not to display a high correlation with the performance of the counterparty) and diversification (collateral should be sufficiently diversified in terms of country, markets, and issuers).

[60]However, according to the research carried out by Pérignon et al. (2014) on a sample of 164 ETFs managed by Deutsche Bank (db x-trackers ETF) with a 40.9 billion USD collateral portfolio, there was a good fit between the asset exposure of the fund, e.g., equity or fixed income, and the collateral used to secure the swap. The match between exposure and collateral turned out to be lower for geographic exposures, especially in ETFs tracking Asia-Pacific or North-American indexes which might have been a consequence of home bias. Moreover, the correlation between the returns of the ETF and of its collateral was, on average, positive.

[61]Other types of conflicts of interest can occur also in other types of ETFs—they can reveal themselves wherever several ETF functions are located within one financial group. For example, this applies to a situation in which an ETF issuer is also involved in the design and/or calculation of the reference index, or it acts as a liquidity provider on the secondary market of the ETF (Financial Stability Board 2011).

[62]ESMA guidelines (2014) indicate that a UCITS fund's prospectus should clearly inform investors of its collateral policy.

Table 3.2 The main differences between physical and synthetic (derivative) ETFs

Characteristic	Physical replicating ETF	Synthetic (derivative) replicating ETF
Investment strategy	Replicate the index by holding index constituents	Swap agreement (funded or unfunded) or equity- or credit-linked note to receive index exposure
Vehicle/issuer risk	Assets held in ring-fenced, segregated accounts or a ring-fenced fund company	Assets in a collateral basket held in ring-fenced, segregated accounts or a ring-fenced fund company
Counterparty risk exposure	Minimal counterparty risk. Possible exposure within securities lending (can be reduced through over-collateralization)	Credit exposure diversified with multiswap counterparties. Risk exposure restricted to 10% (in UCITS funds). It can be reduced through collateralization
Fee structure	Transparent—all fees included in the total expense ratio (TER). Securities lending can reduce the total cost of ownership (TCO)	Swap spread (positive or negative) and TER are reduced from the fund performance
Performance	Tracking difference results from trading, optimization, and rebalanced costs from holdings	Swap counterparty guarantees the index return—TER and swap spread reduces index return
Transparency	Holdings published daily	Publication of holdings, fees, risk exposure, and collateralization varies
Listing and cross listing process (in UCITS funds)	Passportable across the EU under the UCITS Directive—significant effort and cost	Passportable across the EU under the UCITS Directive—significant effort and cost

Source BlackRock (2012)

transactions, which are usually perceived (often rightly) as complex and unclear. The consequence of this may be a lack of confidence in this replication method, which in turn may lead to the abandonment of synthetic

ETFs. This particularly refers to periods of growing uncertainty on financial markets, when a significant number of investors almost automatically stop using more complex financial products, which may only seem or which are actually riskier, in favor of relatively simple instruments, which they believe to be more secure.

In Table 3.2, there is a comparison of physical and synthetic exchange-traded funds, taking into account attributes both already described and not discussed, e.g., fee structure or listing.

3.5 Securities Lending

Securities lending, i.e., the process of temporarily loaning securities to a third party in exchange for a fee, is widely recognized as playing an essential function in the global capital market nowadays by improving market efficiency and liquidity. Securities are usually lent on an open basis with no fixed maturity date, which gives lenders the flexibility to recall them at any time; sometimes, they may be granted for a specific term.

The biggest lenders of assets are typically institutional investors with long investment horizons, such as pension and retirement funds, registered investment funds, insurance companies, endowments, sovereign wealth funds, central banks, and government bodies. This activity primarily helps them to generate additional income. In turn, among borrowers of securities, there are also large financial institutions, such as investment banks, market makers, broker-dealers, and hedge funds. The latter, however, ordinarily borrow through the prime brokerage arms of investment banks or broker-dealers, rather than directly from lending agents or fund managers. These entities borrow securities for a variety of reasons, mostly tactical ones, including ensuring the settlement of trades (avoiding settlement failure), profiting from arbitrage opportunities, as well as facilitating market-making and other trading activities, such as hedging and short selling (Bioy and Rose 2012; McCullough 2018). To mitigate counterparty risk, borrowers are carefully selected, and their creditworthiness is closely monitored. Additionally, to reduce the risk of borrower default, lenders require that borrowers post collateral, usually of greater value than the lent security. Two major collateral types are commonly used to back securities-lending transactions: cash and securities (often treasuries). While securities are on loan, normal interest and dividends still accrue to the beneficial owner. However, the voting rights of equity securities can be used by the securities borrower.

Securities lending is rarely undertaken directly between lenders and borrowers of securities. This activity is generally performed by large custodian banks or third-party specialists. They benefit from economies of scale, expertise, technology, as well as borrower access, which enables them to secure the most competitive pricing. In exchange for matching these two groups of entities, intermediaries receive a part of the lending revenue.

It is no wonder then that securities lending—which can benefit so many participants—is becoming more widespread around the world. According to EquiLend, one of the leading providers of trading, post-trade, market data, and clearing services for the securities finance industry, the global securities finance industry generated just under 10 billion USD in revenue for lenders in 2018. It was a record year in terms of revenue generated for investors that lend out securities from their portfolios. The largest share was entities from the Americas (47%), followed by EMEA (31%) and Asia-Pacific (22%) (DataLend 2019). Volume-weighted average fees[63] to borrow US and European equities amounted to, respectively, 48 bps and 58 bps in 2018 (Benedict 2019).

Mutual fund managers, including ETF managers, engage in securities lending to enhance the yield on their investment portfolios and improve fund performance. The income generated through this activity can help ETFs to improve the quality of index-tracking and offset fund costs, which is a benefit primarily for fund shareholders. However, since the total expense ratios for many ETFs are getting lower, securities-lending programs can also elevate their performance and serve as a point of differentiation for fund sponsors in an increasingly competitive market (McCullough 2018).

According to IHS Markit, a global business information provider, 2018 was the best year on record for ETF lending, with almost USD 400 million in revenue. The vast majority of the income from securities lending went to American ETFs (72% in Q2 2019), which is the obvious consequence of them having the highest assets; they are also characterized by the highest average value on loans[64] (USD 46 bn in Q2 2019). However, the highest weighted average fee applies to European and Asian ETFs (1.48% and 1.46%, respectively, in Q2 2019); the globally weighted average fee amounted to 0.53% (IHS Markit 2019). Higher average fees in the case of these ETFs are the result of the lower supply of securities and their scarcity,

---

[63]The volume-weighted average fee is calculated by summing the value of each transaction (the loan value multiplied by the fee) and dividing it by the total loan value.

[64]Term "securities on loan" means the total amount of securities currently loaned out in the market. As of April 1, 2019, DataLend tracked approximately USD 2.3 trillion worth of securities on loan across the global securities finance market.

especially in some asset classes. Securities lending by equity ETFs provide the largest total income (about 60–70%), followed by fixed-income ETFs (about 15–25%); the importance of other types of ETFs—commodity, alternative, and currency—are negligible. The highest lending revenues are generated by ETFs managed by BlackRock (40–50%) and State Street (15–20%).[65]

The most significant issues that must be considered in relation to the potential income arising from securities lending are:

- the amount of securities that a fund can make available for lending and the actual size of the fund's portfolio on loan,
- the share of revenues generated by securities lending returned to the fund,
- other benefits from securities lending.

Prior to enrolling a security in a lending program, an ETF manager must assess a number of factors—notably regulatory, legal, tax, and liquidity restrictions. They determine the amount of securities that a fund can make available for lending. Among them, legal restrictions are of key importance. In some jurisdictions, strict limits have been imposed on ETF securities lending (e.g., in the USA[66]), while in others (e.g., in the European Union[67]), there are no such regulations, although some companies have set internal limits in this respect. According to a study by Morningstar,[68] in practice, the average percentage of a fund's portfolio on loan in the USA is quite small—usually below 10%. It is also worth noting that asset classes influence the average portfolio percentage on loan—the highest values occur in the case of US small-cap funds and taxable bond funds. In turn, international equity funds, similar to US large-cap funds, are characterized by a relatively low average portfolio percentage on loans, ranging from 1.5 to 3.6%. Differentiation can also be seen when it comes to the funds' sponsors—TIAA and State Street were among the most aggressive lenders before the financial crisis in 2009, while Vanguard, First Trust, Invesco, and Schwab (apart from 2007)

[65]Approximate values based on IHS Markit data from the last few quarters.

[66]Generally, ETFs may not lend more than one-third of total assets, but in calculating this limit, the SEC has taken the view that collateral may be included as part of the lending fund's total assets. Thus, an ETF could lend up to 50% of its asset value before the securities loan. In practice, they do not use this limit, as shown in McCullough (2018).

[67]In the ESMA guidelines (ESMA 2014), any limits for the proportion of assets that may be subject to securities lending were not recommended. ESMA only indicated that a UCITS fund "should ensure that it is able at any time to recall any security that has been lent out or terminate any securities lending agreement into which it has entered." Additionally, ESMA specified a number of requirements related to "efficient portfolio management techniques" which also include securities lending.

[68]The research sample covered almost 3000 observations from 2007 through the first half of 2018. It included 440 unique index mutual funds and ETFs from 10 fund sponsors.

have, on average, consistently lent out a smaller portion of funds' portfolios (McCullough 2018).

In European ETFs, differences in lending levels are much higher. They can range between 0 and 100%, and the amount of assets that can be lent out varies not only from provider to provider, but also from fund to fund. The survey conducted by Morningstar in 2011–2012 among 10 European providers of physical ETFs[69] indicated that 85% of funds lent less than half their assets on average, and around two-thirds lent less than 20%. On the other hand, a few providers lent up to 100% of the assets held by their ETFs (Bioy and Rose 2012).

A very interesting and atypical case is the Japanese market, where individual stocks that constitute ETFs held by the Bank of Japan (BoJ), under the ETF purchasing program implemented in 2010, can be lent freely by ETF managers. Maeda and Shino (2019) found that the expansion of the ETF purchasing program has caused the substantial growth of stock lending markets. It also turned out that each ETF seems to have an "upper limit" on stock lending rates, which ranged from 10 to 80%. Some funds have raised their upper bound during the period from 2014 to 2018.

The primary source of income generated by ETFs engaged in securities lending is a fee charged to borrowers. However, this income does not go only to the lenders. Because funds employ lending agent services, gross securities-lending revenue is reduced by the fees charged by entities engaged in this activity and the costs associated with lending programs. The fees retained by lending agents cover a number of functions, including, but not limited to, arranging lending transactions, monitoring the quality of borrowers, managing collateral, and in some cases, providing indemnification. The degree to which revenues generated via securities lending are split between the fund provider and/or the lending agent (or management company) is determined by a revenue-sharing agreement. This may significantly affect the amount of potential profits from securities lending and, thus, the scale of benefits derived by investors. Interestingly, these issues are sometimes regulated by law. For example, in accordance with EU law, all the revenues arising from efficient portfolio management techniques (including securities lending), net of direct and indirect operational costs (which should be disclosed in the prospectus) should be returned to the UCITS (ESMA 2014).

The portion of lending revenues returned to the fund varies across markets and providers. Morningstar's survey carried out among European ETF

[69]It included almost 200 ETFs engaged in securities lending, both equity and bond funds.

providers showed that the share of revenues returned to the fund ranged from 45 to 70% of gross revenue, although few providers revealed that they return 100% of the revenues (net of costs). The level of fees charged by lending agents varied from 10 to 40% of gross revenues and depended on the scope of the services offered, as well as the size and the securities-lending revenue-generating potential of the funds included in the programs (Bioy and Rose 2012). In the USA, most fund sponsors state that 100% of net securities-lending revenue is passed back to the fund. According to the Morningstar research,[70] the range of the percentages of securities-lending revenue passed along to fundholders varied from 69.2% for the BlackRock US equity funds to 100% for the Fidelity taxable-bond funds. Most securities-lending agents applied a consistent revenue split across asset classes. In the case of international equity funds, the above-mentioned indicators ranged between 74.1% (WisdomTree) and 93.4% (Vanguard). However, as Morningstar emphasizes, it is difficult to draw definite conclusions based only on the percentage of gross securities-lending revenue passed to fundholders. Some entities with less generous "splits" may generate more total lending revenue by lending more aggressively. For example, some fund sponsors lend out only opportunistically, putting on loan only securities that command high lending fees, while others lend out a greater portion of the portfolio regardless of the lending fee level (McCullough 2018). In turn, Better Finance,[71] in their latest study conducted in 2018–2019 on the European market,[72] showed that the "split" of gross revenues varied widely from 51% (Deka) to 95% (Vanguard) allocated to the funds, and therefore 49–5% to the management company and/or to the securities-lending agent. Although the distribution of revenues from securities lending to funds may seem relatively high at first glance, in Better Finance's opinion, the results of the study raise serious concerns regarding compliance with the ESMA rule that 100% of the net income must be returned to the funds (Better Finance 2019).

A typical lending transaction also involves, among others, the lender collecting or paying the rebate rate depending on the difference between the lending rate and funding rate. When the securities-lending fee is lower than

[70]The research was conducted in 2018 on a sample including 250 funds from the 10 largest US index fund and ETF sponsors.

[71]Better Finance, the European Federation of Investors and Financial Services Users, is the public interest, non-governmental organization advocating and defending the interests of European citizens as financial services users at the European level to lawmakers and the public in order to promote research, information, and training on investments, savings and personal finances.

[72]The research sample included 30 mainstream equity ETFs managed by the 10 biggest European ETF providers.

the cash funding fee, the lender pays a rebate to the borrower to compensate the borrower for forgone income from investing cash collateral. The rebate rate is a function of the funding rate of the cash and lending rate of the borrowed security. Lower rebate ratios are a sign of less aggressive lending programs, while more aggressive lending programs tend to make greater use of rebates in order to drive higher loan volumes. According to the Morningstar study conducted in the US market, average rebates paid as a percentage of gross securities-lending revenue varied significantly across index fund and ETF providers and asset classes. In the case of international equity funds, they ranged from 3.5% (First Trust) to 44.1% (Fidelity). Rebates in this category were usually lower than in U.S. equity funds (McCullough 2018).

Although lenders generate revenue primarily by charging borrowers a fee, it is not the sole source of benefits for ETFs. Many European ETF providers willingly use securities lending within the dividend tax arbitrage (tax optimization) strategy. During the dividend season, they lend stocks that are subject to dividend withholding tax to counterparties located in more tax-efficient jurisdictions. In this way, ETFs can avoid a portion of the withholding taxes levied on dividends by European countries, whose rates are usually high.[73] This, in turn, can increase their returns and improve index-tracking quality.

Among ETFs, those most engaged in securities lending, for obvious reasons, are funds employing physical replication. However, this activity is not the exclusive domain of these kinds of ETFs, as it may seem. Synthetic ETFs may also lend out the securities contained within the substitute basket or the fund's collateral. However, it is not widespread across this category of funds, because the securities that usually make up substitute baskets, i.e., large-cap, liquid shares, and collateral do not command high lending fees. Banks prefer to lend securities directly where lending fees are high and to use the remaining inventory to provide collateral to the ETF under the swap arrangements. It is also worth highlighting, that in the case of swap-replicated ETFs, securities lending is usually done at the level of their parent bank, not at the fund level (as is the case for physically-replicated ETFs). This means that the bank, not the ETF, directly assumes the counterparty risk (Johnson et al. 2012a).

ETFs, like index funds, are very desirable lenders for several reasons. Firstly, they usually track broadly diversified indexes; therefore, they can offer a

[73]According to Deloitte (2019), in 2019, withholding tax rates for dividends in some European countries reached 20% or even more—e.g., 27.5% in Austria, 20% in Finland, 30% in France, 25% in Germany, 25% in Portugal, and 35% in Switzerland.

vast inventory of securities which borrowers find attractive. Equity ETFs, in particular, are considered to be entities that offer a wide selection of securities. What is more, the enormous growth of capital flowing into index funds and ETFs in recent years has deepened the pool for prospective borrowers (McCullough 2018). Additionally, the dynamically increasing use of ETFs by institutional investors, especially in the USA,[74] is reflected by the growth of lendable assets[75] in securities lending. In mid-2019, global ETFs' lendable assets reached USD 300 billion for the first time. However, it is still much less than in the case of government or corporate bonds (USD 3.0 trillion and 3.1 trillion, respectively), not to mention equities (USD 13.3 trillion).

The second reason is that ETFs and index funds have a significantly lower turnover ratio[76] than actively managed funds.[77] The borrower in this situation is exposed to a lower risk of the lender (fund manager) suddenly requesting that the borrowed instruments be returned when it would like to sell them or exercise their voting rights. In other words, a relatively static portfolio with low securities turnover is more attractive to securities borrowers because it minimizes recalls of loaned securities (Baklanova et al. 2015).

Although securities-lending returns typically vary by asset class and the underlying demand for securities, corporate bond ETFs and international equity ETFs seem to be particularly welcome lenders and can generate relatively high profits. This is mainly due to the relative scarcity of such financial assets on the global financial market. In the case of emerging/frontier equity ETFs, this is firstly the result of relatively small AUM,[78] which limits the lendable assets base. The smaller potential of these funds is also because securities lending is still prohibited or severely limited in many emerging and frontier markets. Emerging markets are very differentiated and idiosyncratic in their financial regulations and practices. Some countries have adopted

[74]According to a Deutsche Bank study, almost two-thirds of the US ETF market at the end of 2018 was controlled by institutional investors (USD 2.1 trillion), representing a fourfold increase in institutional use over the past 5 years (ETF Stream 2019).

[75]The term "lendable assets" means the total gross inventory of a securities. As of April 1, 2019, DataLend tracked approximately USD 19.9 trillion in lendable assets across the global securities finance market.

[76]Turnover ratio is a measure of the fund's trading activity. It is usually computed by taking the lesser of purchases or sales and dividing by the average monthly net assets. A low turnover figure (20–30%) would indicate a buy-and-hold strategy. High turnover (more than 100%) would indicate an investment strategy involving considerable buying and selling of securities (http://www.morningstar.com/InvGlossary/turnover_ratio.aspx).

[77]According to Morningstar data, the median turnover among cap-weighted passive ETFs and passive mutual funds in the USA over the three years through 2018 was, respectively, 17 and 19%, while among active ETFs and active mutual fund it was 55 and 48%, respectively (Johnson and Bryan 2019).

[78]According to ETFGI data (as of April 2019), the assets of ETFs and ETPs with emerging markets exposure amounted to USD 549 billion, which accounted for only 9.8% of their total assets.

securities-lending standards closer to those that prevail in developed markets, while others have implemented lending, but with their own specific market requirements. In many of these markets, the development of the securities-lending industry must also defer to regulatory concern over short selling, specifically relating to the issues of market and settlement efficiency (Citibank 2012).

Consequently, according to IHS Markit data (as of 2018), lendable assets exceed USD 100 billion in only one EM country (South Korea), while in other top lending EM markets (Taiwan, South Africa, Singapore), it fluctuates around USD 60 billion, and in the others they are much lower. On the other hand, borrow demand for emerging market equities is growing—it was USD 33.4 billion at the end of Q1 2018. This is mainly due to the high volatility in EM equity markets, along with some stock-specific risks. Moreover, the relative scarcity of EM equities also translates into higher fees to be gained from securities lending (the value-weighted average fee for a top lending EM sometimes exceeds 2% or even 3%) (Pierson 2018).

In equity markets, borrowers find it much more difficult to find small-cap, emerging/frontier markets or niche sector/thematic stocks relative to blue chips or developed markets shares.[79] This is reflected in the level of income that owners of these assets can earn, because lending fees are obviously a function of supply and demand. Generally, hard-to-borrow, small, and illiquid securities command considerably higher fees than widely available, large, and heavily traded securities.[80] According to BlackRock calculations conducted for a sample of European iShares ETFs, in the case of funds tracking large-cap equity indexes exposed to developed markets, average yearly securities-lending returns for the period 2014–2018 ranged between 0.6 bps (for iShares S&P 500 UCITS ETF USD [Dist]) and 3.0 bps (iShares MSCI World UCITS ETF USD [Dist]). Meanwhile, securities-lending returns for emerging large-cap equity ETFs ranged from 6.7 bps (iShares MSCI EM UCITS ETF USD [Dist]) to 14.2 bps (iShares MSCI Turkey UCITS ETF USD [Dist]). Lending profits turned out to be significantly higher in two ETFs replicating the indexes of small-cap equity developed and emerging markets (iShares MSCI Japan Small Cap UCITS ETF USD [Dist] and iShares MSCI EM Small

---

[79]For instance, according to IHS Markit data, in mid-2019, the average value of lendable EM equities was significantly below USD 100 bn, while in the case of most developed European and Asian markets it was usually several hundred billion USD and in the case of US equities over 8.5 trn USD.

[80]Moreover, lending fees also depend on considerations unique to each transaction, including the nature, size, and duration of the transaction, the type of collateral offered, and the credit quality of the counterparty involved in the transaction.

Cap UCITS ETF USD [Dist])—19.4 bps and 44.3 bps, respectively.[81] In recent years, iShares small-cap US ETFs achieved slightly lower profits from securities lending (on average), although they were still relatively high.[82] Their average yearly securities-lending returns for the fiscal years 2016–2018 ranged between 8.7 bps (iShares Core S&P Small-Cap ETF) and 30.7 bps (iShares Russell 2000 Growth ETF). Relatively high income on loans was also generated by a sector ETF (iShares Nasdaq Biotechnology ETF)—18.3 bps.[83]

The relevance of income for the previously mentioned types of ETFs is best demonstrated when comparing lending profits with management fees. According to the same BlackRock data, securities-lending income generated had the equivalent effect of offsetting management fees by between 9 and 80% in the case of 5 European emerging equity iShares ETFs and between 29 and 146% (!) in the case of 6 US small-cap equity iShares ETFs (all data for 2018). It is thus evident that income from lending securities—especially in the case of a significant number of international equity ETFs—can significantly improve their investment results and index-tracking efficiency. The revenue stream from lending activities can either reduce an ETF's negative tracking difference relative to its index or even, as indicated above, turn a negative tracking difference into a positive one, in which case the fund will outperform its index. Thus, asset managers may strengthen their competitive position on the market, and investors can more effectively achieve their investment goals.

The potential to generate relatively high lending income by US small-cap and international stocks was confirmed by the results of the previously mentioned Morningstar study carried out among US equity index funds and ETFs. For example, the average net securities-lending yield in the 2007–2018(1H) period across funds investing in international stocks, ranged between 1.3 bps and 4.8 bps, and was only worse than yields in US small-cap funds. Moreover, it was noted that securities-lending yields peaked across all categories during the global financial crisis. This was driven by a surge in demand from short-sellers. When the market subsequently rebounded, demand from these entities decreased, and lending yields declined (McCullough 2018).

[81] Own calculations based on BlackRock (2018).

[82] Funds with more than USD 5 billion in AUM and securities lending returns of at least 0.05% were analyzed.

[83] Own calculations based on BlackRock (2019).

Although securities lending can offer many different benefits to ETFs and investors, it is important to remember that such transactions are accompanied by various types of risk. Two main sources of risk are counterparty risk (borrower default risk) and reinvestment risk. The first type is similar to that which occurs in swap-based ETFs. In the case of securities lending, borrower default risk is the risk that the counterparty fails to return the borrowed security to the lender (ETF). Although counterparty defaults are very rare and their impact is negligible in practice, lenders should carefully select borrowers through constant monitoring of their creditworthiness, especially in the case of a deterioration of their financial situation or the turbulent situation on the market.

The securities-lending agreement counterparty risk may be reduced in three ways:

- collateral management—loans are usually overcollateralized. High-quality and diversified collateral, i.e., government (sovereign) bonds and liquid equities, and less frequently corporate bonds, certificates of deposit, or simply cash, is marked-to-market daily with the counterparty to guarantee that collateral levels are sufficient. Depending on the type and quality of the securities, appropriate margins/haircuts are applied to ensure maximum liquidation value for ETF shareholders in the event a borrower defaults. Moreover, collateral is held in a segregated custodial account in the name of the fund and is not re-used;
- callable loans—lenders can call back securities on loan at any time;
- lending limits—as mentioned earlier, in some countries, regulatory authorities or supervisory agencies restrict the percentage of securities on loan. Sometimes internal limits are imposed by asset managers (McCullough 2018).

However, if these safeguards happen not to work, some lending agents offer indemnification from potential losses resulting from a counterparty default. However, the extent and the method of the coverage of the indemnification may vary a great deal depending on the entity.

The source of reinvestment risk is that the securities in which the cash collateral is subsequently invested, incur losses or underperform relative to other investment options or relative to rebates paid. This is the consequence of the fact that the lending agent may try to squeeze out more investment income by taking an excessive risk when reinvesting cash collateral. As a result, the value of the reinvested collateral cannot cover the value of the lent security, and the ETF suffers losses. The risks associated with cash collateral reinvestment may be mitigated if the investment vehicle is invested in high quality, short-dated instruments.

This type of risk applies mainly to the US market, where cash collateral represents the vast majority of the collateral received in securities-lending programs. In Europe, securities prevail as collateral. After the financial crisis, the SEC introduced more conservative regulations, and currently, nearly the entire cash collateral portfolio must be invested in US Treasuries, or short-term commercial papers rated AA or higher. These activities have largely reined in the reinvestment risk faced by ETFs (Bioy and Rose 2012; McCullough 2018).

References

Anadu, K. E., Kruttli, M., McCabe, P., Osambela, E., & Shin, C. H. (2018). *The Shift from Active to Passive Investing: Potential Risks to Financial Stability?* (Working Paper RPA 18-04). https://www.bostonfed.org/-/media/Documents/Workingpapers/PDF/2018/rpa1804.pdf. Accessed 25 July 2019.

Aramonte, S., Caglio, C., & Tuzun, T. (2017). *Synthetic ETFs, FEDS Notes 2017-08-10, Board of Governors of the Federal Reserve System (U.S.).* https://www.federalreserve.gov/econres/notes/feds-notes/synthetic-etfs-20170810.htm. Accessed 11 Aug 2019.

Atkinson, H. J., & Green, D. (2005). *The New Investment Frontier III: A Guide to Exchange Traded Funds for Canadians.* Toronto: Insomniac Press.

Baklanova, V., Copeland, A., & McCaughrin, R. (2015). *Reference Guide to U.S. Repo and Securities Lending Markets* (Federal Reserve Bank of New York Staff Reports, Staff Report No. 740). https://www.newyorkfed.org/medialibrary/media/research/staff_reports/sr740.pdf. Accessed 1 Sept 2019.

Beasley, J. E., Meade, N., & Chang, T.-J. (2003). A Evolutionary Heuristic for the Index Tracking Problem. *European Journal of Operational Research, 148,* 622–623.

Benedict, C. (2019). *Amidst Global Trade Wars, the Securities Markets Response.* The Purple, Issue 6, DataLend. https://datalend.com/amidst-global-trade-wars-the-securities-finance-market-responds/. Accessed 26 Aug 2019.

Better Finance. (2017). *Better Finance Helps Investors Identify Potential Falsely Active Funds ("Closet Indexers"), and Asks Regulators to Investigate Further.* https://betterfinance.eu/wp-content/uploads/publications/EN_-_Press_Release_and_Annexes_2_3_-_Better_Finance_replication_of_ESMA_study_on_Closet_Indexing.pdf. Accessed 20 June 2019.

Better Finance. (2019). *Efficient Portfolio Management Techniques: Attribution of Profits Derived from Securities Lending by UCITS Exchange-Traded Funds.* https://betterfinance.eu/wp-content/uploads/BETTER-FINANCE-Research-Paper-Securities-Lending-11062019.pdf. Accessed 30 Aug 2019.

Bhattacharya, A., & O'Hara, M. (2020). *ETFs and Systemic Risks*. https://www.cfainstitute.org/-/media/documents/article/rf-brief/etfs-and-systemic-risks.ashx. Accessed 2 Feb 2020.

Bioy, H., Garcia-Zarate, J., Lamont, K., Boyadzhiev, D., & Kang, H. (2019). *A Guided Tour of the European ETF Marketplace*. https://www.morningstar.com/lp/guided-tour-european-etf-marketplace. Accessed 24 July 2019.

Bioy, H., & Rose, G. (2012). *Securities Lending in Physical Replication ETFs: A Review of Providers' Practices, Morningstar ETF Research*. https://media.morningstar.com/uk/media/ETF/SecuritiesLendinginPhysicalETFs.pdf. Accessed 22 Aug 2019.

BlackRock. (2010). *Overview of ETF Structures: How ETFs Track Their Benchmark*.

BlackRock. (2011). *ETF Landscape: Industry Review*. End H1 2011. New York: BlackRock Investment Institute.

BlackRock. (2012). *ETP Due Diligence: A Framework to Help Investors Select the Right European Exchange Traded Products (ETPs)*. https://www.altii.de/media/modelfield_files/dokumente/dokument/datei/etp-due-diligence–report-en-emea-pc-whitepaper.pdf. Accessed 18 Aug 2019.

BlackRock. (2018). *iShares Securities Lending: Unlocking the Potential of Portfolios*. https://www.ishares.com/uk/professional/en/literature/brochure/ishares-securities-lending-en-emea-pc.pdf. Accessed 6 May 2019.

BlackRock. (2019). *iShares Securities Lending: Unlocking the Potential of Portfolios*. https://www.ishares.com/us/literature/brochure/securities-lending-unlocking-portfolios-en-us.pdf. Accessed 2 Sept 2019.

Bloomberg. (2019). *MSCI Urges China Ease Ownership Limits After Dropping Stock*. https://www.bloomberg.com/news/articles/2019-03-07/msci-drops-foreign-favorite-from-china-gauges-on-access-concern. Accessed 24 June 2019.

CESR. (2010). *CESR's Guidelines on Risk Measurement and the Calculation of Global Exposure and Counterparty Risk for UCITS* (CESR/10-788). https://www.esma.europa.eu/sites/default/files/library/2015/11/10_788.pdf. Accessed 12 Aug 2019.

Citibank. (2012). *Securities Lending in the Emerging Markets*. https://citi.com/mss/docs/09_12_securities_lending_emerging_markets.pdf. Accessed 2 Sept 2019.

Cunningham, M. (2017). *The Australian Exchange-Traded Funds Market*. https://www.rba.gov.au/publications/bulletin/2017/jun/pdf/bu-0617-6-the-australian-exchange-traded-funds-market.pdf. Accessed 16 Aug 2019.

DataLend. (2019). *Securities Finance Industry Generated $9.96 Billion in Revenue in 2018*. https://datalend.com/securities-finance-industry-generated-9-96-billion-in-revenue-in-2018/. Accessed 26 Aug 2019.

Deloitte. (2019). *Withholding Tax Rates 2019*. https://www2.deloitte.com/content/dam/Deloitte/global/Documents/Tax/dttl-tax-withholding-tax-rates.pdf. Accessed 30 Aug 2019.

Deutsche Bank. (2010). *Do ETFs Trackers Track? European Equity ETF Tracking Error Under the Microscope*. Deutsche Bank Global Equity Index & ETF Research.

Deutsche Bank. (2012). *db X-Trackers ETFs Under the Microscope: A Guide to ETF Structures and Risks, with an In-Depth Look at db X-Trackers ETFs*. https://www.wertpapier-forum.de/applications/core/interface/file/attachment.php?id=86190. Accessed 1 Aug 2019.

Deutsche Bundesbank. (2018, October). *The Growing Importance of Exchange Traded Funds in the Financial Markets* (Monthly Report). https://www.bundesbank.de/resource/blob/766600/2fd3ae4f0593fb2ce465c092ce40888b/mL/2018-10-exchange-traded-funds-data.pdf. Accessed 27 July 2019.

Dhanraj, C. (2018). *Potential Benefits and Risks of Preferred Stocks*. https://www.ishares.com/us/insights/potential-benefits-and-risks-of-preferred-stocks. Accessed 22 July 2019.

Dickson, J. M., Mance, L., & Rowley, J. J., Jr. (2013). *Understanding Synthetic ETFs*. Vanguard. https://www.vanguard.com.hk/documents/understand-synthetic-etfs-tlrv.pdf. Accessed 11 Aug 2019.

Elia, M. (2012). *Tracking Error of Traditional and Synthetic European Exchange-Traded Funds* (Working Paper). University of Turin. http://papers.ssrn.com/sol3/papers.cfm?abstract_id=2003976. Accessed 13 Aug 2019.

ESMA. (2011). *ESMA's Policy Orientations and Guidelines for UCITS Exchange Traded Funds and Structured UCITS, ESMA/2011/220*. https://www.esma.europa.eu/sites/default/files/library/2015/11/2011_220.pdf. Accessed 24 July 2019.

ESMA. (2014). *Guidelines for Competent Authorities and UCITS Management Companies.* Guidelines on ETFs and Other UCITS Issues, ESMA/2014/937EN. https://www.esma.europa.eu/sites/default/files/library/2015/11/esma-2014-0011 01 00_en_0.pdf. Accessed 4 Aug 2019.

ESMA. (2016). *Supervisory Work on Potential Closet Index Tracking, ESMA/2016/165*. https://www.esma.europa.eu/sites/default/files/library/2016-165_public_statement_-_supervisory_work_on_potential_closet_index_tracking.pdf. Accessed 20 June 2019.

ETF Stream. (2019). *How Institutional Investors Are Using ETFs*. https://www.etfstream.com/news/7680_how-institutional-investors-are-using-etfs/. Accessed 1 Sept 2019.

ETFdb.com. (2019). *Preferred Stock ETF List*. https://etfdb.com/etfs/asset-class/preferred-stock/. Accessed 22 July 2019.

ETFGI. (2019). *ETFGI Reports That Assets Invested in Actively Managed ETFs/ETPs Reached a New Record High of US$151.24 Billion at the End of November 2019*. https://etfgi.com/news/press-releases/2019/12/etfgi-reports-assets-invested-actively-managed-etfsetps-reached-new. Accessed 3 Jan 2020.

European Systemic Risk Board. (2011). *ESRB Response to the ESMA Discussion Paper on "Policy Orientations and Guidelines for UCITS Exchange-Traded Funds and Structured UCITS"*. https://www.esrb.europa.eu/pub/pdf/other/ESRB_response_to_ESMA_consultation_exchange_traded_funds.pdf?19949ead0d7d404b93ae1dcd57ed9d2b. Accessed 24 July 2019.

Evans, J. L., & Archer, S. H. (1968). Diversification and the Reduction of Dispersion: An Empirical Analysis. *Journal of Finance, 23*(5), 761–767.

Fang, K., & Heinrichs, J. (2017). *Understanding the Regulation of Exchange-Traded Funds Under the Securities Exchange Act of 1934*. Investment Company Institute. https://www.ici.org/pdf/ppr_17_etf_listing_standards.pdf. Accessed 13 June 2019.

Ferri, R. A. (2009). *The ETF Book: All You Need to Know About Exchange-Traded Funds*. Hoboken: Wiley.

Ferri, R. A. (2011). *The Power of Passive Investing: More Wealth with Less Work*. Hoboken: Wiley.

Financial Stability Board. (2011). *Potential Financial Stability Issues Arising from Recent Trends in Exchange-Traded Funds (ETFs)*. https://www.fsb.org/wp-content/uploads/r_110412b.pdf. Accessed 24 July 2019.

FTSE Russell. (2015). *How Indexes Change*. https://content.ftserussell.com/sites/default/files/research/how_indexes_change_final.pdf. Accessed 22 June 2019.

Fuhr, D. (2014). *Depositary Receipt Structures Open ETF Horizons*. https://www.fnlondon.com/articles/depositary-receipt-structures-open-etf-horizons-20141020. Accessed 24 July 2019.

Gastineau, G. L. (2010). *The Exchange-Traded Funds Manual* (2nd ed.). Hoboken: Wiley.

Grill, M., Lambert, C., Marquardt, P., Watfe, G., & Weistroffer, C. (2018, November). *Counterparty and Liquidity Risks in Exchange-Traded Funds* (Financial Stability Review). https://www.ecb.europa.eu/pub/financial-stability/fsr/special/html/ecb.fsrart201811_3.en.html. Accessed 25 July 2019.

Hill, J. M., Nadig, D., & Hougan, M. (2015). *A Comprehensive Guide to Exchange-Traded Funds (ETFs)*. Charlottesville: CFA Institute Research Foundation.

Hurlin, C., Iseli, G., Pérignon, C., & Yeung, S. (2019). The Counterparty Risk Exposure of ETF Investors. *Journal of Banking & Finance, 102*(May), 215–230.

IHS Markit. (2019). *Securities Finance Quarterly Review. Q2 2019*. https://cdn.ihs.com/www/pdf/0719/SecuritiesFinanceQ2Review.pdf. Accessed 28 Aug 2019.

International Monetary Fund. (2011). *Global Financial Stability Report: Durable Financial Stability: Getting There From Here*. https://www.imf.org/-/media/Websites/IMF/imported-flagship-issues/external/pubs/ft/GFSR/2011/01/pdf/_textpdf.ashx. Accessed 24 July 2019.

International Monetary Fund. (2015). *Global Financial Stability Report: Navigating Monetary Policy Challenges and Managing Risks*. https://www.elibrary.imf.org/doc/IMF082/22119-9781498372930/22119-9781498372930/Other_formats/Source_PDF/22119-9781475596588.pdf. Accessed 25 July 2019.

Investment Company Institute. (2019). *Investment Company Fact Book 2019: A Review of Trends and Activities in the Investment Company Industry*. https://www.ici.org/pdf/2019_factbook.pdf. Accessed 16 June 2019.

Investment Industry Association of Canada. (2019). *IIAC Market Insights—Canadian ETF Dynamics, Risks and Outlook*. https://iiac.ca/wp-content/uploads/Canadian-ETF-Market-Jan2019.pdf. Accessed 24 July 2019.

IOSCO. (2012). *Principles for the Regulation of Exchange Traded Funds* (Consultation Report). http://www.iosco.org/library/pubdocs/pdf/IOSCOPD376.pdf. Accessed 24 July 2019.

IOSCO. (2013). *Principles for the Regulation of Exchange Traded Funds* (Final Report). https://www.iosco.org/library/pubdocs/pdf/IOSCOPD414.pdf. Accessed 30 June 2019.

Jagannathan, R., Farnsworth, G., Bushonville, A., & Puma, G. (2015). *Index Replication: Principles and Applications*. DSC Quantitative Group. https://www.dscqg.com/wp-content/uploads/2018/04/IndexReplication.pdf. Accessed 2 August 2019.

Johnson, B., Bioy, H., Garcia-Zarate, J., Choy, J., Gabriel, J., Rose, G., & Kellett, A. (2012a, May). *Synthetic ETFs Under the Microscope: A Global Study, Morningstar ETF Research*. http://media.morningstar.com/eu/ETF/assets/SyntheticETFsUnderTheMicroscope_AGlobalStudy_Morningstar.pdf. Accessed 10 Aug 2019.

Johnson, B., Bioy, H., Kellett, A., & Davidson, L. (2012b). *On the Right Track: Measuring Tracking Efficiency in ETFs, Morningstar ETF Research*. https://media.morningstar.com/uk/MEDIA/Research_Paper/Morningstar_Report_Measuring_Tracking_Efficiency_in_ETFs_February_2013.pdf. Accessed 13 Aug 2019.

Johnson, B., & Bryan, A. (2019). *Measuring ETFs' Tax Efficiency Versus Mutual Funds, Morningstar Manager Research*. https://www.morningstar.com/lp/etf-tax-efficiency. Accessed 1 Sept 2019.

JPMorgan. (2009). *Optimization vs. Full Replication, ETF Quarterly 3Q 2009*. https://www.jpmorgan.com/tss/DocumentForEmail/ETF_Quarterly_3Q09_Optimization_vs_Full_Replication/1253320931154. Accessed 28 July 2019.

JPMorgan Chase. (2005). *JPMorgan Depositary Receipt Guide*. http://quantlabs.net/academy/download/free_quant_instituitional_books_/%5BJP%20Morgan%5D%20Depositary%20Receipts%20Reference%20Guide.pdf. Accessed 22 July 2019.

Kilbert, M., & Subramanian, R. A. (2010). *Revisiting Global Small Caps, MSCI Index Research Group*. https://www.msci.com/documents/10199/3378e77e-556f-4c6a-8b47-421149cc3f4d. Accessed 1 Aug 2019.

Kupiec, P. H. (1990). A Survey of Exchange-Traded Basket Instruments. *Journal of Financial Services Research, 4*, 175–190.

Lamont, K. (2015). *How Foreign Ownership Rules Impact Passive Funds*. http://www.morningstar.co.uk/uk/news/141049/how-foreign-ownership-rules-impact-passive-funds.aspx. Accessed 24 June 2019.

Lee, S. (2014). *An Aggressive Quality and Value Dividend Fund*. https://www.morningstar.com/articles/665373/an-aggressive-quality-and-value-dividend-fund Accessed 1 Aug 2019.

Liu, S., Sheikh, A., & Stefek, D. (2001). Optimal Indexing. In A. S. Neuberg (Ed.), *Indexing for Maximum Investment Results*. London: Routledge.

Lyxor. (2019). *Guide to Pragmatic Replication*. https://www.lyxoretf.co.uk/pdfDocuments/Lyxor_Pragmatic%20replication%20guide.pdf. Accessed 11 Aug 2019.

Maeda, K., & Shino, J. (2019). *Stock Lending Market and the BOJ's ETF Purchasing Program: Micro-Evidence from ETF Balance Sheet Data and Equity Repo Trading Data* (WINPEC Working Paper Series No. E1811). https://www.waseda.jp/fpse/winpec/assets/uploads/2019/01/No.E1811.pdf. Accessed 29 Aug 2019.

Mateus, C., & Rahmani, Y. (2017). Physical Versus Synthetic Exchange Traded Funds. Which One Replicates Better? *Journal of Mathematical Finance, 7*(4), 975–989.

Maurer, F., & Williams, S. O. (2014). Physically Versus Synthetically Replicated Trackers: Is There a Difference in Terms of Risk? *Journal of Applied Business Research, 31*(1), 131–146.

McCullough, A. (2018). Securities Lending: An Examination of the Risks and Rewards. *Morningstar*. https://www.morningstar.com/lp/securities-lending-risks-rewards. Accessed 22 Aug 2019.

McLeavey, D., & Solnik, B. (2009). *International Investments*. Boston: Pearson Prentice Hall.

Meinhardt, C., Mueller, S., & Schoene, S. (2015). Physical and Synthetic Exchange Traded Funds: The Good, the Bad or the Ugly. *The Journal of Investing, Summer, 24*(2), 35–44.

Naumenko, K., & Chystiakova, O. (2015). An Empirical Study on the Differences Between Synthetic and Physical ETFs. *International Journal of Economics and Finance, 7*(3), 24–35.

Olma, A. (2001). Implementing Equity Index Portfolios. In A. S. Neuberg (Ed.), *Indexing for Maximum Investment Results*. London: Routledge.

Osaki, S. (2001). The Development of Exchange-Traded Funds (ETFs) in Japan. *Capital Research Journal, 4*(3), 45–51.

Pagano, M., Sanchez Serrano, A., & Zechner, J. (2019, June). *Can ETFs Contribute to Systemic Risk?* (ESRB Reports of the Advisory Scientific Committee No 9). https://www.esrb.europa.eu/pub/pdf/asc/esrb.asc190617_9_canetfscontributesystemicrisk~983ea11870.en.pdf. Accessed 25 July 2019.

Pan, K., & Zeng, Y. (2017, December). *ETF Arbitrage Under Liquidity Mismatch* (European Systemic Risk Board Working Papers Series, No. 59). https://www.esrb.europa.eu/pub/pdf/wp/esrb.wp59.en.pdf?c32ad640616557344d67f09d62590646. Accessed 30 July 2019.

Pérignon, C., Yeung, S., Hurlin, C., & Iseli, G. (2014). *The Collateral Risk of ETFs* (HEC Research Papers Series 1050). https://ideas.repec.org/p/ebg/heccah/1050.html. Accessed 18 Aug 2019.

Pierson, S. (2018). *Rising High, Securities Lending Times, No. 204*. http://www.securitieslendingtimes.com/sltimes/SLT_issue_204.pdf. Accessed 2 Sept 2019.

PricewaterhouseCoopers. (2004). *Entering the United States Securities Markets: A Guide for Non-U.S. Companies*. https://www.pwc.pl/en/rynki-kapitalowe/enteringtheus.pdf. Accessed 23 July 2019.

PricewaterhouseCoopers. (2019, September). *European ETF Listing and Distribution*. https://www.pwc.lu/en/asset-management/etfs/etf-poster-2019.html. Accessed 26 Sept 2019.

Ramaswamy, S. (2011). *Market Structures and Systemic Risks of Exchange-Traded Funds* (Bank for International Settlements Working Papers, No 343). https://www.bis.org/publ/work343.pdf. Accessed 24 July 2019.
Reuters. (2019). *MSCI Deletes Shenzhen Stock from Indexes Due to Foreign Ownership Limits*. https://www.reuters.com/article/china-stocks-msci/update-2-msci-deletes-shenzhen-stock-from-indexes-due-to-foreign-ownership-limits-idUSL3N20U1BP. Accessed 24 June 2019.
Rey, D. M., & Seiler, D. (2001). *Indexation and Tracking Errors* (Working Paper, No. 2). University of Basel/University of St. Gallen.
SCM Direct. (2015). *Closet Indexation*. The UK Epidemic Continues. https://scmdirect.com/wp-content/uploads/2019/06/Closet-Indexation-Epidemic-Continues-Report-February-2015-SCM-Direct.pdf. Accessed 20 June 2019.
Seddik Meziani, A. (2006). *Exchange-Traded Funds as an Investment Option*. Hampshire: Palgrave Macmillan.
Seddik Meziani, A. (2016). *Exchange-Traded Funds: Investment Practices and Tactical Approaches*. London: Palgrave Macmillan.
SET. (2018). *SET Lists First Depositary Receipt Representing Overseas ETF on December 18*. https://www.set.or.th/set/newsdetails.do?newsId=15446582077540&sequence=0&language=en&country=US. Accessed 24 July 2019.
SFC. (2018). *Research Paper on Hong Kong ETF Market and Topical Issues in the ETF Space*. https://www.sfc.hk/web/EN/files/PCIP/Research/Research%20Paper_20180116.pdf. Accessed 16 Aug 2019.
Statman, M. (2004). The Diversification Puzzle. *Financial Analyst Journal, 60*(4), 44–53.
Stevenson, D. (2010). *The Financial Times Guide to Exchange Traded Funds and Index Funds: How to Use Tracker Funds in Your Investment Portfolio*. Pearson Education: Harlow.
Sushko, V., & Turner, G. (2018, March). The Implications of Passive Investing for Securities Markets. *BIS Quarterly Review*. https://www.bis.org/publ/qtrpdf/r_qt1803j.pdf. Accessed 25 July 2019.
The Business Times. (2019). *First Abu Dhabi Bank Proposes to Remove Foreign Ownership Limit*. https://www.businesstimes.com.sg/banking-finance/first-abu-dhabi-bank-proposes-to-remove-foreign-ownership-limit. Accessed 24 June 2019.
The Economist. (2017, August 24). *Private-Equity Returns Can Be Replicated with Public Shares*. https://www.economist.com/finance-and-economics/2017/08/24/private-equity-returns-can-be-replicated-with-public-shares. Accessed 2 Aug 2019.
Vanguard. (2015). *ETF Structures At-a-Glance*. https://advisors.vanguard.com/iwe/pdf/FASTR.pdf?cbdForceDomain=true. Accessed 4 Feb 2016.
Vanguard. (2016). *Exchange-Traded Funds: Clarity Amid the Clutter*. https://www.vanguardinvestments.se/documents/etfs-clarity-amid-clutter.pdf. Accessed 14 June 2019.
Vanguard. (2019). *Exchange-Traded Funds: Clarity Amid the Clutter*. https://personal.vanguard.com/pdf/ISGETFC.pdf. Accessed 14 June 2019.

Vanguard Mexico. (2019). *How Are ETFs Regulated?* https://www.vanguardmexico.com/institutional/en/etf-knowledge-basics/how-are-etfs-regulated-tab. Accessed 17 June 2019.

Wiandt, J., & McClatchy, W. (2002). *Exchange Traded Funds*. New York: Wiley.

4

The Operation and Microstructure of Exchange-Traded Funds

4.1 Introduction

In order to better understand both the pitfalls and potentials of investing in ETFs, it is worth thoroughly exploring their operation and microstructure. Thus, in this part of the book, we will explain and discuss the most important issues related to the primary and secondary ETF markets, the liquidity of these financial instruments, as well as ETF trading. Most of these issues are particularly significant for investors, but some of them are also of key importance for ETF providers, authorized participants, market makers, financial advisors, and other participants of the ETF market.

In the first part of this chapter, the main focus will be on the following topics: launching an ETF, the creation and redemption of ETF shares, and ETF share pricing and valuation. The second part of the chapter will be devoted mainly to the issue of ETF liquidity. Finally, we will look at the trading and execution of ETF orders, including the characteristics of ETF trading with exposure to international equity markets. For all the issues discussed, we will draw particular attention to the specifics of these financial instruments, especially the specificity of equity ETFs with exposure to the international market, funds cross-listed on foreign platform venues, or ETFs traded in exchanges in time zones different than their underlying assets.

T. Miziołek et al., *International Equity Exchange-Traded Funds*,
https://doi.org/10.1007/978-3-030-53864-4_4

4.2 Launching an ETF

The ETF inception process is multi-stage and formally starts[1] when an ETF sponsor (or any other financial institution authorized to manage investment funds) files a request to register an ETF with the financial watchdog. Depending on the legal regulations in force in a given country and how the supervisory authorities function, this procedure can be more or less complicated and, therefore, also costly[2] and time-consuming. In practice, it may last from several months to even over a year.

In the case of the US market, the registration procedure was additionally impeded until recently because an ETF sponsor had to file for exemptive relief with the SEC's Division of Investment Management. Only getting this exemption from certain provisions of the Investment Company Act of 1940 has allowed mutual funds to operate as an ETF (since 1992, the SEC has issued more than 300 exemptive orders). In September 2019, the SEC adopted a new rule and formed amendments designed to modernize the regulatory framework for ETFs (however, only for ETFs organized as open-end funds) by establishing a clear and consistent framework for the vast majority of these funds.[3] Under Rule 6c-11 (ETF Rule), ETFs that satisfy certain conditions are able to operate within the scope of the Investment Company Act of 1940 and come directly to market without the cost and delay of obtaining an exemptive order. The rule's standardized conditions were designed to level the playing field among most ETFs and protect investors, while disclosure amendments adopted by the SEC will provide investors who purchase and sell ETF shares on the secondary market with new information (SEC 2019).

[1]This short description of the ETF launching process focuses mostly on the formal and legal steps related to the creation of an ETF. However, it seems obvious that before starting these activities it is necessary to specify many other relevant and essential issues related to both the product itself (e.g., choosing its objective, investment strategy, methods of management, risk management, etc.) and how it functions (e.g., domicile and jurisdiction, taxation, accounting, auditing, distribution, technology, custody, advisory services, etc.). They are usually similar to those that should be considered when creating any other open-end fund, but there are also some aspects that are specific only to ETFs. They concern, e.g., index licensing, listing platforms, and certain agreements (e.g., with market makers, authorized participants, liquidity providers, index vendors, counterparties (in the case of synthetic ETFs), NAV and iNAV calculation agents, or security borrowers). An interesting analysis of the above issues can be found in Lewellyn (2016).

[2]Murphy (2016) presents a detailed discussion of the costs associated with both the launch of an ETF together with its introduction to the secondary market (including registration costs, costs of legal services, index licensing costs (except self-indexing), seeding costs, and initial ETF listing costs) and its subsequent functioning and maintenance on the listing platform (e.g., annual listing and index fees, marketing costs, audit costs, depositary costs), from the point of view of US ETF market.

[3]The ETF rule is effective since December 23, 2019.

After obtaining the financial supervisory body's decision authorizing the launch of a fund, and upon its registration, an ETF provider may commence actual steps to set it up. However, to make it possible, this usually requires raising seed capital from a third party, without which the fund cannot start any further operations, in particular, creating ETF shares. The main third-party providers of this capital are banks and broker-dealers. In some cases, especially when it comes to the large asset managers, the ETF sponsor provides new money itself, or it ports capital from existing investment vehicles to the newly created fund.

Seed capital is the initial investment that enables the creation of the first shares (units) that underlie the ETF, so that the shares can then be offered to investors on a stock exchange. The amount of capital needed varies, depending mostly on the market and type of fund. In the USA, the general rule of thumb is that seed capital amounts to approximately USD 2.5 million, as a new ETF is usually launched with a minimum of 100,000 shares and a share price of around USD 25. After launching the ETF, the seed capital provider recovers the invested money through the sale of its shares on the secondary market. This process takes, on average, about 30 days, but it can take between one day and six months[4] (Esposito 2018).

Upon raising seed capital, the ETF provider can construct an investment portfolio of a fund using financial instruments suitable to its type, e.g., stocks in the case of equity ETF. This will also allow it to carry out the first issue of the fund's shares on the primary market.[5]

However, the ETF launch process does not end when the first shares are issued. According to the main idea of this investment vehicle, they must be placed on the secondary market. Therefore, the ETF provider has to choose a primary exchange that best suits its needs. Key considerations that should be taken into account include reputation, product support, liquidity, trading volume, and cross-listing arrangements. After submitting the application for admission to exchange trading[6] and it's acceptation, the ETF may debut on a selected platform. This listing is referred to as the primary listing.[7] Sometimes, for example, in the case of European ETFs and certain Asian ETFs, where multiple listings are quite common, ETFs go public simultaneously on several exchanges, which are referred to as secondary listings. As

[4]A detailed analysis of seeding ETF is presented by Abner (2016).

[5]The process creating ETF shares will be discussed in detail later.

[6]The rules for admitting securities to trading on the secondary market, including ETF shares, may vary considerably depending on the stock exchange. Detailed guidelines and tips on this matter are usually available on their websites.

[7]For some ETF markets, especially in Europe, the dominant part of secondary trading falls not on the stock exchange, but on the OTC market (for more information, see the ETF liquidity description).

a rule, however, they are introduced on other exchanges after a few weeks or months. Sometimes it can take even years, e.g., when the ETF provider enters a new market in another region of the world and introduces funds to the local exchange. For ETFs listed on other stock exchanges, their shares are also sometimes denominated and/or traded in other (national) currency or hedged against currency risk.[8] This is to enable or facilitate local investors to access these products and remove currency barriers. ETFs available on other markets can also share their earnings with investors in a different way than in the primary exchange (accumulation vs. distributing share classes).

4.3 Creation and Redemption of ETF Shares

The process of creating and redeeming shares in an ETF is undoubtedly unique and possibly the most important component of ETF mechanics. The creation/redemption mechanism takes place in the primary market.[9] Despite the same labels, the functioning and key functions of the ETF primary market vary greatly from the primary market for other popular securities like stocks or bonds. The latter is where new securities are created, and there is a movement of capital between their issuers and investors that usually allows the former to raise new money (unless the subject of sale is only existing securities). Meanwhile, the ETF primary market enables both the creation and redemption of ETF shares, and this activity takes place between the fund and a large financial institution or specialized market maker—an authorized participant (AP). Moreover, the issuance of, e.g., stocks is carried out only one time on a given primary market, i.e., at the time of the IPO, while the creation of ETF shares is continuous, even daily (as ETFs are mostly structured as open-end funds). It looks similar in the case of the sporadic buybacks of a company's shares and the continuous redemptions of ETF shares (Marszk and Lechman 2019).

[8]In the case of large stock exchange groups, especially those that operate in various countries and have an international investor base, it is possible to trade ETFs in many currencies—e.g., Euronext supports ETF trading in 20 different currencies (AUD, CAD, CHF, CNY, DKK, EUR, GBP, HKD, HUF, ISK, JPY, MXN, NOK, NZD, PLN, RON, SEK, TRY, USD, ZAR).

[9]Sometimes, this market is called the "underlying market" (see, e.g., BlackRock [2010]). However, this term may be misleading, because it is usually used in reference to market a fund's underlying assets (more details will be given when discussing the liquidity of ETFs).

ETF shares are created or redeemed on the primary market at the end of the day at the fund's net asset value (NAV).[10] This is done in the same way as the traditional open-end (mutual) fund, but unlike closed-end funds, where the supply of shares is essentially constant, and thus, the creation of new shares is, as a rule, impossible (unless the law allows for a new issue). However, there are two aspects of these processes which differ between ETFs and mutual funds. Firstly, in the case of ETFs, these end-of-day transactions are facilitated by a pre-approved group of institutions—authorized participants—who enter into an agreement with the ETF's distributor; this is not the case with traditional open-end funds. Secondly, in some ETFs, shares are created in exchange for a basket of securities, not for money as in mutual funds (Novick et al. 2017b).

The process of creating new ETF shares and redeeming existing shares[11] is generally initiated by a market maker, who engages an AP when there is an imbalance of orders to buy or sell ETF shares that cannot be met through the secondary market. To make this possible, each business day, an ETF makes available current fund full holdings and a basket of securities, called a portfolio composition file (PCF) or "basket file," that it will accept for creations (or deliver for redemptions) for trading (Novick et al. 2017b).[12]

ETF shares are created when an AP submits an order for one or more "creation units"—a basket of securities identical (or very similar) to the ETF's holdings. The creation unit consists of a specified number of ETF shares, typically ranging from 25,000 to 200,000 shares (usually 50,000 shares). Then, AP delivers the specified creation unit(s) to the ETF, and then, the ETF's shares of the exact value are transferred to the AP (Antoniewicz and Heinrichs 2014). It is worth emphasizing that this exchange takes place on a fair-value basis. The AP delivers a certain amount of underlying securities and receives the same equivalent value in ETF shares, priced based on their

[10]It is worth noting that NAV-based trading is different in ETFs that invest domestically or internationally. In the latter case, pricing is usually based on next-day execution. This issue will be discussed in detail later.

[11]This description applies, in particular, to the US market. Regional differences may exist for other ETF markets in some aspects of the creation/redemption process.

[12]Full holdings replication during the creation/redemption process is unfortunately often too unwieldy and cost inefficient. However, Rule 6c-11 adopted by the SEC introduced significant changes in this aspect of the creation/redemption process. To reduce transaction costs and minimize tracking error, some ETF issuers are able to publish a portfolio composition file, which represents only a sample of an ETF's full holdings that they will accept for creation. Like this, the PCF aims to match an ETFs risk/reward profile. This is important, in particular, for ETFs whose portfolios have thousands of constituents or which track less liquid asset classes, geographic regions, or strategies, thus for a large part of international equity ETFs.

NAV, not the market value.[13] Both sides of the transaction benefit—the ETF provider gets securities that are needed to precisely track the index, and the AP receives ETF shares that it can hold or resell for profit to other clients' OTC or on-exchange. After the transaction is concluded, it is cleared and settled.[14]

The creation mechanism of ETF shares described above is commonly referred to as in-kind creation or in-specie creation. It is applied usually by ETFs employing physical replication, i.e., holding a portfolio of securities included in the tracked index. However, in the case of funds that use swap replication, and do not need to have securities from replicated index in their portfolios, this way of creating shares is usually not possible. Therefore, by their own nature, these funds most often employ so-called cash creation. This process starts when an AP delivers cash received from an investor (client) to the ETF provider, who buys the underlying securities, usually through program trading. Then, ETF provider creates the ETF's shares and delivers them to the AP, which subsequently passes them to the investor. Some APs prefer cash creation, as this saves the logistics of having to actually deliver the physical basket of securities. However, they may also rely on in-house global cash trading platforms to execute in the underlying markets themselves.

The redemption of ETF shares, carried out on the primary market, usually when the supply of ETF shares on the secondary market increases, runs exactly in reverse to the creation process. In-kind redemption, which is used mostly by physical ETFs, starts when an AP buys up (through purchases on exchanges, principal transactions, or private transactions) the number of ETF shares specified in the ETF's creation unit. Then, it delivers them back to the ETF issuer, who redeems them. In return, the AP typically receives a daily redemption basket of underlying securities, or possibly cash or other financial assets. The AP usually then sells them in the market to flatten its inventories. The total value of the redemption basket is equivalent to the value of the creation unit based on the ETF's NAV at the end of the day on which the transaction was initiated (Antoniewicz and Heinrichs 2014).

Cash redemption is typically employed by synthetic ETFs. In this case, the AP acquires a basket of the ETF's shares and returns them to the ETF sponsor, usually in exchange for the equivalent value in cash. In turn, the ETF sponsor can sell a slice of the constituent portfolio to recover the cash

[13]APs can use an internet-based matching platform to advertise buy and sell interest anonymously and execute with other counterparties. Crossing transactions in this manner reduces the need to create and redeem in the primary market (BlackRock 2012a).

[14]The clearing and settlement process of primary market ETF shares, including the specifics of internationally focused ETFs, is a very important issue, but it is not the subject of book. Detailed information on this matter can be found, e.g., in Antoniewicz and Heinrichs (2014).

paid to the APs (Pagano et al. 2019). This kind of redemption may happen, for example, for exotic equity ETFs, when the underlying securities are less liquid and, therefore, more expensive to trade, e.g., emerging/frontier equity ETFs. A similar situation can arise in times of financial stress, when ETF shares tend to become less liquid than normal, particularly for ETFs with illiquid underlying securities and that are traded OTC.

Selecting the way to redeem shares is important from a tax point of view, because ETFs can use the redemption mechanism to remove capital gains and permit non-redeeming shareholders to defer taxes on their gains. Using the in-kind redemption model means that ETFs do not have to liquidate securities to generate cash to pay the redeeming investor. Additionally, they may use appreciated securities for this kind of redemption. In this case, provided certain requirements are met, ETFs do not recognize gain on the transaction. Thus, there is no need for them to make a taxable distribution of gains to its other non-redeeming shareholders. Typically, there are more opportunities for ETFs with appreciated and liquid portfolio holdings to defer gain recognition by shareholders. However, it should be emphasized that while the in-kind redemption may foster tax efficiency by deferring tax on gains, it generally does not enable those gains to escape taxation (KPMG 2016).[15]

Also, due to the stability of the financial system, the in-kind redemption mechanism is favorable since ETFs that use it do not face redemption risk, nor do they require cash reserves to handle large redemptions. As researchers indicate, physical ETFs should be less likely to experience investor runs if they operate exclusively via in-kind redemptions. Since the composition of the creation unit does not change in response to redemption requirements, there is no first-mover advantage in the sense of entitling those who first ask to redeem the most liquid assets, as is possibly the case in some open-ended mutual funds. On the other hand, cash redemptions are funded by subsequent or contemporaneous sales of the constituent assets by the ETF sponsor. This should reduce the potential for significant decoupling of NAV and ETF market prices and also mitigate investors' incentives to run (Pagano et al. 2019).

Apart from the methods of creating and redeeming ETF shares, there are many other detailed aspects related to these processes that should be taken into account when trading in the primary market. These include (BlackRock 2010):

---

[15]This characteristic applies, in particular, to the US market. For other markets, the tax aspects of the ETF redemption process may be different.

- ETF price execution (the most common is NAV),
- execution style,[16]
- underlying market restrictions,
- currency (underlying currency, ETF base currency, and trading currency),
- timing (trading hours).

Some of them will be discussed later in this chapter; however, now it is worth paying closer attention—given the subject of this book—to the last of the abovementioned aspects. While the functioning of domestically-listed equity ETFs with international exposure is similar to other domestic equity ETFs, there are unique elements to the creation/redemption process of the former. International equity ETFs differ from locally-focused equity funds in that the underlying securities markets are usually closed during domestic trading hours[17] unless the funds invest abroad but in the same time zone. In order to facilitate buying and selling in such ETFs, APs often hold an inventory of an ETF's shares. By owning them, the AP can hedge the exposure through a variety of financial instruments or transactions such as futures, shorting the underlying basket of stocks, or other similar ETFs. However, when the AP lacks ETF shares in its inventory, the price that buyers are quoted from an AP is based on where they believe the securities can be purchased the next day that the markets are open. Thus, the role of an AP in the creation and redemption process of international ETFs is much more complicated than in domestic funds (Ahern and Ruppenstein 2014).

According to Credit Suisse estimations cited by Mackintosh (2019), ETF creations plus redemptions run at around USD 2.8 trillion per year on the US market. Although that is a huge number, it is negligible compared to the total value of exchange-traded products (ETPs), stocks, and futures traded (USD 46, 118, and 156 trillion, respectively).[18]

---

[16]The four main types of execution styles are: Volume-Weighted Average Price (VWAP, the price weighted by the volume at that time), Time-Weighted Average Price (TWAP, the average price weighted by time), Market On Open (MOO, the price from the opening auction or, when there is no opening auction, the first print of the security), and Market On Close (MOC, the price from the closing auction or, when there is no closing auction, the last print of the security) (BlackRock 2010).

[17]There will be more on the importance of trading hours for international equity ETFs later in this chapter.

[18]More data concerning ETF primary market liquidity will be given later in this chapter.

4.4 Authorized Participants

The authorized participant is undoubtedly a key entity involved in the process of creating and redeeming ETF shares on the primary market.[19] An AP is typically a large financial institution, such as a bank (especially an investment bank), broker/dealer, or principal trading firm, which, as the name suggests, meets certain criteria and is authorized by an ETF's sponsor (or distributor) to participate in the creation and redemption of the fund's shares. APs play a critical role in these processes and, thus, in the ETF's primary market liquidity because they have the exclusive right to change the number of the fund's shares (supply of shares) on the market. Accordingly, they are sometimes referred to as liquidity providers.[20] Most active APs act as agents to facilitate creations or redemptions on behalf of their clients—namely, end investors, mostly institutional ones, seeking to access primary market liquidity and market makers,[21] or other entities that perform similar functions on the secondary markets who regularly provide two-sided (buy and sell) ETF share quotations.

APs do not receive compensation from an ETF or its sponsor. Additionally, they have no legal obligation to create or redeem the ETF's shares. Indeed, APs pay fees for any creation or redemption orders submitted to the fund's distributor. Instead, APs derive their compensation from commissions and fees paid by clients for creating and redeeming ETF shares on their behalf. They can also make profits while engaging in arbitrage between an ETF's NAV and its market price. For example, when an ETF is trading at a premium to the NAV,[22] APs may find it profitable to sell short the ETF during the day while simultaneously buying the underlying securities. APs then deliver the basket of securities and/or cash to the ETF in exchange for ETF shares that they use to cover their short sales. In turn, when an ETF is trading at a discount to the NAV, APs may find it reasonable to buy the ETF's shares and sell short the underlying securities. APs then return the

[19]Depending on the market, such an entity may have different names; in the USA, they are called "authorized participants," while in other markets terms such as "designated brokers" or "participating dealers" are employed.

[20]It should be emphasized, however, that this term is also used in relation to other entities (described later) whose task is to provide liquidity on the secondary market.

[21]Interestingly, some APs are also registered market makers and provide liquidity on the secondary market, as well. This means that some firms are both an AP and a market maker in a given ETF. However, an AP does not have to be a market maker in a given ETF, nor does a market maker need to be an AP. According to Antoniewicz and Heinrichs (2015), ETFs with more AUM have more APs that are registered market makers than ETFs with fewer AUM. In turn, international and emerging market equity ETFs tend to have more APs that are registered market makers than domestic equity ETFs.

[22]Premiums and discounts in ETF pricing will be explained later in this chapter.

ETF shares to the fund in exchange for the redemption basket of securities and/or cash, which they use to cover their short positions (Antoniewicz and Heinrichs 2014). However, it should be emphasized that the above activity is important primarily from the point of view of the ETF price discovery mechanism.[23] Thanks to these transactions, APs help keep the market-determined price of an ETF's shares close to its underlying value, i.e., to approximate the underlying market value of an ETF's assets.

Large and broad market ETFs are likely to have a broad set of APs, whereas smaller and more narrowly-exposed funds may have a smaller number of APs with specialized trading skills. According to a survey carried out by ICI in the US ETF market in 2014,[24] each ETF in the sample had 34 AP agreements, on average, and half had at least 36 (median). In the case of international equity ETFs and emerging market equity ETFs, these numbers were similar—they amounted to (in both categories) 35 and 36, respectively. In fact, the average number of APs actively (i.e., a minimum of once in the last six months) creating and redeeming ETF shares proved to be much smaller and was five for the whole sample and three for international equity ETFs and emerging market equity ETFs. The number of active APs on any given day is directly related to the demand for their service. APs create and redeem ETF shares in response to supply and demand, and the inventory management needs of secondary market participants (Antoniewicz and Heinrichs 2015).

The above results were generally confirmed by BlackRock's latest study conducted in the US ETF market.[25] On average, US-domiciled ETFs had 26 "contracted" APs and 5 "active" APs in 2019. There are, in total, 52 contracted APs and 36 active APs in the US-listed ETF universe. Larger funds (AUM above USD 500 million) typically have higher trading volumes; thus,

[23]Price discovery is a hallmark of ETFs and describes how these instruments can provide a mechanism for market participants to accurately price assets or markets that otherwise are not trading (e.g., during suspensions of stocks or markets). Thanks to that, ETFs may be the primary, invaluable source of pricing information available to market participants. Price discovery is especially vital for the smaller or less liquid segments of equity domestic markets, foreign equity markets (especially when they are closed), and many corners of the fixed-income market; it can also be useful during flash crashes. Since the late 1990s, single-country ETFs have played an important role in providing both liquidity and price discovery, especially on emerging/frontier markets, e.g., in the Malaysian market during the 1997–1998 Asian financial crisis (iShares MSCI Malaysia ETF), in the Russian market when the two main exchanges (RTS and Micex) were closed in 2008 during the financial crisis (Market Vectors Russia ETF), in the Egyptian market during the Arab Spring in 2011 (Market Vectors Egypt Index ETF), or in the Greek market when it shut downs its stock exchange in 2015 (Global X FTSE Greece 20) (Hill et al. 2015; BlackRock 2019a).

[24]The survey included 15 ETF sponsors that collectively offered two-thirds of the number of ETFs and represented about 90% of the ETF's total net assets as of November 2014.

[25]It draws on data disclosed by fund companies annually (Form N-CEN), as required by the Securities and Exchange Commission. Completion of the form has been required since June 2018 after the close of an investment company's fiscal year.

they tend to be supported by a greater number of contracted and active APs (32 contracted and eight active) than funds with smaller AUMs (under USD 50 million) (21 contracted and three active APs). Small ETFs have limited or no primary market activity; according to the mentioned study, there were no creations or redemptions over the reporting period in 82% of funds with USD 50 million or less in assets. The average number of contracted and active APs in international equity ETFs (25 and 4 APs, respectively) turned out to be very similar to domestic equity ETFs (27 and 6 APs). The top five APs (BofA, Credit Suisse, JP Morgan, Goldman Sachs, and Citadel) have contracts for 1530 to 1800 ETFs each, and they actively engage with anywhere between 550 and 1550 ETFs. The AP with the highest percentage of activity, Bank of America Securities, accounted for less than one-quarter of all ETF creations and redemptions by dollar value. What is interesting is that subsidiaries of large European banks play a relatively significant role in the US ETF market as APs. Among the top firms by ETF coverage, five of the top 11 by contracted and active tickers were European banks. Four European institutions were among the top ten in gross creation/redemption ETF activity (BlackRock 2019b).[26]

The European ETF industry is characterized by a smaller number of APs, which is the consequence of lower assets and especially smaller trading volumes. However, as the European ETF market is less transparent, there is no comparable data to the US market. The largest ETF provider in Europe—BlackRock—has an average of 30 APs per fund umbrella and, on average, six active APs in EMEA (Novick et al. 2017b).

4.5 ETF Pricing and Valuation

The unique way ETFs function also manifests itself in the area of pricing and valuations. This issue is very important from the point of view of both the ETF sponsors and investors carrying out ETF shares transactions on the

[26]The degree of AP market concentration is quite high, on both the US and European ETF markets. According to the BlackRock study, the top five APs accounted for 65% of all creations and redemptions, while the other 30 APs accounted for the remaining 35% (BlackRock 2019b). Only slightly different results were obtained by the research conducted by the Financial Conduct Authority. It covered the daily creation and redemption of units in a sample that consisted of 257 EU-domiciled ETFs managed by 4 of the largest global issuers, with assets under management of USD 381 billion, and representing about 7% of the global ETF market. The five most active APs accounted for around 75% of the observed primary market volumes and the remaining 25% was spread across 29 APs. The FCA data showed the primary market in ETFs is highly concentrated, especially in typical trading periods. This research revealed also that in times of stress, other APs step into provide alternative liquidity, taking up the extra redemptions and taking a higher than typical proportion of redemption volumes (Aquilina et al. 2019).

primary or secondary markets. For the former, this is significant primarily because of the credibility of their business, which is largely based on the transparency of the valuation of shares. Legible, transparent pricing principles, compliant with the applicable law, are a guarantee of trust in ETF issuers. Meanwhile, for investors, especially those who actively use different opportunities offered by ETFs, it is important to understand the different types of valuation mechanisms for ETFs and the nuances of each type of pricing. This, in turn, makes it possible to avoid many of the pitfalls and investment mistakes that result from misunderstanding valuation mechanisms. Investors with in-depth knowledge of these issues can get the best execution on ETF orders and thus more effectively achieve their investment goals.

4.5.1 Net Asset Value

The main notion associated with the ETF valuation is net asset value (NAV). Generally, it is the total value of an ETF's assets less than the total value of its liabilities. In simplified terms, in funds employing physical replication to mirror the performance of their benchmarks, the assets are composed mainly of index constituent securities, various types of receivables, and some cash.[27] Since the NAV should reflect the market value of the assets in the fund, it is based on the closing market prices of the securities that make up the ETF portfolio and which are calculated immediately after closing. For example, for an ETF that tracks US equities, the NAV is calculated soon after the US market's 4:00 p.m. ET close. The components of assets may also accrue income generated through securities lending and income from securities held, especially dividends in the case of funds investing in shares. The liabilities for ETFs largely consist of management fees owed to the asset management company and sometimes other various types of payables. An ETF's NAV per share is calculated by dividing the total NAV of the fund by the number of outstanding shares. The NAV and NAV per share are calculated by the ETF issuer (in practice, by a custodial bank) and disseminated daily. The calculation process is presented in Picture 4.1.

Although the method of calculating the NAV seems relatively simple and intuitive, in practice, this may not be the case. Sometimes, it turns out that the various inputs, which refer mostly to the method of closing price determination, can be opaque, counterintuitive, and not standardized across asset classes or products. In particular, this applies to non-equity asset classes, e.g.,

[27]Assets of synthetic ETFs include securities contained in the collateral (substitute) basket and derivatives.

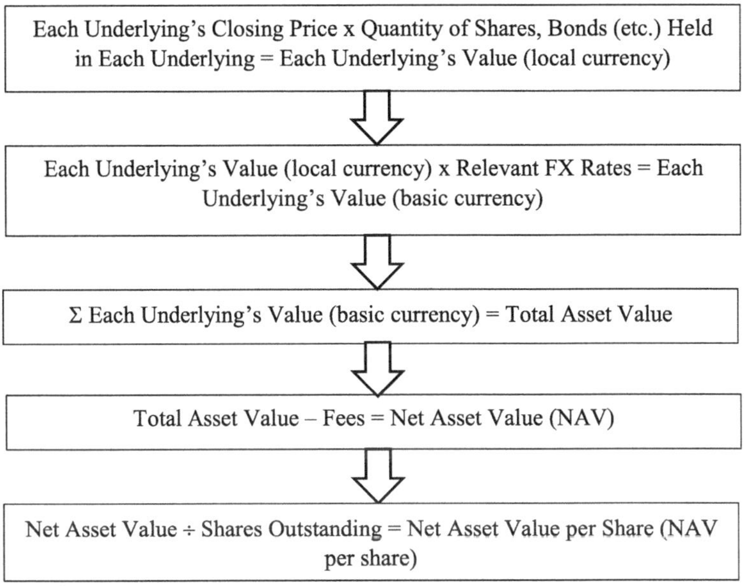

Picture 4.1 Basic steps in the ETF's NAV and NAV per share calculation process (*Source* Jane Street 2018a)

fixed-income ETFs, commodity ETFs that invest in futures contracts, or minimum volatility ETFs.[28]

In the case of certain international equity ETFs, e.g., single-country or single-region funds, which are priced in the same currencies as their underlying assets and whose portfolios constituents are typically traded in the same time zone, NAV calculation also usually does not present much difficulty. However, some problems arise in funds whose underlyings are traded in different time zones (and thus have different trading hours), and/or which are denominated in various currencies, or whose ETF base currency is different from the currency (currencies) in which the portfolio components are denominated.

The main challenge in determining the NAV of international equity ETFs is when their underlying assets are traded, and thus priced, in multiple time zones, often different than the time zone in which the ETF is listed. This refers to when an ETF is listed on an exchange in a particular time zone, but it tracks an index that comprises securities traded on an exchange which

[28]Minimum volatility ETFs attempt to reduce exposure to volatility by tracking indexes that aim to provide lower-risk alternatives, investing especially in securities that exhibit relatively low volatility and concentration risk.

closes earlier during the day (e.g., a US-listed ETF that mirrors the performance of an index comprised from European or Asian stocks), as well as when an ETF is listed on an exchange in a given time zone, but it replicates an index whose constituents are traded on an exchange which closes later (e.g., European-listed ETF that tries to reflect the performance of an index that consists of American stocks). The problem is similar when an ETF is listed on a trading venue in one country (time zone) but has exposure to global or multi-regional equity markets (e.g., a US-listed or European-listed ETF that tracks global equity index). Therefore, it is quite a common challenge—it can refer both to international single-country and single-region equity ETFs that make it possible to invest in non-domestic equity markets and global and multi-region equity ETFs.

When an ETF is listed on an exchange, but its underlyings are not *already* traded (the stock exchange has been closed), a NAV that is determined after an exchange has closed remains unchanged for the next few hours, although the market value of the ETF may still change. Similarly, when the ETF is listed on an exchange, but its portfolio constituents are not *yet* traded (the stock exchange has not opened yet), its NAV reflects the prices of the securities from the previous day. In both cases, the NAV is almost always partially "stale" which can result in differences between the ETF's trading price and its NAV. Thus, some international equity ETFs' NAVs can be determined only the next day, and if it is a weekend or a public holiday in a given region, its NAV may be published in a further one or two days.

Accordingly, some issuers adjust their funds' NAVs to account for market movements that occur between the time the underlying markets close and the time the NAV is actually struck. This adjustment is usually called a fair-value adjustment. This operation involves the issuer increasing the NAV when it believes the underlyings have increased in value in the hours between the market close and the NAV calculation, or decreasing the NAV when it believes the underlyings have decreased in value during those hours. However, since issuers' fair-valuing methods are sometimes opaque, fair valuing may create uncertainty for dealers (Jane Street 2018a).

A fund's NAV is calculated in the base (accounting) currency. If an ETF invests in securities denominated in another currency, or even a few different currencies, it has to use the FX rate to convert the underlyings' market values into the home or base currency for NAV calculation purposes. Currency conversion is also necessary when the ETF has various share (unit) classes denominated in different currencies. While the securities in an international equity ETF's assets often close at various times of the day, most ETF providers use the WM/Reuters 4 p.m. London fix to make this conversion. Thus, in such cases, the NAV does not reflect the currency values at the time the underlyings close, nor do they reflect currency values "now." Instead, it reflects the currency values from a single, arbitrarily chosen point in time that day. Interestingly, such a situation can create unusual, additional ETF trading dynamics (Jane Street 2018a). In conclusion, investors should be aware of the above pitfalls before making NAV trading decisions, especially in international ETFs that invest in underlying securities traded in different time zones and denominated in various currencies.[29]

4.5.2 Intraday NAV (INAV)

Considering the above-described characteristics of NAV, it is worth emphasizing that some of its drawbacks are devoid of another ETF valuation measure—intraday, or indicative net asset value (iNAV).[30] It provides information about the intraday value of an ETF based on the market value of its underlying constituents. In other words, it gives a "real-time" measure of an ETF's fair value based on its assets minus its liabilities. This indicator is calculated by a third-party vendor (typically by the stock exchange) and disseminated to the public every 15 seconds. As a result, investors—especially the most active ones—and other participants of the market (e.g., market makers and liquidity providers) continuously have a reference point that enables them to evaluate their intraday trading opportunities during the trading session by comparing the iNAV with the current market price of ETF. This seems to be a huge advantage, especially for transaction reasons, over the NAV valuation, which is carried out only once a day.

The calculation formula of iNAV is slightly more complicated than NAV. Generally, iNAV is calculated by multiplying the latest available price of each security in the creation unit (CU) (sometimes called the calculation basket) by the number of shares included in the basket. The aggregate value of all securities in the CU is then adjusted by estimated cash components. In order to obtain iNAV per share, the final result is divided by the number of ETF

[29]Apart from the previously mentioned drawbacks, relying on the NAV for trading may also negatively impact the cost of trading due to factors such as order size, direction of the order, and the market maker's own position. Additionally, cutoff times for trading ETFs vary per ETF, provider, and custodian, which raises the cost and undermines the efficiency of trading. Finally, NAV trading may also result in settlement issues in countries where negative interest rates are prevalent, such as Japan or some European countries.

[30]This measure is sometimes called also intraday indicative value (IIV), indicative optimized portfolio value (IOPV), or portfolio indicative value (PIV).

shares in a CU (ETF.com 2014). The detailed formula for calculating iNAV per share is presented below.[31]

$$\text{iNAV} = \sum \frac{(\text{Number of shares of each underlying security} \times \text{Last avaiable market price})/\text{FXrate}}{\text{Number of ETF shares in the CU}} + \frac{\text{Estimated Cash Component}}{\text{Number of ETF shares in the CU}}$$

Although this measure has undeniable advantages, especially for intraday traders, unfortunately, it also has limitations. iNAV, like NAV, may not reflect the true value of an ETF if the underlying prices become "stale."[32] It refers mainly to when an ETF trades in a different time zone than its underlying securities. In such a case, the last traded market prices of securities that are used for the iNAV calculation are essentially "stale" (e.g., they are based on the previous day's close) and therefore do not allow to assess the fair value of ETF.[33] As described earlier, this shortcoming refers to funds investing in foreign financial markets, especially in international equity ETFs.[34] The second limitation is that iNAV is disseminated "only" every 15 seconds. During volatile periods, this time lag may, unfortunately, misrepresent the actual value of the ETF.

Due to the above inconveniences, the SEC, adopting ETF Rule, lifted the duty of disseminating an iNAV every 15 seconds during the trading day, which was a condition of launching an ETF. Nowadays, ETF providers in the US ETF market must disclose on their website each business day the

[31]In practice, investors often do not have to calculate iNAV on their own, as these data are available on the websites of some professional financial services, stock exchanges, and ETF issuers. Some ETF providers offer their clients the ability to calculate ETFs using special algorithms. For example, in 2019, HSBC launched iNAV algo, which makes it possible to execute ETF trades based on their estimated real-time iNAV and investor trading preferences. The algo has been primarily designed to provide clients with greater price transparency and optionality for ETF trading on exchanges, and to help them decide whether to trade on an exchange, OTC, or via a request-for-quote (RFQ) platform (HSBC 2019).

[32]According to ETF.com (2018), the iNAV measure is inaccurate for 80% of all US ETFs, i.e., ETFs holding securities that do not trade precisely contemporaneously with US equity markets.

[33]As discussed earlier, this shortfall can be mitigated by fair valuation done in-house by market makers, authorized participants, or liquidity providers. They may use a proxy to determine the best estimate of fair value for underlying securities that aren't currently trading, e.g., futures contracts, options, or depositary receipts, provided, however, that such instruments exist and are effectively valued (which raises doubts in some emerging and frontier markets due to their low liquidity). When neither the underlying market nor a liquid future is available, general practice is to multiply broad index movements (e.g., the S&P 500 index or Euro Stoxx 50 index) with the beta of the broad index to the closed market, in order to estimate where the underlying market would be trading if it were open.

[34]A detailed explanation of the valuation rules and practices in the case of international ETFs (i.e., funds with international constituents) can be found in Abner (2016).

current NAV per share, the market price per share, and the premium/discount between them as of the end of the preceding business day.

4.5.3 Market Price and Premiums & Discounts

The third measure used in the ETF valuation is the market price, i.e., the price at which investors can buy or sell an ETF's shares on an exchange or OTC. It is expressed as a "bid price," i.e., the price a buyer is willing to pay for an ETF's share and an "ask/offer price," i.e., the price that a seller is willing to accept for a share of an ETF. The difference between the best bid price and the best ask price is known as a spread. The spread of an ETF generally reflects the average spread of the fund's underlying securities; however, in many cases, it can more closely reflect the investors' ability to trade closer to the fair value of the portfolio.

The ETF's market price, determined mostly by the level of supply and demand, and the value of the fund's holdings (underlying securities), usually deviates from its NAV. When the market price exceeds the NAV, it is said that the ETF is traded at a premium. When the market price is below the NAV, it is said that the ETF is traded at a discount.[35] Premiums and discounts are usually negligible for the majority of ETFs, especially funds holding liquid, domestic securities, due to market makers who act on small arbitrage opportunities between the ETF market price and the NAV and the authorized participants who can create and redeem an ETF's shares. However, even in these funds, they can be relatively large during short-term supply and demand imbalances for ETF shares on the secondary market, e.g., during volatile times and rapid news cycles. Additionally, they may be a result of transaction costs that are not reflected in NAV calculations. Especially significant premiums and discounts apply for ETFs with illiquid and international holdings, when their NAVs can be "stale" due to their different trading hours. Another factor that determines the behavior of the premium/discount is the impact of local taxes on the underlying securities at entry-level. The creation of new shares in the ETF may mean that the investor has to pay tax on the underlying securities. On the other hand, if the ETF is bought on the secondary market, no additional tax will be charged to the investor (BlackRock 2012b).

[35]An alternative approach to detecting inefficiencies in ETF pricing was proposed by Petajisto (2017). Instead of comparing ETF prices with NAVs, he measured them relative to the current market prices of a peer group of similar funds. This approach eliminates the problem of stale NAVs.

The most comprehensive study of the pricing efficiency of US-listed ETFs was carried out by Petajisto (2017). He used a sample of 1813 funds (including dead ones) over the period 2007–2014 and with USD 1.97 trillion in assets. Using the standard approach (i.e., comparing ETF prices with NAVs), he found that the average price premium/discount was only six basis points (bps), which indicates that the typical ETF is neither underpriced nor overpriced. However, the time-series volatility of the premium/discount (equal-weighted) was 49 bps, which suggests that ETF prices fluctuate considerably around NAVs, even if the average level of the premium/discount is small. The smallest premiums/discounts generally exist in diversified US equities, US government bonds, and the shortest maturity bonds. At the other end of the spectrum, international equities, international bonds, and illiquid US-traded securities, such as municipal bonds and high-yield bonds, exhibit volatilities of up to 144 bps. When employing a novel approach (ETF premiums/discounts relative to the peer group, as explained earlier in the footnote), the results varied significantly, as this method is unaffected by staleness in the reported NAVs. The equal-weighted volatility of the premium was 26 bps, which was 32% lower than the estimation from the NAV data, and the value-weighted volatility fell by 51% to 18 bps.

For international equity ETFs (the sample consisted of 351 funds), the average price premium/discount calculated using the first method was 20 bps, but it ranged from −4 bps and −1 bps for diversified Pacific/Asia ETFs and foreign small/mid-growth ETFs, respectively, to 37 bps for foreign small/mid-blend ETFs. The equal-weighted and value-weighted volatility of premiums/discounts amounted to 87 bps and 84 bps. The volatility of premiums/discounts measured using the second method was much smaller in this group of ETFs: The equal-weighted volatility was 38 bps and value-weighted 24 bps, i.e., 54 and 71% lower than the estimation from the NAV data. The main source of these funds' greater inefficiency is the more complicated, risky, and costly arbitrage mechanism that occurs in international transactions.

Much larger and more persistent premiums/discounts for international equity ETFs were also observed in other research conducted by both academics and professionals. According to Engle and Sarkar (2006), the average premium for 16 US-listed, single-country ETFs tracking MSCI indices was 34.8 bps (end-of-the-day) and 23.3 bps (intra-daily), while for 17 domestic equity ETFs it was 1.1 and 0.3 bps, respectively. Hilliard (2014) found that various barriers to the arbitrage mechanism that are noticeable in international equity ETFs, such as decreased liquidity of the underlying securities, stale pricing, and currency exchange rate issues, decrease the efficiency of the arbitrage pricing and result in their higher premiums (discounts), higher volatility, and lower speed of adjustment. Interestingly, a positive premium in international equity ETFs (18 bps on average) indicates that there is a great demand among investors for this financial instrument. This observation was also confirmed by Picotti (2018), who claims that investors are willing to pay relatively large premiums for ETFs that invest in underlying assets that are illiquid (e.g., international equity ETFs) because those funds offer easy access to such asset classes that would be otherwise limited to them. In Vanguard (2019) research, higher premiums/discounts (for the median, but especially for the minimum and maximum values) for international equity ETFs rather than US equity ETFs were explained by higher transaction costs in underlying markets. Additionally, the authors of this study indicate that the variability of the premium/discount largely reflects time-zone differences between an ETF's trading hours and the trading hours of the underlying securities, as well as the propensity of the underlying market's transaction costs to fluctuate.

4.6 ETF Liquidity

Exchange-traded funds differ from open-end investment funds in that, among others, no direct trading takes place between the ETF provider and investors. As already indicated, ETFs are investment vehicles, whose units—as their name clearly implies—are traded on regulated stock exchanges (or over-the-counter secondary markets). So, as with many other financial instruments listed on cash markets, trading takes place between investors using trading platforms, particularly stock exchanges.

However, this is only part of the whole story about ETF trading. Trading these financial instruments also occurs, as discussed earlier in this chapter, on the primary market. The key to understanding the liquidity of ETFs is recognizing that it is multi-layered (Golub et al. 2013). Regardless of why we invest in ETFs and whether we decide on a short or long investment horizon, we need to know and clearly understand how an ETF's shares are traded and how their liquidity is assessed. This is particularly important for two groups of investors: those who use them as a speculation tool or for tactical moves, and those who invest in ETFs with exposure to relatively less liquid markets, often international (especially emerging and frontier equity markets) and niche markets (e.g., high-yield corporate bond markets).

4.6.1 Primary Market Liquidity

The primary ETF market is where—as presented in detail earlier in this chapter—an ETF's underlying basket of securities can be exchanged for an ETF's shares (units), or vice versa, through the creation and redemption process carried out by authorized participants. The primary ETF market is always equivalent to the liquidity of the underlying basket; therefore, the funds themselves cannot be less liquid than their underlying assets (Madhavan 2016). The liquidity of an ETFs' underlying securities, known as primary market liquidity, is undoubtedly the most important part of total ETF liquidity. This is the result of the creation process, which enhances ETF liquidity by regulating the supply of ETF shares in the secondary market, as needed, to meet investor expectations.

If the underlying market (e.g., equity market) is liquid enough,[36] authorized participants could seamlessly create new ETF shares in exchange for a basket of appropriate securities, and thus respond to increased demand. So, it allows especially large investors to execute large buy orders for ETFs with relatively low secondary trading volumes and—what is extremely notable—with little or even no market impact. This, in turn, is significant in terms of reducing costs. The whole story is similar in the case of the redemption process and executing sell orders (Vanguard 2015).

However, when the authorized participant cannot efficiently trade the securities in the ETF basket due to their insufficient liquidity, the entire process of supporting liquidity can fail and cause problems for investors—starting from the increase in transaction costs and ending, in extreme situations, with the inability to execute ETF buy or sell orders. Unfortunately, this may apply especially to some international equity ETFs, particularly funds investing in early-stage emerging/frontier markets and international sector/thematic ETFs. According to a study by the WFE and Oliver Wyman (2016), emerging markets' (EM) exchanges (as defined in the FTSE Russell classification[37]) have grown dramatically in both size and activity in recent years[38]; however, this growth has been uneven and has not been associated

[36]To help investors quantify the potential underlying liquidity in an ETF, some third-party data providers and exchanges publish an ETF's implied liquidity figures. They indicate how much of an ETF they can trade on a daily basis without having a price impact on the underlying securities, when looking through the ETF at the liquidity of the underlying securities.

[37]The FTSE Russell country classification will be discussed in detail in Chapter 6.

[38]Market capitalization increased by 148% between 2004 and 2015, from USD 3 trillion to nearly USD 7.5 trillion, while the annual value traded has increased in the same period by 67%, from USD 1.8 trillion to just over USD 3 trillion.

with a commensurate growth in liquidity. It is still lower than in developed markets' exchanges,[39] taking into account, e.g., turnover velocity, i.e., value traded relative to the overall market capitalization.[40] Furthermore, EM exchanges vary greatly, with differing investor bases, issuers, geographical links, product mixes, and regulatory and legislative frameworks. Therefore, even if the liquidity of some (the largest) emerging markets is comparable to developed ones, in many other markets (or segments of markets), it differs significantly from them.

Additionally, it is noteworthy that even in the case of the satisfactory liquidity of a given EM equity market as a whole, there may be a problem with the liquidity of some of its segments, especially mid-caps and small-caps or some sectors. This applies particularly to already available ETFs with exposure to various segments of the Chinese equity market, but also to the Indian or Brazilian equity markets, for example. Though EM exchanges introduce a range of mechanisms to improve liquidity,[41] one should be aware that when investing in emerging/frontier equity ETFs, one can still encounter the liquidity problem of underlying securities.

The role of primary market liquidity is quite similar in the two main ETF markets in the world—the US and European markets—despite the fact that they differ significantly. In the USA, the Investment Company Institute found[42] that daily aggregate creations and redemptions are, on average, only a small fraction (11%) of their total primary and secondary market trading. The primary ETF market in the USA is even less important for international equity ETFs, and especially for emerging markets equity ETFs. Daily aggregate creations and redemptions of these categories of ETFs constituted only 8 and 5% of their total trading, respectively (Investment Company Institute 2018). According to a similar study carried out earlier by ICI, the proportions between primary and secondary ETF market may vary from day to day,

---

[39]Characteristics and determinants of liquidity in emerging markets are discussed, e.g., in IOSCO (2007) and PwC (2015).

[40]Please note that this metric, as well as other popular turnover measures (such as volume and value traded) or bid-ask spreads, are only a proxy of liquidity, but they are commonly employed due to their simplicity and the ready availability of data.

[41]These activities include mostly promoting the development of a diverse investor base with a focus on attracting local and international institutional investors, including enhancing retail participation, increasing the pool of available securities and associated financial products, and investing in the creation of an enabling market environment through the improvement of trading technology, market and reference data, the implementation of market maker schemes, or developing securities lending and borrowing schemes. Much more information about this can be found in Oliver Wyman and World Federation of Exchanges (2016).

[42]ICI analyzed daily ETF market activity for all ETFs from January 2015 to December 2017 (755 daily observations in the sample).

with aggregate daily creations and redemptions of an ETF's shares through an AP ranging from 4 to 25% relative to their total trading.

What is more, the vast majority of ETFs do not have *any* creations or redemptions on any given day, i.e., no primary market activity (Antoniewicz and Heinrichs 2014). In turn, as Vanguard's (2016) study[43] for European ETFs showed, the median ratio of trading volume that took place on the primary market was only 1% for both equity ETFs and fixed-income ETFs. In recent years, however, there is a noticeable trend toward greater activity on the European ETF primary market.[44] In conclusion, from the above data, it follows that the overwhelming majority of ETF trading results in no portfolio management impact and no trading in underlying securities, no matter which market is considered.

4.6.2 Secondary Market Liquidity

The ETF secondary market typically refers to organized stock exchanges (but also to request-for-quote [RFQ] platforms or OTC), where end investors buy and sell ETF shares intraday using common orders at market-determined prices via trading with other investors, market makers, or liquidity providers. This feature gives investors a relatively high level of liquidity, significantly higher than in the case of mutual (open-end) investment funds not traded on the exchange. However, it should be noted that there are two different levels (layers) of ETF liquidity on the secondary market: visible (displayed, on-screen) liquidity and "hidden" (non-displayed, reserve, contingent) liquidity.

The first type concerns the trading activity that actually takes place on the exchange. Its measure is usually the average daily volume (ADV), which is widely considered to be an ETF's secondary market liquidity proxy (see Fig. 4.1 for US exchanges). Although this is an appropriate measure of liquidity, understood as market depth, for shares or bonds (because their supply is generally fixed), the ADV provides only a partial indication of ETF liquidity. It is because their supply is flexible—new ETF's shares can be created and existing ones redeemed at any time on investor demand since they are open-end funds. Therefore, although ADV is popular, and the most often used measure of liquidity,[45] it may not be sufficient when gauging *real*

[43]Vanguard's research covered the period from October 2012 to September 2015 (daily data).

[44]This is demonstrated, for example, by Euronext data which indicate the increasing number of days on which ETF subscriptions or redemptions were recorded (AMF 2017).

[45]ADV is used by both ETF data providers (e.g., ETFGI) and stock exchanges (e.g., NYSE). However, some entities and researchers have introduced their own, proprietary ETF liquidity measures. For example, Deutsche Boerse employs the Xetra Liquidity Measure (XLM) and the intraday Xetra

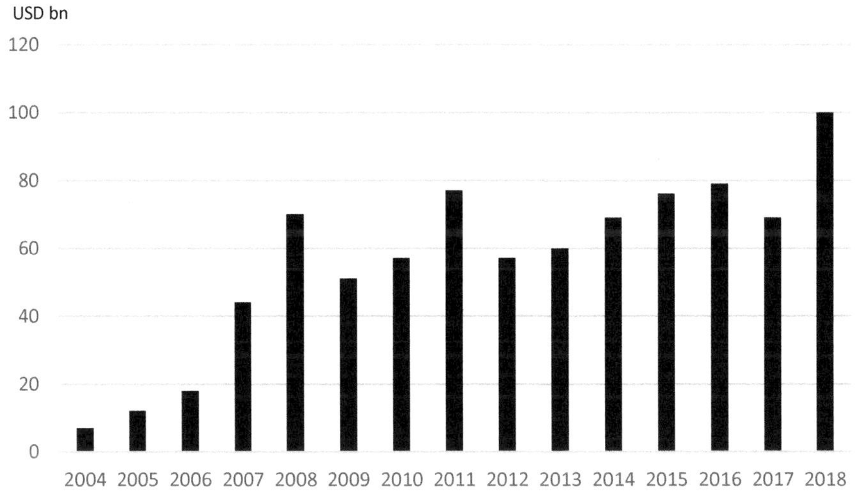

Fig. 4.1 Average daily notional liquidity of ETPs in US exchanges (*Source* Mackintosh 2019)

ETF liquidity. It only measures visible ETF trading activity on the stock exchange, while total ETF liquidity is made up of both ETF shares that can be created and redeemed in the primary market and shares traded in the secondary markets (regulated and OTC). Additionally, ADV data can be misleading because their distribution is sometimes heavily skewed.[46]

Using the ADV as an ETF liquidity measure has another adverse consequence in international equity ETF investing. Many institutional investors in some markets—mostly emerging and frontier markets—employ this metric to assess the level of liquidity in ETF markets and, thus, liquidity risk. On this basis, they often decide on which stock exchange to invest in. This applies to ETFs with a particular exposure (e.g., single-country) that are listed on many markets around the world. In such a situation, they typically choose exchanges where secondary market liquidity—expressed as the ADV—is the highest; meanwhile, the primary market liquidity is negligible. They give up locally-listed ETFs, mistakenly assessing them to be low liquid (ADVs are unattractive compared to more developed exchanges), while, in fact, the local

Liquidity Measure (iXLM). The former measures the average implicit transaction costs (bid-ask spread and market impact) in basis points for a given order size and the latter provides information on how the trading costs of an ETF have developed over the course of the day. In turn, Roncalli and Zheng (2014) proposed both absolute and relative measures of ETF liquidity, i.e., measures which, respectively, do not and do refer to the liquidity of the underlying index.

[46]According to research conducted by Petajisto (2017), the median ADV on the US ETF market was USD 1.2 million in 2014, while in the case of the most active ETF (SPY), it was USD 21 billion.

market is a better choice considering the liquidity of the underlying securities. An example would be Asian institutional investors, most of whom (up to 90%) favor US-listed ETFs, despite higher fees, time-zone inefficiencies, and a high withholding tax. However, they invest in these products because the ADV values on US trading venues are much higher than in domestic markets (DigFin 2018).

Secondary market liquidity is enhanced by market makers (sometimes called designated brokers or official liquidity providers [OLPs]), whose aim is to maintain a fair and orderly market by selling ETF shares to potential buyers and by buying ETF shares from potential sellers (Vanguard 2015). Market makers not only provide liquidity on the ETF secondary market, thus maintaining market equilibrium. They also help to ensure that the market price of each ETF share reflects the value of its underlying securities intraday. For the most popular ETFs and on most mature exchanges, there are often multiple competing market makers.[47] This usually positively translates into spread size reducing costs incurred by investors.[48]

The liquidity of an ETF's underlying index is the main factor affecting its bid-ask (bid-offer) spread[49] and thus trading costs on the secondary market. For funds tracking very liquid indexes, spreads tend to be very narrow. For instance, according to Morningstar analysis, asset-weighted average bid-offer spreads for European large-cap, US large-cap, and global ETFs were 0.11, 0.15, and 0.16%, respectively (Bioy and Garcia-Zarate 2013). However, there is a huge discrepancy in the spreads between fund groups and individual funds, which reflects the wide disparity in trading volumes across them. For example, Petajisto (2017) found that the median ETF closing bid-ask spread for the US market in 2014 was 15 bps, varying from as low as 1 bp for the most liquid funds to several hundred bps for the least liquid funds (the maximum recorded spread was 711 bps!).

Relatively wide spreads usually occur in the case of most international equity ETFs, particularly those investing in stocks listed on emerging/frontier

[47]For example, according to the Euronext analysis conducted in 2015, more than 80% of ETF assets are invested in funds with at least four market makers. The two largest equity ETFs (in asset terms) accept quotes from eight and nine different market makers, respectively (AMF 2017). According to data from the Investment Company Institute (2018), in the USA, ETFs had an average of 17 OLPs, with large differences across classes of ETFs. In Ireland, the majority of equity ETFs have around 32 OLPs (Central Bank of Ireland 2017).

[48]Narrower spreads are not necessarily a result of strong competition among multiple market makers. Some are simply more aggressive than others, regardless of the number of competitors they face.

[49]The bid-ask (offer) spread is the difference between the highest price someone is willing to pay for a given security (the bid) and the lowest price someone is willing to sell that same security for (the ask [offer]). Bid-ask (offer) spreads are commonly quoted as a percentage of the relevant security's market price.

exchanges. The relatively low liquidity of these markets, i.e., the liquidity of the ETF underlying components, makes it difficult for market makers to hedge their exposure. Consequently, the market makers' costs increase, resulting in wider bid-ask spreads than usual or compared with ETFs in other asset classes. In the equity funds category, this also applies to small-cap and mid-cap ETFs, as well as ETFs that track sector/thematic indexes. Morningstar calculations showed that asset-weighted average bid-ask spreads for emerging market ETFs and sector ETFs (0.34 and 0.42%, respectively) are considerably higher than in developed market and broad market ETFs (Bioy and Garcia-Zarate 2013). According to Petajisto (2017), equal-weighted and value-weighted bid-ask spreads for international equity ETFs in the US market were 57 and 6 bps, respectively, indicating the tremendous trading activity that the larger ETFs have generated. The study showed the lowest spreads (in value-weighted terms) in this category applied to "Foreign Large Blend" and "Latin America stock" (4 bps) and the highest to "Foreign Small/Mid Growth" (30 bps) and "Foreign Small/Mid Value" (20 bps) categories.

What is noteworthy is that the average equal-weighted bid-offer spreads were substantially higher than asset (value)-weighted average spreads in the above studies. It follows that the larger the fund, the tighter the spread. Many studies have confirmed a high inverse correlation between fund size (in AUM terms) and the spread and depth of the market, and it is primarily related to the trading and hedging costs faced by market makers. Additionally, ETFs trade with much tighter spreads than the underlying stocks in their portfolios—average spreads for ETFs investing in large-cap, mid-cap, and small-cap US stocks are significantly narrower (0.5, 2.7, and 1.3 bps, respectively) than for stocks belonging to these categories (4.3, 12.7, and 33.3 bps) (Mackintosh 2019).

Bid-ask spreads may vary significantly between funds within each asset class (much higher spreads occur in the case of less liquid indexes), between ETFs tracking the same benchmark, across different listings of the same ETF, and even depending on the time of day. Factors that impact different spreads include market volatility, local and cross-listing trading volume, depth of order book, and the number of market makers in each exchange (Rose 2012). One should also not forget that market makers holding ETF shares run certain risks that need to be hedged. They use a variety of financial instruments to achieve this goal, including futures, options, and ETF shares. The more instruments they have to choose from, the lower their hedging costs and the tighter the bid-ask spread. Since the abovementioned factors are worse in emerging/frontier markets, it results in much wider spreads and, thus, higher costs for investors.

The size of the spread is a very important factor in assessing the liquidity of ETFs for institutional investors. According to a Jane Street global survey (2018b), an ETF's bid-offer spread is the second most important criterion that institutions use to evaluate the liquidity of this instrument—after the liquidity of the underlying assets, and before the ADV of the ETF and its size (AUM). Similar results were obtained among Asian investors in a survey conducted in 2019 by Hong Kong Exchanges and Clearing (HKEX 2019).

Although data on ETF spreads are usually available on the websites of stock exchanges and ETF data providers, as well as through professional financial data suppliers, some researchers believe that this information is insignificant and useless (Angel et al. 2016). In their opinion, the spread observed by investors on a screen, in practice, is usually wider than the reported "average" spread. This is because the published "average" spreads are weighted by an undisclosed measure of the size and density of the bids and offers that are available at various times during the day. This scheme means that a heavier weight is assigned to the spread when the bid and offer sizes are larger, which ordinarily coincides with times when trading volume is highest, and spreads are tightest, i.e., close to the market opening or closing (Gastineau 2017).

Other entities responsible for ensuring liquidity—both on the primary and secondary (especially OTC) markets—are liquidity providers (in the USA—Lead Market Makers [LMM]). They are technologically advanced financial institutions that undertake to provide liquidity by offering reliable and competitive pricing (quotes) to buy and sell ETF shares. In this case, they play a similar role to market makers; however, they are not committed to stock exchanges, and they specialize in executing large trades while simultaneously mitigating their market impact and information leakage. Access to liquidity with competitive pricing is provided via electronic request-for-quote (RFQ) platforms. On the one hand, they automate and thus simplify and accelerate the whole process, and on the other hand, they ensure the highest level of transparency and efficiency for investors. The most important liquidity providers (market makers) on the US ETF market are Virtu, Jane Street, Susquehanna, Cantor Fitzgerald, and IMC (Moody's 2019).

Liquidity providers offer their services mostly to large financial institutions, to which they also provide other complementary services, such as investment research or trading expertise in complex or illiquid markets. The latter is important, e.g., when investing in international equity ETFs, because the majority of financial institutions have insufficient knowledge not only about

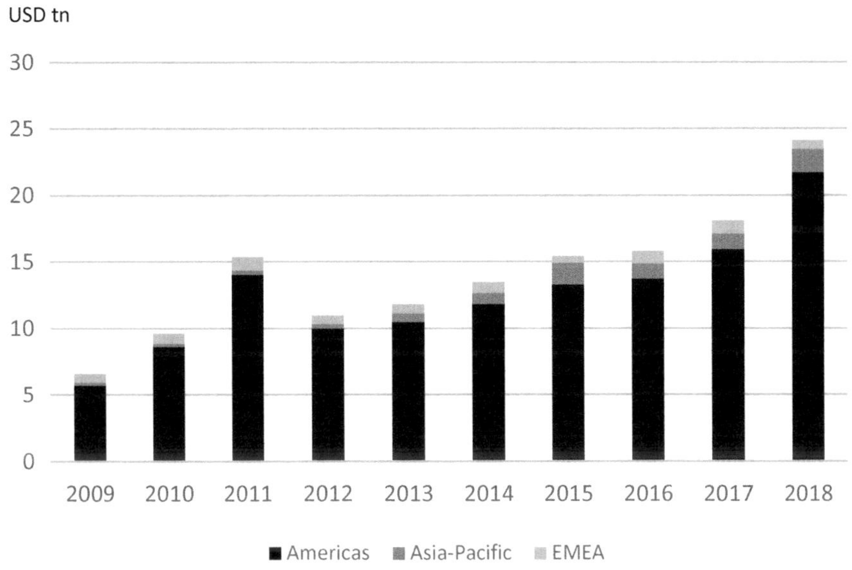

Fig. 4.2 Total value of ETFs traded on stock exchanges worldwide, 2009–2018 (*Source* Own elaboration based on the World Federation of Exchanges statistics)

foreign markets, particularly difficult-to-navigate emerging/frontier markets, but also about the specifics of the ETF shares trading on them.

Summarizing the reflections on ETF secondary visible market liquidity, it is worth looking at the statistics on ETF turnover on the global market. The World Federation of Exchanges (WFE) data regarding the value and volumes of trade in ETF shares in the last ten years clearly indicate that trading in these financial instruments on stock exchanges is systematically growing, although the geographical structure does not change significantly (Fig. 4.2). The total ETF annual turnover increased from USD 6.6 trillion to USD 24.1 trillion, i.e., by 265%, between 2009 and 2018. The stock exchanges from the Americas (primarily US exchanges) have a dominant role in ETF trading—their share in the whole analyzed period exceeded 80% (in 2018, it was 90.0%). The importance of trading platforms from the Asia-Pacific and EMEA regions remains small—in 2018, their shares were only 7.2 and 2.8%, respectively.[50] The increase in ETFs' trading value was caused by their rapidly growing popularity among individuals and various types of

[50]The main reasons for the relatively negligible share of European markets in global ETF trading are the highly fragmented market, the small share of retail investors, and the decentralized infrastructure (trades are settled on the local central securities depositories [CSDs]). Some of these issues will be discussed in more detail later.

institutional investors (as evidenced mostly by data on the net inflows of capital), as well as the wider and more diverse ways of institutional investors using these instruments in the short term—mainly as tactical tools (e.g., cash equitization, manager transitions, portfolio rebalancing, liquidity sleeves, and tactical moves) (Balchunas 2016).

A very high level of ETF trading concentration on the largest stock exchanges in the world can be observed (Table 4.1). According to WFE data, only three exchanges—NASDAQ US, NYSE, and BATS Global Markets—which had the largest ETF trading value in 2018, accounted for as much as 90.3% of total turnover. This means that the role of the remaining 45 exchanges where these financial instruments are listed (according to WFE

Table 4.1 Stock exchanges with the largest ETF trading value in 2018

	Stock exchange	Region	Total ETF trading value[a] (USD million)	Share in total ETF trading (%)	Relation of the total ETF trading value[a] to the total equity trading value[a] (%)
1	NASDAQ (USA)	Americas	11,465,833	45.59	26.26
2	NYSE	Americas	5,671,503	22.55	24.71
3	BATS Global Markets	Americas	5,575,954	22.17	34.77
4	Japan Exchange Group	Asia-Pacific	514,966	2.05	7.13
5	Shenzhen Stock Exchange	Asia-Pacific	407,265	1.62	5.60
6	Korea Exchange	Asia-Pacific	320,491	1.27	12.75
7	LSE Group	EMEA	306,601	1.22	9.13
8	Shanghai Stock Exchange	Asia-Pacific	241,213	0.96	4.11
9	Deutsche Boerse	EMEA	144,172	0.57	8.02
10	Hong Kong Exchanges and Clearing	Asia-Pacific	140,092	0.56	5.98

[a]Both EOB trading and negotiated deals
Source Own elaboration based on the World Federation of Exchanges statistics

statistics[51]) is virtually negligible. One should, therefore, be aware that only a few American trading venues are responsible for the high level of global total ETF turnover on secondary markets, while the trading value on the vast majority of stock exchanges is still often symbolic. It is enough to say that out of the 48 analyzed exchanges, on 15 trading value was below 100 USD million (!), while on eight exchanges did not surpass USD 1 billion in 2018. This applies, in particular, to emerging and frontier market exchanges, but also to some trading platforms in developed countries (e.g., in Ireland and Austria).

In addition to analyzing the absolute values of ETF trading on stock exchanges, it is worth scrutinizing what role the ETF segment plays against the background of the equity market. As evidenced by the data in Table 4.1, the three largest exchanges (in terms of ETF trading value) are also clearly distinguished from the others. The value of ETF secondary market trading in relation to equity trading on these exchanges exceeds 20% (the highest—almost 35%—is on the BATS Global Markets), while on most others it does not exceed 10% (as of 2018). According to the Credit Suisse data cited by Wigglesworth (2017), the share of ETF trading as a percentage of overall US trading oscillated between 25 and 35% (by value), and between 15 and 25% (by volume) from 2008 to 2016.

The uniqueness of US stock exchanges should also be remembered when we see information about the enormous liquidity of some of the ETFs listed there.[52] Although data of this kind are undoubtedly impressive, they relate to a very small group of the most popular domestic equity ETFs, which are often used by institutional investors for tactical purposes. Meanwhile, in the case of the vast majority of other ETFs listed on stock exchanges, the value of their turnover lags behind most traded shares. This applies to EM exchanges, in particular. Although ETF secondary liquidity admittedly steadily growing in these markets—the annual ETF trading value increased from less than USD 200 billion to almost USD 800 billion between 2010 and 2015 (Oliver Wyman, World Federation of Exchanges 2016)—it is still significantly lower than in DM exchanges.

[51]Data providers publish different data on the number of exchanges on which these financial instruments are listed, which is probably due to different approaches in classifying ETFs and other types of ETPs. For example, according to ETFGI (2020), ETFs and ETPs were listed on 70 exchanges in 58 countries at the end of 2019.

[52]For example, in 2016, in the group of the 15 most actively traded instruments on the US stock market, as many as 14 were ETFs (in terms of both volume and turnover value). The most heavily traded ETF was the SPDR S&P 500 ETF Trust (SPY). Its average trading value amounted to USD 19 billion (almost 90 million shares), which was more than five times the second most popular instrument (also an ETF) (Vlastelica 2017). According to Euroclear (2017), in the USA, ETFs regularly make up half or more of the ten most active securities on any given day.

On the sidelines of considerations regarding the secondary market liquidity of ETFs, it is also worth briefly discussing the role of passive funds in stock exchange trading. Although it might seem that the increased popularity of index funds and ETFs is reflected in their growing share in US trading activity compared to active market participants (including—but not limited to—individual investors, HFT traders, and hedge funds), and thus lead to a decrease in price discovery, the truth is completely different. Since most indexing strategies have low turnover (as discussed earlier) and they trade on the margins across a large list of securities, their impact on trading activity is minimal. As various studies indicate, index funds and index ETFs account for approximately 5% of the overall daily trading volume on US exchanges (Novick et al. 2017a; Rowley et al. 2018), and according to the latest research, they account for as little as 1% (Rowley et al. 2019). Even after taking into consideration indexed portfolio management outside of registered funds and removing trading volume due to High Frequency Trading (HFT) and shares of ETFs, estimates show that indexing represents less than 5% of the overall US trading volume.[53]

"Hidden" ETF liquidity refers first to limit orders and reserve orders away from the best quoted (publicly available on the order book) bid or offer prices. These quotes represent the depth of the order book and are another source of ETF liquidity (sometimes called "instantaneous liquidity") because they present additional prices at which an ETF's shares can be traded (Vanguard 2015). Non-displayed liquidity also occurs when ETF units are cross-listed on different exchanges. "Ordinary" investors can usually only see the liquidity coming from one market, their own, although it could be larger since the same instrument is also listed on other exchanges. This applies particularly to the European ETF market, which is fragmented across many stock exchanges; to some extent, it also concerns the Asia-Pacific ETF market.[54] According to PwC data concerning the European market, only 29% of ETFs have one listing, while 45% of ETFs have two or three listings, 25% of ETFs have four or five listings, and 1% of ETFs have six or more listings, as of June 2019 (PwC 2019).

[53]It should be emphasized that these data relate only to the US market and are not necessarily representative of other equity markets, especially less liquid ones. For example, the share of passive investors in Austria's Vienna Stock Exchange (the ATX Prime market) accounted for 18.3% in 2018 (Wiener Boerse 2019).

[54]ETFGI data show that European ETFs and ETPs were listed on 27 exchanges as of February 2020, while Asia-Pacific (ex-Japan) ETFs and ETPs were listed on 17 exchanges, as of September 2019.

Moreover, the most popular indexes are replicated by tens or even more than one hundred (!) ETFs (e.g., Euro Stoxx 50 Index—59 ETFs; Stoxx Europe 50 Index—91; S&P 500—122; and MSCI World Index—123); therefore, trading on ETFs replicating some most desirable indexes is spread not only over various markets but also many funds. Although the highest liquidity usually occurs on the primary market (i.e., the main market for listing), some other exchanges on which a given ETF is listed may also record a relatively high trading volume (e.g., amid different trading currency or different treatment of dividends). Moreover, ETF trading in Europe can take place in many different types of venues,[55] which also contributes to their fragmentation.

The most important non-displayed ETF secondary liquidity occurs in the OTC market. These transactions are often not (or, until recently, they were not) visible in the ETF market statistics, while in some regions of the world, they play a significant or even dominant role. First of all, this applies to the European ETF market, which is dominated by institutional investors.[56] Because of the fragmented nature of the European ETF listings and their apparent lack of on-exchange liquidity, institutional investors often prefer to trade over-the-counter. Other advantages of the OTC market are lower costs and greater flexibility in terms of transaction conditions. For example, the spread dynamics on the OTC market are slightly different than in a stock exchange.

Additionally, trading through an electronic order book (EOB) incurs commission costs and brokerage fees.[57] Institutional investors may also choose to transact at the ETF's daily closing NAV, rather than incurring a bid-offer spread when trading intraday. They may also be subject to creation/redemption fees if they want to buy (or sell) a large block of ETFs (Bioy and Garcia-Zarate 2013). Meanwhile, bilaterally negotiated OTC trading involves no exchange costs and allows for much bigger trades (larger

---

[55]BlackRock distinguishes six different trading venue types in European equity markets: primary exchange (e.g., the LSE), pre-trade transparent Multilateral Trading Facilities (MTFs) (e.g., Turquoise), systematic internalisers (including electronic liquidity providers—e.g., Jane Street), periodic auctions (e.g., CBOE), dark MTFs (e.g., ITG Posit), and dark large-in-scale or conditional venues (e.g., CBOE large-in-scale) (Cohen et al. 2019).

[56]According to Euroclear (2017), retail investors account for around 10–15% of the European ETF market, while in USA, this figure equals about 45%.

[57]It should also be remembered that these costs differ significantly depending on the region (country) in which an invest is made, as well as the market capitalization of companies. Detailed quarterly statistics on trading costs (IS costs, commission costs, and broker costs) in relation to most developed equity markets (USA, UK, Japan, and Canada) and various regions of the world are published by Virtu Financial.

deals). When interacting directly, investors can agree to trade any volume of an ETF's shares, as opposed to being subject to minimum clip sizes in the case of exchange trading through an EOB. Exceptions are trades carried out through negotiated deals, which are confirmed through a system managed—directly or indirectly—by the exchange, where both the seller and buyer agree on the transaction conditions (i.e., price and quantity) (Thomadakis 2018).

Consequently, in Europe, around 70% of ETF trades are done OTC, and only about 30% on-exchange. In the USA, the statistics are reversed—only 30% of trades are executed over-the-counter and 70% on-exchange. Institutional investors have large ticket sizes—on average, about EUR 3.5 million—and they are more familiar with OTC trading (the average on-exchange trade is less than EUR 500,000) (M'Rabti 2018). MiFID I Directive, implemented in 2007, did not recognize ETFs as an asset class, and therefore, not all transactions had to be reported. For this reason, it was not necessary to report ETF trading off-exchange, which greatly hindered the visibility of total ETF trading in Europe. It was not until January 2018, when the MiFID II Directive/MIFIR Regulation came into force. Its general transparency requirements include pre-trade and post-trade disclosures of the details of orders submitted to and transactions conducted on various trading venues (regulated markets, multilateral trading facilities, and organized trading facilities). The implication for EU-domiciled ETFs is the mandatory trade reporting for OTC trades and a consolidated tape (Deloitte 2017). It is similar to the US market, where trades executed on the second layer of liquidity (reserve liquidity) are reported on the consolidated tape required by the US National Market System.

It is little wonder that the mandated trade reporting under MiFID II revealed record trading volumes and liquidity in the European ETF market. According to research conducted by BlackRock in the lead up to the one-year anniversary of MiFID II's implementation, visible ETF liquidity in Europe quadrupled, from approximately USD 500 billion in 2017 to over USD 2 trillion in 2018 (Lord 2018).[58] Although the visibility of ETF liquidity is improving all the time in Europe, investors are still unable to see the full picture. The abundance of trading data is currently not readily available for all portfolio managers (not to mention individual investors), and it needs to be aggregated. The inability to fully assess each ETF's liquidity may mitigate

[58]Another factor helping to drive ETF demand on the European ETF market, especially among retail investors, is the development of fractional trading in ETFs. This makes it possible to remove the obstacle of the high price of many ETF units, not only in the case of retail investors, but also advisers who manage model portfolios (more about fractional trading later in this chapter).

its competitiveness in relation to other investment vehicles. Therefore, it is necessary to create a "consolidated tape" for the European ETF market that will aggregate and report the total trading volume in one place. This solution can further enhance the liquidity, increase transparency, and strengthen the best execution in the UCITS ETF market, which should increase confidence in the European ETF sector, among both EU-domiciled and international investors (Eckett 2019).

4.7 ETF Trading and Execution[59]

Investing in ETFs requires profound knowledge, not only of the various aspects related to the liquidity of these financial instruments but also in the field of best practices concerning trading. Although ETFs have changed the way individuals and institutions invest, and they are now core building blocks of investor portfolios, not all investors utilize the full potential of these vehicles. This is due to the fact that they are not able to execute their trades (orders) in the best possible way, especially when equity markets are volatile and/or not liquid enough. It seems especially important now when ETF trading is becoming more and more complex amid the growing number of ETFs, there is increasing competition in this market segment (many new market participants), and there are new technological opportunities but also risks arising from them. This applies particularly to investing in international equity ETFs and/or investing in foreign markets, due to the specificity of this trading.

4.7.1 Best Practices

There are many rules of thumb that make it possible to improve the efficiency of ETF transactions conducted on the secondary market—selected ones are presented in Table 4.2. Some have a universal dimension (they apply to every security), while others relate only to ETF shares (units).

[59]This subchapter provides practical guidance for ETF trading in secondary market (especially stock exchanges), which can be useful especially for individual investors. For more detailed criteria addressed to more sophisticated investors and also usable for investing in primary markets, including execution styles, see e.g., Abner (2016), Gastineau (2017), and BlackRock (2010).

Table 4.2 Basic best practices for trading ETF shares (units) on stock exchanges

Type of order[a]	When your priority is to secure a certain price, use limit orders. You set a price and execute your trade only if shares are available at that price or better. When you place a market order, your priority is speed of execution, but you may pay more or receive less than you would have liked. When you place a stop-limit order, your priority is to try to limit a loss or protect a profit without the unpredictability of a market order
Type of price	ETF shares are traded on the secondary market, usually intraday, at the market price, but on some exchanges, trading is also possible at the end of the day (like mutual funds) at the net asset value. Trading at the market price is convenient especially for most active investors, but ETF share price can deviate from its fair value as implied by its underlying components (i.e., at a discount or a premium). Therefore, it is very important to check the prices in both markets before executing an order to achieve the best execution. Investors who are afraid of intraday risk or who cannot trade this way may also place an order at any point during a trading session, but their order can be executed at the closing auction[b] at the NAV. That price reflects the end of day NAV of the ETF, plus or minus the costs of creating or redeeming shares. There is also a cutoff point for each fund when no more orders are collected for that day
Execution time (period)	It is worth avoiding trading during most volatile periods. Volatile market conditions can lead to a sharp divergence between an ETF's intraday price and the fund's NAV (an ETF is then often traded at a high premium or at a high discount). Market volatility can also increase bid-ask spreads and, thus, transaction costs. During such periods, fewer shares may be listed at best bid and best ask prices, increasing the importance of using the appropriate order type and monitoring trades

(continued)

Table 4.2 (continued)

	If you want to avoid increased volatility, do not trade when information appears that could change market prices dramatically. This includes releases of a country or sector's economic indicators, statements from central banks or other important institutions, earnings and other price-setting information from companies that are large constituents of an ETF portfolio, as well as the tweets of influential people or entities. In the case of ETFs, this also applies to the specific type of information published by index providers, e.g., a change of tracking index, modifications in the methodology for constructing or calculating the index, reclassification of a specific country, sector or company, etc.
	You should be cautious of trading in the first and last 15–30 minutes of the trading session. At the open, not all securities included in the ETF portfolio may have traded yet (e.g., because of material news about a security) leading to pricing inefficiencies, cause spreads to widen and make ETF pricing difficult. At the end of the day, investors can expect greater volatility as market makers balance their books. Additionally, fewer firms are then available, which can also lead to pricing inefficiencies and, in turn, increased trading costs
	Similarly, special care must be taken on certain days of the year, e.g., when index futures expire (this often leads to increased volatility of their quotations and quotations of index constituents), when the index is reconstituted or rebalanced, or when the stock exchange is closed in a given country (it limits primary liquidity)
Liquidity issue	When an ETF's underlying securities are difficult to trade (i.e., the primary market liquidity is insufficient), the market maker's costs may increase, resulting in wider bid-ask spreads. So, you should be careful conducting ETF transactions that have exposure to illiquid (or even niche) assets or markets (especially foreign ones)
	It is also necessary to pay attention to secondary market liquidity—in the case of ETFs measured by ADV. When the volume is small, the ETF's bid-ask spread is usually wider and, thus, transaction costs are higher[c]

(continued)

Table 4.2 (continued)

Transaction size	Trading large blocks of ETFs may reduce market impact risk and facilitate achieving the best possible average trading price. To execute block trades effectively, order sizes may be calculated by dividing the shares by the ADV, which reduces liquidity bias. Investors can also rely on algorithms and automated platforms to execute the best possible trade. Block trades are usually made through specialized intermediaries that help investors weed out volatility when trading large blocks of an ETF's shares

[a]Only basic, commonly utilized order types were described. Stock exchanges offer a much broader spectrum of orders—for example, NYSE Arca handles over 30 different order types

[b]Closing auction mechanics can be vague and intricate due to issues such as order types, order handling in the pre-matching session, auction matching rules, auction extension rules, and price limits. Such difficulties are further exposed when a trader wants to execute a global basket and needs to account for the regional differences in the auction mechanisms. Additionally, when investing in different markets, an investor needs to account for regional differences in auction mechanisms

[c]In European markets, the volume is typically highest right after the European open (and later, after the US open), and then, it drifts lower and peaks once again at the close

Source Own elaboration based on Dickson and Rowley (2014), Vanguard (2015), Bourgi (2016), and Phadnis et al. (2016)

Significant differences in ETF trading between US and European market should also be pointed out. Investors making transactions on US exchanges are assured that they will receive the best possible price when executing trades through their broker, without worrying about aggregating quotes from multiple exchanges or market makers before placing a trade. SEC regulations require brokers to trade at the best (lowest) available ask price and the best (highest) available bid price when buying and selling securities for customers. This is done by Securities Information Processors (SIPs) collecting real-time quote data from execution venues and exchanges; it is then disseminated as a consolidated National Best Bid and Offer (NBBO). Thus, NBBO regulation helps level the playing field for retail investors who may not always have the resources to seek out the best prices across multiple exchanges. However, one should keep in mind that this may not apply to all trading platforms, including dark pools and other alternative trading systems.[60] Unfortunately, Europe has no equivalent of NBBO in its equity market.

[60]Although NBBO quotations represent liquidity (price and size) available from market makers who post quotes through a stock exchange, they do not reflect the full depth of the ETF marketplace (it can be accessed by broker/dealers' ETF block desks or by placing a limit order that is beyond the NBBO).

Although many market participants use a self-calculated European Best Bid and Offer (EBBO), there is still no prescribed standard, as in the USA. An official EBBO should increase pre-trade transparency, improve the public availability of pricing information to investors, and solve some regulatory market structure concerns (Cohen et al. 2019).

Another issue regarding ETF trading, which is important for both individual and institutional investors, is fractional trading. The possibility of buying or selling not only whole ETF shares, but also fractions of them (even to four decimal places) is available to a limited extent in the USA (through some brokerages and robo-advisors) and Europe (it is offered by, e.g., Nutmeg and Winterflood). Firstly, it makes it possible to allocate money with even greater precision, which is game-changing, particularly when reinvesting dividends and managing smaller (even micro) portfolios. In Europe, fractional trading can be a liquidity booster of sorts, opening ETFs up to relatively modest regular savings plans (M'Rabti 2018). Secondly, the high price of many ETF shares is an obstacle to including them in smaller model portfolios managed by financial advisers. Therefore, this solution enables not only them, but also robo-advisors, traditional platforms, and discretionary fund managers to fully invest in ETFs and ensure that these instruments can be used effectively through model portfolios of all sizes (not only big ones). Thirdly, it helps smaller investors to access markets which may previously have been impractical to invest in. Finally, fractional trading may increase the number of ETFs that one can invest in (especially high-priced ones), which increases the number of securities in an investment portfolio and, in turn, providing better diversification.

4.7.2 Trading International ETFs[61]

Although ETF trading is generally not an easy task, transactions on the secondary market in the case of international ETFs are particularly demanding. This is mainly due to the time differences—an ETF's shares and their underlying securities (companies' shares, depositary receipts, and ETF's shares) are often traded in various time zones. As a result, the opening hours of stock exchanges on the Asia-Pacific, EMEA, and American exchanges either slightly overlap (e.g., the US markets are open from 9:30 a.m. to 4:00 p.m. ET, while most European exchanges close by 1:00 p.m. ET) or they are completely different (e.g., in the case of the Asian and American markets) (Picture 4.2).

[61]This subchapter focuses exclusively on secondary market transactions.

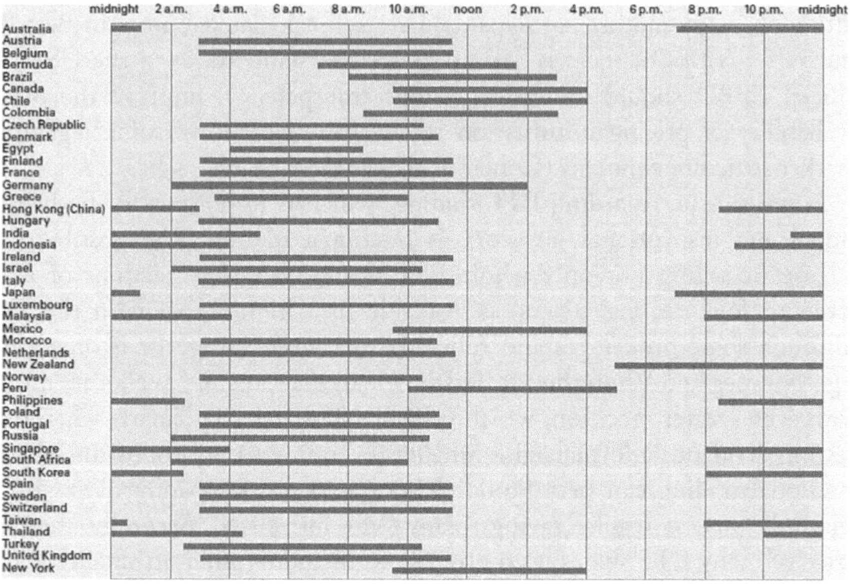

Picture 4.2 Global overlap in the opening hours of stock exchanges (US ET) (*Source* Sharp 2018)

Although the pricing mechanism of ETFs enables trading before the market opens or after it has closed, it is generally recommended to buy/sell shares of international ETFs at times that coincide with the trading hours of the underlying securities' local markets. For example, the prices of international ETFs traded on European exchanges tend to be closer to the value of the underlying securities and they typically trade with narrower bid-ask spreads when their respective markets are open and overlap with European trading hours (Vanguard 2015).

When foreign markets are closed, information continues to flow, which may affect the prices of an international ETF's underlying securities, even though the security prices themselves do not yet reflect this information. For international ETFs whose local markets are closed while the domestic market is open, this may mean that new information is incorporated into the ETF's market price, leading to seemingly greater premiums and discounts. However, the ETF's market price may better reflect the true value of its underlying securities, whose last available set of prices has not yet had the chance to adjust to the latest news (Dickson and Rowley 2014).

However, the lack of synchronization between an ETF's market price and its underlying assets is not the only problem. The other major and inherent challenge when trading international ETFs is currency exposure, and currency risk. The discrepancy between an ETF's trading currency, i.e., the currency (currencies) in which the ETF itself is bought and sold on a particular exchange,[62] and the base currency, i.e., the official currency that the ETF's NAV is calculated in and/or the currency (currencies) of the fund's underlying securities[63] means that an investor may lose or profit due to exchange rate fluctuations between them.[64]

References

Abner, D. J. (2016). *The ETF Handbook: How to Value and Trade Exchange Traded Funds* (2nd ed.). Hoboken: Wiley Finance.

Ahern, B., & Ruppenstein, C. (2014). *ETF Trading Fallacies and Best Practices.* http://kraneshares.com/resources/2014_5_the_roach_motel.pdf. Accessed 18 Sept 2019.

AMF. (2017). *ETFs: Characteristics, Overview and Risk Analysis—The Case of the French Market.* https://www.amf-france.org/technique/multimedia?docId=workspace://SpacesStore/2d61ede7-b0be-40fa-8654-fe438a33ad00_en_1.0_rendition. Accessed 11 Oct 2019.

Angel, J. J., Broms, T. J., & Gastineau, G. L. (2016). ETF Transaction Costs Are Often Higher Than Investors Realize. *The Journal of Portfolio Management, Spring, 42*(3), 65–75.

Antoniewicz, R., & Heinrichs, J. (2014, September). Understanding exchange-Traded Funds: How ETFs Work. *ICI Research Perspective, 20*(5). https://www.ici.org/pdf/per20-05.pdf. Accessed 15 Sept 2019.

Antoniewicz, R., & Heinrichs, J. (2015, March). *The Role and Activities of Authorized Participants of Exchange-Traded Funds.* ICI. https://www.ici.org/pdf/ppr_15_aps_etfs.pdf. Accessed 20 Sept 2019.

Aquilina, M., Croxson, K., Valentini, G. G., & Vass, L. (2019). *Fixed Income ETFs: Primary Market Participation and Resilience of Liquidity During Periods of Stress.* Financial Conduct Authority. https://www.fca.org.uk/publication/research/fixed-income-etfs-primary-market-participation-resilience-liquidity-during-periods-stress.pdf. Accessed 21 Sept 2019.

Balchunas, E. (2016). *The Institutional ETF Toolbox: How Institutions Can Understand and Utilize the Fast-Growing World of ETFs.* Hoboken: Wiley & Bloomberg Press.

---

[62]On some exchanges, especially European ones, certain ETFs are traded in several different currencies.

[63]In the case of global or multi-regional equity ETFs, their portfolio constituents can be denominated in several or even a dozen or so currencies.

[64]More information on the practical aspects of neutralizing currency risk in different types of international equity ETFs by investing in currency-hedged ETFs will be presented in subsequent chapters.

Bioy, H., & Garcia-Zarate, J. (2013). Every Little Helps: Comparing the Costs of Investing in ETPs Versus Index Funds. *Morningstar*. http://media.morningstar.com/uk/Research/Morningstar_Report_Every_Little_Helps_Comparing_the_Cost_of_Investing_in_ETPs_versus_Index_Funds_September_2013.pdf. Accessed 20 Oct 2019.

BlackRock. (2010, November). *Trading ETFs*. Key Factors and Issues.

BlackRock. (2012a). *Trading ETFs*.

BlackRock. (2012b). *ETP Due Diligence: A Framework to Help Investors Select the Right*. European Exchange Traded Products (ETPs). https://www.altii.de/media/modelfield_files/dokumente/dokument/datei/etp-due-diligence–report-en-emea-pc-whitepaper.pdf. Accessed 18 Aug 2019.

BlackRock. (2019a). *Index Investing Supports Price Discovery*. https://www.blackrock.com/corporate/literature/whitepaper/policy-spotlight-index-investing-supports-price-discovery-april-2019.pdf. Accessed 20 Sept 2019.

BlackRock. (2019b). *iShares Investigates: The ETF Ecosystem*. Part 2—Authorized Participants by the Numbers. https://www.blackrock.com/corporate/literature/investor-education/ishares-investigates-authorized-participants-market-makers-part-2-en-us.pdf. Accessed 12 Oct 2019.

Bourgi, S. (2016). *6 Best Practices for Executing ETF Orders*. https://etfdb.com/etf-education/6-best-practices-for-executing-etf-orders/. Accessed 5 Dec 2019.

Central Bank of Ireland. (2017). *Exchange Traded Funds* (Discussion Paper). https://www.centralbank.ie/docs/default-source/publications/discussion-papers/discussion-paper-6/discussion-paper-6—exchange-traded-funds.pdf?sfvrsn=6. Accessed 15 Oct 2019.

Cohen, S., De Jesus, H., Fisher, S., Mayston, D., Rosenblum, A., & Jackson, A. (2019). *Mark-to-Market Structure: An End-Investor Perspective on the Evolution of Developed Equity Markets*. BlackRock Viewpoint. https://www.blackrock.com/corporate/literature/whitepaper/viewpoint-mark-to-market-structure-an-end-investor-perspective-on-the-evolution-of-developed-equity-markets.pdf. Accessed 20 Nov 2019.

Deloitte. (2017). *ETF Market in Europe*. https://www2.deloitte.com/ie/en/pages/financial-services/articles/etf-market-in-europe.html. Accessed 28 Nov 2019.

Dickson, J. M., & Rowley, J. J. (2014). *Best Practices for ETF Trading: Seven Rules of the Road*. Vanguard. https://www.vanguard.com/pdf/ISGETF.pdf. Accessed 5 Dec 2019.

DigFin. (2018). *ETF Players Assess Robo-Driven Growth*. https://www.digfingroup.com/etf/. Accessed 15 Oct 2019.

Eckett, T. (2019). *ETF Insight: Consolidated Tape Crucial to Next Stage of ETF Growth in Europe*. https://www.etfstream.com/feature/9088_etf-insight-consolidated-tape-crucial-to-next-stage-of-etf-growth-in-europe/. Accessed 28 Nov 2019.

Engle, R., & Sarkar, D. (2006). Premiums-Discounts and Exchange Traded Funds. *The Journal of Derivatives, 13*(4), 27–45.

Esposito, M. (2018). *What It Takes to Seed an ETF*. https://www.fa-mag.com/news/what-it-takes-to-seed-an-etf-39975.html. Accessed 12 Sept 2019.

ETF.com. (2014). *Understanding iNAV*. https://www.etf.com/etf-education-center/etf-basics/understanding-inav?nopaging=1. Accessed 3 Oct 2019.

ETF.com. (2018). *The ETF Rule: ETF.com's Comment Letter*. https://www.etf.com/sections/blog/etf-rule-etfcoms-comment-letter?nopaging=1. Accessed 3 Oct 2019.

ETFGI. (2020). *ETFGI Reports Assets in the Global ETFs and ETPs Industry Which Will Turn 30 Years Old in March Started the New Decade with a Record 6.35 Trillion US Dollars*. https://etfgi.com/news/press-releases/2020/01/etfgi-reports-assets-global-etfs-and-etps-industry-which-will-turn-30. Accessed 10 Feb 2020.

Euroclear. (2017). *A New Dawn for Europe's Retail ETFs*. https://www.euroclear.com/dam/Perspective%20articles%20pdfs/MA4098%20ARTICLE-ANewDawnForEuropeRetailETF.pdf. Accessed 11 Nov 2019.

Gastineau, G. L. (2017). *How to Reduce Your Cost of Trading Exchange-Traded Funds (ETFs)*. http://www.etfconsultants.com/Reducing_Your_ETF_Trading_Costs.pdf. Accessed 26 Oct 2019.

Golub, B., Novick, B., Madhavan, A., Shapiro, I., Walters, K., & Ferconi, M. (2013). *Exchange Traded Products: Overview, Benefits and Myths*. BlackRock. https://www.blackrock.com/corporate/literature/whitepaper/viewpoint-etps-overview-benefits-myths-062013.pdf. Accessed 28 Nov 2018.

Hill, J. M., Nadig, D., & Hougan, M. (2015). *A Comprehensive Guide to Exchange-Traded Funds (ETFs)*. Charlottesville: CFA Institute Research Foundation.

Hilliard, J. (2014). Premiums and Discounts in ETFs: An Analysis of the Arbitrage Mechanism in Domestic and International Funds. *Global Finance Journal, 25*(2), 90–107.

HKEX. (2019). *Asia's ETF Assets on the Rise—HKEX Presents the Results of Asia ETF Survey 2019*. https://www.risk.net/exchanges/6933441/asias-etf-assets-on-the-rise-hkex-presents-the-results-of-asia-etf-survey-2019. Accessed 20 Oct 2019.

HSBC. (2019). *HSBC Launches First ETF Fair Value Algo*. https://www.gbm.hsbc.com/insights/markets/inav-algo-launch. Accessed 3 Oct 2019.

Investment Company Institute. (2018). *2018 Investment Company Fact Book: A Review of Trends and Activities in the Investment Company Industry*. https://www.ici.org/pdf/2018_factbook.pdf. Accessed 11 Oct 2019.

IOSCO. (2007). *Factors Influencing Liquidity in Emerging Markets*. https://www.iosco.org/library/pubdocs/pdf/IOSCOPD258.pdf. Accessed 10 Oct 2019.

Jane Street. (2018a). *Important Considerations for NAV-Based ETF Trading*. https://www.janestreet.com/wp-content/themes/janestreet/pdf/Important_Considerations_for_NAV_Based_ETF_Trading.pdf. Accessed 2 Oct 2019.

Jane Street. (2018b). *Institutional ETF Trading: Liquidity Improving, Trade Sizes Growing*. https://www.risk.net/asset-management/6008081/institutional-etf-trading-liquidity-improving-trade-sizes-growing. Accessed 20 Oct 2019.

KPMG. (2016). *ETF Tax Efficiency: Fact of Fiction?* https://assets.kpmg.com/content/dam/kpmg/us/pdf/etf-tax-efficiency-web.pdf. Accessed 17 Sept 2019.

Lewellyn, D. (2016, May). *Looking Behind the ETF Curtain* (ETF Report, pp. 22–23).

Lord, J. (2018). *MiFID II Reveals Record ETF Trading Volumes in Europe, Finds BlackRock*. https://www.etfstrategy.com/mifid-ii-unveils-record-etf-trading-volumes-in-europe-finds-blackrock-65487/. Accessed 28 Nov 2019.

Mackintosh, P. (2019). *Are ETFs Eating Liquidity?* https://www.nasdaq.com/articles/are-etfs-eating-liquidity-2019-12-05. Accessed 10 Dec 2019.

Madhavan, A. N. (2016). *Exchange-Traded Funds and the New Dynamics of Investing*. New York: Oxford University Press.

Marszk, A., & Lechman, E. (2019). *Exchange-Traded Funds in Europe*. London: Academic Press/Elsevier.

Moody's. (2019). *ETFs Track Liquidity Risk on Top of Asset Performance*. http://www.moodys.com/researchdocumentcontentpage.aspx?docid=PBC_1161529. Accessed 26 Oct 2019.

M'Rabti, M. (2018). *More Transparency Equals More Liquidity in ETFs*. https://www.euroclear.com/content/dam/euroclear/news%20&%20insights/Format/PDFs/2018/MA4189%20-%20More%20transparency%20equals%20more%20liquidity%20in%20ETFs.pdf. Accessed 28 Nov 2019.

Murphy, C. (2016). *Launching an ETF Is No Cheap Endeavor*. https://www.etf.com/sections/features-and-news/cost-run-etf?nopaging=1. Accessed 10 Sept 2019.

Novick, B., Cohen, S., Madhavan, A., Bunzel, T., Sethi, J., & Matthews, S. (2017a). *Index Investing Supports Vibrant Capital Markets*. BlackRock Viewpoint. https://www.blackrock.com/corporate/literature/whitepaper/viewpoint-index-investing-supports-vibrant-capital-markets-oct-2017.pdf. Accessed 12 Nov 2019.

Novick, B., Madhavan, A., Cohen, S., Samandar, S., Van Nugteren, S., & Rosenblum, A. (2017b). *A Primer on ETF Primary Trading and the Role of Authorized Participants*. https://www.blackrock.com/corporate/literature/whitepaper/viewpoint-etf-primary-trading-role-of-authorized-participants-march-2017.pdf. Accessed 14 Sept 2019.

Oliver Wyman, World Federation of Exchanges. (2016). *Enhancing Liquidity in Emerging Market Exchanges*. https://www.world-exchanges.org/storage/app/media/research/Studies_Reports/liquidity-in-emerging-market-exchanges-wfe-amp-ow-report.pdf. Accessed 10 Oct 2019.

Pagano, M., Sanchez Serrano, A., & Zechner, J. (2019, June). *Can ETFs Contribute to Systemic Risk?* (ESRB Reports of the Advisory Scientific Committee No. 9). https://www.esrb.europa.eu/pub/pdf/asc/esrb.asc190617_9_canetfscontributesystemicrisk~983ea11870.en.pdf. Accessed 25 July 2019.

Petajisto, A. (2017). Inefficiencies in the Pricing of Exchange-Traded Funds. *Financial Analysts Journal, 73*(1), 24–54.

Phadnis, K., Park, S., & Kan, G. (2016). *Intelligently Allocate to Benchmark the Closing Price—Part I*. https://www.bloomberg.com/professional/blog/intelligently-allocate-benchmark-closing-price/. Accessed 5 Dec 2019.

Picotti, L. R. (2018). ETF Premiums and Liquidity Segmentation. *Financial Review, 53*(1), 117–152.

PwC. (2015). *Global Financial Markets Liquidity Study*. https://www.pwc.se/sv/pdf-reports/global-financial-markets-liquidity-study.pdf. Accessed 10 Oct 2019.

PwC. (2019). *European ETF Listing and Distribution*. PricewaterhouseCoopers. https://www.pwc.lu/en/asset-management/etfs/etf-poster.html. Accessed 20 Nov 2019.

Roncalli, T., & Zheng, B (2014). *Measuring the Liquidity of ETFs: An Application to the European Market*. http://www.thierry-roncalli.com/download/Liquidity-European-ETF.pdf. Accessed 11 Oct 2019.

Rose, G. (2012). *Total Cost of ETF Ownership: The Bid-Offer Spread*. https://www.morningstar.co.uk/uk/news/69355/total-cost-of-etf-ownership-the-bid-offer-spread.aspx. Accessed 15 Oct 2019.

Rowley, J. J., Hirt, J. M., & Wang, H. (2018). *Setting the Record Straight: Truths About Indexing*. Vanguard. https://personal.vanguard.com/pdf/ISGBEL.pdf. Accessed 12 Nov 2019.

Rowley, J. J., Zorina, I., & Zhu, C. (2019). *A Drop in the Bucket: Indexing's Share of US Trading Activity*. Vanguard. https://advisors.vanguard.com/iwe/pdf/ISGINDX.pdf. Accessed 12 Nov 2019.

SEC. (2019). *SEC Adopts New Rule to Modernize Regulation of Exchange-Traded Funds*. https://www.sec.gov/news/press-release/2019-190. Accessed 1 October 2019.

Sharp, D. R. (2018, Summer). *Why International ETFs Cost More to Trade, ETF Perspectives*. https://advisors.vanguard.com/iwe/pdf/FAETFPSU.pdf. Accessed 10 Mar 2019.

Thomadakis, A. (2018). *The European ETF Market: What Can Be Done Better?* (ECMI Commentary, No. 52). European Capital Markets Institute. https://www.ceps.eu/ceps-publications/european-etf-market-what-can-be-done-better/. Accessed 28 Nov 2019.

Vanguard. (2015). *Understanding ETF Liquidity and Trading*. https://www.vanguard.nl/documents/understanding-etf-liquidity.pdf. Accessed 10 Oct 2019.

Vanguard. (2016). *Exchange-Traded Funds: Clarity Amid the Clutter*. https://www.vanguardfrance.fr/documents/etfs-clarity-amid-clutter.pdf. Accessed 11 Oct 2019.

Vanguard. (2019). *Exchange-Traded Funds: Clarity Amid the Clutter*. https://personal.vanguard.com/pdf/ISGETFC.pdf. Accessed 14 June 2019.

Vlastelica, R. (2017). Here's How Much ETFs Are Dominating on the Trading Floor. *MarketWatch*. https://www.marketwatch.com/story/heres-how-much-etfs-are-dominating-on-the-trading-floor-2017-01-10. Accessed 11 Nov 2019.

Wiener Boerse. (2019). *Institutional Investors and Austrian Stocks in 2018*. https://www.wienerborse.at/en/issuers/shares/investors/institutional-investors-and-austrian-stocks/?c16845%5Bfile%5D=qHseyEP2g8JUXeTooCIO9g&fileId=143770. Accessed 12 Nov 2019.

Wigglesworth, R. (2017). ETFs Are Eating the US Stock Market. *Financial Times*. https://www.ft.com/content/6dabad28-e19c-11e6-9645-c9357a75844a. Accessed 11 Nov 2019.

Part III

International Equity Exchange-Traded Funds

5

Global Equity Exchange-Traded Funds

5.1 Introduction

Investing internationally in equity exchange-traded funds is an excellent way to diversify investment portfolios and mitigate the negative effects of home bias.[1] The global financial market currently offers a variety of opportunities in this area for institutional and individual investors, both for tactical and strategic purposes. Although the wide range of funds available allows investors to choose the investment strategy best suited to their needs, it can also create problems related to the difficulty in choosing a product that would best meet their expectations. This applies not only to traditional key investment parameters such as the expected rate of return, investment risk, or level of liquidity but also to other factors that have recently become more important, such as compliance with ESG principles. When there is a wealth of choice (there are several hundred equity ETFs currently operating on the global market with international exposure), this does not always result in better investment decisions or ensure greater satisfaction.[2] Therefore, the main purpose of this part of the book is to help investors navigate the complex world of international equity ETFs with different exposures. Although the main focus will be on ETFs listed on US stock exchanges, there will also be characteristics of the

[1]The theoretical foundations regarding portfolio diversification and home bias were presented in Chapter 2.

[2]As shown by the results of modern research in the field of social sciences, excess choice can even be harmful to human well-being; it can be a source of unrealistic expectations and even guilt after making a decision. For more on this topic, see, e.g., Schwartz (2004).

T. Miziołek et al., *International Equity Exchange-Traded Funds*,
https://doi.org/10.1007/978-3-030-53864-4_5

market offer of funds domiciled in other jurisdictions and traded on stock exchanges or OTC in other regions of the world.

This part of the book consists of four chapters, each describing one segment of the international equity ETF market. The basis for distinguishing these segments is primarily the degree of market coverage by funds. Accordingly, this chapter is devoted to global equity ETFs, which allow investors to obtain the broadest and often the most diverse possible exposure to the global stock market through listed passive instruments, although this is not always the case. In the next chapter, attention will focus on multi-country equity ETFs, including funds with economic, regional (geographical), and other exposures. Chapter 7 will allow us to get acquainted with the specifics of single-country equity ETFs, mostly funds with broad market coverage and tracking large-cap indexes. A slightly different approach will be presented in Chapter 8, where the subject of analysis will be sector ETFs and thematic ETFs that invest in companies from countries all over the world.

5.2 Global Diversification

Developments in equity markets and asset management have led many investors, particularly institutional ones, to desire very broad and diversified coverage and size-segmentation of the international equity markets. Investing in equity exchange-traded funds with global exposure ensures the highest possible degree of geographical diversification of passively managed portfolios. Global equity ETFs make it possible to invest indirectly in shares or equity-like financial instruments issued by companies from various countries. As these countries differ in the level of economic development and the degree of development of the financial system, and they are often in different phases of the business cycle, it can be a great way to mitigate the investment risk associated with equity home (or regional) bias.[3] Additionally, global equity ETFs are also generally highly diversified in terms of currency exposure, as they usually invest in financial instruments denominated in various currencies. Thus, they make it possible to reduce currency risk to a greater extent than funds that are focused on investments in one region, as those instruments are often strongly correlated.

[3]There are many factors that contribute to home-country or home-region portfolio bias in global equity investing. The most significant are inertia, return opportunity, and risk control. Others include a preference for familiar, corporate governance, liability hedging, multinational companies, and currency (Scott et al. 2017). Some of these aspects will be discussed later in this chapter.

There are many rationales for geographical diversification. First of all, there is always a big divergence across the best and worst performing countries in any given period (Table 5.1). Returns in domestic equity markets over the last seven decades have varied considerably, while equally-weighted portfolios

Table 5.1 Countries' rankings of equity excess returns by decade

1950s	1960s	1970s	1980s	1990s	2000s	2010s
Germany 739%	Spain 312%	Korea 456%	Sweden 503%	Switzerland 231%	Norway 48%	USA 182%
Japan 662%	Australia 148%	Japan 66%	Korea 354%	USA 217%	Brazil 45%	New Zealand 149%
Italy 484%	EW 75%	Canada 30%	Japan 310%	Sweden 190%	Canada 52%	Sweden 146%
France 484%	Japan 74%	EW 10%	Spain 188%	France 117%	Australia 36%	Japan 105%
EW 384%	Canada 71%	UK 8%	EW 185%	UK 110%	Korea 22%	Germany 99%
USA 376%	USA 41%	Switzerland −5%	Germany 179%	Spain 96%	Spain 17%	Switzerland 97%
Australia 277%	Sweden 31%	Australia −12%	UK 173%	Germany 92%	EW 1%	France 92%
UK 270%	UK 28%	USA −17%	Italy 169%	Australia 59%	New Zealand −3%	UK 83%
Sweden 240%	Germany 21%	France −20%	France 158%	EW 53%	Switzerland −4%	Norway 78%
Canada 222%	Italy −1%	Sweden −22%	Switzerland 96%	Canada 52%	Sweden −13%	EW 74%
Spain 98%	France −6%	Germany −31%	USA 96%	Italy 40%	Taiwan −23%	Taiwan 55%
		Spain −69%	Australia 39%	Norway 2%	UK −23%	Canada 54%
		Italy −74%	Norway 23%	New Zealand −6%	USA −27%	Australia 41%
			Canada −4%	Japan −47%	France −32%	Korea 27%
				Taiwan −49%	Italy −35%	Italy 20%
				Korea −66%	Germany −36%	Spain 11%
					Japan −41%	Brazil −26%

Note EW—Equal weight
Source Saphier et al. (2019)

performed much better. Taking into consideration two measures—cumulative excess returns and 10-year rolling return-to-risk ratios—the results for equally-weighted portfolios from the beginning of the 1950s to the end of the 2010s proved to be better than in the cases of most individual countries (Saphier et al. 2019).

Thus, if we want to achieve the best investment results, bearing in mind that no country consistently outperforms another (outperformance in one period typically leads to relative overvaluation and a subsequent reversal), investing in various markets seems to be the best solution. Truly global diversification gives investors the possibility to participate in whatever region, group of countries, or individual country is outperforming at a given time. A portfolio invested solely within an individual equity market, typically the investor's home market, regardless of his/her domicile, excludes a large portion of the global opportunity set.

Secondly, exposure to both domestic and international equity markets typically makes it possible to mitigate portfolio risk. Investing in foreign stocks, e.g., through international equity ETFs, comes with diversification benefits because of the less-than-perfect correlations between various countries. This is caused mainly by differences in economic cycles, fiscal and monetary policies, currency performance, and sector weighting. There are many examples in which geographic diversification was an effective tool in limiting the level of risk. One of the most interesting is the Bridgewater research (Saphier et al. 2019),[4] which showed that an investment portfolio (equally-weighted) composed of stocks derived from various countries experienced relatively shorter and much shallower drawdowns than most domestic equity markets. Moreover, such diversified investments tended to recover faster from losses than most individual countries.

A study carried out by Vanguard provides more compelling evidence of global diversification benefits—from the perspective of American investors.[5] An internationally diversified equity portfolio (60% USA, 40% international

[4]This analysis covered cases of the worst equity excess return drawdowns (in USD terms) across 17 countries since (in most cases) 1900. The magnitude of losses varied from 51 to 100%, and the length of drawdown periods ranged from two to 17 years.

[5]Although most of the analyses regarding international portfolio diversification referred to in this chapter are carried out from the point of view of an American investor, the benefits of such diversification differ across countries. Driessen and Laeven (2007) found that the merits of investing abroad are largest for investors in developing countries, including when controlling for currency effects. Most of the benefits are obtained from investing outside the region of the home country. Global diversification benefits remain large when controlling for short-sales constraints in developing stock markets. The gains from international portfolio diversification appear to be largest for countries with high country risk. Additionally, diversification advantages vary over time as country risk changes. This will be discussed later in this chapter.

Table 5.2 Real (inflation–adjusted) equity returns in selected markets, regions, and globally (1900–2019)

Country/region	Geometric mean (%)	Standard deviation (%)	Minimum return (%)	Minimum year	Maximum return (%)	Maximum year
Europe	4.3	19.7	−47.5	2008	75.2	1933
Japan	4.2	29.2	−85.5	1946	121.1	1952
Switzerland	4.6	19.4	−37.8	1974	59.4	1922
UK	5.5	19.6	−56.6	1974	99.3	1975
USA	6.5	19.9	−38.6	1931	55.8	1933
World	5.2	17.4	−41.4	2008	67.6	1933

Source Dimson et al. (2020)

stocks[6])[7] would have consistently lowered volatility relative to a portfolio that held only US or international equities over the last five decades (January 1970–December 2018). Additionally, such a portfolio produced the highest risk-adjusted return (or the highest return per unit of risk) (0.63), while USA and international portfolios experienced lower outcomes—0.59 and 0.50, respectively (Dinucci 2019).

Even in the very long term, one can clearly see the advantages offered by global diversification, especially for risk reduction. It was proved by Credit Suisse analysis conducted for a period covering 120 years (1900–2019) (Table 5.2). Real annualized equity returns for a world portfolio amounted to 5.2% (geometric mean) in the analyzed period. They were slightly lower than in the UK and especially in the USA, but higher than in Europe, Japan, and Switzerland. The world portfolio turned out to be the most effective in risk mitigation. It recorded the lowest value of the standard deviation of equity market returns (17.4%) and one of the best results (−41.4%), i.e., the lowest loss, taking into account returns in the worst year in the research period (Dimson et al. 2020).

---

[6]International equity returns, as measured by the MSCI World ex US Index (it captures large- and mid-cap representation across 22 of 23 developed markets (ex-US)), and US equity returns, as measured by the MSCI USA Index (it measures the performance of more than 600 companies representing the large- and mid-cap segment of the US equity market). Interestingly, very similar proportions of American and international shares occur in the most popular global stock indexes (cf. Table 5.3).

[7]Determining an appropriate portfolio allocation, whether for a global allocation or for an allocation within a specific region or country, assumes (in accordance with financial theory) investing proportionally according to market capitalization. This method assumes that markets are reasonably efficient and, thus, stock prices reflect all the available information, investment positions, and expectations of investors.

For American investors, global investing offers a much broader opportunity set, not just considering that the world's most dominant and profitable companies in some sectors are domiciled in the various regions of the globe.[8] Applying this approach may also provide greater dividend opportunities, as many non-US firms tend to pay dividends more consistently, and their stocks have higher dividend yield.[9] Additionally, non-US developed markets and emerging markets also usually offer better valuations in the long term, e.g., the 15-year average P/E ratio for US companies is 14.8, while for DM and EM it is 13.3 and 11.1, respectively. These stocks are traded at lower valuations compared to their US-domiciled counterparts, mainly due to political or economic issues in their home countries (Lovelace and Polak 2019).

Interestingly, the advantages of global diversification in the context of reducing portfolio risk may prove to be particularly important nowadays, when global financial market volatility is relatively high (and is expected to remain heightened in the near future[10]), mostly due to the elevated market valuations on some equity markets at the end of 2010s, the high level of geopolitical and economic policy uncertainty[11] (e.g., US monetary policy, the consequences of Brexit, and instability of Chinese economy), and specific risks typical of the late phase of the economic cycle in many countries.[12]

During the last few decades, countries' economies and financial markets have become increasingly connected, mostly amid globalization processes and progressing free flow of capital. The surge of globalization after World War II, with rising trade and capital ties between countries globally, led to unprecedented high correlations among the equity returns of different countries and regions, especially after the 1980s. For example, in the last 25 years, most of the cross-regional correlations (North America, EMEA, Asia-Pacific, and

[8]For example, many flagship pharmaceutical, chemical, and luxury companies are located in Europe, robotic firms in Japan, and technology companies in South Korea and China. What is more, on average, as many as 74% of the 50 top stocks globally (i.e., with the best annual return) in the 2010s were non-US companies.

[9]More on dividends in Chapter 6.

[10]According to Vanguard estimations, the projected ten-year median volatility of global 100% equity portfolio is 15.1% (Davis et al. 2019).

[11]In 2019, economic policy uncertainty (measured by the Economic Policy Uncertainty Index, which provides a real-time measure of policy uncertainty in the economy by incorporating a variety of factors such as tax policy, spending policy, monetary policy, and government shutdowns) was at its highest level since 2011 and the second-highest level in the past three decades (Aliaga-Díaz et al. 2019).

[12]Late stage expansion periods have typically been marked by greater market and economic volatility as well as uncertainty over its persistence. Vanguard estimates a 47% increase in US equity market volatility (measured by the annualized standard deviation of equity returns) when moving from the middle stage of expansion to the late stage, as measured by the CBOE Market Volatility Index (VIX) since 1990 (Wang et al. 2019).

emerging markets) were between 0.7 and 0.8; in one case (North America-EMEA), they even amounted to 0.86. Although average inter-regional equity correlations between the four mentioned regions have increased over recent decades—especially in times of financial turmoil—one can observe a clear benefit from diversification across regions and from adding EM exposure in a global equity portfolio (MSCI 2019). Also, research conducted by Viceira and Wang (2018)[13] implied that despite the secular increase in global stock correlations, the benefits of global equity diversification have not declined for long-horizon investors.

MSCI's (2019) analysis also showed that pairwise country correlations in emerging markets were, on average, lower than in developed markets; thus, the benefits of country diversification in emerging markets were more significant than in developed markets. Interestingly, correlations in both markets showed similar cyclical behavior. Likewise, stock return dispersion[14] was higher in emerging markets than in developed markets, and in turbulent markets, there was more dispersion in returns than in calm markets. In both regions, the majority (65–90%) of the cross-sectional volatility of returns was explained by stock-specific return contributions. Similarly, the assessment of the diversification ratio[15] showed similar cyclical behavior as the aforementioned analysis. Stock diversification was the largest contributor to diversification, followed by regional diversification and country contribution, which was the smallest contributor. Concluding, the increased correlations among stocks, relatively low levels of dispersion, and lower values of the diversification ratio during financial distress indicate that in these circumstances, the potential for diversification is relatively smaller.

While diversification across regions and sectors is important, another important driver for diversification was the number of securities in the global benchmark. Limiting the opportunity set over the past 25 years (from December 1994 to February 2019) would have negatively affected the risk and performance characteristics of a global portfolio. For example, omitting small-caps from a global equity portfolio represented by the MSCI ACWI IMI would have reduced performance by over 4% during the period,

[13]They carried out an empirical investigation of global portfolio diversification in equities and sovereign bonds in the period 1986–2016.

[14]The dispersion of equity returns was measured by their cross-sectional volatility of returns.

[15]The diversification ratio of a set of securities measures the ratio between the weighted sum of the individual security volatilities (using portfolio weights in the sum) and the volatility of the entire portfolio. More about this measure and the theoretical and empirical properties of diversification as a criterion in portfolio construction can be found in Choueifaty and Coignard (2008).

depriving investors of the premium (over large-cap securities) offered historically by the segment. Likewise, omitting emerging markets altogether had an even more substantial impact on a global equity portfolio, as MSCI Emerging Markets Index outperformed the MSCI World Index (which includes developed markets) by almost 3% per year for the past 32 years (December 1987–February 2019) (Melas 2019).

According to the MSCI (2019) research, concentration risk[16] in global equity portfolios increased over the past decade. It was visible mainly at the country level due to the dominant role of the US equity market in developed markets (its share increased from about 40% to almost 60%) and China's dominance in emerging markets (its weight surged from zero to almost 30%)[17] in the period 1993–2018. However, this can also be observed at a security level due to the rise of so-called mega-caps, i.e., Facebook, Apple, Amazon, Netflix, Google (FAANG) and Baidu, Alibaba, Tencent (BAT) stocks. Their total weights in respective indexes (the MSCI USA Index and MSCI China Index) almost doubled in the last six and three years. Mitigating concentration risks is crucial for limiting investors' exposure to potential regional bubbles in equity markets and in averaging out regional differences in fundamental long-term performances. This may be relevant from the global investors point of view, who face the risk of a reversal in the US equity market and the risk that emerging markets' economic growth may falter.

There are many signs that geographic diversification is likely to be more significant in the immediate future. There has been increasing anti-globalization sentiment in many countries in recent years, which is most clearly demonstrated by tensions in world trade. It is likely that the world will probably become less intertwined and also more multipolarized in coming years and even decades, as relatively new economic and financial powers will gain more importance (e.g., China, India); additionally, quite new powers will emerge (e.g., Indonesia, Brazil, Mexico, and Nigeria) (PwC 2015). The increasing risk of political and military conflicts within and across countries also may increase the likelihood of divergent performances. Furthermore, since returns exhibit a strong tendency to regress to the mean, i.e., good years (decades) are often followed by mediocre (or worse) ones, and vice versa, the 2020s may be much worse than the previous decade for some developed equity markets, especially for USA. Expected returns for the US stock market

---

[16]Concentration risk is defined as the risk of a large weight in a portfolio to be exposed to a single source of risk.

[17]The weight of the MSCI USA Index in the MSCI World Index and the weight of the MSCI China Index in the MSCI Emerging Markets Index.

are significantly lower than for other markets,[18] underscoring the benefits of global equity strategies for American investors. Thus, the importance of portfolio diversification and effective risk management at the international level will increase considerably in subsequent years. Under these circumstances, investing in global equity ETFs is a simple, flexible, and accessible way to take advantage of the benefits of geographical diversification.

Although global equity investing has become common practice, particularly among investors from developed countries in recent years, one should expect that more and more investors, including those from developing economies, will explore the advantages of global diversification in the future. Many investors from high growth economies,[19] amid strong wealth accumulation from fast economic growth, the limited capacity of local equity markets, as well as the risk associated with excessive home country concentration, may decide to benefit from the global investment opportunity set. Chia and Ho (2013) indicated three substantial benefits for investors from high growth countries who adopt a global equity allocation framework. First, it provides investors with broad access to the full diversity of global investment opportunities and represents the natural starting point for any equity allocation. Second, home-biased equity allocations of investors from high growth countries have produced mixed performance results compared to diversified market portfolios. In the 1990s, most (87%) domestic equities from growth economies underperformed in at least one of the four geographically diversified portfolios, though in the 2000s, it was only 57%.[20] Third, reducing home bias by increasing the allocation to global equities contributed to visible

[18]According to most analysts, equity returns over the 2020s are anticipated to be modest at best. Forecasts from Barings (2019) indicate that equity returns in the USA (in local currency terms) will amount 3.2% per annum, while for the UK, Europe, Japan, and emerging markets, it will be 8.0, 6.8, 6.6, and 7.2%, respectively (in the latter—in USD terms). Although global ex-US equities are likely to perform moderately well, these returns are likely to be lower than the high single-digit annual returns that many investors are accustomed and expect in the future. Vanguard presented only slightly better forecasts for the US market and similar forecasts for other equity markets. According to the analysis, the annualized return over the next ten years is likely to be between 3.5 and 5.5%. It pales in comparison with the 10.6% annualized return generated over the last 30 years on the US equity market, and is much lower than expected returns in non-US equity markets, which are likely to be about 6.5–8.5% (from a US investors' perspective) thanks to relatively more reasonable valuations (Davis et al. 2019).

[19]A high growth economy is defined as an economy that displays above-average GDP growth on a sustainable basis.

[20]Domestic equity portfolios were proxied by their respective MSCI country indexes. Four geographically diversified portfolios (global, developed, emerging markets, and regional) were represented by the MSCI ACWI, MSCI World, MSCI Emerging Markets, and MSCI AC Asia ex Japan/MSCI EM EMEA/MSCI EM Latin America indexes, respectively.

portfolio risk reduction (18–39%) and return-to-risk improvements (13–28%). Global diversification is particularly useful during a domestic market crisis.

While outlining the advantages of international diversification, we must not forget about the potential threats arising from this strategy. Currently, as mentioned earlier, geopolitical and economic risks seem to be the most significant. Regarding the former, the main drawbacks are internal or external instability (political and social), weakness of state institutions and legal structures, discriminatory practices (e.g., restrictions related to taxation of foreign investors' income or dividends), and corruption. Among the economic threats, irresponsible monetary and fiscal policies may have the greatest negative impact on the macroeconomic situation and, thus, the financial health and valuations of domestic companies. Macroeconomic factors can also elevate currency risk (exchange rate fluctuations)[21] and thus adversely affect the size and volatility of nominal stock returns. An important disadvantage when investing in some markets may also be their low transparency. A lack of information, or its insufficient scope or quality (e.g., in the case of accounting, it is not compliant with generally applicable standards), may considerably increase the risk of investing capital in a given country or region. Finally, random events in certain parts of the world, mainly of a climatic and geographical nature (such as drought, flood, fire, earthquake, tsunami), or which are technical (e.g., blackout, disaster in nuclear plant) or biological (such as epidemics—e.g., coronavirus), may constitute a significant argument against investing internationally.[22]

Additionally, some question the need for international diversification by claiming that domestic multinational companies have enough coverage of foreign markets reflected in their prices as they generate a significant portion of their revenue from foreign operations. Actually, as a result of globalization, many companies now derive a significant part of their income from operating outside their own country[23]; however, this does not rule out the benefits of international diversification. First, when investing globally, we

[21]Currency exposure, which affects return volatility, especially in the short-term, can be hedged or removed from international holdings. Primary factors to consider in the equity-hedge decision include currency contribution to volatility, currency correlation with the underlying asset, and investor risk tolerance. Currency-hedging decision is affected by, for example, local market size, currency liquidity in a crisis, hedging costs, and home bias (Roberts et al. 2018).

[22]Global diversification of the equity portfolio also often results in increased risk and costs as a consequence of lower liquidity of some foreign equity markets and higher transaction costs. These issues, in relation to ETF investing, were discussed in detail in the previous chapter.

[23]For example, the 10 largest companies in Europe generate less than a third (30%) of their revenue from their home region (Lovelace and Polak 2019). More on this subject will be presented in Chapter 7.

have the opportunity to benefit from leading global companies that are domiciled outside our home market. Secondly, we can thus diversify the portfolio in currency terms, which we will not achieve by investing only in the shares of domestic companies. Thirdly, a global equity market portfolio makes it possible to have more diversified sector exposure than in the case of only domestic investing (Scott et al. 2019).

However, almost all of these adverse factors (except for those of a random and sudden nature) can be predicted and prepared. More importantly, in the case of passive investing, index providers take responsibility for monitoring the political, social, or economic situation in a given country or region. Their duty is to create an appropriate methodology for the construction of a global or regional equity index, including, in particular, the rules governing the exclusion from the portfolio of specific countries that no longer meet the criteria set by the index provider. Quickly and effectively implementing these tasks can significantly reduce the adverse effects of the factors described above from the investor's point of view. However, even if these safeguards do not work properly and do not protect the investor from losses, a global equity portfolio will usually offer better hedging against local unfavorable events—mainly over the long term—than single-region, and especially country-specific investment portfolios. Irrespective of the circumstances, global investing always tends to offer exposure to a wider array of economic and market forces than local investments, which tend to be more exposed to narrower factors specific to a given market.

5.3 Broad Global Equity Indexes

Any analysis of investment opportunities related to global equity ETFs should begin with a thorough examination of the characteristics of the indexes that are replicated by these funds and then comparing them with each other in order to select the ETF that best meets the investors' expectations. In the case of global passive investing, this is important as the entity creating the index determines all key parameters related to the index, and therefore often—particularly in the case of full physical replication—also the composition and structure of the fund's investment portfolio. A good knowledge of the index methodology[24] and all its nuances, which are presented in the box below, makes investing in index-tracking ETFs more aware and makes

[24]Documents containing index methodology are generally available free of charge on index providers' Web sites.

it possible to avoid possible mistakes and misunderstandings related to them being incorrectly interpreted.[25]

Index methodology

The two main areas concerning the functioning of equity indexes, regardless of their type, are their **construction** and maintenance. However, due to their special properties, i.e., the plurality and diversity of the countries they cover (some of them include companies from 50 countries!), these activities are particularly complex and varied in the case of global equity indexes.

The process of creating a global equity index, as a rule, consists of the three main steps.[26] The first stage involves **defining the equity universe.**[27] The equity universe is defined by two elements: identifying eligible equity securities and classifying these eligible equity securities into the appropriate country. Typically, all listed equity securities are eligible for inclusion in the equity universe. This applies primarily to common (ordinary) shares (also usually including preferred shares) and depository receipts, but it may also refer to, e.g., REITS or equivalent structures, income trusts, some limited partnerships, limited liability companies, etc. Conversely, mutual funds, ETFs, equity derivatives, and most investment trusts are usually not eligible for inclusion in the equity universe. The equity universe may vary depending on how the index providers treat different securities that function in various countries.[28] Then, each company and its securities are classified in one country, which allows for a distinctive sorting of each company by its respective country.[29]

In the second stage, the **market investable equity universe** (MIEU) **is determined**. From an investment point of view, one of the most important features of indexes is their investability and replicability. These two features are crucial for index-based financial product providers and, thus, for investors, especially institutional ones. This stage starts with identifying eligible listings for each security in the equity universe. Securities may be represented by either a local listing or a foreign listing (including a depositary receipt)—in the latter case, only if they met certain conditions. Next, investability screens are used to

[25]These mistakes can be of a various natures and scales—starting from misinterpreting the name of the index, to misconceptions of its some features (e.g., regarding market capitalization of the index constituents).

[26]This procedure is described using the example of the MSCI Global Investable Markets Indexes (MSCI 2020). In the case of other index providers, it may differ from the one presented here.

[27]These steps refer to each individual financial market. They are usually individual countries, but, e.g., in the MSCI methodology, Developed Markets Europe (15 countries) and West African Economic and Monetary Union (WAEMU) (8 countries) are treated as single markets for the purpose of index construction.

[28]Definitions and properties (e.g., from a tax point of view) of equity-like instruments may vary from country to country or even from one company to another, so index providers often analyze them on a case by case basis.

[29]A detailed description of the procedure in this and subsequent stages of the procedure has been omitted.

determine the investable equity universe in each market.[30] The most important ones are size screens and liquidity screens. Size screening starts with equity universe minimum size requirement (EUMSR) (i.e., minimum full market capitalization; companies with capitalizations below specified level are not included in the MIEU), and it then employs equity universe minimum free float-adjusted market capitalization requirements (i.e., to be eligible for inclusion in the MIEU, a security must have a free float-adjusted market capitalization equal to or higher than a defined percent of the EUMSR—in the case of MSCI, it is 50%). Liquidity screening refers to the Minimum Liquidity Requirement (MLR). To be eligible for inclusion in an MIEU, a security must have at least one eligible listing (as defined in Step 1) that meets the MLR measured by specified liquidity ratios (e.g., annual traded value ratio (ATVR), frequency of trading or the averaged daily traded volume (ADTV)).[31] Other investability screens include the following requirements: minimum foreign inclusion factor, minimum foreign headroom (both refer to the possibility of international investors purchasing shares), and minimum length of trading.

The final stage involves **defining market capitalization size-segments**, i.e., the MIEU is segmented into size-based indexes. The most popular approaches to this issue in the case of global equity indexes—as shown in Table 5.3—are large and mid-cap indexes (including large and mid-cap companies), all-cap (investable market) indexes (including large, mid and small-cap companies) and total market indexes (including large, mid, small and micro-cap companies). There are also global indexes that focus only on one specified size-segment—e.g., large-cap or small-cap. In order to create size-segments that can be aggregated into composites, the individual market size-segments need to balance two objectives: achieving global size integrity and achieving consistent market coverage. Regarding the first objective, a composite index[32] should include only companies of comparable and relevant sizes that are included across all markets. The second goal is to ensure that each market's size-segment is represented in its proportional weight in the composite universe. Since it is not possible to achieve both of these objectives consistently and simultaneously across all markets, to balance these objectives, index providers set a minimum size cutoff for each size-segment in each market.[33]

---

[30]Most of the investability requirements are applied at the individual security level, but some at the overall company level, represented by the aggregation of individual securities of the company.

[31]Additional requirements may apply to specific markets (e.g., China).

[32]Composite indexes refer to market capitalization-weighted indexes created by combining individual market indexes.

[33]Creating the size-segment indexes involves the following steps: defining the market coverage target range for each size-segment (e.g., MSCI large-cap indexes cover 70% ± 5% of the free float-adjusted market capitalization MIEU, large- and mid-cap indexes cover 85% ± 5%, and large-, mid-, and small-cap indexes cover 99% ± 1% (0.5)%), determining the global minimum size range for each size-segment, determining the market size-segment cutoffs and associated segment number of companies, assigning companies to the size-segments, and finally applying final size-segment investability requirements.

Once created, a global equity index should be properly maintained in order to correctly reflect the evolution of the underlying equity markets and segments on a timely basis. The main objectives of **index maintenance** are:

- index continuity, as it avoids the temporary inclusion or exclusion of market indexes in composite indexes at different times,
- the continuous investability of constituents and replicability of the indexes,
- index stability and low index turnover.

All the above features are extremely important not only for index providers but also for investors, since the attractiveness of index-related products (e.g., from the point of view of transaction costs) depends significantly on how these goals are achieved in practice.

Index maintenance involves two main activities: periodic index reviews and ongoing, events-related index changes. Periodic index reviews are carried out several times a year (usually 2–4), and they differ in both the form and scope of the changes made, depending on the index provider. Global equity index revisions cover a wide variety of activities. During semi-annual index reviews—in the case of MSCI Global Investable Markets Indexes, it includes both size-segment indexes and global value and growth indexes—the following activities are undertaken:

- updating the equity universe and MIEU,
- recalculating the global minimum size references and the corresponding ranges,
- reassessing the segment number of companies and the corresponding market size-segment cutoffs,
- assigning companies to appropriate size-segments, taking into account buffer zones,
- assessing conformity with final size-segment investability requirements.

Quarterly index reviews in the MSCI Global Investable Markets Indexes relate only to size-segment indexes. They are designed to ensure that indexes continue to be an accurate reflection of the evolving equity marketplace. These reviews may result in:

- additions or deletions due to migration to another size-segment index,
- the addition of significant new investable companies to the standard index,
- the deletion of companies from the investable market indexes due to low liquidity.

Additionally, during semi-annual and quarterly reviews, changes in foreign inclusion factors and the number of shares can be made.

Ongoing event-related changes are the result of mergers, acquisitions, spin-offs, bankruptcies, reorganizations, and similar corporate events. They can also result from capital reorganizations in the form of rights issues, bonus issues, public placements, and other corporate events that take place on a continuing basis. These changes are generally implemented in the indexes at the time of the event. Corporate events affect many aspects of an index and its constituents, including the inclusion or deletion of companies outside of the index reviews (such as significant IPOs), weight changes due to changes in foreign ownership limits, foreign inclusion factors or the number of shares, and changes in size, style and/or industry classification.

Regardless of the investor's country of origin, global equity indexes are those that should include exhaustive coverage of the investable opportunity set on the global equity market. In practice, this generally means that such indexes include public companies from several dozen (usually between 30 and 50—cf. Table 5.3) countries—both developed ones and emerging ones,[34] although companies from frontier and other markets are excluded.[35] It means, therefore, that not all indexes containing terms suggesting global equity exposure (e.g., "world" or "global") in their names can be considered *truly* global. Some of them are not diversified in the manner described above, but include only companies from a specific group of countries, for example. Recognizable indexes such as the MSCI World Index, S&P Global 100 Index, Dow Jones Global Titans 50 Index, or Solactive Global Equity Index, contrary to appearances, do not capture the whole world but confusingly only encompass developed countries. The heavy use of acronyms by index providers (e.g., the MSCI ACWI) does not help either. The names of only some global indexes contain expressions indicating explicitly that they include companies both from developed and emerging markets (e.g., STOXX Developed and Emerging Markets Total Market Index). In conclusion, what is crucial for ETF investors is that they should be aware that definitions of the "world" can vary among the index providers and indexes.

Very broad country exposure of a global equity index usually results in the widest possible coverage of the global investable equity market and a huge number of constituents. Typically, such indexes cover over 90%, and sometimes even 99% of global equity markets (e.g., the MSCI ACWI IMI, FTSE Global All Cap Index). Only for some indexes is there less coverage (e.g., the MSCI ACWI—85%, S&P Global 1200 Index—70%). The portfolios of global equity indexes usually include a few thousand companies (e.g., the MSCI ACWI, FTSE All-World Index), but some include shares of even over ten thousand constituents (e.g., the MSCI ACWI All Cap, S&P Global BMI)

[34]The lists of countries belonging to developed and emerging markets is determined by a given index provider based on its countries classifications. They will be presented in Chapter 6. As a result, coverage in global equity indexes that cover both developed and emerging markets may vary.

[35]Such restrictive criteria mean that relatively few providers create such indexes; hence, their number and diversity are relatively small compared to regional indexes, for example, as will be described in the following chapter.

Table 5.3 Main characteristics of key index providers' flagship global equity broad market indexes (as of 31 December 2019)

Index	Size segments[a]	Number of countries[b]	Coverage of global investable equity market[c]	Number of constituents	Median capitalization (USD bn)	Percentage in top 10 (%)	Top 3 stocks (%)[d]	Top 3 countries (%)
MSCI ACWI	Large and mid-cap	49 (23 DM + 26 EM)	85%	3050	5.317	11.94	1. Apple—2.61 2. Microsoft—2.25 3. Alphabet—1.61	1. USA—55.59 2. Japan—7.17 3. UK—4.81
MSCI ACWI IMI	Large, mid and small-cap	49 (23 DM + 26 EM)	99%	9033	1.074	10.49	1. Apple—2.29 2. Microsoft—1.97 3. Alphabet—1.41	1. USA—54.93 2. Japan—7.62 3. UK—5.04
MSCI ACWI All Cap	Large, mid, small and micro-cap	49 (23 DM + 26 EM)	99%	14,825	0.325	10.40	1. Apple—2.27 2. Microsoft—1.96 3. Alphabet—1.41	1. USA—54.67 2. Japan—7.79 3. UK—5.08
FTSE All-World	Large and mid-cap	49	90–95%	3931	3.044	11.88	1. Apple—2.56 2. Microsoft—2.34 3. Alphabet—1.58	1. USA—54.47 2. Japan—7.73 3. UK—5.10

Index	Size segments[a]	Number of countries[b]	Coverage of global investable equity market[c]	Number of constituents	Median capitalization (USD bn)	Percentage in top 10 (%)	Top 3 stocks (%)[d]	Top 3 countries (%)
FTSE Global Total Cap	Large, mid, small and micro-cap	49	99%	17,121	0.225	10.40	1. Apple—2.24 2. Microsoft—2.04 3. Alphabet—1.38	1. USA—54.72 2. Japan—7.57 3. UK—5.06
FTSE Global All Cap	Large, mid and small-cap	49	98%	8872	1.051	10.62	1. Apple—2.28 2. Microsoft—2.09 3. Alphabet—1.40	1. USA—54.93 2. Japan—7.59 3. UK—5.08
S&P Global 1200	Large-cap	30	70%	1219	20.097	13.8	1. Apple—2.8 2. Microsoft 3. Alphabet	1. USA—60.8 2. Japan—7.3 3. UK—5.6
S&P Global BMI	Large, mid and small-cap	50	–	11,915	1.340	10.2	1. Apple—2.1 2. Microsoft 3. Alphabet	1. USA—53.5 2. Japan—8.3 3. UK—4.9
STOXX Global TMI	–	–	–	9064	1.100	10.81	1. Apple—2.10 2. Microsoft—2.08 3. Alphabet—1.42	1. USA—55.0 2. Japan—8.3 3. UK—5.0

(continued)

Table 5.3 (continued)

Index	Size segments[a]	Number of countries[b]	Coverage of global investable equity market[c]	Number of constituents	Median capitalization (USD bn)	Percentage in top 10 (%)	Top 3 stocks (%)[d]	Top 3 countries (%)
STOXX Developed and Emerging Markets TMI	–	–	–	8867	1.200	10.08	1. Apple—2.10 2. Microsoft—2.08 3. Alphabet—1.42	1. USA—55.1 2. Japan—8.4 3. UK—5.0

[a]According to the size (capitalization) methodology of the index provider
[b]DM and EM countries—according to the country classification of the index provider
[c]As defined by index provider
[d]Alphabet A and C share classes counted together
Source Factsheets of indexes

(cf. Table 5.3). The number of participants in the index is generally variable and is not specified in its name, but there are also indexes where the number is fixed and indicated in their names (S&P Global 1200 Index, STOXX Global 3000 Index).

The huge number of components in global equity indexes suggests that they offer a very high degree of portfolio diversification—in terms of countries, sectors, and individual holdings. As it turns out, however, this is not entirely the case in market capitalization-weighed indexes. Let us analyze how it looks in the three aspects mentioned above.

Although some of these indexes include shares of companies from almost 50 countries, US equities alone make up around 55% of the global stock universe (at the end of 2019). Overconcentration in the global equity indexes is also visible taking into account the total weight in their portfolios of the three largest countries (approx. 67–68%) and the ten largest countries (approx. 85%). This means that the weights of most countries in these indexes, in particular emerging ones, are negligible (definitely below 1%), which means that the actual benefits of global diversification become questionable.[36] Moreover, such significant overweighting of some markets (developed markets in general) and underweighting of others (emerging markets in general) not only reduces the merits of global diversification but it also often conflicts with the economic importance of individual countries or regions. The most conspicuous example is US stocks, which represent more than 50% of the global equity universe, while the US economy comprises just 23.9% of the 2018 global economy as measured by the World Bank. To a lesser extent, this also applies to e.g., Japan (ca. 8% vs. 5.8%), UK (ca. 5% vs. 3.3%), and Canada (ca. 3% vs. 2.0%). On the other hand, the weights of some emerging countries are disproportionately smaller in relation to their economic importance. This applies in particular to China[37] (ca. 4% vs. 15.8% respectively), but also, e.g., India (1.2% vs. 3.2%), Brazil (1.0% vs. 2.2%) or Russia (0.5% vs. 1.9%).

Significant differences between the size of a country's equity market and the size of its economy—in both directions—derive from some aspects of the index methodology. The first one is the typically applied method of index weighting—capitalization weighting. This means that stocks' weights, and thus countries' weights, are largely determined by stock prices, and are

[36]Interestingly, at the end of the nineteenth century, the global stock market was more diversified as the three largest countries (the UK, USA, and Germany) accounted for around 53% of world capitalization. The total weight of the 10 largest countries was around 88% (Dimson et al. 2020).

[37]This discrepancy in the case of China has recently been diminished as a result of major index providers starting to introduce more Chinese companies to global equity indexes.

therefore susceptible to speculative activities or imbalances occurring in some markets or regions. Consequently, stock prices can depart from fundamentals (e.g., measured by the cyclically adjusted price/earnings (CAPE) ratio), and thus investors' preferences and biases can periodically affect capitalization.[38] Since, on a global scale, developed economies with well-developed stock markets usually attract more capital than emerging countries with less-developed stock markets, the weights of the former are often overstated, while the latter are underestimated. This is exacerbated by the fact that cap-weighted global indexes are calculated using "free-float" capitalization, may curb the weightings of some emerging markets due to the significant share of the government in the shareholding structure of large companies, e.g., in China or Russia (Morgan 2019). Additionally, the weights of certain markets may also be limited due to other restrictions resulting from the activity of index providers that care about index investability and replicability and countries themselves restricting foreign investors' access to their markets.

The sector diversification of broad global equity indexes[39] seems appropriate as, in most of them, the weight of no sector exceeded 20% of the total portfolio, and only a few of them weigh more than 10% (at the end of 2019). Companies from sectors that play the largest role in the contemporary global economy (among public companies) and which enjoy the greatest interest among investors have the highest weights in this type of indexes, i.e., financials, information technology (IT), health care, industrials and consumer discretionary. Companies representing real estate, utilities, materials, and energy sectors have the smallest weights.[40] However, there are notable differences in the sector breakdown of these indexes. For example, the individual weights of the top three sectors—IT, financials, and health care—in the MSCI ACWI (17.2, 16.7, and 11.8%, respectively), and S&P Global BMI

[38]Not all international equity indexes are subject to this drawback. For example, this does not apply to fundamental indexes in which portfolio constituents are weighted by fundamental variables, e.g., book value, cash flow, revenues, sales, dividends, or employment. They can also be an attractive alternative to traditional capitalization-weighted indexes for international investments. The first fundamental indexes were designed and put into practice as far back as the 1990s, but the real growth of interest in the fundamental indexation started in the middle of the first decade of twenty-first century (Miziolek and Zaremba 2017). Equal-weighted global indexes also are devoid of these disadvantages. For instance, the largest weights in MSCI ACWI Equal Weighted Index have Chinese stocks (24.6%), US stocks (20.6%), and Japanese stocks (11.6%).

[39]This does not apply to international equity indexes covering companies exclusively from one selected sector or representing a specific investment theme. Such indexes will be described in Chapter 8.

[40]This characteristic applies, in particular, to broad global equity indexes maintained by MSCI and S&P Dow Jones Indices as they use the Global Industry Classification Standard (GICS). In the case of indexes calculated by providers that use other classifications, the role of individual sectors in these indexes may vary slightly. Definitions and coverage of individual sectors are defined by sector classifications—the most important will be described in Chapter 8.

(16.4, 16.5, and 11.6%, respectively[41]) are quite varied. This, of course, ultimately translates into the diverse investment results of the ETFs that replicate these indexes, in particular, over the longer term.

It is also worth noting that the sector diversification of global equity indexes is usually slightly higher than that of domestic indexes, taking into account, e.g., the weight of the largest industry in the index. This is because in single-country indexes—and, in particular, in countries whose economy is based on one or only a few industries—the share of the dominant industry often exceeds 20%, sometimes 30%, and in extreme cases, even 50%. This applies to developed markets (e.g., UK indexes have a heavy weighting in resources, German and Japanese indexes in manufacturing industries, and German indexes in basic materials), but in particular to emerging economies (EM indexes are often overweight in financials, basic materials, oil and gas, and telecoms)[42] (Dimson et al. 2015). Meanwhile, in global indexes (and, to some extent, regional ones, although emerging market indexes may be an exception here), when grouping companies from various countries with diversified economic profiles, these overweights are endured.[43] These observations clearly prove that global diversification across countries is essential in order to effectively diversify equity portfolios across industries.

For global equity investors, it is also extremely important to answer the question of whether countries or industries have a greater impact on investment results. Although the results of relatively older studies indicated that country-specific factors dominated industry factors (Heston and Rouwenhorst 1994), globalization reduced distinctions between countries. As a result, industries have become more important relative to countries in explaining sources of return and volatility. From the most recent research conducted by Menchero and Morozov (2012) and Menchero and Nagy (2014),[44] it appears that asset allocation and active positions in Europe should focus primarily on industries, and in emerging markets, they should focus on countries (although the difference between countries and industries has been

[41]All data as of the end of 2019.

[42]More on this in Chapter 7.

[43]It is worth adding that country equity indexes (particularly emerging and frontier ones) are sometimes dominated by a handful of industries, and many international sector indexes are dominated by only a few countries. These issues will be discussed in Chapters 7 and 8.

[44]Menchero and Morozov used a global factor model (Barra Global Equity Model (GEM2)) and investigated a large universe of global stocks—all the constituents of the MSCI All Country World Investable Market Index—over the period 1994–2010. Menchero and Nagy applied the Barra Emerging Markets Equity Model (EMM1)—a risk model tailored to emerging markets. In both studies, the MAD measure (i.e., the mean absolute deviation of factor returns) was used to evaluate the relative strength of industries versus countries. MAD is defined as the cap-weighted average of the absolute value of country or industry factor returns.

declining). On a global scale, however, industries and countries are roughly equally important. In turn, according to a study by Empirical Research Partners, as cited by Lovelace and Polak (2019), most (64%) emerging markets and developed markets' stock returns can be explained by company fundamentals, while only about one-third can be explained by region and country or sector and industry.

Despite the significant degree of diversification of global equity indexes, it should be recalled that in the past, the weights of some sectors temporarily rose more than average. It happened during periods of speculative bubbles, for example, at the end of the nineteenth century during the railway stock bubble (as a result, the weight of transportation companies increased),[45] and in the late 1990s during the dotcom bubble (consequently, the weights of technology and communication stocks increased). These cases also illustrate another phenomenon that is significant from the point of view of sector diversification of global or regional equity portfolios. Investors often place too high a value on new technologies, overvaluing new ones, and undervaluing old ones. This results in an excessive concentration of new, "fashionable" sectors in indexes and the relatively low significance of old, traditional sectors. Many studies show that an industry's rotation strategies—employed globally, regionally, or within a country—may help lean against these tendencies. For example, Dimson et al. (2015) proved that an industry value rotation strategy that helps avoid periods of overvaluation for growth industries and exploit periods of undervaluation for value industries historically generated a premium. Also, an industry momentum rotation strategy, which involves buying previous years' best-performing industries while shorting the quintile of the worst performers would, since 1900, have generated an annualized winner-minus-loser premium of 6.1% in the USA, and 5.3% in the UK. However, it works most effectively for patient, long-rung investors. Since the rotation strategies, even when combined, have failed in around one year in three (especially at market turning points), they should be used with caution in short periods.[46]

At first glance, diversification in broad global equity indexes in terms of individual holdings seems to be flawless. As most of them cover several thousand constituents (and some even more), the problem of excessive concentration should not occur. However, when we look more closely at the

[45]In 1900, the share of railway companies in the USA and Great Britain in the total stock market capitalization amounted to approximately 60 and 50%, respectively (Dimson et al. 2020). Even earlier, the US stock market (public companies) was dominated by the financial sector.

[46]In practice, active sector rotation strategies have been used so far in passive investments exclusively in relation to the US market by investing in shares of sector ETFs (e.g., the SPDR SSGA US Sector Rotation ETF, the Anfield US Equity Sector Rotation ETF, and the Main Sector Rotation ETF).

structure of such indexes, we notice that the vast majority of companies have a minimum, i.e., less than 0.1%, weight in a portfolio. Meanwhile, the weights of the largest stocks exceed 1%, and some (Apple, Microsoft) even 2%, i.e., they are many times larger. Although the significance of individual companies is still relatively small,[47] particularly compared to regional or country-specific indexes where individual holdings can have even double-digit weights, the total weight of the biggest constituents in broad global equity indexes is fairly large and usually slightly exceeds 10% (cf. Table 5.3). Global indexes with a relatively smaller number of constituents have more concentration—e.g., the total weight of the top ten stocks in the S&P Global 1200 Index amounts to nearly 14 percent.

The differences between broad global equity indexes when it comes to individual allocations are minimal. The greatest refer only to the biggest positions. For example, the weight of the largest company—Apple—is relatively larger in indexes with a smaller number of constituents, e.g., the FTSE All-World Index and the MSCI ACWI (about 2.6%), than in indexes with a larger number of stocks, e.g., the S&P Global BMI and the STOXX Global TMI (about 2.1%) (cf. Table 5.3). Although this difference seems to be negligible (and in the case of other companies they are even smaller), it may, especially in the long run and in times of market stress, translate into quite noticeable differences in ETF returns that mimic various indexes. There is also a significant overlap in the companies the indexes encompass—for example, the top ten stocks in the MSCI ACWI, the FTSE All-World, and the S&P Global BMI indexes are identical; there are only slight differences in their positions on this list.[48]

[47]Incidentally, despite the small weights of individual companies, they can sometimes be greater than the weight of a particular country (countries). For example, the weight of the largest company (Apple) in the S&P Global BMI (2.1%) is greater than the individual weights of 41 countries (82% of all countries in the index portfolio) including, e.g., South Korea, Taiwan, India, the Netherlands, or Brazil. The total weight of the two largest firms (Apple and Microsoft) in the main broad global equity indexes presented in Table 5.3 is greater than the individual weights of 47 countries (except USA, Japan, and the UK), including, e.g., France, China, Canada, and Germany. Four US companies (Apple, Microsoft, Alphabet, and Amazon) make up more of the global stock market than any single country apart from the USA.

[48]An exception is, e.g., the Global Dow Index. This is an equally weighted index designed to measure the stock performance of about 150 leading companies from around the world—both from developed and emerging markets. There are only three companies among its top ten constituents that overlap with portfolios of the above-mentioned indexes (as described in factsheet).

5.4 Exchange-Traded Funds with Global Exposure

The spectrum of investment opportunities offered by the market of global equity ETFs is quite moderate compared to funds with regional, single-country, and international sector/thematic exposure. The basic group of funds within this category are those whose aim is to track the investment return of broad (all country) global equity indexes, i.e., benchmarks that cover both developed (well-established) and emerging (still-developing) stock markets. As we showed earlier, these products enable the broadest possible diversification of an investment portfolio, from geographical, size, interest rate, and currency perspectives. They usually invest in large-cap and mid-cap (sometimes also small-cap and micro-cap) stocks from dozens of countries from around the world, listed in different exchanges, and often denominated in various currencies. They typically aim to mirror capitalization-weighted indexes[49] (including those described in the previous subchapter) applying physical replication, mainly in the form of representative sampling.[50]

Due to the serious challenges associated with creating and managing these types of financial instruments and their comparatively low popularity among international ETFs—compared to regional and single-country funds—relatively few companies offer this type of ETF. These funds are mainly listed on US exchanges (e.g., ETFs provided by BlackRock (iShares), Vanguard and SSGA (SPDR)) and European exchanges (e.g., ETFs provided by BlackRock (iShares), Deutsche Bank (Xtrackers), Lyxor, SSGA (SPDR), and UBS). Several funds of this type are also listed on stock exchanges in the Asia-Pacific region (e.g., in South Korea and New Zealand) and in Africa (e.g., in South Africa). Table 5.4 presents selected global equity ETFs, and Table 5.5 shows the largest funds of this kind in the world in terms of AUM.

Another proposal, which is aimed mainly at investors from the most developed countries who invest independently in the domestic market, but who also want to complement it with global equity exposure, is global ex-country ETFs.[51] These products can also be useful for those investors who want global equity exposure, but—for various reasons—they do not intend to invest in

---

[49] One of the few examples of using a different weighing method is the SPDR Global Dow ETF listed on NYSE Arca. This fund seeks to provide investment results that, before fees and expenses, generally correspond to the total return performance of the equally weighted Global Dow Index. This index is made up of 150 constituents, both from developed and emerging countries, which are selected not just on size and reputation, but also on their promise of future growth.

[50] A detailed description of this replication method was presented in Chapter 3.

[51] Some index providers offer also global ex-region indexes (e.g., the MSCI ACWI ex-Europe, the MSCI ACWI ex-Latin America). However, no ETFs tracking these indexes have been created so far.

Table 5.4 Broad global equity ETFs and global ex-country equity ETFs listed on exchanges in various regions of the world

American exchanges	EMEA exchanges	Asia-Pacific exchanges
Global equity exchange-traded funds		
iShares MSCI ACWI ETF, SPDR Global Dow ETF, SPDR MSCI ACWI IMI ETF, Vanguard Total World Stock ETF	Ashburton Global 1200 Equity ETF, iShares MSCI ACWI UCITS ETF, Lyxor ETF MSCI ACWI - C-USD, Lyxor ETF MSCI All Country World ETF, SPDR MSCI ACWI UCITS ETF, SPDR MSCI ACWI IMI UCITS ETF, UBS ETFs PLC - MSCI ACWI SF UCITS ETF, UBS ETFs plc MSCI ACWI SF UCITS ETF (USD), Vanguard FTSE All-World UCITS ETF, X-trackers MSCI AC World Index UCITS ETF DR	Hanwha ARIRANG SYNTH-MSCI AC World ETF, Smartshares Total World ETF
Global ex-country equity exchange-traded funds		
iShares MSCI ACWI ex US ETF, SPDR MSCI ACWI ex USA ETF, iShares Core MSCI Total International Stock ETF, iShares Core MSCI All Country World ex Canada Index ETF, SPDR MSCI ACWI ex-US ETF, Vanguard FTSE All-World ex-US ETF, Vanguard Total International Stock ETF, Vanguard FTSE All-World ex-US Small-Cap ETF, Xtrackers MSCI ACWI ex USA ESG Leaders Equity ETF, Xtrackers MSCI All-World ex-US High Dividend Yield Equity ETF	Xtrackers FTSE All-World ex-UK ETF	Nikko Listed Index Fund World Equity MSCI ACWI ex-Japan, Vanguard All-World ex-US Shares Index ETF

Source Own elaboration

Table 5.5 Largest global equity ETFs in the world

Fund (ticker)	Index	Exchange	Assets (USD bn)	Expense ratio (%)
Vanguard FTSE All-World ex-US ETF (VEU US)	FTSE All-World ex US Index	NYSE Arca	26.352	0.09
Vanguard Total World Stock ETF (VT US)	FTSE Global All Cap Index	NYSE Arca	14.097	0.09
iShares MSCI ACWI (ACWI US)	MSCI ACWI Index	NASDAQ	10.743	0.32
UBS ETFs PLC - MSCI ACWI SF UCITS ETF (ACWIU SW)	MSCI ACWI with Developed Markets 100% hedged to EUR Index	SIX Swiss Exchange[a]	7.131	0.21
iShares Edge MSCI Min Vol Global ETF (ACWV US)	MSCI All Country World Minimum Volatility Index	Cboe BZX	5.871	0.20

[a]Primary exchange
Note As of 19 February 2020. Sector (thematic) ETFs are excluded
Source Bloomberg

stocks from a given country. Examples of these types of funds listed on exchanges in various parts of the world are presented in Table 5.4. In addition to funds that exclude the most representative companies for a given country, there are also ETFs that do not invest in companies from a given country with specific characteristics (e.g., with higher dividend income). An interesting case is also Vanguard FTSE All-World ex-US Small-Cap ETF, which provides broad exposure to non-US small-cap equity markets around the world with relatively significant weights of emerging stocks.

As mentioned earlier, global ETFs are also diversified in currency terms; however, this creates additional risk for investors. Fortunately, investors looking for instruments free of currency risk also have the opportunity to invest in ETFs hedged against it. This applies particularly to US investors, who can mitigate exposure to fluctuations between the value of the fund's component currencies and the USD by investing in the iShares Currency

Hedged MSCI ACWI ex US ETF or the Xtrackers MSCI All World ex US Hedged Equity ETF.

Investors looking for ways to outperform traditional global ETFs that replicate market cap-weighted indexes—on an absolute and risk-adjusted basis—have the opportunity to invest in smart-beta global equity ETFs. For example, European investors who focus on risk premia offered by exposure to factors such as value, momentum, quality, size, and low risk on a global scale may invest in the actively managed fund HSBC Multi Factor Worldwide Equity UCITS ETF. The Invesco Goldman Sachs Equity Factor Index World UCITS ETF explores a similar strategy. Its goal is to maximize exposure to those five factors while controlling the country and sector risk versus market cap-weighted benchmarks. Another actively managed global equity ETF is the HSBC Economic Scale Worldwide Equity UCITS ETF. It aims to invest in companies according to their economic scale, as measured by their contribution to the Gross National Product. Some ETFs listed on European exchanges focus their investments on minimum volatility. The Lyxor FTSE All World Minimum Variance UCITS ETF offers exposure to global large and mid-caps from both developed and emerging markets. The fund selects stocks with a low correlation with one another. The Ossiam World Minimum Variance NR UCITS ETF invests in stocks whose volatility is among the lowest in the S&P Global 1200 Index. The Vanguard Global Minimum Volatility UCITS ETF employs an active management strategy that uses a quantitative model to evaluate the securities in the benchmark (the FTSE Global All Cap Index) by referring to characteristics that are designed to measure their exposure to a variety of factors that drive a security's volatility, such as industry sector, liquidity, size, value, and growth. Examples of funds that allow investing in dividend companies on a global scale are the Vanguard FTSE All-World High Dividend Yield UCITS ETF (it invests in stocks of the largest higher-yielding companies in developed and emerging markets) and the SPDR S&P Global Dividend Aristocrats UCITS ETF (its portfolio encompass companies that have increasing or maintaining dividends for at least ten consecutive years and that simultaneously have a positive return on equity and cash flow from operations).

American investors oriented to high-dividend-yielding companies in the USA, other developed, and emerging equity markets have at their disposal the WisdomTree Global High Dividend Fund. Global X SuperDividend ETF invests in 100 of the highest dividend-yielding equity securities in the world. Those who want to gain exposure to dividend-paying companies with growth characteristics in developed (ex-US) and emerging equity markets may choose the WisdomTree Global ex-US Quality Dividend Growth Fund (all of the above ETFs are listed on NYSE Arca), while the iShares Edge MSCI Min Vol Global ETF gives exposure to global stocks with potentially less risk (listed on Cboe BZX, formerly known as BATS).

References

Aliaga-Díaz, R., Patterson, A., Raithatha, S., Hirt, J., & Maciulis, V. (2019). *Known Unknowns: Uncertainty, Volatility, and the Odds of Recession.* Vanguard Research. https://personal.vanguard.com/pdf/ISGUVR.pdf. Accessed 17 Dec 2019.

Barings. (2019). *Forecasting the Next Decade: An Analysis of Asset Returns.* https://www.barings.com/assets/user/media/04.2019_ForecastingTheNextDecade.pdf. Accessed 14 Dec 2019.

Chia, C. P., & Ho, B. (2013). *The Next Generation of Global Investors: Global Investing for Investors from High Growth Countries.* MSCI Index Research. https://www.msci.com/documents/10199/93355b8c-1a98-45f2-a446-ff58232c6c7c. Accessed 21 Dec 2019.

Choueifaty, Y., & Coignard, Y. (2008). Toward Maximum Diversification. *Journal of Portfolio Management, Fall, 35*(1), 40–51.

Davis, J., Aliaga-Diaz, R. A., Westaway, P., Wang, Q., Patterson, A. J., DiCiurcio, K. et al. (2019). *Vanguard Economic and Market Outlook for 2020: The New Age of Uncertainity.* Vanguard Research. https://advisors.vanguard.com/iwe/pdf/ISGVEMO.pdf. Accessed 15 Dec 2019.

Dimson, E., Marsh, P., & Staunton, M. (2015). *Credit Suisse Global Investment Returns Yearbook 2015.* Credit Suisse Research Institute. https://www.credit-suisse.com/media/assets/corporate/docs/about-us/research/publications/global-investment-returns-yearbook-2015.pdf. Accessed 5 Jan 2020.

Dimson, E., Marsh, P., & Staunton, M. (2020). *Summary Edition Credit Suisse Global Investment Returns Yearbook 2020.* Credit Suisse Research Institute. https://www.credit-suisse.com/media/assets/corporate/docs/about-us/research/publications/credit-suisse-global-investment-returns-yearbook-2020-summary-edition.pdf. Accessed 28 Feb 2020.

Dinucci, T. (2019). *The Case for Global Equity Investing (and a Happy Marriage).* https://vanguardblog.com/2019/02/14/the-case-for-global-equity-investing-and-a-happy-marriage/. Accessed 19 Dec 2019.

Driessen, J., & Laeven, L. (2007). International Portfolio Diversification Benefits: Cross-Country Evidence from a Local Perspective. *Journal of Banking & Finance, 31*(6), 1693–1712.

Heston, S. L., & Rouwenhorst, K. G. (1994). Does Industrial Structure Explain the Benefits of International Diversification? *Journal of Financial Economics, 36*(1), 3–27.

Lovelace, R., & Polak, D. (2019). *Guide to International Investing: How to Go Global in an Uncertain World.* Capital Group. https://www.capitalgroup.com/

content/dam/cgc/shared-content/documents/brochures/Capital-Group-Guide-to-International-Investing.pdf. Accessed 22 Dec 2019.

Melas, D. (2019). *The State of Global Investing.* https://www.msci.com/www/blog-posts/the-state-of-global-investing/01639564375. Accessed 18 Dec 2019.

Menchero, J., & Morozov, A. (2012). The Relative Strength of Industries Versus Countries in Global Equity Markets. *Journal of Investment Management, 10,* 75–87.

Menchero, J., & Nagy, Z. (2014, September). *The Relative Strength of Industries and Countries in Emerging Markets, MSCI Global Market Report.* Industries and Countries in Emerging Markets. https://www.msci.com/documents/10199/6669d7e7-7768-4948-82b8-237bec0613e7. Accessed 7 Jan 2020.

Miziolek, T., & Zaremba, A. (2017). Fundamental Indexation in European Emerging Markets. *Romanian Journal for Economic Forecasting, 20*(1), 23–37.

Morgan, E. (2019). Morningstar Investment Management Insights. What Is the Right Weighting to U.S. Equities? Morningstar. https://www.morningstar.co.uk/uk/news/181313/what-is-the-right-weighting-to-us-stocks.aspx. Accessed 3 Jan 2020.

MSCI. (2019). *Selected Geographical Issues in the Global Listed Equity Market*. Analysis for the Norwegian Ministry of Finance. https://www.regjeringen.no/globalassets/upload/fin/aff/2019-10-03-msci_report-for-the-norwegian-gpfg.pdf Accessed 18 Dec 2019.

MSCI. (2020). *MSCI Global Investable Market Indexes Methodology*. https://www.msci.com/eqb/methodology/meth_docs/MSCI_Feb20_GIMIMethod.pdf. Accessed 13 Feb 2020.

PwC. (2015). *The World in 2050: Will the Shift in Global Economic Power Continue?* https://www.pwc.com/gx/en/issues/the-economy/assets/world-in-2050-february-2015.pdf. Accessed 12 Dec 2019.

Roberts, D. R., Bosse, P. M., Donaldson, S. J., & Tufano, M. C. (2018). *The Portfolio Currency-Hedging Decision, by Objective and Block by Block*. Vanguard Research. https://personal.vanguard.com/pdf/ISGPCH.pdf. Accessed 22 Dec 2019.

Saphier, M., Karniol-Tambour, K., & Margolis, P. (2019). *Geographic Diversification Can Be a Lifesaver, Yet Most Portfolios Are Highly Geographically Concentrated, Bridgewater Associates.* https://www.bridgewater.com/research-library/daily-observations/geographic-diversification-can-be-a-lifesaver/Geographic_Diversification_Can_Be_a_Lifesaver.pdf. Accessed 12 Dec 2019.

Schwartz, B. (2004). *The Paradox of Choice: Why More Is Less*. New York: HarperCollins.

Scott, B. J., Balsamo, J., McShane, K. N., & Tasopoulos, C. (2017). *The Global Case for Strategic Asset Allocation and an Examination of Home Bias.* Vanguard Research. https://personal.vanguard.com/pdf/ISGGAA.pdf. Accessed 12 Dec 2019.

Scott, B. J., Stockton, K. A., & Donaldson, D. J. (2019, February). *Global Equity Investing: The Benefits of Diversification and Sizing Your Allocation.* Vanguard Research. https://www.vanguard.com/pdf/ISGGEB.pdf. Accessed 22 Dec 2019.

Viceira, L. M., & Wang, Z. (2018). *Global Portfolio Diversification for Long-Horizon Investors* (Working Paper). https://scholar.harvard.edu/files/zwang/files/vw-intldiv-2018-07-07.pdf. Accessed 17 Dec 2019.

Wang, Q., Hirt, J., Raithatha, S., & Lepigina, O. (2019). *As the Cycle Turns: Late-Cycle Macro Risks and Asset Allocation.* Vanguard Research. https://advisors.vanguard.com/iwe/pdf/ISGCYCLE.pdf. Accessed 17 Dec 2019.

6

Regional Equity Exchange-Traded Funds

6.1 Introduction

One can find passive international equity investing in a wide variety of forms, among which, regional equity exchange-traded funds are undoubtedly one of the most popular. The passive investing in shares of companies from a given group of countries is a response to investors' needs. They often look for exposure to a group of markets with shared traits such as a similar level of economic and financial development, geographical neighborhood, common currency, participation in economic integration agreements, etc. Similarly, investors can enjoy comparable benefits of geographical diversification, as in the case of global investing, but in a more targeted way. Thus, it is possible to mitigate the country-specific idiosyncratic risk[1] that occurs in single-country investing while avoiding the possible over-diversification of the investment portfolio in the case of global investing.

The opportunities offered by this form of international equity investing are enormous and constantly increasing. Investors may include in their portfolio shares of companies from countries that are at a different level of economic development, e.g., from emerging markets, to benefit from the faster growth characteristics of these countries, or from developed markets when they want to limit risk in times of uncertainty, as it is usually relatively smaller in this group of countries. They can invest in equity markets from their own region

[1]Country-specific idiosyncratic risk (called also specific risk, unsystematic risk, or residual risk), analogous to firm-specific idiosyncratic risk, is the risk specific to an individual country that can be reduced or eliminated through diversification.

T. Miziołek et al., *International Equity Exchange-Traded Funds*,
https://doi.org/10.1007/978-3-030-53864-4_6

when they also want to get exposure to companies from neighboring countries but limit a home country specific risk (e.g., Pacific countries, Central and Eastern European [CEE] countries), or in multiple regions in other parts of the world when they look for an effective, broad geographical diversification, but not necessarily on a global scale (e.g., Europe, Australasia, Far East [EAFE]).

Finally, regional equity ETFs make it possible to diversify the portfolio by investing in a group of countries from the same region that have a strictly formal, usually economic and/or political character and usually joint interests (e.g., European Monetary Union [EMU], Association of Southeast Asian Nations [ASEAN], Gulf Cooperation Council [GCC]), or group of countries from all over the world without any formal connections, but which have some common economic, demographic, or cultural features (the most widely known is BRIC—Brazil, Russia, India, and China). Moreover, the above "specializations" may overlap; hence regional investments are possible, e.g., in emerging markets in Asia or developed markets in Europe.

The remainder of the chapter proceeds as follows. The next part discusses the pros and cons of regional diversification. The subsequent section explores investing in developed, emerging, and frontier market ETFs, while the next subchapter describes investing in geographically focused regions. The last section outlines other opportunities in the scope of regional equity ETFs.

6.2 Regional Diversification

The rationales for the regional equity diversification of an equity portfolio are essentially the same as for global equity diversification described in detail in the previous chapter. The most important thing is mitigating the level of investment risk by smoothing the volatility. Return drawdowns are typically shorter and shallower than in the case of single-country returns. Additionally, regional diversification may provide the opportunity to participate in whichever single country (or even region or group of countries in multi-region investing) is currently outperforming. It also often makes it possible to profit from leading companies from various countries that are attractively priced and pay high dividends.

However, it should be emphasized that regional diversification merits vary and depend on many factors. First, the number of countries where we invest is significant. Multi-country ETF investing may encompass from only a few (even only two) countries (e.g., ETF investing only in China and India) to over twenty countries (e.g., in DM and EM funds). Generally, the more countries in the regional portfolio, the more pronounced the benefits of diversification. However, this general principle does not always hold, for at least two reasons. Firstly, although the number of countries in the portfolio usually implies the number of companies in the portfolio (i.e., the more countries, the more companies), this is not always the case. There are, in fact, multi-country equity indexes that include even a dozen or so countries, but the number of companies is relatively small (e.g., the S&P Global 100 Index covers about 100 stocks from 10 developed countries, while the Dow Jones Global Titans 50 Index includes only 50 blue-chip stocks from 12 developed countries). However, even when the index portfolio is fairly concentrated, the effectiveness of diversification can be meaningful, provided there is a relatively low correlation between its components. On the other hand, some regional indexes cover only a few countries, but the number of constituents is relatively large (e.g., the FTSE Developed Asia Pacific ex Japan Index, which comprises about 380 stocks from five countries, or the MSCI BRIC Index, which embraces about 860 stocks from only four countries).[2]

However, undoubtedly the crucial factor from the point of view of effective portfolio diversification is the degree of correlation between index components. When the correlation coefficients between (even numerous) countries are relatively high, the benefits of its dispersion may be negligible. According to MSCI research, the biggest average intra-region correlations[3] in the last 20 years (December 1998–October 2019) were observed within developed markets. This applies especially to the Americas (specifically, to the two North American countries—the USA and Canada—which are economically very closely integrated)—0.89, but also in EMEA (Europe, Middle East, Africa) region,[4] ranging from 0.56 to 0.77 (with the exception of Israel—0.46), and the APAC (Asia-Pacific) region, which ranges from 0.56 to 0.67 (Giese and Kozumenko 2019). A high degree of correlation also occurs between regions consisting of developed markets (DMs)—from 0.71 between DM EMEA and DM APAC, as well as DM Americas and DM APAC, to even 0.86 between DM Americas and DM EMEA (MSCI 2019).

Meanwhile, much lower levels of correlation between countries occur within emerging markets. This regards the Americas (in particular, five Latin American countries), which ranges from 0.46 to 0.60, the APAC region, which ranges from 0.46 to 0.55 (with exception of Pakistan—0.24), and the EMEA region, which ranges from 0.42 to 0.56. However, cross-regional correlations between the EM region (as a whole) and DM regions (the

[2]All data as of end of February 2020.

[3]Correlations measured using MSCI country or regional indexes.

[4]Regions as defined by MSCI.

Americas, EMEA, and APAC) are relatively high (from 0.72 to 0.76). Additionally, they are typically higher (exceeding even 0.9) in times of financial turmoil. In conclusion, the potentially greatest diversification benefits may appear when investing in EMs and in calm times, while the lowest appear when investing in DMs and during turbulent periods.

It is also worth noting that within geographical regions, average pairwise correlations declined from the peak reached during the global financial crisis, and—as of August 2019—have been at levels close to their values 20 years ago in most regions. This may reflect the decreasing economic dependency within the home region and the increasing dependency on other regions. The best example is EM EMEA countries that are increasingly economically integrated with DM EMEA countries (Giese and Kozumenko 2019). A similar downward trend was also observed in the 2010s in the case of developed markets and emerging markets. The average pairwise correlation between countries declined from about 0.75 to about 0.6 at the end of the 2010s decade within DMs, and from about 0.5 to about 0.35 within EMs (MSCI 2019).

Multi-country investing may also vary as regards levels of sectoral diversification. Portfolios of some regional equity indexes are very differentiated in this respect, just like in the most recognizable broad global equity indexes described in Chapter 5, in which the weight of no sector exceeds 20%. The situation is similar in broad regional equity indexes that cover several regions or numerous countries. For example, the weight of the largest sector in the MSCI EAFE Index is 18.4%, and the largest three sectors represent 46.0% of its total capitalization; in the FTSE Developed Index, it is 18.1 and 40.8%, respectively. Meanwhile, sectoral concentration can be significant in narrow-based regional equity indexes that encompass a relatively small number of countries with less-diversified economic potential and/or with similar economic characteristics (e.g., whose economies are based mainly on a few industries). For example, the weight of the largest sector in the MSCI GCC Index is 61.8%, and the largest three sectors are responsible for 83.5% of its total capitalization; in the S&P Emerging Europe BMI Index, it is 36.1 and 73.8%, respectively. Likewise, in regional equity indexes with a small number of constituents, sectoral concentration can be quite large. For example, the weight of largest sector in the S&P BRIC 40 Index is 36.8%, and the total weights of the three largest sectors amount to 75.4% of its capitalization.[5] An example of a regional equity index that uses sector-specific weights is Morningstar Developed Europe 100 Index. It is designed to provide exposure to largest and most liquid companies in the developed

[5]All data as of end of February 2020.

market Europe region. The maximum weight of an individual sector in the index is capped at 4% plus its corresponding weight in the broad benchmark (Morningstar Developed Europe Index).

Excessive country or sectoral concentration in multi-country equity indexes is one of the most important challenges in international investing.[6] To provide greater country diversification, some index providers—either on their own initiative or as a result of applicable legal regulations—impose restrictions (capped weights) on the indexes so that the total weight of companies from any country does not exceed a certain level. This applies to indexes covering a few countries or indexes that contain a relatively large number of countries in which one or several countries have a significant share in the capitalization of the region (group). Examples include the MSCI EM Beyond BRIC Index and the MSCI FM 15% Country Capped Index, in which the weight of each country is capped at 15% (this refers to Taiwan and South Korea in the former, and Kuwait and Morocco in the latter).[7]

Although regional equity indexes offer many similar benefits to global equity indexes, they are not free from disadvantages, including various types of economic and geopolitical risks, as well as threats arising from extraordinary events (e.g., of a geographical of biological nature). They are also susceptible to speculative bubbles, or they may be tilted toward new, "fashionable" sectors that are often overvalued in relation to traditional industries.[8] The impact of these risks on investment performance may vary. In indexes covering several regions, their impact is generally similar to that of global indexes. However, it is different in the case of indexes with exposure to one region (especially small or highly integrated) or to several countries with similar economic, social, cultural, or demographic characteristics that are often treated by international investors as one entity. Then, geographical diversification may, unfortunately, prove to be illusory. Therefore, regional investing—regardless of whether it concerns a group of countries with common economic characteristics or countries located in a specific part of the world—seems to be a much more serious challenge for investors than global investing. It requires thorough knowledge and understanding not only of the potential merits but also the drawbacks and even the pitfalls associated

[6]Overconcentration is also a significant problem in some single-country equity indexes; however, they use capping to ensure diversification among companies, and to the lesser extent to sectors.

[7]An interesting, and simultaneously an untypical example of capping is the MSCI EFM Africa Capped + GCC Countries Capped Special Weighted 10/40 Index. To avoid excess concentration, the weight of each country is first capped in two component indexes (the maximum weight of any country is limited to 70%), following which, the composite index is capped as per the MSCI 10/40 Indexes methodology (this methodology will be explained in the next chapter).

[8]All the above aspects of international equity investing were described in Chapter 5.

with it. Additionally, such investing is complicated by the various definitions used by index providers, e.g., for emerging markets and even regions of the world.

6.3 Developed, Emerging, and Frontier Markets

Probably the most popular and widespread form of regional equity investing applies to investing in countries according to their economic and financial status. In the case of passive investing, this is done by investing in financial instruments—including index ETFs—whose purpose is to track the performance of an index that comprises stocks from countries with a similar level of economic and capital market development. For this purpose, major index providers develop country classification methodology[9] that aims primarily to define the categories of countries (equity markets) and specify initial and additional eligibility criteria for the different groups of countries. Then, based on the analysis of quantitative and qualitative criteria,[10] each country is assigned to a specific category. The fulfillment of criteria is periodically reviewed, and, as a result, countries that cease to meet the criteria in a given category are assigned to a lower category, while countries that have managed to meet the more demanding criteria are promoted to a higher category.

All leading index providers—S&P Dow Jones Indices, MSCI, FTSE Russell, STOXX (Qontigo), and Solactive—distinguish two basic groups of countries (equity markets): developed and emerging.[11] Most of them also differentiate a third category—frontier markets (FMs). Additionally, some index providers (S&P Dow Jones Indices and MSCI) distinguish a fourth group—standalone markets. Although index providers' opinions on individual countries are consistent in most cases, there are also exceptions when

[9]Classifications of countries are made by various international institutions (e.g., International Monetary Fund), but from the point of view of passive investing, the most important are classifications made by index providers.

[10]Quantitative and qualitative factors may vary between index providers. For example, the quantitative criteria applied by the S&P Dow Jones Indices cover a range of factors that reflect macroeconomic conditions (e.g., GDP per capita, non-occurrence of hyperinflation), and capital market development (e.g., minimum full domestic market capitalization, domestic turnover value, and exchange development ratio). Qualitative criteria include factors such as political stability, investment conditions (e.g., no significant foreign ownership restrictions and freely traded foreign currency), legal property rights and procedures, and trading and settlement processes. Final decisions on classification are made by the S&P Dow Jones Indices Global Equity Index Committee based on both the consultation and the quantitative criteria (S&P Dow Jones Indices 2019).

[11]FTSE Russell additionally divides emerging countries in two subcategories: advanced emerging and secondary emerging.

some countries are classified differently by different entities. This applies to, e.g., South Korea and Poland (classified by some providers as DMs, but by others as EMs), or Argentina, Kuwait, and Vietnam (classified as EMs or FMs).

6.3.1 Developed Markets

In the context of international equity investing, developed markets are usually defined as markets that meet the highest criteria for the development of the economic and financial system as well as the capital market. Depending on the index provider, this category includes between 23 and 26 countries, as presented in Table 6.1. Most of them—almost two-thirds—are from the EMEA region, but the two largest economies in the world that belong to this group come from the Americas (USA) and Asia-Pacific region (Japan). Despite being part of a group of developed countries, they are quite diverse. This refers not only to strictly macroeconomic indicators (e.g., GDP in the USA is USD 20.544tn and in Luxembourg only USD 71bn) and financial market indicators (e.g., the market capitalization of listed domestic companies ranges from USD 49bn in Luxembourg to USD 30.436tn in the USA),[12] but also to demographic or civilization issues. However, from the point of view of the international investment community, these differences are of secondary importance. Factors such as a high degree of economic development and its sustainability, well-developed capital market (in terms of its size, organization, and infrastructure), a high level of openness to foreign ownership, the ease of capital inflows/outflows, and the stability of the institutional framework play a key role.

Despite the indisputable dominant importance of developed countries in the world economy and on the global financial market, their position in the last four decades has clearly decreased. For example, their share in world GDP measured at market exchange rates declined from just over 70 to 57%,[13] while their share in world Purchasing Power Parity (PPP) dropped from just

[12]World Bank data as of 2018.

[13]Although advanced economies and emerging economies grew at about the same pace at 1980s and 1990s, the GDP growth rates in the 2000s and 2010s in the former were significantly lower. The growth gap between the two economies increased, particularly in 2000s, peaking at 6.1 pp in 2009, then it declined and stabilized at 3 pp over the past decade. It is also worth noting that though economic growth rates in recent years were much lower for DMs than EMs, the former also showed lower levels of dispersion in growth rates (European countries and Japan developed most slowly). A detailed trend analysis of global economic activity and global trade broken down into developed and emerging countries in the last three decades is presented by MSCI (2019).

Table 6.1 List of developed countries (markets) according to the S&P Dow Jones Indices, FTSE Russell, MSCI, STOXX, and Solactive country (market) classifications

Country	S&P Dow Jones Indices	FTSE Russell	MSCI	STOXX	Solactive
Americas					
Canada	•	•	•	•	•
USA	•	•	•	•	•
EMEA					
Austria	•	•	•	•	•
Belgium[a]	•	•	•	•	•
Denmark	•	•	•	•	•
Finland	•	•	•	•	•
France	•	•	•	•	•
Germany	•	•	•	•	•
Ireland	•	•	•	•	•
Israel	•	•	•	•	•
Italy	•	•	•	•	•
Luxembourg[a]	•	•		•	
Netherlands	•	•	•	•	•
Norway	•	•	•	•	•
Poland		•		•	•
Portugal	•	•	•	•	•
Spain	•	•	•	•	•
Sweden	•	•	•	•	•
Switzerland	•	•	•	•	•
UK	•	•	•	•	•
Asia-Pacific					
Australia	•	•	•	•	•
Hong Kong	•	•	•	•	•
Japan	•	•	•	•	•
New Zealand	•	•	•	•	•
Singapore	•	•	•	•	•
South Korea	•	•			

[a]According to the FTSE Russell classification, Belgium and Luxembourg are treated together

Source Own elaboration based on index providers' country (market) classifications

over 60 to 37%, and their share in world investable equity market capitalization fell from nearly 100 to 88%. The relatively large share of developed countries in the global equity market is since leading index providers still exclude or underweight market segments that are difficult to access (e.g., Chinese A-shares), they apply free-float weighting to indexes (the average level of free-float in DMs is much larger than in EMs), and screen out individual stocks deemed hard to deal in (a greater proportion of EM stocks than DM stocks fail the free-float and liquidity hurdles) (Dimson et al. 2019). This means that easily accessible and transparent developed markets are preferred, while the importance of other markets is constantly underestimated.

Investing in equity markets in developed countries is recognized by most investors as relatively safe, stable, and predictable compared to emerging markets, not to mention even less-developed markets. This is a consequence of these countries' better economic, social, and political situations, as well as better regulations, which affect both fundamentals of listed public companies and investment conditions. Despite this, developed markets have been delivering lower returns over the past three decades than emerging markets. Annualized returns for the period January 1988 to February 2019 for DMs and EMs were 7.8 and 10.7%, respectively (MSCI 2019).[14] DMs outperformed EMs only in two longer periods for a total of about ten years (September 1994–January 1999 and September 2010–January 2016),[15] while for the rest of the period, they usually achieved lower nominal returns (except for relatively short periods in recent years).[16] Given the annual returns, DMs outpaced EMs in seven out of the last 16 years (2008, 2011, 2013–2015, and 2018–2019). The overperformance of developed markets for a considerable period of the 2010s resulted largely from the outstanding performance of US stocks, which represented more than 50% (and sometimes even over 60%) of their market capitalization during the last decade. Annualized returns for the 10-year period ended in February 2019 for DMs and EMs were 13.7 and 10.7%, respectively. This also was confirmed by the better performance of the MSCI World Index (a proxy of developed markets that includes the USA) than the MSCI World ex USA Index in eight years in the 2010s (except 2012 and 2018).[17] (Fig. 6.1). In general, DM equities outperformed EM equities during the 2010s due to the faster expansion of equity valuations in DMs.[18]

Interestingly, in the much longer time horizon, developed markets outperformed emerging markets as well. The annualized return from a 119-year

[14]In regional terms, EMEA and Pacific countries outperformed North America in the run-up to the financial crisis in 2008, but considerably underperformed North America after the crisis. Eventually, North American countries delivered the highest, and Pacific countries the lowest levels of returns during the whole period.

[15]MSCI Emerging Markets Index vs. MSCI World Index.

[16]It should be emphasized that developed markets perform much better against emerging markets when considering real (i.e., inflation-adjusted) returns, as nominal returns are often greatly devalued by high inflation on the latter.

[17]The MSCI World Index captures large- and mid-cap representation across 23 developed markets. The MSCI World ex USA Index captures large- and mid-cap representation across 22 out of 23 developed markets, excluding the USA. Both indexes cover approximately 85% of the free float-adjusted market capitalization in each country.

[18]The underperformance of emerging markets in USD terms was also partly explained by currency effects, as EM currencies underperformed both USD and other DM currencies.

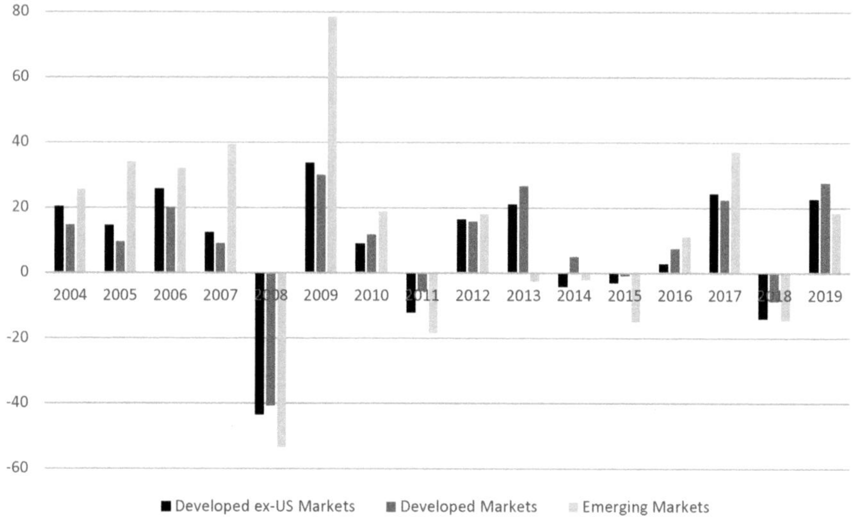

Fig. 6.1 Annual returns of developed ex-US, developed and emerging markets in 2004-2019 (%) (*Note* Developed ex-US markets—MSCI World ex USA Index Net [USD], developed markets—MSCI World Index Net [USD], emerging markets—MSCI Emerging Markets Index Net [USD]. *Source* Own elaboration based on factsheets of the MSCI indexes)

investment (starting in 1900) in DMs was 8.2% compared with 7.2% in EMs (Dimson et al. 2019). This means that 1 USD invested in 1900 in developed equity markets was worth more than three times more in 2019 than a US dollar invested in emerging markets.

An important argument for investing not in *selected* DM countries but across *all* developed markets is the fact that—as was already pointed out in Chapter 5 in the case of global investing—no country consistently outperforms (Table 6.2). What is more, there are also examples of unpredictability in short-term equity returns in these markets. For example, after posting the highest developed market return in 2015, Denmark had the lowest return in 2016. In 2000, New Zealand had the lowest return among developed markets, followed by the highest return in both 2001 and 2002 (Dimensional Fund Advisors 2019). Thus, broad diversification provides a possibility to participate in whatever country or group of countries is outperforming at a given time. As Table 6.2 indicates, in some years, disparities between annual returns across ten selected developed countries (in USD terms) reached over 30 percentage points in the 2000–2019 period![19] In this context, it should

[19]The divergences would be even greater if all developed countries were included. According to Dimensional Fund Advisors (2019), the difference between the best and worst performers among

Table 6.2 Annual returns (in USD) of 10 selected developed equity markets, ranked in order of performance (%)

Rank	2000	2001	2002	2003	2004	2005	2006	2007	2008	2009	2010	2011	2012	2013	2014	2015	2016	2017	2018	2019
1	CH	AU	AU	DE	AU	CA	DE	HK	JP	AU	HK	US	DE	US	US	JP	CA	HK	US	CH
	5.85	1.68	−1.34	63.80	30.34	28.31	35.99	41.20	−29.21	76.43	23.23	1.36	30.90	31.79	12.69	9.57	24.56	36.17	−5.04	32.32
2	CA	US	JP	CA	HK	JP	FR	DE	CH	HK	CA	GB	HK	DE	HK	NL	AU	NL	HK	NL
	5.34	−12.39	−10.28	54.60	24.98	25.52	34.48	35.21	−30.49	60.15	20.45	−2.56	28.27	31.37	5.07	1.34	11.45	32.20	−7.83	32.10
3	NL	GB	CH	AU	CA	CH	NL	CA	US	CA	JP	CH	AU	NL	CA	US	US	FR	CH	US
	−4.09	−14.05	−10.31	49.46	22.20	16.33	31.38	29.57	−37.57	56.18	15.44	−6.77	22.07	31.30	1.50	0.69	10.89	28.75	−9.08	30.88
4	FR	HK	CA	FR	GB	AU	AU	AU	FR	GB	US	AU	FR	JP	CH	CH	FR	DE	AU	CA
	−4.31	−18.61	−13.19	40.22	19.57	16.02	30.86	28.34	−43.27	43.30	14.77	−10.95	21.29	27.16	−0.09	0.44	4.88	27.70	−11.99	27.50
5	AU	CA	GB	HK	FR	NL	GB	NL	CA	NL	AU	NL	NL	CH	AU	FR	NL	JP	FR	FR
	−9.95	−20.43	−15.23	38.10	18.48	13.85	30.61	20.59	−45.51	42.25	14.52	−12.12	20.59	26.61	−3.41	−0.11	4.82	23.99	−12.76	25.72
6	GB	CH	HK	JP	DE	DE	HK	FR	DE	FR	CH	CA	CH	FR	NL	HK	DE	CH	JP	AU
	−11.53	−21.38	−17.79	35.91	16.17	9.92	30.35	13.24	−45.87	31.83	11.79	−12.71	20.35	26.33	−3.46	−0.54	2.75	22.51	−12.88	22.92
7	US	NL	NL	CH	JP	FR	CH	GB	NL	US	GB	JP	US	GB	JP	DE	JP	GB	NL	GB
	−12.84	−22.10	−20.83	34.08	15.86	9.88	27.40	8.36	−48.22	26.25	8.76	−14.33	15.33	20.67	−4.02	−1.89	2.38	22.30	−13.11	21.05
8	HK	FR	FR	GB	CH	HK	CA	US	GB	CH	DE	HK	GB	HK	GB	GB	HK	US	GB	DE
	−14.74	−22.36	−21.18	32.06	14.96	8.40	17.80	5.44	−48.34	25.31	8.44	−16.02	15.25	11.09	−5.39	−7.56	2.27	21.19	−14.15	20.77
9	DE	DE	US	US	NL	GB	US	CH	AU	DE	NL	FR	CA	CA	FR	AU	GB	AU	CA	JP
	−15.59	−22.39	−23.09	28.41	12.24	7.35	14.67	5.29	−50.67	25.15	1.74	−16.87	9.09	5.63	−9.92	−9.95	−0.10	19.33	−17.20	19.61
10	JP	JP	DE	NL	US	US	JP	JP	HK	JP	FR	DE	JP	AU	DE	CA	CH	CA	DE	HK
	−28.16	−29.40	−33.18	28.09	10.14	5.14	6.24	−4.23	−51.21	6.25	−4.11	−18.08	8.18	4.16	−10.36	−24.16	−4.87	16.07	−22.17	10.34

Note Designations of country names according to the ISO country codes
Source Lazard Asset Management (2020a)

also be recalled (as we showed earlier in this chapter) that, overall, average country correlations within DMs (especially in the Americas and EMEA region) are considerably higher than in EMs. Thus, the effectiveness of diversification when investing in a few markets within one region is significantly limited.

As already mentioned in the previous chapter in the global context, the relative importance of country effects and industry effects also has direct implications for diversification potential. In developed markets, country effects were more dominant until the turn of the century, after which the roles of country and industry have been more balanced. Currently, both dimensions are almost equally important for diversification. The decline in the historical dominance of country effects coincided with a much greater role for industry effects during the market downturns associated with the tech bubble and the global financial crisis.

Developed markets' returns were achieved with substantially lower levels of financial risk than those of emerging markets. According to MSCI (2019), the volatility of returns for DMs and EMs was 14.6 and 22.5, Value-at-Risk (VaR) at 99% amounted to −10.6 and −15.7, and Conditional Value-at-Risk (CVaR) at 99% was −13.8 and −22.5%, respectively. Maximum drawdown also proved to be significantly lower for developed markets (−53.7%) than for emerging ones (−61.4%).[20] Ultimately, developed markets performed slightly worse than emerging markets on a risk-adjusted basis measured by the Sharpe ratio (0.29 vs. 0.32).[21] DMs, on average, underperformed EMs given an equity risk premium but showed a lower level of dispersion.

For some investors, especially income-oriented ones, another important factor to consider in investing is dividend. First, according to Janus Henderson's study into dividend trends,[22] global dividends amounted to a record USD 1.43tn in 2019. Over the 2010s, global dividend payments

developed markets over the last 20 years (1999–2018) ranged from as low of 24 percentage points in 2018 (Finland −3% and Austria −27%) to as much as 81 percentage points in 2009 (Norway 87% and Japan 6%).

[20]North American countries experienced the lowest levels of risk among developed countries, and Pacific countries the highest (except maximum drawdown).

[21]However, there were considerable disparities between the regions. The Sharpe ratio for North American countries was 0.49, while for EMEA countries it was 0.27, and −0.03 for Pacific countries.

[22]This study is based on the Janus Henderson Global Dividend Index (JHGDI). The JHGDI measures the progress global firms are making in paying their investors an income on their capital. It analyzes dividends paid by the world's largest 1200 firms by market capitalization (representing 90% of global dividends paid); dividends paid by the next 1800 firms are estimated. The index is calculated in USD, and its base year is 2009. It is broken down into regions, countries, industries, and sectors.

totaled USD 11.4tn and grew 97% in underlying terms,[23] i.e., 7.0% per annum, meaning that income investors received USD 694bn more in dividends in 2019 than they did ten years before. Among the world's largest 1200 firms by market capitalization, dividends paid out in developed markets represented approximately 89% of total dividends in 2019. The largest share belongs to North American (42% of total), and European companies (28%) (Janus Henderson Investors 2020).

Second, it should be noted that dividends and dividend growth accounted for the overwhelming majority of stock returns in the past, both in developed and emerging markets. For example, over the past 25 years, notional returns for the MSCI World Index (developed markets proxy) were 8.3% annually, including dividend reinvestment, versus 5.9% without reinvesting dividends.[24] According to SG Cowen Cross Asset Research, dividend yield and growth have generated nearly all the total return for stocks in the UK and France since 1970, while stocks in Germany, Canada, and Australia have also been highly dependent on dividends (Su 2018).

Third, income-oriented passive investing—not only in developed markets—may rely on tracking "traditional," broad-based regional equity indexes (e.g., presented in Table 6.3) or specially constructed regional dividend indexes. In the first case, investors can benefit from the simple fact that companies from DMs usually pay dividends more often than those from EMs.[25] Despite this, the dividends paid in DMs are relatively low. For example, Robeco research showed that the average dividend yield of the MSCI World Index ranged between 2 and 3% in October 2006–December 2017, only reaching a higher level (ca. 4%) during the 2008 crisis; at the end of 2019, its dividend yield was 2.32%. Interestingly, net dividend return accounted for less than 40% of its total return (2.1%); the rest (3.5%) came from price returns (van Vilet et al. 2018). A closer look shows that among developed markets, the higher-yielding companies come now mainly from other countries than the USA, while in the past, US stocks paid higher dividends (over the past century, the average dividend yield of US stocks was about 4.5% per year). Capital Group found that there were more than three times as many non-US stocks (498) than US stocks (158) with dividend yields over 3%[26] (Lovelace and Polak 2019). This example conveys a

[23]Underlying dividend growth is headline dividend growth (change in total gross dividends) adjusted for special dividends change in currency, timing effects and index changes.

[24]As of the end of the first quarter 2018.

[25]According to CLSA data, over 80% of companies from DMs have paid dividends in the last 20 years (1998–2017), while in the case of EMs, this percentage has only recently reached this level (Su 2018).

[26]As of August 31, 2019.

Table 6.3 Main characteristics of key index providers' flagship developed and emerging equity broad market indexes (as of 31 December 2019)

Index	Size segments[a]	Number of countries	Coverage of market capitalization	Number of constituents	Median capitalization (USD bn)	Percentage in top 10 (%)	Top 3 stocks (%)[d]	Top 3 countries (%)
Developed equity indexes								
MSCI World Index	Large-cap and mid-cap	23	85%[b]	1646	11.092	13.52	1. Apple—2.97 2. Microsoft—2.56 3. Alphabet—1.84	1. USA—63.33 2. Japan—8.17 3. UK—5.48
MSCI World IMI	Large-cap, mid-cap, and small-cap	23	99%[b]	5976	1.592	11.84	1. Apple—2.60 2. Microsoft—2.24 3. Alphabet—1.61	1. USA—62.42 2. Japan—8.66 3. UK—5.73
FTSE Developed Index	Large-cap and mid-cap	25	98[c]	2167	7.455	13.20	1. Apple—2.87 2. Microsoft—2.62 3. Alphabet—1.76	1. USA—61.07 2. Japan—8.67 3. UK—5.71
S&P Developed BMI	Large-cap, mid-cap, and small-cap	25	–	7788	1.365	11.5	1. Apple—2.3 2. Microsoft 3. Alphabet	1. USA—60.3 2. Japan—9.4 3. UK—5.5

Index	Size segments[a]	Number of countries	Coverage of market capitalization	Number of constituents	Median capitalization (USD bn)	Percentage in top 10 (%)	Top 3 stocks (%)[d]	Top 3 countries (%)
STOXX Global 1800 Index	Large-cap and mid-cap	21	–	1800	ca. 10.200	13.04	1. Apple—2.70 2. Microsoft—2.68 3. Amazon—1.64	1. USA—60.7 2. Japan—9.6 3. UK—5.8
Emerging equity indexes								
MSCI Emerging Markets Index	Large-cap and mid-cap	26	85%[b]	1404	1.687	24.54	1. Alibaba—5.77 2. Tencent—4.44 3. Taiwan SC—4.37	1. China—34.28 2. South Korea—11.72 3. Taiwan—11.70
MSCI Emerging Markets IMI	Large-cap, mid-cap, and small-cap	26	99%[b]	3057	0.508	21.97	1. Alibaba—5.17 2. Tencent—3.98 3. Taiwan SC—3.92	1. China—31.81 2. Taiwan—12.61 3. South Korea—12.12
FTSE Emerging Index	Large-cap and mid-cap	24	–	1764	0.809	24.57	1. Alibaba—6.70 2. Tencent—4.99 3. Taiwan SC—4.81	1. China—37.35 2. Taiwan—13.04 3. India—10.33
S&P Emerging BMI	Large-cap, mid-cap, and small-cap	25	–	4127	1.296	19.3	1. Alibaba—5.0 2. Tencent 3. Taiwan SC	1. China—36.4 2. Taiwan—13.3 3. India—11.6

(continued)

Table 6.3 (continued)

Index	Size segments[a]	Number of countries	Coverage of market capitalization	Number of constituents	Median capitalization (USD bn)	Percentage in top 10 (%)	Top 3 stocks (%)[d]	Top 3 countries (%)
STOXX Emerging Markets 1500 Index	Large-cap and mid-cap	21	95%[b]	1500	ca. 1.300	19.20	1. Taiwan CS—4.81 2. Samsung—4.51 3. China CB—1.51	1. India—17.4 2. Taiwan—15.6 3. South Korea—15.2

[a]According to the size (capitalization) methodology of the index provider
[b]Approximate coverage of the free float-adjusted market capitalization in each country
[c]Approximate coverage of the world's investable market capitalization
[d]Alphabet A and C share classes counted together; Taiwan SC—Taiwan Semiconductor, China CB—China Construction Bank
Source Own elaboration based on the factsheets of the indexes

strong case for international diversification for American dividend-oriented investors.

Another opportunity is investing in an ETF that aims to mirror dividend indexes that focus either on capturing high dividend yields or dividend growth,[27] and with exposure to a specific region or country. Portfolios of such indexes gather dividend stocks, i.e., stocks with an above-average dividend yield or that pay increasing (or at least maintaining) dividends.[28] The Vanguard study proves that companies from DMs have most recently been averaging a dividend yield of about 2–4%, depending on the country. But more importantly, yields from these strategies are also about 50% higher, on average, than those available in local broad equity markets. This is largely confirmed by Robeco's research—the average dividend yield of the MSCI World High Dividend Yield Index[29] was 4.0% (ranging from 3% to almost 6% during the crisis). However, the net dividend return contribution (3.5%) to its total return was significantly bigger (almost 80%) than the price return (0.9%) (van Vilet et al. 2018). These data also show that higher yields do not necessarily always translate into higher returns.[30] Consequently, according to the Vanguard study, the highest- and lowest-yielding companies within developed markets—represented by the constituents of the MSCI World Index—achieved very close total returns (income capital plus capital return). The same research also proves that, in the last two decades (1997–2016), the two mentioned approaches to dividend investing[31] generated higher returns,

[27]Generally, there are two methods of dividend investing. The first one, known as high dividend-yielding equities, relies on investing in companies with above-average dividend yields. The second approach, known as dividend growth-oriented equities, assumes investing in companies that have a history of maintaining or increasing their dividends (though they usually tend to yield less than global broad market equities) (Schlanger and Kesidis 2017). In the case of passive investing, the requirements for dividend growth index inclusion (on an example S&P Dow Jones Indices) range—depending on the market/region—from five years (Canada) to even 20 years (USA). According to S&P DJI research, foreign (i.e., outside the USA) dividend growth-oriented stocks generally offer higher yields and higher dividend growth, and they outperform in the long run (Cheng et al. 2019).

[28]It is worth adding that high-dividend stocks have different characteristics compared to low-dividend stocks. Usually, they tend to be more mature firms, with conservative management. Systematically investing in stocks which pay a high dividend is an effective way to reduce volatility, while at the same time enhancing returns.

[29]The MSCI World High Dividend Yield Index is based on the MSCI World Index and includes large-cap and mid-cap stocks across 23 developed markets. The index is designed to reflect the performance of equities in the parent index with higher dividend income and quality characteristics than average dividend yields that are both sustainable and persistent. It also applies quality screens and reviews 12-month past performance to omit stocks with potentially deteriorating fundamentals that could force them to cut or reduce dividends.

[30]More on this in the next section.

[31]High dividend-yielding equities from DMs represented by MSCI World High Dividend Yield Index, and "normal" DMs equities represented by MSCI World Index.

with less volatility, than "normal" investing in developed markets. As a result, it translates into higher risk-adjusted returns (Schlanger and Kesidis 2017).

Another important factor taken into account when assessing the attractiveness of investing in stock markets is company valuations. Of the various fundamental valuation indicators, the ones probably most often applied in practice include classical and most recognized ratios like Price-To-Earnings (P/E) (including Forward P/E (F P/E) and Trailing 12 Months P/E (TTM P/E)), Price-To-Book Value (P/BV), Cyclically Adjusted Shiller-PE (CAPE, Shiller P/E), Price-Cash Flow (P/C), Price-Sales (P/S), and Dividend Yield (DY).[32] An analysis of these ratios is important for investors, as many studies have shown that long-term stock market returns can be predicted from its valuation.

Of the numerous studies regarding regional valuations of stocks, it is worth drawing attention to the comprehensive research conducted by MSCI. They assess valuations using two complementary measures: the aggregate price-to-book value ratio and the aggregate price-to-trailing 12-month earnings ratio. In the case of P/BV, they noticed that EMs have been trading at a discount relative to DMs for most of the last 20 years (December 1998–January 2019), averaging close to 20%.[33] They also found that at the beginning of 2019, the discount was closer to 30%, suggesting that emerging markets had moderately attractive valuations compared to developed markets and relative to the historical relationship between the valuations of the two markets. Likewise, an analysis of the P/E indicator proved that in the last two decades, stocks from DMs have been trading at a premium (even slightly bigger on average than in the case of P/BV) relative to EMs.[34] However, relative valuations of EM stocks at the beginning of 2019 were close to the average level from the period considered (Melas 2019). Examining the relationship between these measures and subsequent performance showed that relative valuations have historically been associated with subsequent performance over long horizons (five years). However, in the short term (one year), the relationship was negative but weak.

Keimling (2016) investigated the fundamentals of developed equity markets that apply various indicators, including the cyclically adjusted price-to-earnings (CAPE) ratio. His empirical research, based on 17 MSCI country

[32]There are many different versions of these indicators, as well as many other ratios, but these issues are not the subject of the book and will not be discussed.

[33]Valuations (P/BV) of stocks from developed markets have fallen relative to emerging markets until 2010 (with the exception of the crisis) but have been systematically growing since then.

[34]P/E ratios of stocks from developed markets (relative to emerging markets) grew suddenly from 1999 to 2001, then fell gradually until 2008, grew again until 2014, and have remained relatively stable in the last few years.

indexes and carried out for 35 years (December 1979–May 2015), demonstrated that the average CAPE ratio for analyzed DMs was 21.0, CAPE adjusted for different payout ratios was 23.8, P/B ratio was 2.0, P/E 21.3, P/C 8.9, and DY 3.2. However, the average ratios for the 17 individual countries varied significantly—e.g., for the CAPE ratio, it ranged from 14.8 to 43.2, with a relative standard deviation of 31.7% across all the countries.[35] He also proved that the CAPE ratio has fairly reliably predicted long-term returns in MSCI DMs country indexes for periods of more than ten years, and also enabled equity market risks to be estimated. Low market valuations were followed by above-average market returns and lower drawdowns, while high market valuations led to lower returns and faced higher market risks.

The latest research of this indicator (as of the end of 2019) revealed that in the case of the US large-caps, the current CAPE ratio of 30.8 was very high in relation to its historical values (96th percentile) and almost twice higher than the historical median (16.2). It was even higher for the US small-caps (over 50). While US stocks were trading at very stretched valuation levels, stocks from other developed markets (e.g., EAFE equities) were not only much cheaper (CAPE below 20), but their current valuations are also lower than historical values (Arnott and Treussard 2020).

The offer of ETFs with exposure to developed markets is extensive and diversified, in particular on the US and European exchanges.[36] It includes funds that mimic the performance of the most recognizable, broad-based capitalization-weighted developed market indexes, as well as ETFs that try to mirror returns of indexes that, in various ways, limit a broad investment spectrum that focuses on companies from only some developed countries or with specific investment characteristics. Due to the huge wealth of DMs ETFs that use a variety of investment strategies and the limited volume of the book, we will focus primarily on the first group of funds and on ETFs that have similar features. We will omit narrow-focused index-tracking DM funds that are oriented on, e.g., capitalization segments (large-caps, mid-caps, or small-caps) and investment style (value, growth, blend). We will not focus on funds that apply alternative methods of stock weighting or replicating, e.g., equally weighted or fundamentally weighted DMs indexes. We will not deal with either smart-beta (strategic-beta) and factor (multi-factor) DM ETFs, nor leveraged, short (inverse), and leveraged short funds.[37] In-depth information

[35] A similar degree of differentiation between countries occurred in other indicators.

[36] Assets of equity exchange-traded products with exposure to broad DMs amounted to USD 707 billion at the end of 2019, which accounted for 14.5% of total assets invested globally in equity ETPs (BlackRock 2020).

[37] International sector funds and thematic international equity ETFs, including those with regional exposure, will be described in Chapter 8.

on these kinds of funds is available in other books, papers, and brochures on ETFs,[38] while recommended sources of current data and their offer are available from professional financial services that deliver business and financial data, news, and insight (e.g., Bloomberg, Refinitiv) or Web sites that contain ETF search engines and screeners—e.g., etf.com, etfdb.com (US ETFs), and justetf.com (European ETFs).

Taking into account countries, sectors, and individual holdings, the most diversified ETFs are those that replicate broad-based DM indexes. Selected popular benchmarks of this type that are managed by major index providers are presented in Table 6.3. Their characteristics are largely similar to global indexes, as their composition largely overlaps. They apply market capitalization-weighted methodology (free-float adjusted) and typically represent the performance of large-cap and mid-cap companies (sometimes also small-caps). They give extensive coverage of the investable developed markets and a huge number of constituents (usually a few thousand). Though their portfolios include stocks from over 20 developed markets, US companies dominate within—their total weight exceeds slightly 60%.[39] No other country exceeds 10%; only two (Japan and UK) exceed 5%. The total weight of the ten smallest countries usually does not surpass 3% (e.g., in the S&P Developed BMI, it is 2.5%). In terms of sectors, these indexes are—as with the global indexes—well diversified. The weight of the largest sector does not exceed 20%, and the total weight of the three largest sectors (information technology, financials, and health care[40]) varies between 40 and 50% (e.g., 46.1% in the MSCI World Index). There is also no problem of the excessive concentration of stocks in these indexes. The weights of only two (Apple and Microsoft) exceeds 2%, and the total weight of the ten largest companies ranges between 11 and 14% (cf. Table 6.3).[41]

The most popular broad-based developed equity market index applied by ETF issuers is probably the MSCI World Index,[42] as evidenced by the fact

[38]Information on these sources is also available in the references at the end of Chapters 3–8.

[39]All data as of the end of 2019.

[40]Sector definitions in accordance with the GICS classification, applied by the S&P Dow Jones Indices and MSCI.

[41]Various aspects related to country, sectoral, and company concentration of equity indexes are outlined in detail in Chapter 5.

[42]The MSCI World Index was the first international performance benchmark designed to track the world's developed markets. It was created in 1968 by Capital International, the Swiss subsidiary of the Capital Group (base date is January 1, 1970). The rights to the index were acquired by Morgan Stanley in 1986 (Shilling 2018).

that it is the most often used by European ETF providers[43] (e.g., BlackRock [iShares], Deutsche Bank [X-trackers], Lyxor [Lyxor and ComStage], Amundi, UBS, Invesco, SSGA [SPDR], HSBC, and Deka), but also some major US (e.g., BlackRock) and APAC (e.g., Samsung) asset managers.[44] The FTSE Developed Index is used slightly less often, but it is a benchmark in the two largest developed markets ETFs in the world managed by Vanguard (cf. Table 6.4).

Similar investment characteristics are offered by quite a large group of ETFs that exclude a specific country or group of countries from the portfolio. They are usually addressed to investors from a given country or to those who want to bypass—for various reasons—a specific country or group of countries. However, they are usually characterized by a lower level of diversification due to the slightly limited geographical exposure. Investors have at their disposal ETFs excluding:

- US stocks (e.g., tracking the FTSE Developed All Cap ex-US Index, the FTSE Developed ex-US Index, the MSCI World ex USA IMI Index, the S&P Developed Ex-U.S. BMI),
- Japanese equities (e.g., replicating the MSCI Kokusai Index[45]),
- Australian stocks (e.g., mirroring MSCI World ex Australia Index, the S&P Developed Ex-Australia LargeMidCap Index),
- North American equities (e.g., tracking the FTSE Developed All Cap ex North America Hedged to CAD Index),
- stocks from European countries that belong to the European Monetary Union (EMU), i.e., countries using the euro currency (e.g., replicating the MSCI World ex EMU Index),
- European stocks (e.g., mirroring the MSCI World ex Europe Index).

Some ETFs are targeted to specific groups of countries within the DM—e.g., EAFE stocks.[46]

Finally, investors seeking to mitigate currency risk while investing in developed markets can invest in currency-hedged ETFs. They have the possibility

[43]According to PwC research (2019), the MSCI World Index was an underlying index in 123 EU-domiciled ETFs with EUR 73.5bn in assets as of the end of June 2019.

[44]It should be remembered that some terms used in the names of equity indexes and, consequently, in ETFs offered (mainly on the US market) can be misleading, as they suggest global investing. This applies to term "world," which refers only to developed markets, and the term "international," which refers to developed markets ex-USA.

[45]MSCI Kokusai Index (also known as the MSCI World ex Japan Index) captures large-cap and mid-cap representation across developed markets excluding Japan.

[46]They will be described later in this chapter.

Table 6.4 Largest developed markets equity ETFs in the world

Fund (ticker)	Index	Exchange	Assets (USD bn)	Expense ratio (%)
Vanguard FTSE Developed Markets ETF (VEA US)	FTSE Developed All Cap ex US Index	NYSE Arca	81.087	0.05
iShares Core MSCI World UCITS ETF (SWDA LN)	MSCI World Index	London Stock Exchange[a]	25.423	0.20
Schwab International Equity ETF (SCHW US)	FTSE Developed ex US Index	NYSE Arca	20.968	0.06
Sygnia Itrix MSCI World Index ETF (SYGWD SJ)	MSCI World Index	Johannesburg Stock Exchange	8.971	0.68
Xtrackers MSCI World UCITS ETF (XDWD LN)	MSCI World Index	London Stock Exchange[a]	6.499	0.19
iShares MSCI World UCITS ETF (IWRD LN)	MSCI World Index	London Stock Exchange[a]	5.781	0.50
iShares International Select Dividend ETF (IDV US)	Dow Jones EPAC Select Dividend Index	Cboe BZX	5.193	0.49
iShares Edge MSCI World Minimum Volatility UCITS ETF (MVOL LN)	MSCI World Minimum Volatility Index	London Stock Exchange[a]	4.999	0.30
Schwab Fundamental International Large Company Index ETF	Russell RAFI Developed ex US Large Company Index	NYSE Arca	4.881	0.25

(continued)

Table 6.4 (continued)

Fund (ticker)	Index	Exchange	Assets (USD bn)	Expense ratio (%)
Lyxor MSCI World UCITS ETF (WLD FP)	MSCI World Index	Euronext Paris[a]	4.342	0.30

[a]Primary exchange
Note As of 19 February 2020. Sector and thematic ETFs are excluded
Source Bloomberg

of investing in funds hedged to a single currency (mainly to the USD, e.g., a fund that tracks the FTSE Developed ex North America 50% Hedged to the USD Index), or to multiple currencies (e.g., a fund that replicates the WisdomTree Dynamic Currency Hedged International Equity Index[47]). Furthermore, Cboe Options Exchange (CBOE) trades options on some equity ETFs with DM exposure.

The ten largest equity ETFs in terms of AUM investing in developed markets are presented in Table 6.4.

6.3.2 Emerging Markets

Emerging markets[48] are an increasingly essential part of the global economy and financial markets. However, in the investing world, they are typically defined as countries whose level of economic and financial (including capital market) development has not yet reached the level of developed markets. It refers to these countries' economic conditions, capital market maturity, legal regulations concerning particularly financial operations, and openness to foreign investments. Additionally, governmental institutions in emerging markets are generally considered to be weaker and less stable than those of developed countries. Likewise, corporate governance standards in most developing countries are not as robust as they are in the developed world. Thus, investing in emerging markets generally involves a higher level of risk than investing in developed ones.

[47]This index is designed to remove from index performance the impact of changes to the value of foreign currencies relative to the US dollar with a hedge ratio ranging from 0 to 100% on a monthly basis.

[48]The term "emerging markets" was coined by Antoine van Agtmael in 1981 when he was working for the International Finance Corporation (IFC), a division of the World Bank. This term was to more positively describe countries previously referred to as "third world," suggesting their progress, uplift, and dynamism.

On the other hand, factors such as favorable demographics, urbanization, and a rapidly growing middle (consumer) class—at least in some emerging countries—may provide better investment opportunities going forward than in developed countries. It is also worth emphasizing that EMs have made great strides in many areas of the economy in the past few decades, which has not always been noticed or sufficiently appreciated by investors. As a result, the term "emerging" does not seem to be the right nomenclature for most of these markets today.

Many of these countries have drawn lessons from past crises and have carried out ambitious and often difficult reforms, the positive effects of which are already visible or will be noticeable in the future. First, numerous EMs have made policy improvements that should contribute to increased resilience during times of stress, e.g., they significantly increased their currency reserves and abandoned currency pegs to the US dollar, making them less vulnerable to speculation or a strengthening of the USD. Second, EM economies have evolved and have become more diversified in the last two decades. They are already not merely commodity and low-cost product exporters who are reliant on DMs for growth. Their new drivers of economic expansion are the consumption and technology sector (especially in China). Third, in some ways, EMs' weaknesses have become their strengths. EM companies are leapfrogging established models in developed markets through innovation and technology, e.g., in areas such as e-commerce, digital payments, mobile banking, and electric vehicles (they decisively have overtaken the USA and Japan in terms of patent applications) (Sekhon et al. 2019). Taking all this into account, EMs may potentially generate higher returns—especially in the long run—both in absolute and risk-adjusted terms.

Depending on the index provider, the list of emerging markets encompasses between 21 and 26 countries, as presented in Table 6.5. Most of them—about half—are from the EMEA region, about one-third come from the Asia-Pacific region, and the rest are from Latin America. This large group of countries is also highly differentiated, both in terms of economic parameters and financial market indicators. For example, GDP ranges between USD 13.608tn (China) and USD 141bn (Kuwait), and market capitalization of listed domestic companies ranges from USD 29bn (Hungary) to USD 6.235tn (China).[49]

Although the economic fundamentals of emerging countries are still lagging developed countries, their position has considerably improved in recent decades. Over the period 1980–2018, their share in global GDP

[49]World Bank data as of 2018.

Table 6.5 List of emerging countries (markets) according to the S&P Dow Jones Indices, the FTSE Russell, MSCI, STOXX, and Solactive country (market) classifications

Country	S&P Dow Jones Indices	FTSE Russell	MSCI	STOXX	Solactive
Americas					
Argentina			•		•
Brazil	•	• (A)	•	•	•
Chile	•	• (S)	•	•	•
Colombia	•	• (S)	•	•	•
Mexico	•	• (A)	•	•	•
Peru	•	• (S)	•		•
EMEA					
Czech Republic	•	• (A)	•	•	•
Egypt	•	• (S)	•	•	•
Greece	•	• (A)	•	•	•
Hungary	•	• (A)	•	•	•
Kuwait	•	• (S)			•
Poland	•		•		
Qatar	•	• (S)	•		•
Russia	•	• (S)	•	•	•
Saudi Arabia	•	• (S)	•		•
South Africa	•	• (A)	•	•	•
Turkey	•	• (A)	•	•	•
United Arab Emirates	•	• (S)	•		•
Asia-Pacific					
China	•	• (S)	•	•	•
India	•	• (S)	•	•	•
Indonesia	•	• (S)	•	•	•
South Korea			•	•	•
Malaysia	•	• (A)	•	•	•
Pakistan	•	• (S)	•	•	•
Philippines	•	• (S)	•	•	•
Taiwan	•	• (A)	•	•	•
Thailand	•	• (A)	•	•	•
Vietnam				•	

Note (A)—Advanced Emerging, (S)—Secondary Emerging
Source Own elaboration based on the index providers' country (market) classifications

measured at market exchange rates almost doubled from 18 to 35%. Likewise, their share in world PPP increased from about 25 to 49%. Despite the rapid economic growth of many (though not all) EMs, their growing position in the world's economy has not yet been adequately reflected in the global stock market. The share of these countries in the world investable free-float market capitalization (i.e., their weight in the capitalization of global equity indexes) amounts to only 12%,[50] i.e., is at the level three times lower than their share in GDP (Dimson et al. 2019). It is due to two factors. Firstly, market accessibility and openness are still weaker for EMs than for DMs (e.g., China A-shares are only partially included in the benchmarks). Secondly, EM equities underperformed DM equities during the 2010s (as will be presented later), due to the slower expansion of equity valuations (MSCI 2019).

Since emerging markets differ enormously in terms of, e.g., economic potential (including competitiveness and innovation of economies), population size and demographic structure, society's affluence, the abundance of natural resources, the consumption of commodities, the sectoral structure of the economy, and the state of public finances (to name but a few),[51] the investment opportunities that emerging countries offer to investors are wide, but also very diverse. This is confirmed by data regarding the enormous differences in returns between countries—much larger than in developed markets. Among EMs, over the last 20 years, differences between the best and worst performers (countries) range from 38.9 percentage points (pp) in 2013 to 201.2 pp (!) in 2002 (Table 6.6). In fact, this difference exceeded 100 pp in six years, and on average, it was 93.0 pp.[52] There are also examples of unpredictability in short-term equity returns in emerging markets. For example, after posting the highest return in 2003, Thailand had the lowest return in 2004. Morocco, after being the best-performing country in 2008, experienced the worst result in 2009. Conversely, Pakistan had the lowest return among EMs in 2001, followed by the highest return in 2002. Additionally, good results rarely persisted for long. Only once did it happen that a country which had the highest return in a given year was among the three countries with the best results in the following year (Colombia 2004–2005).

Thus, broad country diversification is essential in investing, particularly in emerging markets. However, according to many studies, the importance of country effects on diversification potential across EMs has declined over the last few decades. Despite the longer-term attenuation of country effects,

---

[50] Interestingly, share of EM countries in total equity market capitalization is more than 10 pp higher than share in free-float market capitalization—according to MSCI (2019) it amounted 23.4% as of end of February 2019.

[51] It is worth noting that for some of these parameters, emerging markets—as a whole—dominate the world. For example, they represent 68% of the world's population. Additionally, the seven largest emerging markets (Brazil, China, India, Indonesia, Mexico, Russia, and Turkey) accounted for 92% of the increase in metals consumption, 67% of the increase in energy consumption, and 39% of the increase in global food consumption over the past two decades (Baffes et al. 2018).

[52] Interestingly, the average difference in the 2010s (63.7 pp) was almost half smaller than in the 2000s (122.2 pp). All data refer to differences in annual returns (in USD) between best and worst country equity index across emerging markets in the period 2000–2019.

Table 6.6 Annual returns (in USD) of the 5 best and 5 worst performing emerging equity markets, ranked in order of performance (%)

Rank	2000	2001	2002	2003	2004	2005	2006	2007	2008	2009	2010	2011	2012	2013	2014	2015	2016	2017	2018	2019
Top 5 performing single-country indexes																				
1	IL	RU	PK	TH	CO	EG	CN	PE	MA	BR	TH	ID	TR	TW	EG	HU	BR	PL	QA	RU
	24.75	53.17	150.53	143.51	132.44	161.59	82.87	94.37	−11.08	128.06	55.71	6.00	64.21	9.06	29.33	36.31	66.24	54.72	29.84	50.91
2	VE	KR	CZ	TR	EG	CO	ID	BR	CO	IN	PE	MY	EG	EG	ID	RU	PE	CN	PE	GR
	0.78	45.97	43.66	125.30	126.23	107.15	73.78	79.56	−25.10	126.24	53.32	0.12	47.10	8.18	26.59	4.21	55.61	54.07	1.56	43.17
3	CZ	CO	ID	BR	HU	JO	MA	TR	IL	RU	CL	PH	PH	MY	PH	IN	RU	KR	BR	EG
	0.71	37.07	41.87	114.41	91.49	73.64	67.98	74.09	−29.26	104.22	44.16	−0.89	46.44	7.68	25.59	−6.12	54.82	47.30	−0.49	41.75
4	PL	JO	HU	AR	CZ	RU	AR	IN	CL	IN	CO	TH	PL	KR	IN	KR	HU	CL	RU	TW
	−4.59	29.02	30.32	100.35	85.62	73.12	67.31	73.11	−35.79	102.81	43.41	−2.72	39.24	3.94	23.87	−6.66	35.37	42.23	−0.70	36.37
5	PK	MX	PE	PE	JO	PK	PE	CN	ZA	TR	MY	CO	CO	CN	TR	PH	TH	HU	CZ	CO
	−13.26	15.93	29.11	96.16	61.13	63.81	62.11	66.24	−37.89	97.51	37.01	−5.02	35.89	3.64	18.71	−6.80	26.61	39.95	−4.45	30.84
Bottom 5 performing single-country indexes																				
1	ID	PK	AR	MY	TH	VE	JO	AR	PK	MA	HU	EG	MA	PE	RU	GR	GR	PK[a]	TR	AR[a]
	−63.04	−35.00	−50.70	26.61	−1.24	−24.07	−30.88	−4.02	−74.18	−5.31	−9.58	−46.86	−11.98	−29.85	−46.27	−61.33	−12.13	−24.44	−41.40	−20.93
2	TH	TR	TR	HU	CN	MY	TR	TW	RU	CZ	CZ	IN	BR	TR	GR	CO	EG	QA	GR	CL
	−56.70	−33.73	−35.83	32.03	1.89	2.29	−7.21	8.38	−73.88	26.52	−2.53	−37.17	0.05	−26.76	−39.96	−41.80	−11.53	−11.51	−36.84	−16.94
3	KR	IL	IL	MX	PE	TW	IL	MX	IN	EG	CN	TR	CZ	ID	HU	BR	MX	AE	PK	PL
	−50.35	−32.28	−31.28	32.81	3.02	6.38	−5.31	12.15	−64.63	39.74	4.63	−35.41	2.47	−23.48	−27.44	−41.37	−9.16	2.93	−34.79	−5.87
4	TR	PL	BR	KR	RU	TH	PK	CO	TR	PL	BR	HU	ID	CL	CO	TR	TR	EG	ZA	MY
	−46.16	−28.69	−30.65	35.02	5.46	8.72	3.04	14.99	62.29	41.50	6.54	−33.65	4.65	−21.98	−19.81	−31.87	−8.46	5.13	−24.76	−2.00
5	TW	CN	PH	PL	TW	MA	TH	HU	HU	MY	EG	PL	CL	CO	PL	PE	PH	RU	KR	QA
	−45.35	−26.04	−29.46	35.12	8.99	13.44	11.11	16.80	−61.53	52.06	12.42	−30.12	7.77	−21.14	−14.21	−31.66	−6.58	5.20	−20.94	−0.99

Note Designations of country names according to the ISO country codes

[a]Return numbers represent the entire year, even if a country entered mid-year

Source Lazard Asset Management (2020b)

they are still considerably higher, on average, compared with developed markets—the average value of emerging market country effect volatility is approximately twice as large as the value for developed markets (NBIM 2019).[53]

A strong case for investing in emerging markets—as a group of countries—is their better performance than developed markets in the last three decades, most of the time.[54] As presented earlier (cf. subchapter about developed markets), annualized returns for the January 1988–February 2019 period were 2.9 pp higher for EMs (MSCI 2019). Emerging markets outperformed DMs particularly in the late 1980s and early 1990s (December 1987–September 1994) and 2000s (January 1999–September 2010), as for most of this period they offered faster economic growth driven by globalization (increasing cross-border trade), commodity supercycles, and the rise of global supply chains.

However, EM stocks were mostly laggards over the past decade. Annualized total returns of EM stocks have been just over 1% (or 4% including dividends); given the annual returns, they underperformed DMs in six out of the last ten years (2011, 2013–2015, 2018–2019).[55] This was mainly a consequence of the bull market in the USA (as the most important DM market)—the MSCI EM Index underperformed the S&P 500 by 9.8 pp on an average annual basis in the 2010s (11.0% vs. 1.2% CAGR, respectively). The most important factors that contributed to poorer performance were slowed economic growth (especially in Russia, Brazil, and South Africa) and the collapse in commodities prices of 2014–2015. EMs did not recover after the global financial crisis mainly due to stagnation in total factor productivity and de-globalization pressures (no further trade integration) (Leverenz 2020). Moreover, the underperformance of EM equities in USD terms was partly explained by currency effects (EMs' currencies underperformed both USD and other DMs' currencies).

Additionally, a thorough analysis points out that the different cyclical behavior of EMs versus DMs during the past two decades provides evidence for the added value that EM stocks have offered investors for diversifying their global investments. EM equity returns were clearly more cyclical across

---

[53] Additionally, as we showed earlier, the effectiveness of diversification when investing in emerging markets is potentially higher, as average pairwise country correlations within EMs are distinctly lower than in DMs.

[54] However, this is not the case over a much longer period. Research carried out by Dimson et al. (2019) demonstrated that emerging markets have underperformed developed markets since 1900—the annualized return from a 119-year investment in EMs was 1 pp lower than in DMs (7.2% vs. 8.2%).

[55] All analyses are based on the MSCI World and MSCI Emerging Markets indexes' returns.

the macroeconomic cycle than DM returns. EM countries exhibited higher equity risk premia than DMs, compensating investors for higher levels of risk in terms of business cyclicality and market price volatility. At the same time, however, they demonstrated a higher level of dispersion in this respect (MSCI 2019).

Investment risk is a particularly serious challenge for investors in emerging markets, which is confirmed by data from the last 30 years. The values of all risk measures were significantly bigger for EMs than DMs: volatility (22.5 vs. 14.6), Value-at-Risk at 99% (−15.7 vs. −10.6), Conditional Value-at-Risk at 99% (−22.5 vs. −13.8%), and drawdown (−61.4% vs. −53.7%). Despite the higher level of risk, emerging markets achieved better results in returns on a risk-adjusted basis measured by the Sharpe ratio (0.29 vs. 0.32) (MSCI 2019).

The analysis of emerging markets' investment potential must not ignore dividends, as they are a very important component of stock returns and deliver a stable positive contribution to equity performance.[56] EM stocks have demonstrated strong dividend growth over the past ten years. The total value of dividends has almost exactly doubled in USD terms during this period and amounted to almost USD 140bn in 2019, which accounted for 11% of global paid dividends. The three largest markets in this respect were China (29% of total EMs dividends), Russia (20%), and India (13%) (Janus Henderson Investors 2020).

Over the last decade, EM dividend payments have totaled USD 1.14tn. However, there was considerable volatility in dividend values during this time[57] and large divergences in dividend policies across emerging markets. This is because dividends on EMs are paid mainly by companies from cyclically sensitive industries like mining and oil (thus, their dividends tend to have high variability), and EM firms tend to pay special, one-off payouts that are separate from their regular dividend cycle. Income from dividend stocks in emerging markets decreases, especially in turbulent times when firms are not so willing to share profits with investors or may not generate any profits at all. During financial crises, many companies cut their dividends or even stop

[56]Basic information on the strategy of investing in dividend companies was described in the previous section.

[57]According to Janus Henderson data, the total value of dividends in emerging markets in the 2010s ranged from USD 87bn in 2010 to USD 140bn in 2019 (in percentage terms—from 8.6% of total dividends in 2016 to 14.0% in 2013).

payouts altogether. This is not a convenient situation for passive, income-oriented investors who value predictability and progressive dividend policies that deliver steady dividend growth over time.[58]

Bearing in mind the volatility in the value of EM dividends paid, it should be noted that in the long run, it is not only their value that increases but so, too, does the number of companies paying them. The number of EM companies paying dividends has doubled over the past 20 years (1998–2017)—from just over 40% to over 80% (Su 2018). Increasingly, they can also boast relatively high dividend yields—in 2019 (as of August 31), there were more EM stocks (518) with dividend yield over 3% than DM (ex-US) stocks (498) (Lovelace and Polak 2019). In the last 25 years (December 1994–February 2019), the average dividend yield in emerging markets was 2.56%, i.e., it was higher than in developed markets in North America (1.92%) and the Pacific (2.15%), but lower than the EMEA region (3.14%). In the last decade (December 2008–February 2019), the average dividend yield in EMs (2.73%) was higher than in North America 2.18%, but lower than in the Pacific (2.85%) and EMEA (3.68%) (MSCI 2019).

Aggregate valuations of emerging equity markets have generally improved over the past two decades and have remained at a relatively attractive level compared to developed markets for several years. In the case of the aggregate price-to-trailing 12-month earnings ratio, emerging equities have been trading at slightly about 20% discount relative to developed equities (i.e., TTM P/E was lower in EMs than in DMs), although historically there have been significant fluctuations in this respect. Discounts even reached more than 40% between 2001 and 2003, but it turned into a premium in 1999 and again at the turn of 2007 and 2008. Similarly, the aggregate price-to-book value ratio for emerging stocks has been trading at a discount (20% on average) relative to developed stocks, i.e., the P/BV ratio for EMs was lower than for DMs. For this indicator, historical value fluctuations were even greater—the discount amounted to more than 50% at the turn of the new millennium, but it turned into a premium in 2007–2011 (Melas 2019). At the beginning of 2019, relative valuations of EM equities were close to the average level from the last 20 years, indicating that emerging markets have quite attractive valuations compared to developed markets.

[58]The golden rule in investing in dividend stocks is to systematically monitor them and apply multiple screens to avoid the dividend trap. Unfortunately, often a rise in a share's yield is a function of its falling price. That may be a sign that a company is in danger of cutting its payouts, or that it is unlikely to grow its payouts further from their already high levels. The investor's goal should, therefore, be to identify companies trading at low valuations which have the ability to deliver not only solid yield today, but which also have underlying growth and stability in cash flows to grow that income into the future.

Similar conclusions can be drawn by analyzing historical values of the cyclically adjusted price-to-earnings (CAPE) ratio developed by Robert Shiller (thus also known as the Shiller P/E ratio). Emerging market equities have been trading at a CAPE ratio of 13.4 (the 28th percentile of historical values), below both historical median (15.4) and fair value (14.0, at the 37th percentile) at the end of 2019, which implies that EM stocks are relatively cheap (Arnott and Treussard 2020).

Other fundamental indicators have also improved since the end of the 1990s and currently look favorable. For example, profitability—as measured by return on equity (RoE)—has been growing significantly recently, reaching levels (12–13%) close to those of developed markets. Interestingly, emerging markets showed the second-highest level of profitability during the 2010s. Additionally, dispersion in profitability levels in EMs (measured as the cross-sectional standard deviation of RoE) declined noticeably during the last two decades (except for 2008–2009) and is lower than in the Americas and EMEA (MSCI 2019).

Considering this and the fact that EM valuations are considerably lower than those for DMs, it should translate into improved performance in the future. Unfortunately for EM investors, this has not been the case in the last few years. Although EM equities have been attractively valued for some time now, they have continued to underperform compared to DM equities. This can be explained by the fact that investors in EMs still exhibiting significant risk aversion after the global financial crisis. However, valuations matter greatly in the long term, and taking such a perspective, it can be assumed that purchasing EM stocks at current valuation levels seems like a good investment idea.

There are numerous ETFs with exposure to emerging markets equities listed mainly on stock exchanges in the USA and Europe.[59] The spectrum of these funds is very diverse. The most popular are those that aim to mimic the performance of the most recognized, broad EM benchmarks presented in Table 6.3, particularly the MSCI Emerging Markets Index.[60] These funds track broad-based indexes that encompass a relatively large number of stocks (even a few thousand) from over 20 emerging markets, mainly large-caps

[59]Assets of equity exchange-traded products with exposure to broad emerging markets equaled USD 251 billion at the end of 2019, which accounted for nearly 5.15% of total assets invested globally in equity ETPs (BlackRock 2020).

[60]Melas (2019) presents detailed information on this index and its history.

and mid-caps (but rarely small-caps).[61] Replicated indexes use the free float-adjusted market capitalization weighting approach. Their portfolios are not so country-concentrated as developed indexes, although one can observe the increasing dominance of Chinese companies (currently over 30%).[62] The top three countries (usually China, Taiwan, and either South Korea or India) account for about 55–60% of total market capitalization (except for the STOXX EM 1500 Index, where it is below 50%). The importance of countries with the smallest share in the indexes is negligible—there are 12 countries with a weight under 1% (5.9% in total) in the S&P Emerging BMI, and 11 countries with a weight below 1% (4.9% in total) in the FTSE Emerging Index.[63] Broad EM equity indexes are also quite well diversified sectorally, although to a slightly smaller extent than in the case of developed countries. The weight of the largest sector equals about 25%, and the total weight of the three largest sectors (financials, information technology, and consumer discretionary) ranges from 50 to 55% (e.g., 54.1% in the MSCI EM Index[64]).[65] The relatively highest degree of portfolio concentration refers to individual holdings. Although these indexes capture a few hundred or over a thousand (and some even more) constituents, the total weight of the three largest stocks (usually Alibaba, Tencent, and Taiwan Semiconductor) is about 15%. The top ten firms account for even more than 20% of total index capitalization, i.e., more than any individual country except for China (cf. Table 6.3). The rising portfolio concentration of EM indexes was largely due to the emergence of BAT stocks (Baidu, Alibaba, Tencent), i.e., Chinese mega-caps. They significantly increased the investment risk of the whole EM indexes, also because of significantly increasing pairwise return correlations

[61] Many critics argue that broad equity EM indexes are structurally biased toward larger markets and larger companies, and thus investors miss out on some of the best investment opportunities in this asset class which are often in smaller countries and small-caps (Stevenson and Tuckwell 2019). More information on investment advantages offered by the international small-caps segment can be found in, e.g., Orzano and Welling (2017), Brzenk and Du (2019) and Bender et al. (2012).

[62] The weight of Chinese equities listed in mainland China and Hong Kong will grow to over 40% of the MSCI Emerging Markets Index, when A shares will be included at full weight.

[63] There are EM equity indexes that apply restrictions to weights of countries. An example is the MSCI Emerging Markets Equal Country Weighted Index that includes the same constituents as its parent index (MSCI EM Index) but applies an equal country weighting at each semi-annual index review date.

[64] All data as of end of 2019.

[65] One of the MSCI Emerging Markets Index variants provides equal weights for all sectors. The MSCI Emerging Markets Equal Sector Weighted Index includes the same constituents as its parent index but applies an equal sector weighting across the GICS sectors at each semi-annual index review date.

(over 0.5) and high valuations (e.g., the relative P/B of BAT stocks was 3–4 times higher than all stocks in the MSCI China Index[66]) (MSCI 2019).

The most popular broad-based EM equity index among ETF issuers is undoubtedly the MSCI Emerging Markets Index.[67] It is mainly used by asset management companies in the EMEA region (e.g., Amundi, BlackRock (iShares), Deutsche Bank (X-trackers), Lyxor (Lyxor and ComStage), Invesco, UBS, SSGA (SPDR), HSBC, Deka, and Satrix). Less commonly, ETFs based on this benchmark are offered by entities from North America (e.g., BlackRock (iShares), BMO)[68] and Asia (e.g., Nikko, Next Funds, Samsung, Hanwha). The performance of the FTSE Emerging Markets All Cap China A Inclusion Index is tracked by the largest regional equity ETF, the Vanguard FTSE Emerging Markets ETF (cf. Table 6.7). The FTSE Emerging Index is also used, e.g., by Charles Schwab and Invesco (in the USA) and Vanguard (in the European market). The S&P Emerging BMI and S&P Emerging LargeMidCap Index are replicated by SPDR ETFs.

There is also a fairly large scope of emerging markets equity ETFs with narrower geographical exposure. The vast majority of them focus on stocks from a specific geographical region or group of countries (they will be described in further subchapters). Only a few invest in broad equity EMs excluding a single country—such products are aimed mainly at investors from a given country who only want to get exposure to other emerging markets.[69] These funds are usually used when we invest in this market in a different way and are treated as "satellites" when a "core-satellite" strategy is applied. It is usually about the largest equity markets that have the widest coverage of investment funds, regardless of whether they are actively or passively managed. The most recognizable example of this approach is a fund that excludes Chinese stocks while tracking the MSCI Emerging Markets ex China Index. Some ETF providers also offer broad equity EM funds that exclude group of stocks with specific characteristics. An interesting example of this approach is a fund that mimics the WisdomTree Emerging Markets

---

[66]Data as of the beginning of 2019.

[67]This does not only apply to ETF sponsors, but also to other financial products providers. According to MSCI data over USD 1.8 trillion in AUM was benchmarked globally to the MSCI Emerging Markets Index suite as of June 30, 2018 (MSCI 2018). In turn in Europe, MSCI Emerging Markets Index was an underlying benchmark in 46 ETFs with EUR 31.4bn in assets (giving way only to S&P 500, MSCI World, Euro Stoxx 50 and STOXX Europe 50 indexes) as of end June 2019 (PwC 2019).

[68]An untypical EM equity listed in the USA is Innovator MSCI Emerging Markets Power Buffer ETF. It aims to track the price return of the MSCI Emerging Markets Index, up to a predetermined cap, while buffering investors against the first 15% of losses over the outcome period.

[69]Sometimes it is dictated by the desire to exclude a particular country from the investment spectrum, when we are convinced that the economic and investment prospects of this country are significantly worse than other countries.

Table 6.7 Largest emerging markets equity ETFs in the world

Fund (ticker)	Index	Exchange	Assets (USD bn)	Expense ratio (%)
Vanguard FTSE Emerging Markets ETF (VWO US)	FTSE Emerging Markets All Cap China A Inclusion Index	NYSE Arca	65.890	0.12
iShares Core MSCI Emerging Markets ETF (IEMG US)	MSCI Emerging Markets Investable Market Index	NYSE Arca	61.103	0.14
iShares MSCI Emerging Markets ETF (EEM US)	MSCI Emerging Markets Index	NYSE Arca	29.169	0.67
iShares Core MSCI EM IMI UCITS ETF (EMIM LN)	MSCI Emerging Markets Investable Market Index	London Stock Exchange[a]	15.426	0.18
Schwab Emerging Markets ETF (SCHE US)	FTSE Emerging Index	NYSE Arca	6.694	0.13
UBS ETF (LU) MSCI Emerging Markets UCITS ETF (EMMUSA SW)	MSCI Emerging Markets Index	SIX Swiss Exchange[a]	6.374	0.225
Amundi MSCI Emerging Markets UCITS ETF (AEEM FP)	MSCI Emerging Markets Index	Euronext Paris[a]	5.775	0.20

(continued)

Table 6.7 (continued)

Fund (ticker)	Index	Exchange	Assets (USD bn)	Expense ratio (%)
iShares Edge MSCI Min Vol Emerging Markets ETF	MSCI Emerging Markets Minimum Volatility Index	Cboe BZX	5.327	0.25
Amundi Index MSCI Emerging Markets UCITS ETF DR	MSCI Emerging Markets Index	Euronext Paris[a]	4.435	0.20
SPDR Portfolio Emerging Markets ETF (SPEM US)	S&P Emerging BMI Index	NYSE Arca	3.822	0.11

[a]Primary exchange
Note As of 19 February 2020. Sector and thematic ETFs are excluded
Source Bloomberg

ex-State-Owned Enterprises Index, which measures the performance of EM stocks that are not state-owned enterprises.[70]

Broad-based equity ETFs do not exhaust investment opportunities in emerging markets. There are many funds listed on stock exchanges, mainly in the USA and Europe, that specialize in emerging markets which simultaneously implement a specific investment strategy. Among them are ETFs that focus on, for example, large-caps, mid-caps, or small-caps, which invest in value or growth stocks, which capture stocks from a given sector, or which represent a specific investment theme.[71] Additionally, there are smart-beta and factor (multi-factor) ETFs, leveraged, short (inverse), and leveraged short funds and ETFs that apply alternative methods of weighting (e.g., equal-weighted[72]). Given the huge number of investment strategies and the limited size of this book, we will not describe these products. Comprehensive information about them is available in various sources, including books, articles, brochures (also referenced in our book), as well as through Web sites

[70]State-owned enterprises are defined as government ownership of more than 20% of a company's outstanding shares.

[71]One of the most interesting is Freedom 100 Emerging Markets ETF that seeks to invest in countries that support life, liberty, and property rights (its methodology results in an emerging market ETF that's vastly different under the hood from competing funds).

[72]For example, the MSCI Emerging Markets (EM) Equal Weighted Index in which all constituents are weighted equally, effectively removing the influence of each constituent's current price.

containing ETF search engines and screeners and via professional companies that provide data and financial insights.

Investing in emerging markets is usually associated with a much higher level of currency risk than in developed markets, as the currencies of these countries are generally very volatile. The antidote may be to invest in funds that are hedged against currency risk. Although they have shown their worth many times, especially during heightened currency variability, interest in them is relatively small. For US investors, such products are offered by, e.g., BlackRock (iShares fund that tracks the MSCI Emerging Markets 100% USD Hedged Index), Deutsche Bank (Xtrackers fund that replicates the MSCI EM US Dollar Hedged Index), and Northern Trust (FlexShares fund that mirrors the Morningstar Emerging Markets Factor Tilt Hedged Index). An interesting proposition for sophisticated investors may also be options on ETFs. CBOE has the largest offer in this respect, offering options on some broad EM ETFs (e.g., the iShares MSCI Emerging Markets ETF and the Invesco BLDRS Emerging Markets 50 ADR Index Fund).

The ten largest equity ETFs in terms of AUM that invest in emerging markets are presented in Table 6.7.

6.3.3 Frontier and Standalone Markets

Although frontier markets (FMs)[73] represent a significant part of the global population (16%) and occupy a meaningful part of the planet's landmass (12%) (Redman and Sai 2016), they constitute the smallest segment of the global equity market in terms of market capitalization (about 0.6% depending on the index provider). They include developing countries with commonly high rates of economic growth, which encourages investors who are looking for global opportunities to diversify their portfolios. However, their economies are often at an early stage of development, cyclically sensible, and often dependent on a single industry. Additionally, frontier and standalone equity markets are small, relatively illiquid, hard to access, and not transparent enough. Mainly, however, they are usually perceived as extremely risky, although they have historically been less volatile than emerging markets. Even though they offer meaningful diversification opportunities, most investors—especially individual ones—omit them in their portfolios. Sometimes this decision is unintentional, as many investors are

[73]The term "frontier markets" was first introduced by the International Finance Corporation (IFC) in 1992 to refer to a subset of smaller markets within its emerging markets database that had lower levels of market capitalization and less liquidity.

not aware of the possibilities these markets offer, or even their existence in the global opportunity set.

The list of frontier markets, depending on the index provider, encompasses from 21 to 32 countries, as presented in Table 6.8.[74] Most of them—about two-thirds—are from the EMEA region, and the rest from Asia and Latin America. Just like emerging markets, they are strongly differentiated, both in terms of GDP (it ranges from USD 13bn (North Macedonia) to USD 520bn (Argentina)) and the market capitalization of listed domestic companies (which ranges from a few to more than one hundred billion USD).[75] Additionally, two major index providers—the MSCI and S&P Dow Jones Indices—distinguish eleven[76] and seven[77] standalone markets, respectively, and calculate their single-country indexes.

There is no doubt that frontier and standalone markets are now on the margins of the world economy and global capital market; thus, they are typically missing within the majority of investment portfolios and global equity indexes.[78] This is confirmed by the following data. The GDP share of frontier markets measured at market exchange rates accounts for 4%, their share of world PPP equals 5%, and their share of world investable market capitalization is as low as 0.5% (Dimson et al. 2019).[79] Despite this, they should not be underestimated, because according to various studies, at least some of them will be among the largest economies in the world in a few decades.[80] For example, PwC (2017) estimates that Bangladesh, Vietnam, and Nigeria will be one of 30 countries with the highest projected GDP at PPP in 2030. Two decades later, Nigeria will even be one of 20 countries with the highest GDP

---

[74]There is less agreement between index providers as to what constitutes a frontier market compared to developed market and emerging market classifications. Other entities classify frontier markets even more differently—e.g., Credit Suisse includes 30 countries in this group.

[75]World Bank data as of 2018.

[76]Jamaica, Panama, Trinidad & Tobago, Bosnia Herzegovina, Bulgaria, Malta, Iceland, Ukraine, Botswana, Zimbabwe, and Palestine. The MSCI Standalone Market Indexes are not included in the MSCI Emerging Markets Index or MSCI Frontier Markets Index. However, these indexes use either the EM or the FM methodological criteria concerning size and liquidity.

[77]Malawi, Palestine, Rwanda, Tanzania, Uganda, Ukraine, and Zimbabwe.

[78]Major global equity indexes, as presented in Chapter 5, omit frontier markets and include only developed and emerging markets.

[79]All data as of 2018. It is worth adding that, at that time, frontier markets also included, e.g., Kuwait and Saudi Arabia, which are now classified by most index providers as emerging markets. Thus, the current importance of FMs may be even smaller.

[80]Let us note that almost all financial markets were once considered frontier markets prior to economic reforms, developing infrastructure, and building platforms and regulations for share trading. This applies to China, for example, which was widely considered a frontier market as recently as 1980. Today it is the second largest economy in the world.

Table 6.8 List of frontier countries (markets) according to the S&P Dow Jones Indices, the FTSE Russell, and the MSCI country (market) classifications

Country	S&P Dow Jones Indices	FTSE Russell	MSCI
Americas			
Argentina	•	•	
Ecuador	•		
Jamaica	•		
Panama	•		
Trinidad & Tobago	•		
EMEA			
Bahrain	•	•	•
Botswana	•	•	
Bulgaria	•	•	
Côte D'Ivoire	•	•	
Croatia	•	•	•
Cyprus	•	•	
Estonia	•	•	•
Ghana	•	•	
Iceland		•	
Jordan	•	•	•
Kenya	•	•	•
Kuwait			•
Latvia	•	•	
Lebanon	•		•
Lithuania	•	•	•
Malta		•	
Mauritius	•	•	•
Morocco	•	•	•
Namibia	•		
Nigeria	•	•	•
North Macedonia		•	
Oman	•	•	•
Palestine		•	
Romania	•	•	•
Serbia		•	•
Slovakia	•	•	
Slovenia	•	•	•
Tunisia	•	•	•
WAEMU[a]			•
Zambia	•		
Asia-Pacific			
Bangladesh	•	•	•

(continued)

Table 6.8 (continued)

Country	S&P Dow Jones Indices	FTSE Russell	MSCI
Kazakhstan	•	•	•
Sri Lanka	•	•	•
Vietnam	•	•	•

[a]WAEMU (West African Economic and Monetary Union): Benin, Burkina Faso, Côte D'Ivoire, Guinea-Bissau, Mali, Niger, Senegal, and Togo
Source Own elaboration based on the index providers' country (market) classifications

at PPP, while Vietnam and Nigeria will make the largest move by 2050.[81] Some frontier markets are projected to have some of the highest economic growth rates in the world over the coming decades.

Promising prospects for frontier markets are derived from a variety of factors. First of all, and mainly in relation to developed countries, they (in aggregate) have competitive macroeconomic growth rates[82]—past and future—that emulate the growth prospects for EMs (excluding China), albeit with higher volatility.[83] However, like emerging markets, they exhibit a fairly high degree of economic dependency on commodities (Redman and Sai 2016). Secondly, the strong growth of FMs is underpinned by their large and relatively young populations. These countries represent nearly one-eighth of the global population, and still rising (they exhibit population growth of up to 3% per annum), and, in contrast to many of the world's advanced economies, most FMs have a higher ratio of working (and soon to be working) population to current or projected retirement population (FTSE Russell 2014). Favorable demographics, together with urbanization dynamics (current urbanization rate is as low as 48%) and growing literacy rates, will result in the expansion in the labor force and, consequently, increased productivity, and they will be catalysts for further economic growth. Frontier markets should achieve gains in economic productivity due to technological advancements, improved levels of education, and the strengthening of the nation's human capital (Redman and Sai 2016). Another important growth factor may arise from the fact that many FMs have an abundant wealth of

[81]These projections do not take account of major events since the date of the report, including, in particular, the global COVID-19 pandemic. Additionally, one must not forget the problems that have afflicted once highly promising countries, such as Argentina, Nigeria, Venezuela, and Zimbabwe.

[82]The latest detailed data on economic growth are available in the World Bank (2020). However, it is worth remembering, that these prospects were developed before the outbreak of the coronavirus pandemic.

[83]Frontier markets are a heterogenous group of countries in terms of economic growth rate. Based on IMF projections up to 2021, some of these countries (Côte d'Ivoire, Bangladesh, Kenya, and Vietnam) are on course for impressive development. Meanwhile, several other markets—mostly in Latin America and EMEA—will likely underperform in growth terms, compared to developed economies.

natural resources. They will benefit from economic development in EMs, which will lead to increased demand for raw materials, especially oil, natural gas, and industrial metals. Additionally, frontier markets may benefit from open trade, as they have at their disposal a plentiful supply of comparatively cheap labor. This will allow them to limit dependence on commodity exports and to focus on more value-adding products and services. Growth in FMs is also supported by their relatively strong fiscal position compared to their more developed counterparts. Compared to developed countries, they have exceptionally low debt-to-GDP ratios. Finally, frontier markets have been characterized by rapid progress in the quality of administrative and corporate governance, especially in smaller nations (FTSE Russell 2014).

Of course, this does not mean that these countries are not facing major challenges. The most important ones are political and social instability (some countries have non-democratic governments, and are plagued with civil and social unrest), low quality of legal regulations, and high levels of corruption, among others. From the investor's point of view, restrictions imposed on foreign investors (including high taxes), insufficient liquidity of the financial market (resulting in higher trading costs), and low levels of transparency can create significant problems and pose a heavy burden. Additionally, rapid economic growth may not necessarily translate to the growth of the financial markets, as many FMs tend to have abundant state-owned enterprises and a large presence of multinational companies within key sectors. Therefore, due to methodological aspects related to the construction of equity indexes, even the high growth of these sectors may not be fully captured in the local equity benchmarks (FTSE Russell 2014).

With this in mind, it is worth considering the inclusion of frontier stocks in investment portfolios, especially since their historical medium-term investment characteristics and current valuations are already quite attractive, e.g., compared to emerging markets. It is important to think about it now when they have not yet attracted the widespread attention of the entire investment world and are currently under-owned by global investors.

HSBC research (Sidani et al. 2018) showed that frontier markets delivered annualized returns of 9.1% between May 2002 and March 2018, with a dividend yield that was typically higher than EMs and DMs. They have had historically higher volatility (18.0%) than developed markets (14.9%), but lower than emerging markets (21.5%).[84] A compelling argument for diversifying an equity portfolio through investing in FMs is also their low

[84]There are two potential explanations for frontier markets' less volatile returns (expressed in USD). First, currency can have a significant impact on the volatility realized. Since FM currencies are not as free-floating as their more developed counterparts (they often closely follow the US dollar or

correlations to EMs and DMs. The average correlation of 36-month monthly returns between frontier markets and emerging markets was relatively small (0.60), just like the correlation between frontier markets and developed markets (0.61) in the same period.[85] Intra-country correlations within frontier markets are even lower. Based on the monthly returns between July 2013 through June 2018, the average equaled 0.20 (Quisenberry 2018). The beta (36-month monthly returns) of FMs versus EMs amounted to 0.50, while the beta of FMs versus DMs equaled 0.73, suggesting that FMs are less more volatile than more developed markets[86] (Sidani et al. 2018). As with EMs and DMs, volatility, correlations, and beta significantly increased during market turmoil.[87]

Generally, frontier markets offer a relatively large choice of highly profitable, value-creating corporations. With a higher cost of equity, frontier stocks usually trade at a considerable discount, mainly to developed equities, and they consistently offer superior yield in comparison with both DMs and EMs (Redman and Sai 2016).[88] For example, trailing P/E amounted to 12.1 as of June 30, 2018, i.e., ca. 10, 21, and 42% lower than the corresponding ratio for emerging equities, developed equities ex-US, and US large stocks, respectively.

These ratios, of course, are constantly changing, but this relationship has typically been the case for frontier stocks (Quisenberry 2018). This was confirmed by previous studies carried out for longer periods. For example, Vanguard found that trailing 12-month P/E ratios for frontier markets in the period from December 1999 through September 2012 were usually slightly lower than in EMs, and considerably lower than in DMs and the USA (Philips and Redding 2013). Research conducted by Credit Suisse in 2016 demonstrated that two-decade average discounts amounted to 28% (vs. developed equities) and 4% (vs. emerging equities). They have persisted due to the frontier markets' more volatile earnings stream and higher cost of

---

other major currencies), it reduces the realized volatility. A second explanation may be lower cross correlations between countries (as will be shown later) (Philips and Redding 2013).

[85]The average correlation to the S&P 500 Index, calculated monthly on a 60-month rolling basis, was even smaller (0.43), offering more diversification potential for US investors (Quisenberry 2018).

[86]Calculations concerning the investment characteristics of frontier, emerging and developed markets are based on the MSCI Frontier Markets Index (USD), the MSCI Emerging Markets Index (USD), and the MSCI World Index (USD), respectively.

[87]Similar conclusions can be drawn from previous studies conducted by MSCI (Maloor 2012) and Vanguard (Philips and Redding 2013) for earlier periods, although specific values may vary.

[88]Frontier markets in this research were represented by a group of the ten largest countries within FMs selected by their respective ranking of current nominal GDP, population and equity market capitalization. This group included Argentina, Bangladesh, Egypt, Iran, Kenya, Morocco, Nigeria, Pakistan, Romania, and Vietnam. They collectively represented between three-quarters and four-fifths of the total economic, demographic, and equity investment opportunity set of frontier markets.

equity (Redman and Sai 2016). As of March 31, 2018, frontier markets had a higher RoE for only a slightly higher P/B valuation versus emerging markets and for a lower P/B valuation versus developed markets (Sidani et al. 2018). According to a Meketa Investment Group study, as of 2018, the CAPE ratio for FMs (12) was also substantially lower than for emerging markets (15), developed markets ex-US (20) and the US (27) (Walsh et al. 2018).

Additionally, frontier equities have historically offered a noticeably more attractive dividend yield relative to their developed and emerging counterparts. This attribute has been true for some 86% of the time over the two decades (1996–2016), with long-term averages of 3.8, 2.2, and 2.5%, respectively. The superior yield offered by frontier market equities is not simply a result of discounted pricing, but also a factor of structurally higher shareholder distributions by frontier corporations. The two-decade average dividend payout ratio equaled 51%, while it was 44% for developed markets and 36% for emerging markets (Redman and Sai 2016).

The list of broad frontier market indexes is definitely not as long as for emerging markets, not to mention developed markets. Their diversity is also much smaller than in the case of their counterparts from more developed markets. They are calculated by a modest number of index providers and have a relatively short track record.[89] Among them, three index providers—the S&P Dow Jones Indices, MSCI, and FTSE Russell—manage the most recognizable and the most used FM indexes in practice. They are mainly large-cap indexes that cover the most liquid and thus investable stocks covering either all frontier markets (as defined by a given index provider—cf. Table 6.8) or only selected ones.

Two flagship frontier market indexes calculated by the S&P Dow Jones Indices are the S&P Frontier BMI (which encompasses more than 500 stocks from 33 countries) and the S&P Select Frontier Index (which encompasses 40 of the largest and most liquid stocks from 11 countries from the S&P Extended Frontier 150 Index). The latter is replicated by the Xtrackers S&P Select Frontier Swap UCITS ETF—the oldest ETF of this kind in Europe. The two leading MSCI frontier market indexes are the MSCI Frontier Market Index (which captures over 90 large-cap and mid-cap stocks within 28 countries) and the MSCI Frontier Markets 100 Index (which includes approx. 100 of the largest and most liquid stocks of the broad-based MSCI Frontier Markets IMI). The latter is applied as a benchmark by the largest ETF of this kind in the world—the iShares MSCI Frontier 100 Index ETF. The most recognizable FM index calculated by FTSE Russell is the FTSE Frontier 50

[89]Standard & Poor's launched the first frontier index (S&P Select Frontier) in October 2007, closely followed by the launch of the MSCI Frontier Markets Index in December 2007.

Index, which comprises the largest 50 companies from 16 countries[90] that are constituents of the broad-based FTSE Frontier Markets Index.[91]

Despite the fact they seemingly have the same exposure, the FMs indexes tracked by ETFs differ significantly. This applies not only to the number of participants (as mentioned earlier), but also to portfolio structure (e.g., major countries, and sectors) or the median capitalization of constituents, for example. The top three countries in the S&P Select Frontier Index are Vietnam, Argentina, and Bahrain (31.8, 28.6, and 10.7%, respectively); the top sectors are financials, consumer discretionary and materials (28.1, 17.0, and 14.1%, respectively); and the median capitalization is USD 1.67bn. Meanwhile, the top countries in MSCI Frontier Markets 100 Index are Kuwait, Morocco, and Vietnam (28.0, 11.4, and 11.1%, respectively); the main sectors are financials, communication services, and consumer staples (51.2, 17.6, and 7.1%); and the median capitalization amounts to USD 0.43bn.[92] Therefore, when investing in frontier market ETFs, it is necessary to scrutinize the basic characteristics of their benchmarks, as the differences between them can also significantly affect performance, especially in the long run.

6.4 Geographical Regions

Another form of regional equity investing concerns investing in equities and equity-like financial instruments, where the main selection criterion is their geographical location. In this case, passive investing is carried out through index funds, index ETFs, and other ETPs, and it aims to mimic the performance (before fees and expenses) of the index that comprises stocks from a given region (or part of a region) or several regions, as accurately as possible. Geographic exposure does not have to coincide with the level of economic and financial development. However, in general, index providers define the region or set requirements for inclusion in the index portfolio so that the

[90]All data regarding indexes and ETFs as of mid-February 2020.

[91]It is also worth mentioning the two ETFs that combine exposure to both emerging and frontier markets. The Global X MSCI Next Emerging & Frontier ETF seeks to provide investment results that correspond generally to the price and yield performance of the MSCI Select Emerging and Frontier Markets Access Index. The index aims to represent the performance of 200 securities from selected countries within the MSCI Emerging and Frontier Markets Indexes, i.e., 150 from EMs and 50 from FMs, while excluding the more developed EMs of Brazil, Russia, India, China, South Korea, and Taiwan. Meanwhile, the Xtrackers MSCI Africa Top 50 Swap UCITS ETF aims to track the MSCI EFM Africa Top 50 Capped TRN Index. The index provides exposure to 50 selected stocks from emerging and frontier African countries.

[92]All data as of March 31, 2020.

composition of the index is quite homogeneous. This means that by buying ETFs with European exposure, for example, we usually invest exclusively (or almost exclusively) in companies from developed European countries, omitting emerging economies. This is worth remembering since the names of some ETFs and indexes contain only a term that identifies the geographical region. However, in practice, the name does not correspond to the entire region (in the geographical or administrative sense), only to a specific part.

A very important aspect regarding this kind of investing is also the distinction between the country exposure of regional indexes, as measured by their constituent companies' country of domicile, and economic exposure, i.e., the source of revenue. When analyzing the attractiveness of regional or country-specific index-tracking investments,[93] the domicile-based classification of stocks that comprise an index portfolio is usually taken into account. Meanwhile, as an increasing number of companies—especially multinationals—generate their revenue abroad, it is essential to assess not only the potential but also the risk associated with this type of investment through the prism of economic exposure, i.e., companies' sources of revenue. Morningstar compared domicile- and revenue-based exposure of the MSCI ACWI Index by region and found that, as of September 2018, regions such as the Eurozone, European emerging countries, Latin America, the Middle East, and Asian emerging countries achieved higher weights under economic exposure than its domicile-based weighting. The opposite situation occurred in the case of the North American region and European ex-Euro countries (Whitelaw et al. 2019).

Similar results were obtained by the MSCI study. Different regions show very different levels of diversification of sales revenues. The least diversified sales revenues were found in EMs, where 86% of sales were within the same region, followed by North America, where 71% of sales were generated in the region. The most diversified sales profile was found in the EMEA and Pacific regions, where only 48 and 60% of sales were generated internally, respectively (as of February 2019). EMs have been experiencing a steady increase in the share of global sales revenue since 2003, while North American countries have been recording the largest decrease in this respect (MSCI 2019).

Two approaches to regional ETF equity investing can be distinguished: multi-regional investing and single-regional investing (including investing in only some countries that represent part of a given region).

Multi-regional investing seems to be the most popular approach (in terms of AUM), especially among US investors. They often strive to achieve

[93]This issue in relation to single-country ETFs will be discussed in Chapter 7.

exposure to foreign equity markets by buying an ETF or other financial instrument that covers all major regions of the world. In this way, they can diversify their portfolio internationally with one simple transaction. That is why ETFs that track EAFE indexes,[94] i.e., indexes that cover stocks from more than 20 developed countries within three regions of the world (Europe, Australasia, and the Far East), while excluding American and Canadian equities, are so popular in North America (cf. Table 6.9). They are offered mostly by American ETF providers (e.g., BlackRock (iShares), BMO, ProShares, Global X, State Street (SPDR), Direxion), but also Asian ones (e.g., Hanwha). As described in Chapter 5, ETFs that invest globally, with the exception of a specific country or region, have similar characteristics.

ETFs with single-region exposure make up the majority of international equity ETFs that are focused on geographical regions.[95] They allow investors to purchase in a convenient way a basket of securities from all countries from a given region (or parts thereof) in a single transaction. These ETFs are aimed both at local investors who want to obtain intra-regional exposure (thus, they are usually listed within this region), as well as foreign investors eager to diversify their portfolio internationally. They are also increasingly used by institutional investors, who can thus easily and quickly, and relatively cheaply, obtain the desired regional exposure without the need for time-consuming and labor-intensive analysis of individual markets.

Probably some of the most popular ETFs of this kind in the world are those that offer exposure to European equities.[96] However, they do not invest in stocks from all European countries, only those that belong to developed markets. An example would be one of the most popular indexes among ETF providers with exposure to the European equity market—the Stoxx Europe 50 Index.[97] This blue-chip index covers 50 stocks from 17 European countries,[98] while there are more than 40 countries in Europe today, according to the United Nations. Other leading broad regional European equity indexes willingly used by ETF providers—both European and American—are the STOXX Europe 600 Index, the MSCI Europe Index, the FTSE Developed

---

[94]The major index providers calculate many versions of this type of index. However, due to the limited size of this book, we will not discuss them in greater detail.

[95]The huge number of these instruments and their providers makes it impossible to characterize them more accurately. Only the most important regional equity indexes will be listed.

[96]More information on the European ETF market can be found, e.g., in Bioy et al. (2019), and Marszk and Lechman (2019).

[97]There were EU-domiciled 91 ETFs with EUR 37.2bn AUM that mirrored this index at the end of June 2019 (PwC 2019).

[98]Austria, Belgium, Denmark, Finland, France, Germany, Ireland, Italy, Luxembourg, the Netherlands, Norway, Poland, Portugal, Spain, Sweden, Switzerland, and the UK.

Table 6.9 Largest regional equity ETFs in the world

Fund (ticker)	Index	Exchange	Assets (USD bn)	Expense ratio (%)
iShares Core MSCI EAFE ETF (IEFA US)	MSCI EAFE IMI Index	Cboe BZX	76.293	0.07
iShares MSCI EAFE ETF (EFA US)	MSCI EAFE Index	NYSE Arca	63.863	0.31
iShares Edge MSCI Min Vol EAFE ETF (EFAV US)	MSCI EAFE Minimum Volatility (USD) Index	Cboe BZX	13.294	0.20
iShares MSCI EAFE Small-Cap ETF (SCZ US)	MSCI EAFE Small Cap Index	NASDAQ	11.094	0.39
iShares MSCI EAFE Value ETF (EFV US)	MSCI EAFE Value Index	Cboe BZX	5.787	0.38
iShares MSCI EAFE Growth ETF (EFG US)	MSCI EAFE Growth Index	Cboe BZX	4.589	0.40
JPMorgan BetaBuilders Europe ETF (BBEU US)	Morningstar Developed Europe Target Market Exposure Index	Cboe BZX	4.517	0.09
Lyxor Core STOXX Europe 600 (DR) UCITS ETF (MEUD FP)	STOXX Europe 600 Index	Euronext Paris[a]	2.393	0.07
FTSE Developed Europe UCITS ETF (VEUR LN)	FTSE Developed Europe Index	London Stock Exchange[a]	2.337	0.10

(continued)

Table 6.9 (continued)

Fund (ticker)	Index	Exchange	Assets (USD bn)	Expense ratio (%)
iShares MSCI Pacific ex Japan ETF (EPP US)	MSCI Pacific ex-Japan Index	NYSE Arca	2.240	0.48

[a]Primary exchange
Note As of 19 February 2020. Sector and thematic ETFs are excluded
Source Bloomberg

Europe Index, and the S&P Europe 350 Index (along with their different versions). Investing in specific regions of Europe is enabled by ETFs that mimic, e.g., the MSCI Nordic Index, and the MSCI EM Eastern Europe Index. The former allow investors to gain exposure to large-cap and mid-cap stocks from four developed Nordic countries (Sweden, Denmark, Finland, Norway), while the latter give them access to large-cap and mid-cap equities from four emerging Eastern European countries (Russia, Poland, Hungary, and Czechia).[99]

Among providers of Asia-Pacific regional equity ETFs, the most popular are indexes with exposure to all the Asia Pacific/Asian countries or all-region indexes excluding individual countries. Examples of the former—with DM exposure—are the S&P Asia 50 Index, the FTSE Developed Asia Pacific All Cap Index, and the MSCI Pacific Index. Examples of the latter include the MSCI AC (All Country) Asia Pacific ex Japan Index, the MSCI AC Asia ex Japan Index, the FTSE Developed Asia Pacific ex Japan Index, the MSCI Asia Apex 50 Index, the MSCI AC Far East ex Japan Index, the MSCI Pacific ex Japan Index, the Morningstar Developed Asia Pacific ex-Japan Target Market Exposure Index, and the Solactive Core Developed Markets Pacific ex Japan Large & Mid Cap Index. Investors looking for opportunities to invest in ETFs that replicate emerging market APAC indexes have at their disposal the MSCI EM Asia Index, the S&P Asia Pacific Emerging BMI Index, the MSCI EM ex China Index, the MSCI EM Far East Index, and the WisdomTree Emerging Asia Equity Income Index, among others. In turn, the WisdomTree Middle East Dividend Index makes it possible to gain exposure to broad Middle Eastern all-cap equities from dividend-paying companies.

ETF investors focusing on regional North American stocks have a fairly small selection of indexes, as most providers offer only single-country (the

[99]There are also ETFs tracking MSCI EM Eastern Europe ex Russia Index that excludes Russian stocks.

USA and Canada) benchmarks of various kinds. In this context, it is worth mentioning the FTSE North America Index, the MSCI North America Index, the Morningstar North America 100 Equal Weight Index, and the MSCI North America High Dividend Yield Index, which are tracked by funds listed on US and European exchanges.

The offer of ETFs that replicate the Latin America (Latam) region indexes is also relatively small. There are funds that seek to provide investment results that closely correspond to the performance of the MSCI EM Latin America Index, the MSCI Emerging Markets Latin America 10/40 Index, the FTSE Latin America Capped Index, the S&P Latin America 40 Index, and the S&P/BNY Mellon Latin America 35 ADR Index.

There is also a modest selection of funds aimed at mapping the returns of African broad indexes. To the best of our knowledge, only three ETFs currently exist that replicate the results of such indexes. Interestingly some of these funds put into practice the previously described idea associated with economic exposure. The Xtrackers MSCI Africa Top 50 Swap UCITS ETF mirrors the MSCI EFM Africa Top 50 Capped Index that provides diversified exposure to the top 50 blue-chip African stocks, with 85% market representation. The Lyxor Pan Africa UCITS ETF attempts to capture the performance of the SGI Pan Africa Index, which comprises the largest 30 stocks listed in Africa or which predominantly explores African assets. The VanEck Vectors Africa Index ETF tracks the MVIS GDP Africa Index. It includes local listings of companies that are incorporated in Africa and listings of companies incorporated outside of Africa but that have at least 50% of their revenues/related assets in Africa.

The ten largest regional equity ETFs in terms of AUM are presented in Table 6.9.

6.5 Other Groups of Countries

In addition to ETFs that invest in markets with a specific level of economic and financial development and funds with a strictly regional focus, the providers of these financial instruments offer products that allow investors to get exposure to specific groups of countries. This applies most often to countries that are members of an economic, political-economic, or trade alliance. Another example is ETFs that invest in the equity markets of several countries, which, according to a particular financial institution, form an informal association of countries with similar economic, demographic, or other features, and with significant investment potential. Some funds invest in neighboring countries that have many common features and can be treated by investors as one investment entity. Equity indexes that cover these groups of countries do not usually cover many countries (usually several); hence, the degree of diversification of the ETF portfolio that tracks their performance is generally limited. The lack of potential in this respect also results from the fact that the economies and financial markets of these countries are usually closely related and susceptible to the same types of investment risk.[100] Therefore, investing in ETFs that replicate these types of indexes is subject to a relatively high degree of investment risk. It can, however, be rewarded with a high return when this investment "bet" proves to be accurate.

ETFs that mirror the performance of indexes which comprise countries that are a part of regional integration groupings include funds that invest in[101]:

- EMU (European and Monetary Union) countries, i.e., Austria, Belgium, Cyprus, Estonia, Finland, France, Germany, Greece, Ireland, Italy, Latvia, Lithuania, Luxembourg, Malta, the Netherlands, Portugal, Slovakia, Slovenia, and Spain. They are offered mainly in Europe, both by European (Deutsche Bank [Xtrackers], Amundi, Lyxor, ComStage, Invesco, UBS, HSBC, and BBVA) and American (BlackRock [iShares], and State Street [SPDR]) providers. The index most frequently used by European ETF providers is the Euro Stoxx 50 Index,[102] which represents the performance of the 50 largest companies from the supersectors in terms of free-float market cap in 8 Eurozone countries.[103] Another popular benchmark with EMU exposure is the MSCI EMU Index, which captures large-cap and mid-cap representation across the 10 European DMs[104];
- ASEAN (Association of Southeast Asian Nations) countries, i.e., Brunei, Cambodia, Indonesia, Laos, Malaysia, Myanmar, the Philippines, Singapore, Thailand, and Vietnam. They are offered by, e.g., Global X, Principal (CIMB), One AM, and Premia Partners;

---

[100]For these types of indexes, their constituents are usually stocks only from developed markets or only from emerging markets.

[101]It should be emphasized that these indexes do not have to include all countries that belong to a given alliance. For example, the MSCI EMU Index captures only 10 developed countries from all 19 members of the EMU.

[102]There were 13 providers offering ETFs that tracked the performance of this index in 2019 (Bioy et al. 2019). AUM in 59 EU-domiciled ETFs that replicate it amounted to EUR 46.6bn at the end of June 2019 (PwC 2019).

[103]Belgium, Finland, France, Germany, Ireland, Italy, Luxembourg, the Netherlands and Spain.

[104]Austria, Belgium, Finland, France, Germany, Ireland, Italy, the Netherlands, Portugal and Spain.

- GCC (Gulf Cooperation Council) countries, i.e., Bahrain, Kuwait, Oman, Qatar, Saudi Arabia, and the United Arab Emirates. They are offered by, e.g., Deutsche Bank (Xtrackers);
- The Pacific Alliance countries, i.e., Chile, Colombia, Mexico, and Peru. They are offered by, e.g., Deutsche Bank (Xtrackers).

Other groups of countries whose indexes are applied by ETF sponsors include:

- BRIC (Brazil, Russia, India, and China)—offered by, e.g., BlackRock (iShares),
- BICK (Brazil, India, China, and South Korea)—offered by First Trust,
- SMIT (South Korea, Mexico, Indonesia, and Turkey)—offered by Lyxor (ComStage),
- Chindia (i.e., China and India)—offered by First Trust.

References

Arnott, R., & Treussard, J. (2020). *Forecasts or Nowcasts? What's on the Horizon for the 2020s*. Research Affiliates. https://www.researchaffiliates.com/documents/772-forecasts-or-nowcasts.pdf. Accessed 30 Jan 2020.

Baffes, J., & Kabundi, A., Nagle, P., & Ohnsorge, F. (2018). *The Role of Major Emerging Markets in Global Commodity Demand* (Policy Research Working Paper 8495). World Bank. https://openknowledge.worldbank.org/bitstream/handle/10986/29948/WPS8495.pdf?sequence=1&isAllowed=y. Accessed 28 Jan 2020.

Bender, J., Briand, R., Fachinotti, G., & Ramachandran, S. (2012). *Small Caps—No Small Oversight*. Institutional Investors and Global Small Cap Equities. https://www.msci.com/documents/10199/255853/RI_Small_Caps_No_Small_Oversight.pdf/35f3c8b5-3d60-4b2b-ad3d-d6217e6d6df0?version=1.0. Accessed 16 Feb 2020.

Bioy, H., Garcia-Zarate, J., Lamont, K., Boyadzhiev, D., & Kang, H. (2019). *A Guided Tour of the European ETF Marketplace*. Morningstar. https://www.morningstar.com/lp/guided-tour-european-etf-marketplace. Accessed 10 September 2019.

BlackRock. (2020). *BlackRock Global ETP Landscape*. Quarterly Highlights Q4 2019. https://cdn.prgloo.com/media/download/ac84a79c8d5b4b5eba637f4418602d01. Accessed 15 Mar 2020.

Brzenk, P., & Du, R. (2019). *Building Better International Small-Cap Benchmarks.* https://us.spindices.com/documents/research/research-building-better-international-small-cap-benchmarks.pdf?force_download=true. Accessed 16 Feb 2020.

Cheng, T., Srivastava, V., & Wang, I. (2019). *A Case for Dividend Growth Strategies.* S&P Dow Jones Indices Research. https://us.spindices.com/documents/research/research-a-case-for-dividend-growth-strategies.pdf?force_download=true. Accessed 22 Jan 2020.

Dimensional Fund Advisors. (2019). *The Randomness of Global Equity Returns.* https://us.dimensional.com/perspectives/randomness-of-global-equity-returns. Accessed 18 Jan 2020.

Dimson, E., Marsh, P., & Staunton, M. (2019). *Summary Edition Credit Suisse Global Investment Returns Yearbook 2019.* Credit Suisse Research Institute. https://www.credit-suisse.com/articles/news-and-expertise/2019/02/en/global-investment-returns-yearbook.html. Accessed 16 Jan 2020.

FTSE Russell. (2014). Frontier Markets: Assessing the next frontier. https://www.ftserussell.com/sites/default/files/research/frontier_markets-accessing_the_next_frontier_final.pdf. Accessed 9 Feb 2020.

Giese, G., & Kozumenko, R. (2019). *Have Regional Equity-Market Correlations Risen?* https://www.msci.com/www/blog-posts/have-regional-equity-market/01644267058. Accessed 12 Jan 2020.

Janus Henderson Investors. (2020). *Janus Henderson Global Dividend Index*. Edition 25. https://cdn.janushenderson.com/webdocs/JHGDI+-+Edition+25+-ASIA.pdf. Accessed 15 Feb 2020.

Keimling, N. (2016). *Predicting Stock Market Returns Using the Shiller CAPE*. StarCapital Research. https://www.starcapital.de/fileadmin/user_upload/files/publikationen/Research_2016-01_Predicting_Stock_Market_Returns_Shiller_CAPE_Keimling.pdf. Accessed 25 Jan 2020.

Lazard Asset Management. (2020a). *Annual Returns of Developed Markets Equity (%; 2000–2019).* https://www.lazardassetmanagement.com/docs/-m0-/174/DevelopedMarketsEquityReturns_LazardInvestmentFacts_2019_en.pdf. Accessed 18 Jan 2020.

Lazard Asset Management. (2020b). *Top 5/Bottom 5 Emerging Markets Equity Returns (%; 2000–2019).* https://www.lazardassetmanagement.com/docs/-m0-/175/Top5-Bottom5EmergingMarketsEquityReturns_LazardInvestmentFacts_2019_en.pdf. Accessed 24 Jan 2020.

Leverenz, J. (2020). *The Past Decade in Emerging Markets and Thoughts on the Future.* Invesco. https://www.invesco.com/us-rest/contentdetail?contentId=145ea1d6c7500710VgnVCM1000006e36b50aRCRD. Accessed 6 Feb 2020.

Lovelace, R., & Polak, D. (2019). *Guide to International Investing: How to Go Global in an Uncertain World*. Capital Group. https://www.capitalgroup.com/content/dam/cgc/shared-content/documents/brochures/Capital-Group-Guide-to-International-Investing.pdf. Accessed 22 Dec 2019.

Maloor, S. (2012). *Market Insight: Diversity on the Frontier*. MSCI. https://www.msci.com/documents/10199/a8d7985e-d8b7-49bc-be63-4848c3c2f34c. Accessed 10 Feb 2020.

Marszk, A., & Lechman, E. (2019). *Exchange-Traded Funds in Europe*. London: Academic Press/Elsevier.

Melas, D. (2019). *The Future of Emerging Markets: 30 Years on from the Launch of the MSCI Emerging Markets Index*. MSCI. https://www.msci.com/documents/10199/239004/Research-Insight-The-Future-of-Emerging-Markets/13e0765f-9506-4011-2d6d-704346c1cc30. Accessed 25 Jan 2020.

MSCI. (2018). *Emerging Markets: Looking to Expand Your Investment Horizon?* https://www.msci.com/documents/1296102/1362201/MSCI-MIS-EM-May-2018.pdf/b1b05adf-4bf3-9acc-404c-9865da3e9997. Accessed 1 Feb 2020.

MSCI. (2019). *Selected Geographical Issues in the Global Listed Equity Market*. Analysis for the Norwegian Ministry of Finance. https://www.regjeringen.no/globalassets/upload/fin/aff/2019-10-03-msci_report-for-the-norwegian-gpfg.pdf. Accessed 18 Dec 2019.

NBIM. (2019). *Country and Industry Effects in Global Equity Returns* (Discussion Note 01/2019). https://www.nbim.no/contentassets/70b80f2f81fb4a3dbd703dde9d568b0f/country-and-industry-effects-in-global-equity-returns.pdf. Accessed 19 Jan 2020.

Orzano, M., & Welling, J. (2017). *Making the Case for International Small Caps*. S&P Dow Jones Indices. https://us.spindices.com/documents/education/education-making-the-case-for-international-small-caps.pdf?force_download=true. Accessed 16 Feb 2020.

Philips, C. B., & Redding, B. (2013). *Exploring the Next Frontier: A Review of Frontier Equity Markets*. Vanguard Research, https://www.vanguardinvestments.dk/documents/exploring-the-next-frontier-tlrv.pdf. Accessed 10 Feb 2020.

PwC. (2017). *The Long View: How Will the Global Economic Order Change by 2050?* https://www.pwc.com/gx/en/world-2050/assets/pwc-the-world-in-2050-full-report-feb-2017.pdf. Accessed 9 Feb 2020.

PwC. (2019). *European ETF Listing and Distribution*. PricewaterhouseCoopers. https://www.pwc.lu/en/asset-management/etfs/etf-poster.html. Accessed 20 Nov 2019.

Quisenberry, C. (2018). *Frontier Markets: A Comparative Analysis, Investments and Wealth Monitor*. Investments & Wealth Institute. https://investmentsandwealth.org/getattachment/10f6792b-8916-43a9-85ef-ec7298662e8a/IWM18NovDec-FrontierMarkets.pdf. Accessed 10 Feb 2020.

Redman, A., & Sai, A. (2016). *The Next Frontier*. Credit Suisse Research Institute. https://www.credit-suisse.com/media/assets/corporate/docs/about-us/research/publications/csri-next-frontier-2016.pdf. Accessed 9 Feb 2020.

S&P Dow Jones Indices. (2019, August). *Country Classification Methodology*. https://us.spindices.com/documents/index-policies/methodology-country-classification.pdf. Accessed 15 Jan 2020.

Schlanger, T., & Kesidis, S. (2017). *An Analysis of Dividend-Oriented Equity Strategies*. Vanguard Research. https://personal.vanguard.com/pdf/ISGADOS.pdf. Accessed 22 Jan 2020.

Sekhon, M., Sehgal, C., & Rajah, S. (2019). *Emerging Markets Come of Age*. Franklin Templeton. https://www.franklintempleton.co.uk/download/en-gb/common/jtcfwj2l/emerging-markets-come-of-age.pdf. Accessed 28 Jan 2020.

Shilling, H. (2018). *The International Guide to Securities Market Indices*. New York: Routledge.

Sidani, R., Tong, S., & Chadha, T. (2018). *Allocating to Frontier Markets Equities*. HSBC Global Asset Management. http://info.emfunds.us.hsbc.com/institutional/insights/Frontier_Markets_Article_Allocating_to_Frontier_Market_equities_Sept_17_update.pdf. Accessed 10 Feb 2020.

Stevenson, D., & Tuckwell, D. (2019). *The Ultimate ETF Guidebook: A Comprehensive Guide to the World of Exchange-Traded Funds*. Petersfield: Harriman House.

Su, G. (2018). *How a Global Approach Can Enhance Dividend Investing*. ClearBridge Investments. https://www.clearbridge.com/perspectives/institutional/2018/global-dividend-investing.html. Accessed 22 Jan 2020.

van Vilet, P., Polfliet, M., & Mosselaar, J.-S. (2018). *High Dividend Investing: Buy Them Stable & Strong*. Robeco. https://www.robeco.com/media/7/2/c/72cc3334288ec33e168cb25a4a7b8f75_high-dividend-investing-buy-them-stable-and-strong_tcm17-11927.pdf. Accessed 23 Jan 2020.

Walsh, E., Yontar, T., Obregon, R., & Benham, F. (2018). *Frontier Markets*. https://meketa.com/wp-content/uploads/2019/07/Frontier-Markets-WP1.pdf. Accessed 10 Feb 2020.

Whitelaw, T., Lucas, A., Greengold, R., Boyadzhiev, D., & Malseed, M. (2019). A *New Perspective on Geographical Diversification: Revenue Exposure by Region*. Morningstar Manager Research. https://www.morningstar.com/lp/revenue-exposure. Accessed 14 Feb 2020.

World Bank. (2020). *Global Economic Prospects: Slow Growth, Policy Challenges*. https://openknowledge.worldbank.org/bitstream/handle/10986/33044/9781464814693.pdf. Accessed 9 Feb 2020.

7

Single-Country Equity Exchange-Traded Funds

7.1 Introduction

Investing in stocks from a particular country seems to be the most obvious and simplest form of the equity portfolio international diversification. It does not require analyzing many markets, which usually is a time-consuming and labor-intensive process. It is much easier to examine the macroeconomic fundamentals of an individual country and the investment potential of companies domiciled in this market. This type of international equity investing is convenient in particular when investing passively. Buying shares of a single-country ETF, whose aim is to track the performance of a given index, makes it possible to achieve a relatively cheap exposure to the entire stock market, or its specific part, through one simple transaction.

The benefits we can get by investing in ETFs focused on a single country are generally similar to those that occur in other forms of international investing described in the two previous chapters. Like in regional and global investing, it is possible to reduce the investment risk of the whole portfolio, although potential in this respect is typically lower, especially when the market we invest on is strongly correlated with ours. In return, however, we can achieve better results than with broader international strategies, particularly when we focus our investment bet on a small number of countries that outperform.

Single-country ETFs are often chosen by professional investors who, having a well-grounded and research-based belief in the potential of a given market, are more likely to make such a targeted investment hoping for a

T. Miziołek et al., *International Equity Exchange-Traded Funds*,
https://doi.org/10.1007/978-3-030-53864-4_7

higher profit (at an acceptable level of risk) rather than diluting their portfolio by investing in too many markets. They may also be an interesting proposition for less experienced investors, tolerating higher investment risk, who would like to benefit from the economic and investment potential of the countries whose perspectives look better than their own country—especially when they are close to us for some reason (geographically, culturally, civilizationally).

Country-specific ETFs are widespread among investors worldwide, not only due to their potential benefits, but also because of the easiest access to these funds and their immense selection. They are listed on stock exchanges in several dozen countries and provide exposure to over 60 equity markets—developed, emerging, and even frontier—on almost all continents. Particularly extensive and varied offer applies to ETFs with exposure to the largest developed markets (e.g., USA, Canada, Japan, Australia, UK, Germany, France) and some emerging ones (e.g., China). Proponents of more sophisticated solutions may, however, invest in funds related to equity indexes in countries such as Jamaica, Iceland, North Macedonia, Bangladesh, or Vietnam.

The rest of this chapter proceeds as follows. First, the most important advantages and drawbacks of investing in single-country equity ETFs, as well as certain aspects and nuances that should be considered when deciding on this type of international exposure, will be discussed. In the next subsections, selected ETFs and indexes with exposure to single-country equity markets will be presented, broken down into three regions—Americas (North America and Latin America), Europe, Middle East and Africa (EMEA), and Asia-Pacific (APAC).

7.2 Country-Specific Investing

The arguments for single-country investing via exchange-traded funds rest mainly on international portfolio diversification (as it was discussed in detail in the previous chapters) and the potentially higher return from investing in selected equity market, instead of investing in a broader range of various markets. Best funds of this kind usually outperform regional and global equity ETFs, especially in the short term. This is an obvious and natural consequence of the fact that the investment portfolios of the latter are more diversified, and therefore, it is more difficult for them to generate an exceptionally high return. Meanwhile, country-specific ETFs with geographically concentrated portfolios[1] may be the preferred investment solution for those who are expecting higher absolute returns, though are ready to take a higher risk. As a result, these funds may also achieve higher risk-adjusted returns compared to multi-country equity ETFs.

Applying single-country strategy, we actually make a "bet" analogous to investing in the shares of an individual company on the domestic market, but in this case our choice refers to a specific country out of a global opportunity set. If this "bet" succeeds, we can gain a lot, but if it fails, we can incur huge losses. To increase the likelihood of implementing the first scenario, we cannot leave this matter to chance. Thus, deciding on such a strategy, we must take conscious actions that will allow us to choose an equity market which is currently relatively cheap, offers favorable prospects for the future, and simultaneously best fits our investments, i.e., complements well the domestic equity portfolio.

Just as an investment in a company's stock is typically evaluated based on the fundamental analysis, an investment in a country-specific ETF should be judged on the same grounds, though with regard to the basket of securities in the replicated index. For this purpose, there could be applied widely used measures for valuing stocks, for example, Price-To-Earnings (P/E) (including P/E Fwd and Trailing 12 Months P/E), Price-To-Book Value (P/BV), Cyclically Adjusted Shiller-PE (CAPE, Shiller P/E), Price-Cash Flow (P/C), Price-Sales (P/S), and Dividend Yield (DY).[2] An in-depth macroeconomic analysis of the country is also necessary to assess the opportunities and threats associated with its current economic environment and its future perspectives, including the business cycle.

It should be emphasized that in the latter analysis it is necessary not to focus attention solely on the country of domiciliation of the stocks making up the given index (it is usually 100% or nearby).[3] This approach often turns out to be insufficient when analyzing the economic and investment potential of a country index. This is mainly due to an increasing level of global economic integration, reflected in the globalization of companies' sales revenues. An analysis taking into account economic exposure of the equity index (precisely speaking—stocks being part of its portfolio), instead of the traditional approach based on the country of domicile, is inevitable, as more

[1]The funds in question may also be concentrated in other respects—e.g., by sector or company. The issue will be further discussed later in the chapter.

[2]Numerous other variations of these indicators are also applied in the investment practice. However, due to the limited scope of the book, they will not be discussed.

[3]All the more, no particular importance should be attached to the place of listing. In the case of some ETFs (e.g., Israeli), they invest in shares listed on various stock exchanges, especially the American ones.

and more companies operate across several countries and regions, and thus, their revenues are exposed to economic activity and risks beyond their home country. Consequently, viewing companies through the lens of revenue offers a significant advantage over their domicile. Additionally, the economic exposure of companies can be a meaningful descriptor for characterizing the macro-factor risks of stocks (Gupta and Subramanian 2014).

Since the performance of single-country ETFs is sensitive to that of the economies to which they are exposed, the disparity between the geographic revenue exposures of tracked country indexes relative to their market capitalization weights should be assessed. Morningstar research demonstrated that among developed markets in such countries as the USA, UK and (to a lesser extent) Japan and France, domicile-based exposure in the MSCI ACWI Index is higher than revenue-based exposure. The opposite is the case of China, whose economic exposure in the abovementioned index is threefold higher than domicile-based exposure (10.6% vs. 3.5%). An analysis of the most important benchmarks on the global equity market, eagerly used by country-specific ETFs sponsors, shows that in the leading European economies, as much as about 80% of their constituents' revenues derive from outside their home countries (the CAC40 Index [France]—82.5%; the DAX Index [Germany]—80.7%; the FTSE 100 Index [UK]—77.7%).[4] European and perhaps most other investors (save Australians) face the challenge of rooting the domestic portion of their portfolios in the revenues generated from their home countries. This applies, to a much lesser extent, to investors in the USA and Australia, where analogous indicators are much lower—38.0% (the S&P 500 Index)[5] and 42.1% (the S&P/ASX 200 Index), respectively (Whitelaw et al. 2019).[6]

Additionally, investors can decrease or increase home country revenue exposure by paying heed to index's market capitalization and style. According to the Morningstar study—regarding the first factor—the higher the average market capitalization of the country index is, the smaller the percentage

[4]According to Capital Group research, the 10 largest companies in Europe (Nestlé, Royal Dutch Shell, Novartis, Roche, HSBC, BP, Total SAP, AstraZeneca, and LVHM) generate on average only 30% of their revenue from their home region. The rest derives from emerging markets (31%), North America (29%), and Asia-Pacific region (10%) (Lovelace and Polak 2019).

[5]The S&P Dow Jones Indices study of the US equity market demonstrates that these indicators, despite some fluctuations, have been at a similar level for years. In 2018, the percentage of S&P 500 sales from foreign countries was 42.90%, down from 2017s 43.62%, and 2016s 43.16%. The recent high mark was 2014s 47.82%, and the recent low mark was 2003s 41.84%. Asia, Europe, UK, Japan, Africa, and Canada accounted for 8.24, 8.24, 1.49, 1.14, 3.82, and 1.98% of all S&P 500 sales, respectively (Silverblatt 2019).

[6]Regardless of the market, companies' geographic sources of revenues matter most in the aftermath of surprising political or macroeconomic events such as the USA' November 2016 presidential election and the UK's June 2016 vote to leave the European Union.

of revenue from its home country becomes and the percentage of revenue deriving from other regions of the world is larger.[7] Thus, investors who want to magnify domicile-based exposure should tilt their investments toward small-cap equity ETFs. Conversely, investors seeking greater revenue diversity within their international portfolios should be biased toward ETFs tracking large-cap and mega-cap equity indexes.[8] Likewise, US investors aiming to widen international exposure should be tilted toward the growth versions of the country equity index, while those who want to be more home-biased should invest in the greater extent in ETFs mirroring US value indexes.

Concluding, ETF investors have three options to increase international revenue diversification within a portfolio. The first one is to invest in local funds encompassing mega-cap growth stocks since these firms are equipped with business models and resources to pursue opportunities irrespective of geography. The second possibility is to create a diversified global portfolio through investing in foreign equity ETFs biased toward small-cap value stocks as these companies tend to have businesses that receive most of their revenues from their home countries. The third option, combining the two above approaches, results in a portfolio characterized by market-cap, style, and geographic diversity, measured by either domicile or revenue source (Whitelaw et al. 2019).

Like any other investment analysis, single-country ETF needs thorough examination of its return, risk, and risk-adjusted measures.[9] Performance measures—in the medium and the long term—may comprise, for instance, annualized and cumulative absolute return (in one-, three-, five-, and ten-year periods and since inception) and the calendar year return. The most common risk measures are annualized standard deviation (typically for the same periods as the abovementioned), maximum drawdown, and beta vs. benchmark index. Among the most widespread risk-adjusted return ratios, there are the Sharpe ratio and information ratio.

---

[7]For example, percent of revenues derived from outside USA is about two times higher in the S&P 500 Index than in the Russell 2000 Index, 20 percentage points higher in the FTSE 100 Index than in the FTSE 250 Ex-Investment Trust Index, and about 10 percentage points higher in the S&P/ASX 200 Index than in the S&P/ASX Small Ordinaries Index.

[8]These conclusions probably also apply to other developed countries, although not necessarily to the same extent. However, it is difficult to say whether this is also applicable to emerging markets.

[9]Only the most important investment parameters taken into account in the ETF analysis, also used for other (equity) financial instruments, are indicated. Description of other features, also very important, that are specific to ETF and taken into account with due diligence, will be omitted here—both quantitative (such as index-tracking quality [including tracking difference and tracking error], total cost of ownership [including total expense ratio, bid-ask spread, premium and discount], secondary liquidity [including average daily turnover value], portfolio turnover [including turnover ratio], etc.), and qualitative (method index replication, legal and tax aspects, place of listing, credibility of fund provider, etc.). Most of them were discussed in the second part of the book.

ETF (index) valuation measures data, as well as their return and risk characteristics, are available in a variety of ways. The basic ratios are usually demonstrated on the websites of ETFs and in the factsheets of indexes tracked by these funds. Other useful data and information can be found through analytical companies, international financial institutions, specialized financial media, and professional financial data providers. Regardless of the source, the methodology used to calculate specific indicators should be carefully checked, as there may be some differences between entities, which may affect their interpretation.

An important factor influencing the scale of potential benefits from equity portfolio international diversification is the correlation of rates of return. This matters, in particular, when buying a country-specific ETF is to serve as an effective tool for diversifying investments. Considering the fact that average pairwise correlation ratios between some countries are typically high (as described in detail in Chapter 6), choosing a fund that significantly reduces the risk of the entire portfolio poses a serious challenge. This regards especially developed markets—mainly in North America and EMEA region—where country correlations are the highest. This is easier to achieve by investing in single-country ETFs from emerging markets, especially the EMEA region, as they are the least inter-correlated regional clusters (MSCI 2019a).

Portfolio diversification through country-specific equity ETFs, in addition to the foregoing merits, also carries various risks. One needs to be aware of them when making such a "bet," especially since they can be particularly severe in the case of targeted investment. First, the narrower the exposure is, the most serious the perils and pitfalls resulting from international equity investing may be. While a wider foreign exposure normally reduces the risk of a failed investment, betting only on one single-country ETF significantly increases this risk. The more targeted the approach is, the more carefully you have to monitor it for sudden events that could turn a potentially profitable investment into a serious loss. Therefore, as we have already pointed out, one should carefully monitor the macroeconomic situation of a given country (or countries to which the fund has economic exposure) and react in advance when alarming signals appear, e.g., weakening economic growth, deteriorating fiscal situation, lowering credit rating, etc. While one can somehow get prepared for, or even forecast, this kind of threat, it is usually difficult to avoid negative consequences of political or social events, and especially random events (e.g., terrorist attack, earthquake, tsunami, flood, ecological disaster) that affect an individual country. Given that, it is important to assess investor's risk tolerance and level of involvement. Single-country ETFs may be appropriate for risk-accepting investors and those who are ready to actively, and closely monitor their investment. These funds are rather not of the "buy and hold" kind, suitable for an auto-pilot type of investor. For those investors the broad-based international equity ETF that provides exposure across several countries will probably prove itself better.

Another threat is the potential overlapping when simultaneously investing in country-specific ETF and in regional or global equity ETF. When a broader-based fund includes geographical exposure to a particular market, actual exposure to this country is greater and potential diversification benefits are smaller. This applies, in particular, to the situations when an investor uses various international ETFs as building blocks for a well-diversified portfolio. For example, having at the same time an ETF with broad emerging markets exposure and China ETF, actual exposure to this country is much larger. It results from the fact that Chinese stocks have a significant weight (over 30%) in the majority of EM funds.[10]

A prerequisite for mitigating portfolio risk via investing in single-country ETFs is not only the choice of an appropriate fund in terms of its geographical and economic exposure. An important role is also played by the selection of such an ETF that will replicate a well-diversified index. Meanwhile, contrary to appearances, numerous ETFs do not provide the level of diversification many investors expect. It is therefore necessary to scrutinize the index portfolio, in terms of both individual holdings and industries.

Country-specific equity ETFs have undoubtedly the most concentrated investment portfolios across various forms of international equity exchange-traded funds described so far.[11] However, the degree of portfolio concentration among them varies greatly. The smallest concentration usually concerns funds replicating broad indexes, with a large number of constituents and exposure to equity markets in developed countries. The largest concentration occurs in funds tracking the performance of indexes focused on a certain segment of the domestic market (e.g., in terms of capitalization, investment style or sector) and smart beta indexes. Overconcentration relates also to benchmarks covering stocks from emerging and frontier markets as their economies are usually quite poorly diversified and often rely on few sectors. In the latter case, both sectoral and individual concentration can be really significant (regardless of its definition and methods of calculation), especially

---

[10]A similar pitfall occurs when investing in various (regarding geographical exposure) international ETFs, while their economic exposure overlaps significantly.

[11]This mainly applies to capitalization-weighted indexes or indexes based on market factors, while it does not refer to equal-weighted indexes.

when the public equity market, or its specific segment, in a given country is based only on a few sectors or companies.[12]

Excessive industry-concentrated country indexes apply to numerous countries. According to the Credit Suisse research, carried out within 47 countries belonging to the FTSE All World Index (as of the beginning of 2015), the weighting of the three largest industries accounts for at least 40% of country capitalization in 42 out of 47 countries; for at least 50% for 33 countries; for at least 60% for 21 countries; and for 70% or more in 15 countries. In the five most concentrated countries (Morocco, Peru, Czechia, Pakistan, and Greece), three or even fewer industries (out of 40 in total) make up the country's entire capitalization; in Portugal and in Ireland, they account for over 80% of country capitalization.[13] Although this trend mainly refers to less developed equity markets, it also manifests itself in developed countries. For example, the three largest industries make up more than 70% of country capitalization in Denmark and Belgium, above 60% in Finland, Switzerland, and Austria, and over 50% in Italy, Sweden, and New Zealand. The smallest degree of industry concentration—below 40%—occurs in UK, Japan, France, and the USA (26%) (Dimson et al. 2015).

The above data clearly indicate that if investors restrict their international portfolios to one equity market, they will end up poorly industry-diversified

[12]It is worth noting that although the concentration of the investment portfolio is generally unfavorable from the point of view of mitigating its risk, this approach also has its advantages. A review of various empirical studies on this topic (in terms of research periods, definitions of concentration, and applied methodologies) from academics, asset managers, and other industry practitioners is presented by Mier (2017). Among recent research regarding portfolio concentration, one of the most comprehensive was carried out by Choi et al. (2017). They found, using data containing security holdings of 10,771 institutional investors' portfolios of various types (e.g., mutual funds, hedge funds, insurance companies) domiciled in 72 countries, that in contrast to traditional asset pricing theory and in support of information advantage theory, concentrated investment strategies in international markets can be optimal. Their results showed that home country, foreign country, and industry concentration are all associated with higher risk-adjusted returns of institutional investors' portfolios. Additionally, higher concentration in a given country (either home or foreign) and in the industries of that country is associated with better performance in the part of the portfolio allocated to that country. This evidence suggests that institutional investors concentrate their holdings in home markets as well as selected foreign markets and industries, as if they possessed an information advantage in these assets.

[13]For some single-country indexes, only largest sector alone accounts for over 40% of total market capitalization. This applies to RTS Index (Russia)—45.0% (energy [oil & gas]); Nikkei 225 Index (Japan)—45.7% (technology); FTSE TWSE Taiwan 50 Index (Taiwan)—49.9% (technology); MSCI Tadawul 30 Index (Saudi Arabia)—50.2% (financials); and FTSE Kuwait All Cap 15% Capped Index (Kuwait)—61.0% (banks) (all data as of March 2020).

foreign investments in most cases.[14] Although the vast majority of country indexes do not have a sectoral cap,[15] some index providers—to prevent excessive industry concentration—create benchmarks that restrict the weight of an individual sector or limits the number of constituents from an individual sector.[16] This approach ensures higher degree of portfolio diversification, but limits the potential merits when capped sector outperforms others.

However, a much more serious problem regards individual stocks. Applying free float-adjusted market capitalization weighting methodology may result—especially in narrow country benchmarks[17]—in excessive company concentration in certain cases. This may happen regardless of market circumstances, but it intensifies during bullish periods in particular, when rising prices of some stocks may lead to a significant increase in their weight in the index. As a result, it may happen that the share of one company in the index may exceed, e.g. 20%, and the total weight of just a few will be greater than 50%.[18] To avoid such situations and help investors meet concentration and diversification requirements,[19] index providers construct capped indexes. They are usually market capitalization-weighted indexes, designed to limit concentration in any single security at a certain level. Single or two-level capping approaches are employed to limit the weight of companies. Single cap refers to maximum allocation to a single constituent, and two-level cap additionally constrains the sum of the weights of all entities representing

---

[14]The sector composition of an equity index may be of primary significance also in terms of performance. For example, S&P Dow Jones Indices research assessed the relative importance of sectors in determining the performance of the S&P 500 Index. As it turned out, in most sectors, around half of daily variation in stock prices could be attributed to changes in sector prices (Edwards and Lazzara 2019).

[15]It is recognized that equity indexes, including country-specific ones, should adequately reflect the structure of the economy, basically the market of public equities. Additionally, such solution is against the grain of free market principles and it may cause that local funds will not be able to attract foreign institutional investors since they typically prefer non-capped indexes. Thus, the vast majority of single-country indexes do not apply sectoral cap.

[16]Sector restrictions are used, for example, in the following equity indexes mirrored by single-country ETFs: SOFIX Index (Bulgaria) (maximum weight of sector—20%) and WIG20 Index (Poland) (may not include more than 5 companies from a single exchange sector).

[17]Unlike global and regional indexes, majority of single-country equity indexes usually encompass a fixed number of stocks, usually not more than 30.

[18]For instance, the weight of the largest constituent in the ISEQ 20 Index (Ireland) is 23.8%, and total weight of three largest stocks is 56.8%; in the case of PX Index (Czech Republic), it is 24.0 and 58.1%, respectively; and in the case of BUX Index (Hungary), it is 30.8 and 87.3%, respectively. In some indexes, the largest stock accounts for over 30% (e.g., BUX Index [Hungary], KOSPI 200 [South Korea]) or even for over 40% (e.g., EGX 30 Index [Egypt], FTSE TWSE Taiwan 50 Index [Taiwan]) of its total capitalization (all data as of March 2020).

[19]These requirements derive usually from legislation referring to diversification requirements for registered investment funds, e.g., regarding Regulated Investment Company (RIC) in the USA or Undertakings for Collective Investments in Transferable Securities (UCITS) in the European Union. Sometimes these limitations are an initiative of the index providers themselves (e.g., stock exchanges).

more than, e.g., 5% weight at, e.g., 40%.[20] A more detailed description of how the capped equity indexes look, together with examples (based on the methodology used by MSCI), is provided in the box below.

Capped Indexes

Capped equity index is constructed on the basis of underlying (parent) index. Index provider defines a criterion for grouping constituents of the parent index and determines the maximum weight to be applied to such groups.

According to MSCI capped indexes methodology (2019b),[21] constituents of the parent index can be grouped by the following criteria:

- country or region,
- sector, industry group, industry or sub-industry (based on the GICS[22]),
- stock exchange or currency of price,
- group entity,
- issuer.

Additionally, each index constituent may be considered as a single group.

During construction and at each rebalancing, if the weight of any group in the parent index is greater than the maximum weight, its weight is capped at the maximum weight. Within the capped group, securities are weighted in proportion to their free float-adjusted market capitalization. The weight of the securities outside the capped group is increased in proportion to their weight prior to capping.

The most commonly used capped indexes are:

- **MSCI 10/40 Indexes**—they constrain the weight of any single group entity at 10%, and the sum of the weights of all group entities representing more than 5% weight at 40%, with a buffer of 10% applied on these limits at each index rebalancing. This capping methodology is applied to help providers of index-linked financial products (including ETFs) meet EU regulatory standards;
- **MSCI 25/50 Indexes**—they constrain the weight of any single group entity at 25%, and the sum of the weights of all group entities representing more than 5% weight at 50%, with a buffer of 10% applied on these limits at each index rebalancing. This capping methodology is applied to help providers of index-linked financial products (including ETFs) meet US Internal Revenue Code investment constraints for a fund to qualify as a Regulated Investment Company (RIC) in the USA;

[20]The capping practices are also applied, for the same reasons, in traditional, non-capped equity indexes replicated by ETFs.

[21]In the case of other index providers, the methodology of creating capped indexes may differ from the one presented hereby.

[22]The GICS methodology will be presented in Chapter 8.

- **MSCI 20/20 Indexes**—they constrain the weight of any single group entity at 20%, with a buffer of 10% applied on this limit at each index rebalancing;
- **MSCI 20/35 Indexes**—they constrain the weight of the largest group entity at 35%, and all other group entities at 20%, with a buffer of 10% applied on these limits at each index rebalancing;
- **MSCI 10/50 Indexes**—they constrain the weight of the largest group entity at 10%, and the sum of the weights of all group entities representing more than 5% weight at 50%, with a buffer of 10% applied on these limits at each index review.

Interestingly, limiting the number of country-specific equity indexes' constituents is sometimes intentional and results from market circumstances. According to some index providers, it guarantees that all the underlying shares of the index have excellent liquidity (or at least sufficient from a point of view of investability), which results in an index that is suitable for investment products, including ETFs. This applies to exchanges in all countries, but in particular to emerging and frontier ones, where equity trading is focused on a small number of large-cap companies, often on a few ones only.[23] This issue is also essential for ETF sponsors, if they want to offer investors a replicable product, and market makers as their possibilities of the hedging position depend on the liquidity of the underlying instruments' market. As a result, the vast majority of major benchmarks tracked by single-country ETFs, even on the developed markets, consist of a relatively small number of securities, i.e., between 10 and 30.

Single-country equity exposure through passive instruments like ETFs also requires an appropriate risk approach. Risk navigation can be a serious and complicated challenge; therefore, some exchanges offer options on ETFs that can help manage country risk exposure. The largest and the most comprehensive offer of single-country ETFs options provides CBOE. Products of this kind are also available in EMEA region (e.g., on Eurex) and in APAC region (e.g., on ASX and JPX). Currency risk can be reduced by investing in country-specific currency-hedged ETFs. These instruments are widespread mainly in the USA, where they are offered, e.g., by BlackRock (iShares), Deutsche Bank (Xtrackers), WisdomTree, Franklin Templeton, and New York Life Investments (IQ). There is also a range of the currency-hedged ETFs

[23]According to OECD (2016), equity market trading concentration applies to countries with varying levels of development. For seven studied countries—five developed (USA, UK, Japan, Germany, and France) and two emerging (Turkey and Indonesia)—the share of total trading volume attributed to the 10% of largest companies in terms of market capitalization was over 70%, with the exception of Indonesia (68%). Moreover, in most of these markets, 20% of all trading was attributed to the largest 1% of companies.

listed on the European exchanges that cover the major single-country equity indexes (iShares, UBS, Xtrackers, Lyxor, and Amundi).

7.3 Americas

The offer of single-country exchange-traded funds providing exposure to the country equity markets in North America, Central America, Caribbean, and South America[24] is relatively modest. According to our analysis, it includes ETFs replicating indexes of 10 countries, including two developed, six emerging, and two frontier.[25] Selected country-specific ETFs are presented in Appendix: with developed markets exposure in Table A.1 (Panel A), with emerging markets exposure in Table A.2 (Panel A), and with frontier markets exposure in Table A.3 (Panel A). Major equity indexes tracked by ETFs focused on American countries, broken down into DM, EM, and FM exposure, are described in Table 7.1.

The ETF offer in this region is extremely concentrated. The vast majority are ETFs investing in US and Canadian stocks and listed mainly on stock exchanges in these two countries—predominantly on NYSE Arca, NASDAQ, CBOE BZX, and Toronto Stock Exchange.[26] Selected US and Canada-focused funds—usually tracking core benchmarks—are available to investors from other parts of the world as they are either cross-listed or registered for sale (mostly in Latin America countries[27]), or their counterparts are traded on European, Asian, and Australian exchanges.[28] Only few funds have exposure to selected Latam countries. They are listed on domestic, US and European stock exchanges.

Undoubtedly, the majority of American (and not only) ETF sponsors offer US-focused funds aiming to mirror the performance of the S&P 500 Index. This is one of the most iconic, core large-cap equity benchmarks globally. Furthermore, it is the world's most frequently used index by assets under

[24]Sub-regions according to the United Nations Statistics Division geoscheme for Americas.

[25]According to country classification of MSCI as of mid-2019.

[26]Assets of equity exchange-traded products with exposure to USA and Canada amounted to USD 2837 bn and USD 53 bn at the end of 2019, respectively, which accounted for 58.2 and 1.1% of total assets invested globally in equity ETPs (BlackRock 2020).

[27]The majority of ETFs listed in Chile, Colombia, and Mexico are cross-listings of funds having their primary listings in the USA or elsewhere. This is due to the fact, among others, that pension funds in many Latam countries have been allowed and encouraged to use foreign-domiciled ETFs to gain exposure to other markets (Fuhr 2015).

[28]Many American asset managers register their ETFs in these regions of the world in accordance with the applicable law (e.g., in the EU mainly in Ireland), which facilitates their distribution on those markets and enables to profile their offer for local investors.

Table 7.1 Major equity indexes tracked by exchange-traded funds in Americas

Country	Index	Description
Developed markets		
Canada	S&P/TSX Capped Composite Index	It is the primary gauge for Canadian-based, Toronto Stock Exchange-listed companies. It imposes capped weights of 10% on all of the constituents included in the S&P/TSX Composite Index that covers approximately 95% of the Canadian equities market
USA	S&P 500 Index	It is widely regarded as the best single gauge of large-cap US equities. The index includes 500 of the top companies in the leading industries of the US economy and covers approximately 80% of available market capitalization
Emerging markets		
Argentina	MSCI All Argentina 25/50 Index	It is designed to represent the performance of the broad Argentina equity universe, while including a minimum number of constituents (currently—25). It takes into account the 25 and 50% concentration constraints required for funds to qualify as a RIC in the USA
Brazil	Ibovespa Index	It is the main performance indicator of the stocks traded in B3 (Brasil, Bolsa, Balcão) and lists major companies in the Brazilian capital market. It accounts for about 80% of the number of trades and the financial volume of the Brazilian capital market

(continued)

Table 7.1 (continued)

Country	Index	Description
Chile	S&P IPSA Index	It seeks to measure the performance of the largest and most liquid stocks listed on the Santiago Exchange
Colombia	COLCAP Index	It is the market capitalization-weighted index, composed of the 25 most liquid stocks listed in the Bolsa de Valores de Colombia (BVC). Maximum stock weight is 20%
Mexico	S&P/BMV IPC Index	It seeks to measure the performance of the largest and most liquid stocks listed on the Bolsa Mexicana de Valores (BMV). The index is designed to provide a broad, representative, yet easily replicable index covering the Mexican equities market
Peru	MSCI All Peru Capped Index	It is designed to represent the performance of the broad Peru equity universe, while including a minimum number of constituents (currently—25). It takes into account the 25% and 50% concentration constraints required for funds to qualify as a RIC in the USA
Frontier markets		
Jamaica	JSE Financial Index	It is a major stock market index which tracks the performance of all ordinary companies listed on the Jamaica Stock Exchange (JSE)
Trinidad & Tobago	All T&T Index	It measures the price movements of listed companies that are registered in Trinidad & Tobago

Source Own study

management (AUM). There were USD 3.61 tn in assets (including USD 0.61 tn in exchange-traded products [ETPs]) indexed to, and USD 5.62 tn in assets benchmarked to the S&P 500 globally. The share of S&P 500 ETFs (excluding sector and style ETFs) in the total ETF assets based on all S&P Dow Jones Indices (USD 1.31 tn) amounted to 52% at the end of 2018 (S&P Global 2019).[29] The S&P 500 Index is the most frequently used single-country equity index in the world, in terms of both assets under management (AUM) and the number of ETFs.[30] For instance, the three largest ETFs in the USA (and worldwide)—SPDR S&P 500 ETF (also the world's most traded ETF), iShares Core S&P 500 ETF, and Vanguard S&P 500 ETF—replicate its performance. The same applies to some other regions of the world: The S&P 500 Index is tracked by the two largest European ETFs (iShares Core S&P 500 UCITS ETF USD (Acc) and Vanguard S&P 500 UCITS ETF USD) (Glow 2020), the largest ETF in Canada (BMO S&P 500 Index ETF) (CETFA 2020), and the third largest ETF in Australia (iShares S&P 500 ETF). The main reasons for huge popularity of ETFs linked to this index are its very high recognition among investors around the world, the fact that it is a representative benchmark for the largest equity market in the world and—last but not least—excellent investment results over the decades, especially in the long run.[31]

Other major US equity market indexes,[32] frequently replicated by most popular ETFs, include:

- CRSP US Total Market Index—it comprises nearly 4000 constituents across mega, large, small, and micro-capitalizations, representing almost 100% of the US investable equity market;
- Dow Jones Industrial Average Index—it is a price-weighted index of 30 US blue-chip companies covering all industries except transportation and utilities. It is the world's most cited equity market benchmark and the oldest continuous barometer of the US stock market. It is employed by ETPs whose total assets are USD 23.1 bn;

[29]S&P 500 Index is also by far the most used benchmark by European-listed ETFs (122 ETFs with EUR 135.9 bn AUM at the end of June 2019) (PwC 2019).

[30]The current full list of ETFs replicating the results of this index is available in S&P Dow Jones Indices (2020).

[31]For instance, according to the data from Crestmont Research, rolling 20-year returns of the S&P 500 Index inclusive of dividends over the past century (1919–2019) were positive, with only two exceptions (1948 and 1949) when they were less than 5% per annum. Meanwhile, it gained at least 10% per year over the trailing 20-year period in more than 40 years, and at least 13% per annum in 20 years (Williams 2020).

[32]Due to the limited scope of the book, this list does not include many other indexes, focused on a particular segment of the US stock market considering capitalization, investment style, etc. It also does not include numerous indexes that use alternative (other than capitalization) weighting methods, smart beta indexes, and strategy (i.e., short and leveraged) indexes. A similar approach will be used to characterize the country-specific ETFs in other regions. A broad overview of the funds linked to the US indexes can be found, e.g., in Balchunas (2016). A comprehensive list of US-specific ETFs is available on professional websites, e.g., etf.com, etfdb.com (US-listed), justetf.com (European-listed).

- Russell 1000 Index—it measures the performance of the large-cap segment of the US equity universe and includes approximately 1000 of the largest US securities;
- Russell 2000 Index—measures the performance of the small-cap segment of the US equity universe and includes approximately 2000 of the US smallest securities;
- S&P MidCap 400 Index—it measures the performance of 400 mid-sized US companies and is employed by ETPs whose total assets are USD 60.5 bn;
- S&P SmallCap 600 Index—it seeks to measure the small-cap segment of the US equity market and is employed by ETPs whose total assets are USD 40.6 bn.[33]

Equity ETFs with US exposure are offered by all major providers of these financial instruments worldwide—Americans (e.g., BlackRock (iShares), Vanguard, State Street (SPDR), Invesco, Schwab, First Trust[34]),[35] Canadians (e.g., BMO AM, Horizons), Europeans (e.g., Amundi, Deutsche Bank [Xtrackers], Lyxor, UBS, HSBC, BNP Paribas), Asians (e.g., Nomura AM, Nikko AM), and from Latin America (e.g., Itau AM).

Among the most popular Canadian-focused equity ETFs, there are those replicating two major indexes widely regarded as the best gauges for Canadian public companies. The S&P/TSX Capped Composite Index covers approximately 95% of the Canadian equities market and includes about 230 stocks listed on Toronto Stock Exchange (TSX). Two out of the three largest ETFs with exclusively Canadian exposure aim to track its performance: iShares Core S&P/TSX Capped Composite Index ETF and BMO S&P/TSX Capped Composite Index ETF. The S&P/TSX 60 Index captures the large-cap market segment of the Canadian equity market. Two of the most popular Canada-specific ETFs aim to track the performance of this index: iShares S&P/TSX 60 Index ETF (the first ETF in the world[36]) and Horizons S&P/TSX 60 Index ETF (all above ETFs are listed on the TSX). Other popular ETFs listed on other exchanges investing in Canada-based

[33]All data concerning assets of ETFs tracking Dow Jones Industrial Average Index, S&P MidCap 400 Index, and S&P SmallCap 600 Index as of end 2018 (S&P Global 2019).

[34]The first three companies are the three largest ETF sponsors in the world. The following three are in the top 10 ETF providers globally.

[35]Many American asset managers—for example, BlackRock, Vanguard, State Street, Invesco—offer US ETFs also in other regions of the world.

[36]Toronto 35 Index Participation Fund was launched in Canada in March 1990. In 2000, it was merged with the Hundred Index Participation Fund to create iUnits S&P/TSE Index Participation Fund, which has been renamed the iShares CDN S&P/TSX 60 Index Fund (Fuhr 2015).

stocks track the FTSE Canada All Cap Index, the MSCI Canada Custom Capped Index, and the Morningstar Canada Target Market Exposure Index. Apart from Canadian and US providers, ETFs with Canadian exposure are offered also by European issuers (e.g., UBS, Deutsche Bank, Lyxor, HSBC).

The catalog of ETFs investing in individual Latin America countries is quite meager, in terms of both the number of countries and the number of funds. These funds are provided by local asset managers (e.g., Itau AM, Caixa), US ETF sponsors (e.g., BlackRock, Global X, Franklin Templeton, VanEck), European issuers (e.g., Lyxor, Amundi, Deutsche Bank, HSBC, Banco Bilbao Vizcaya Argentaria [BBVA]), and Asian managers (e.g., Nomura AM). The most frequently indexed are blue-chip benchmarks comprising the largest and most liquid stocks listed on the domestic exchange. Some of them are maintained by stock exchanges (e.g., Ibovespa, COLCAP) and others by recognized, foreign index providers (e.g., the S&P/BMV IPC, the S&P IPSA, the MSCI Brazil, the MSCI All Argentina 25/50 Index). ETFs investing in Latam equity countries are largely concentrated in two major markets—Brazil and Mexico. Among the most popular single-country funds, in terms of AUM, there are: iShares NAFTRAC,[37] MEXTRAC 09 (both listed on BMV), PIBB—Fundo de Índice Brasil-50 (listed on B3 [Bovespa]), iShares MSCI Brazil ETF, iShares MSCI Mexico ETF (listed on NYSE Arca), iShares MSCI Chile ETF (listed on CBOE BZX), and iShares MSCI Brazil UCITS ETF and Lyxor MSCI Brazil UCITS ETF (the last two listed on European exchanges).

7.4 Europe, Middle East, and Africa (EMEA)

The most extensive offer of single-country equity ETFs applies to the EMEA region. It includes, to our knowledge, funds tracking indexes with exposure to 37 countries, including 16 developed, 11 emerging, and 10 frontier ones. Selected country-specific ETFs are presented in Appendix: with developed markets exposure in Table A.1 (Panel B), with emerging markets exposure in Table A.2 (Panel B), and with frontier markets exposure in Table A.3 (Panels B, C, and D). Major equity indexes tracked by ETFs focusing on European, Middle Eastern, and African markets, broken down into DM, EM, and FM exposure, are described in Table 7.2.

[37]NAFTRAC was the first ETF in Latin America, launched on April 16, 2002, on Bolsa Mexicana De Valores. It was designed to track the Mexican IPC Index (currently S&P/BMV IPC Index). BlackRock acquired the fund from Nacional Financiera on May 14, 2009, and it has since been renamed iShares NAFTRAC (BlackRock 2011).

Table 7.2 Major equity indexes tracked by exchange-traded funds in EMEA countries

Country	Index	Description
Developed markets		
Austria	ATX Index	It is a free float market capitalization-weighted price index made up of the 20 most liquid stocks traded on Vienna Stock Exchange and listed in the "prime market." Constituent weights are capped on a quarterly basis to ensure compliance with UCITS standards for portfolio diversification
Belgium	BEL 20 Index	It is a free float market capitalization-weighted index that reflects the performance of the 20 largest shares listed on Euronext Brussels, and is the most widely used indicator of the Belgian stock market
Denmark	OMX Copenhagen 25 Index	It is a market value-weighted, free float-adjusted and capped index. It contains the 25 largest and most traded shares on NASDAQ Copenhagen
Finland	OMX Helsinki 25 Index	It is the Helsinki Stock Exchange leading share index that consists of the 25 most actively traded stocks on the HSE. It is a capitalization-weighted stock price index
France	CAC 40 Index	It is a free float market capitalization-weighted index that reflects the performance of the 40 largest and most actively traded shares listed on Euronext Paris, and is the most widely used indicator of the Paris stock market

(continued)

Table 7.2 (continued)

Country	Index	Description
Germany	DAX Index	It tracks the segment of the largest and most important companies on the German equities market. It contains shares of the 30 largest and most liquid companies admitted to the FWB Frankfurt Stock Exchange in the Prime Standard segment. The DAX represents 72% of the aggregated Prime Standard's market-cap
Ireland	ISEquation 20 Index	It is a free float market capitalization-weighted index that reflects the performance of the 20 largest shares listed on Euronext Dublin, and is the most widely used indicator of the Irish stock market
Israel	TA-35 Index	It is the Tel Aviv Stock Exchange (TASE) flagship index. It tracks prices of the 35 companies with the highest market capitalization on the exchange that matches the index criteria
Italy	FTSE MIB Index	It is the primary benchmark index for the Italian equity markets and measures the performance of 40 equities. Capturing approximately 80% of the domestic market capitalization, the index is comprised of highly liquid, leading companies across ICB sectors in Italy
Netherlands	AEX Index	It is a free float market capitalization-weighted index that reflects the performance of the 25 largest and most actively traded shares listed on Euronext Amsterdam, and is the most widely used indicator of the Dutch stock market

(continued)

Table 7.2 (continued)

Country	Index	Description
Norway	OBX Index	It consists of the 25 most traded securities on Oslo Børs, based on six months turnover rating. It is a free float-adjusted total return index and is capped to comply with UCITS III Directive, and the total weighting of non-EEA companies is limited to a maximum of 10%
Portugal	PSI 20 Index	It is a free float market capitalization-weighted index that reflects the performance of the maximum 20 most actively traded shares listed on Euronext Lisbon, and is the most widely used indicator of the Portuguese stock market
Spain	IBEX 35 Index	It is made up by the 35 most liquid securities traded on the Bolsas y Mercados Españoles (BME), used as a domestic and international benchmark. It is a price index that is weighted by capitalization and adjusted according to the free float
Sweden	OMX Stockholm 30 Index	It is the Stockholm Stock Exchange's leading share index. It consists of the 30 most actively traded stocks on the Stockholm Stock Exchange and is a market-weighted price index
Switzerland	SMI Index	It is the most important stock index in Switzerland. It comprises the 20 largest stocks from the SPI with weight capping to 20%. It is free float-adjusted and covers approximately 80% of the total capitalization of the Swiss equity market

(continued)

Table 7.2 (continued)

Country	Index	Description
UK	FTSE 100 Index	It is a market capitalization-weighted index of UK-listed blue-chip companies. It measures the performance of the 100 largest companies traded on the London Stock Exchange (LSE) that pass screening for size and liquidity
Emerging Markets		
Czechia	PX Index	It is the official price index of the Prague Stock Exchange (PSE). It is a free float-weighted price index made up of the most liquid stocks. Their number is variable (currently 12)
Egypt	EGX30 Index	It includes the top 30 companies in terms of liquidity and activity listed on the Egyptian Exchange (EGX). It is weighted by market capitalization and adjusted by the free float
Greece	FTSE/Athex Large-Cap Index	It represents the performance of the 25 biggest, in terms of capitalization, listed companies in Athens Exchange (Athex)
Hungary	BUX Index	It is the official index of blue-chip shares with the biggest market value and turnover listed on the Budapest Stock Exchange. It consists of a variable number of stocks (currently—14)
Poland	WIG20 Index	It is a blue-chip index that consists of the 20 biggest and most liquid companies of the Warsaw Stock Exchange (WSE) Main List. It is a price index and may not include more than 5 companies from a single exchange sector. The weighting of a single company in the index may not exceed 15%

(continued)

Table 7.2 (continued)

Country	Index	Description
Qatar	QE Index	It is a free float market capitalization index that measures the 20 largest and most liquid stocks in the Qatar Stock Exchange. The 15% cap is applied to an individual constituent's weight in the index
Russia	RTS Index	It is capitalization-weighted composite index based on prices of the most liquid Russian stocks (ca. 40) of the largest and dynamically developing Russian issuers present on the Moscow Exchange
Saudi Arabia	MSCI Tadawul 30 Index	It targets the top 30 securities, listed on the Saudi Main Equity Market, based on free float market capitalization with capping criteria, screened for liquidity and international investability
South Africa	FTSE/JSE Top 40 Index	It consists of the 40 largest companies, ranked by investable market value in the FTSE/JSE All-Share Index
Turkey	BIST 30 Index	It consists of 30 stocks selected from among the stocks of companies traded on the Stars Market in Borsa Istanbul Equity Market. It is free float market capitalization-weighted index
United Arab Emirates (UAE)	MSCI All UAE Capped Index	It represents the performance of the broad UAE equity universe, while including a minimum number of constituents (currently—28). It takes into account the 25% and 50% concentration constraints required for funds to qualify as a RIC in the USA

(continued)

Table 7.2 (continued)

Country	Index	Description
Frontier markets		
Bulgaria	SOFIX Index	It is the main index of the Bulgarian Stock Exchange (BSE) and consists of the 15 most liquid companies on BSE. Maximum weight of a single issuer and single sector is capped at 15 and 20%, respectively
Croatia	CROBEX Index	It is the main index of the Zagreb Stock Exchange and consists of a variable number (between 15 and 25) of stocks (currently—21). It is a price, free float market capitalization-weighted index
Iceland	OMX Iceland 10 Cap Index	It comprises the 10 shares with the largest volume of trading on NASDAQ Iceland. The largest company in the index must not weigh more than 35% and the next companies may not weigh more than 20% (on a daily basis) or 30 and 15% (on semi-annual capping)
Kuwait	FTSE Kuwait All Cap 15% Capped Index	It is a market capitalization-weighted index designed to represent the performance of Kuwaiti large-cap, mid-cap, and small-cap stocks. Companies are capped at 15% on a quarterly basis to avoid overconcentration
Nigeria	NSE 30 Index	It tracks the top 30 companies listed on the Nigerian Stock Exchange (NSE) in terms of market capitalization and liquidity. It is a price index and is weighted by adjusted market capitalization

(continued)

Table 7.2 (continued)

Country	Index	Description
North Macedonia	MBI10 Index	It consists of up to 10 listed shares, chosen by the Macedonian Stock Exchange Index Commission, according to the index methodology. It is a price-weighted index with the free float market capitalization
Romania	BET Index	It is a free float market capitalization-weighted index of the most liquid Romanian companies listed on Bucharest Stock Exchange's regulated market. It has a variable number of constituents, between 10 and 20 (currently—17). Maximum weight of a single issuer is capped at 20%
Serbia	BELEX15 Index	It is the leading index of the Belgrade Stock Exchange and consists of most liquid Serbian shares. It is a free float market capitalization-weighted index. It has a variable number of constituents, between 7 and 15 (currently—10). Maximum weight of a single component is capped at 20%
Slovakia	SAX Index	It is the official share index of the Bratislava Stock Exchange. It is a capitalization-weighted, total return index. The weight of each company in the index must not exceed the maximum 20%. It comprises currently 7 companies
Slovenia	SBI TOP Index	It is the main index of the Ljubljana Stock Exchange. It measures the performance of the most liquid and highly capitalized stocks. It is a price index, weighted by free float market capitalization. It consists of 5–15 shares (currently—11). Maximum weight of a single company is 30%

Source Own study

The spectrum of EMEA-specific ETFs is very large and diverse. It mainly covers a multitude of funds listed on the five most developed (in this regard) European exchanges—London Stock Exchange, Deutsche Boerse, Euronext Paris, SIX Swiss Exchange, and Borsa Italiana. Some European-domiciled UCITS ETFs, typically aiming to mirror returns of the most popular benchmarks, are cross-listed or registered for sale in other regions (mainly in Asia and Latin America).[38] Access to ETFs investing in European markets is also possible via funds listed on trading platforms in all other regions of the world, though their offer is limited. Relatively few funds aim to provide investment results that closely correspond to the performance of indexes representing the Middle East and African equity markets. They are mainly listed on local, but also on US and some European exchanges.

Within numerous equity indexes replicated by European country-specific ETFs, the most recognized and most frequently employed are the following large-cap benchmarks: the FTSE 100 Index (UK), the DAX (Germany), the CAC 40 (France), the SMI (Switzerland), the FTSE MIB (Italy), the AEX (Netherlands), the OMX Stockholm 30 (Sweden), and the IBEX 35 (Spain) (all these indexes are described in Table 7.2). For instance, the FTSE 100 Index was the first European single-country index used to create ETF that is currently the largest single-country ETF with European exposure,[39] while the DAX Index is the second most used single-country equity index (after S&P 500) in the European ETF market.[40]

Large accessibility of European country-focused ETFs worldwide is due to the three main reasons. Firstly, geographically fragmented European market strongly influences the development of the ETF industry.[41] This results in a market crowded with numerous offerings for the same exposure (Bioy et al. 2019). Both major European and US ETF issuers, like Deutsche Bank, Lyxor (these two firms are in the top 10 ETF providers globally), Amundi, UBS, BlackRock, Vanguard, State Street, and Invesco, usually offer several or even

[38]Some European asset managers register UCITS ETFs in these regions and distribute them on local markets. According to PwC research (2019), the highest number of registrations of cross-border UCITS ETFs outside Europe was in Singapore (291), Chile (103), Japan (37), Mexico (33), and South Africa (21) as of end June 2019. These ETFs are managed mostly by BlackRock (iShares), UBS, Deutsche Bank (Xtrackers), Invesco, Lyxor, Amundi, and BNP Paribas.

[39]iShares FTSE 100 Index Fund was listed on the London Stock Exchange on April 27, 2000, as third ETF in Europe, after LDRS DJ STOXX 50 and LDRS DJ EUROSTOXX 50.

[40]According to PwC (2019), 22 funds with EUR 16.5 bn were listed on the European platforms as of end June 2019. First ETF on DAX—DAX EX—was launched on Deutsche Boerse on January 3, 2001, by Indexchange. Today, as iShares Core DAX UCITS ETF (DE), it is part of the product family of BlackRock (Deutsche Boerse 2020).

[41]More on the European ETF market in Marszk and Lechman (2019).

a dozen or so ETFs with single-country exposures.[42] In this way, they want their offer to reach the widest possible range of clients, especially the most affluent ones, from Western European countries. Although this requires a significant commitment on the part of these companies, increasingly liberal regulations regarding the cross-border distribution of UCITS funds in the European Union and favorable financial environment in some countries (e.g., efficient tax regimes for funds, ease of fund launching and listing) cause that they register funds typically in Ireland or Luxembourg and distribute them in many European countries.[43] Thus, despite the fact that the segment of single-country ETFs is already very saturated, new entrants still keep entering this market, bringing investors additional me-too products. Secondly, there are an increasing number of medium- and small-sized European ETF issuers that launch domestically-focused or regionally-focused funds aimed at attracting local, mostly retail investors.[44] This applies primarily to Nordic countries (e.g., Xact Kapitalförvaltning, DNB, Seligson & Co.) and CEE countries (e.g., Expat Capital, Beta Securities Poland). Thirdly, cross-border UCITS funds distribution makes it possible to offer ETFs globally (as mentioned before), so US companies sell funds investing in European markets worldwide, as well as some local ETF providers bring funds replicating European indexes to their own markets.[45]

The offer of single-country equity ETFs enabling exposure to individual Middle East and African countries is relatively small. They are predominantly funds with exposure to Israel (tracking local indexes, like the TA-35 Index, as well as BlueStar Indexes and MSCI Indexes) and South Africa (tracking FTSE indexes and MSCI indexes—e.g., the FTSE/JSE Top 40 Index and the MSCI South Africa Index). These funds are listed on local exchanges (Tel Aviv Stock Exchange [TASE] and Johannesburg Stock Exchange [JSE]), the US exchanges (NYSE Arca, CBOE Global Markets), and European exchanges (e.g., London Stock Exchange). They are provided by both local (e.g., KSM, Tachlit, Harel [Israel], Satrix, Sygnia, 1nvest, Ashburton [South Africa]) and US (e.g., BlackRock, VanEck, Franklin Templeton, ARK) firms. Some

[42]Many providers of European ETFs, in contrast to the USA, adopted "coffee shop" approach to their offerings; that is, they offer similar products based on the same benchmarks (Fuhr 2015).

[43]According to Morningstar data, cited by Irish Funds (2018), over 70% of the total ETF assets in Europe are domiciled in Ireland and Luxembourg (54 and 17%, respectively). They are followed by France (12%), Germany (9%), and Switzerland (3%). Ireland's leadership position results from the fact that the vast majority of US managers prefer this country as a domicile of choice due to a similar legal system, cultural similarities, and the fact that English is the primary working language in both countries.

[44]There were 70 ETF providers in the European ETF market at the end of 2019 (ETFGI 2020).

[45]For instance, HuaAn AM (Hong Kong) and Tachlit (Israel) offer ETFs that mirror DAX Index, and Tachlit offers ETF tracking CAC 40 Index.

South African ETFs are cross-listed on four African exchanges (Botswana Stock Exchange, Ghana Stock Exchange, Stock Exchange of Mauritius, and Namibian Stock Exchange) (Fuhr 2015).

Other Middle East and African country-specific equity ETFs include funds investing in:

- Egypt (managed by, e.g., VanEck and Beltone Financial),
- Kuwait (offered by Hanetf),
- Nigeria (offered by, e.g., Global X, Stanbic IBTC AM, and Greenwich AM),
- Qatar (managed by, e.g., BlackRock and Masraf Al Ryan),
- Saudi Arabia (managed by, e.g., Falcom, BlackRock, Franklin Templeton, HSBC, and Invesco),
- United Arab Emirates (offered by BlackRock).

7.5 Asia-Pacific (APAC)

Investors have a substantial offer of funds tracking the performance of country equity indexes across APAC region at their disposal. According to our estimates, it encompasses ETFs with exposure to 17 markets, including five developed, nine emerging, and three frontier ones. Selected country-specific ETFs are presented in Appendix: with developed markets exposure in Table A.1 (Panel C), with emerging markets exposure in Table A.2 (Panel C), and with frontier markets exposure in Table A.3 (Panel E). Major equity indexes tracked by ETFs and focused on Asia-Pacific countries, broken down into DM, EM, and FM exposure, are described in Table 7.4.

APAC-focused single-country ETFs are primarily listed on leading local stock exchanges: Japan Exchange Group (JPX) (Tokyo SE and Osaka Exchange), Australian Securities Exchange (ASX), Hong Kong Stock Exchange (HKEX), Singapore Exchange (SGX), Korea Exchange (KRX), Chinese exchanges (Shanghai Stock Exchange (SSE), Shenzhen Stock Exchange (SZSE)), and National Stock Exchange of India (NSE). Investors can trade on these platforms both domestic ETFs managed by local companies, cross-listed European UCITS funds and ETFs managed by branches of major global asset managers, mostly American ones. Passive funds with Asia and Pacific exposure are obtainable too—although in smaller numbers—on the US, Canada, and EMEA exchanges.[46]

[46]More detailed information on ETF market in Asia-Pacific region can be found in Marszk et al. (2019).

Asia-Pacific markets offer numerous globally-recognized equity indexes that are employed by asset managers creating ETFs and other index-linked financial products. The most popular ones comprise blue-chip equity benchmarks, constructed and maintained by stock exchanges: Nikkei 225 and TOPIX (Japan), S&P/ASX 200 (Australia), Hang Seng (Hong Kong), Straits Times (Singapore), S&P/NZX 50 (New Zealand), KOSPI 200 (South Korea), SSE 50 and CSI 300 (China), and Nifty 50 (India) (all these indexes are described in Table 7.4). ETF issuers use also other market barometers calculated by major index providers (MSCI, S&P Dow Jones Indices, and FTSE Russell) as well as by many small index companies specialized in Asian markets.

The largest single-country APAC ETFs are those replicating Japanese large-cap indexes. The first fund of the kind was launched in 1995 on Tokyo Stock Exchange and tracked Nikkei 300 Index (Osaki 2001).[47] Nowadays, Japanese investors may choose from more than 30 Japan-focused equity ETFs (excluding sector and thematic ETF) listed on the JPX. The largest encompass Nomura TOPIX ETF, Nikko Listed Index Fund TOPIX, Nomura Nikkei 225 ETF, Daiwa ETF-TOPIX, Nikko Listed Index Fund 225, Daiwa ETF-Nikkei 225, Maxis Nikkei 225 ETF, and Maxis TOPIX ETF. Most of those funds are larger than any other single-country ETFs, except US-focused ETFs. Nomura AM, Nikko AM, and Daiwa are also the three largest ETF providers in Japan and can be found in the top 15 ETF issuers globally.

Investors from the USA and Europe also have a very wide and diverse selection of ETFs investing in Japanese stocks. The two largest ETFs addressed to American investors are iShares MSCI Japan ETF (it replicates the performance of MSCI Japan Index and is listed on NYSE Arca) and JPMorgan BetaBuilders Japan ETF (it tracks Morningstar Japan Target Market Exposure Index and is listed on CBOE Global Markets). European investors invest most willingly in iShares Core MSCI Japan IMI UCITS ETF seeking to track the performance of MSCI Japan IMI (listed on five European exchanges and cross-listed in Mexico) and Lyxor JPX-Nikkei 400 (DR) UCITS ETF Daily Hedged to EUR that aims to mirror JPX Nikkei Net Total Return Index (listed on three European exchanges). Additionally, ETFs with Japan exposure are traded, inter alia, on stock exchanges in Australia, Hong Kong, Israel, Singapore, South Africa, South Korea, and Taiwan.

The scope of offer of ETFs that are exposed to other Asia-Pacific equity markets is highly diversified. Investors seeking the possibility of passive investing in Australian, Chinese, Indian, and Korean stocks have the widest

[47] Currently, it operates as Nomura Nikkei 300 Stock Index Listed Fund and is managed by Nomura AM.

selection. Those who want to gain exposure to other emerging and frontier markets have a much poorer choice. The largest APAC (ex-Japan) country-specific ETFs available on Asia-Pacific exchanges are:

- China 50 ETF (managed by China AM, listed on SSE, and tracking the SSE 50 Index),
- China CSI 500 ETF (managed by China Southern Fund Management, listed on the SSE, and tracking the CSI 500 Index),
- Hang Seng Index ETF (managed by Hang Seng Investment Management, listed on the HKEX, and tracking the Hang Seng Index),
- Huatai-PineBridge CSI 300 ETF (managed by Huatai-PineBridge Fund Management, listed on the SSE, and tracking the CSI 300 Index),
- Samsung KODEX 200 ETF (managed by Samsung AM, listed on the KSE, and tracking the KODEX 200 Index),
- SBI–ETF Nifty 50 (managed by SBI Funds Management, listed on the NSE, and tracking the Nifty 50 Index),
- SPDR S&P/ASX 200 Fund (managed by State Street Global Advisors, listed on the ASX, and tracking the S&P/ASX 200 Index),
- Tracker Fund of Hong Kong (managed by State Street Global Advisors, listed on the HKEX, and tracking the Hang Seng Index; it is one of the two first ETFs in the Asia-Pacific region outside Japan[48]),
- Vanguard Australian Shares Index ETF (managed by Vanguard Australia, listed on the ASX, and tracking the S&P/ASX 300 Index),
- Yuanta/P-shares Taiwan Top 50 ETF (managed by Yuanta Securities, listed on the TWSE, and tracking the FTSE TWSE Taiwan 50 Index).

Asia-Pacific (ex-Japan) single-country ETFs are quite popular also in the USA. The most used indexes in this respect are MSCI indexes that are employed mainly by BlackRock. The largest ETFs across this category are: iShares MSCI China ETF (listed on the NASDAQ and tracking the MSCI China Index), iShares China Large-Cap ETF (listed on the NYSE Arca and tracking the FTSE China 50 Index), iShares MSCI India ETF (listed on the Cboe BZX and tracking the MSCI India Index), iShares MSCI South Korea ETF (listed on the NYSE Arca and cross-listed on the ASX, tracking the MSCI Korea 25/50 Index), and iShares MSCI Taiwan ETF (managed by BlackRock, listed on the NYSE Arca, and tracking the MSCI Taiwan 25/50 Index). Other North American providers whose funds are traded on the US and Canadian exchanges are: Franklin Templeton (Australia, China,

[48]Tracker Fund of Hong Kong (TraKH) was launched on November 11, 1999.

Hong Kong, India, South Korea, Taiwan), Van Eck (China, India, Indonesia, Vietnam), Wisdom Tree (China, India),[49] Global X (China, Pakistan), State Street (China, Hong Kong), Deutsche Bank (China), KraneShares (China), and BMO (China, India).

European investors primarily have a huge selection of Chinese-focused ETFs at their disposal—they are offered, e.g., by Deutsche Bank, BlackRock, Lyxor, HSBC, Deka, Amundi, L&G, Franklin Templeton, UBS, and Wisdom Tree. Furthermore, they can invest in funds providing exposure to equity markets in Australia, Hong Kong, India, Indonesia, Malaysia, Pakistan, Philippines, Singapore, South Korea, Taiwan, Thailand, and Vietnam. Chinese and Indian equity ETFs are also listed on the stock exchange in Israel.

When investing in ETFs with exposure to the Chinese equity market, it is extremely important to consciously distinguish between different Chinese share classes. China-incorporated companies, listed in the People's Republic of China (PRC), issue different classes of shares, depending on where they are listed and which investors are allowed to own them. The classes are A, B, and H, which are all renminbi-denominated shares but traded in different currencies, depending on where they are listed. In turn, China companies incorporated and listed outside PRC are generally referred to as "Red Chips," "P Chips," "S Chips," or "N Shares," depending on their ownership structure, revenue source, and listing location. These types of shares may have different definitions among index providers or exchanges (FTSE Russell 2019). Detailed information on the Chinese share classes are presented in Table 7.3.

The classification of Chinese shares is crucial from the point of view of foreign investors interested in this market, as only some classes are available to them. This also applies to those investing in ETFs, because access to the Chinese stock market is only possible through funds that track indexes covering share classes available to foreign investors.

[49]Untypical ETFs investing in China and India are WisdomTree China ex-State-Owned Enterprises Fund and WisdomTree India ex-State-Owned Enterprises Fund. They seek to track the investment results of Chinese and Indian companies, respectively, that are not state-owned enterprises, which is defined as government ownership of greater than 20%.

Table 7.3 Characteristics of the Chinese share classes

Share class	Country of incorporation	Country of listing	Trading currency	Other requirements	Available to mainland Chinese investors	Available to other investors
A-share	People's Republic of China (PRC)	China	CNY		Yes	Yes under QFII/RQFII/Stock Connect programs
B-share	People's Republic of China (PRC)	China	USD (Shanghai) HKD (Shenzhen)	None as they are specific share classes issued by the company	Yes (if they have appropriate currency accounts)	Yes
H-share	People's Republic of China (PRC)	Hong Kong	HKD		Yes if QDII approved or under Stock Connect programs	Yes
Red Chip	Non-PRC	Hong Kong	HKD		Yes if QDII approved or under Stock Connect programs	Yes
P Chip	Non-PRC	Hong Kong	HKD	According to index providers' definition	Yes if QDII approved or under Stock Connect programs	Yes
S Chip	Non-PRC	Singapore	SGD		Yes if QDII approved	Yes

(continued)

Table 7.3 (continued)

Share class	Country of incorporation	Country of listing	Trading currency	Other requirements	Available to mainland Chinese investors	Available to other investors
N Share	Non-PRC	USA	USD		Yes if QDII approved	Yes

Note QDII (Qualified Domestic Institutional Investors Scheme)—a scheme that enables domestic (mainland) fund managers to invest onshore capital outside of China; QFII (qualified institutional investors)—large financial institutions having access to the A-share market; RQFII (Renminbi QFII)—program that facilitates foreign investment in the mainland via offshore renminbi accounts
Source FTSE Russell (2019)

Table 7.4 Major equity indexes tracked by exchange-traded funds in APAC countries

Country	Index	Description
Developed markets		
Australia	S&P/ASX 200 Index	It measures the performance of the 200 largest index-eligible stocks listed on the Australian Securities Exchange (ASX) by float-adjusted market capitalization. It is widely considered Australia's preeminent benchmark index
Hong Kong	Hang Seng Index	It is the most widely quoted gauge of the Hong Kong stock market. It includes 50 largest and most liquid stocks listed on the Main Board of the Stock Exchange of Hong Kong. Stocks are free float-adjusted for investability representation. 10% capping is applied to avoid single stock domination
Japan	Nikkei Stock Average (Nikkei225) Index	It is used around the globe as the premier index of Japanese stocks. It is an adjusted price-weighted equity index which consists of 225 stocks in the First Section of the Tokyo Stock Exchange
New Zealand	S&P/NZX 50 Portfolio Index	It is widely considered New Zealand's preeminent benchmark index. It measures the performance of the 50 largest, eligible stocks listed on the Main Board of the New Zealand's Exchange (NZX) by float-adjusted market capitalization (with 5% cap). It covers approximately 90% of New Zealand equity market capitalization
Singapore	Straits Times Index (STI)	It is the most globally-recognized benchmark index and market barometer for Singapore. It is a market capitalization-weighted index that tracks the performance of the top 30 largest and most liquid companies listed on the Singapore Exchange (SGX) Main Board

(continued)

Table 7.4 (continued)

Country	Index	Description
Emerging markets		
China	SSE 50 Index	It consists of the 50 largest and most liquid A-share stocks listed on Shanghai Stock Exchange (SSE). It reflects the overall performance of the most influential leading Shanghai stocks. It is a free float-adjusted market capitalization index with 10% cap
India	Nifty 50 Index	It is a well-diversified index comprising 50 leading companies accounting for 13 sectors of the economy and listed on the National Stock Exchange of India (NSE). It is computed using the free float market capitalization method. It represents 65–70% of the free float market capitalization of the stocks listed on NSE
Indonesia	LQ-45 Index	It measures the stock price performance of 45 stocks listed on the Indonesia Stock Exchange (IDX) with relatively large market capitalization, high liquidity, and good fundamentals. It is free float-adjusted market capitalization-weighted index. The weight of a single issuer is capped at 15%
Malaysia	FTSE Bursa Malaysia KLCI (Kuala Lumpur Composite Index)	It comprises the largest 30 companies listed on the Main Board of Bursa Malaysia by full market capitalization that meet the eligibility requirements of the FTSE Bursa Malaysia Ground Rules
Pakistan	MSCI All Pakistan Select 25/50 Index	It is designed to represent the performance of the Broad Pakistan Equity Universe, while including constituents with minimum level of liquidity and applying the MSCI 25/50 Indexes methodology. It includes 30 constituents

(continued)

Table 7.4 (continued)

Country	Index	Description
Philippines	Philippine Stock Exchange Index	It is the main index of the Philippine Stock Exchange (PSE). It is composed of the 30 largest and most liquid stocks listed on the PSE. It is computed using full market capitalization for domestic companies and the free float market capitalization for foreign companies
South Korea	KOSPI 200 Index	It is widely known as a Korean blue-chip index. It comprises 200 constituents that are market and industry leaders with decent liquidity
Taiwan	FTSE TWSE Taiwan 50 Index	It is a headline index of the Taiwan Stock Exchange (TWSE). It comprises the top 50 Taiwanese companies by market capitalization that meet the relevant investability screening requirements set by FTSE and representing nearly 70% of the Taiwanese equity market
Thailand	SET50 Index	It is a market capitalization-weighted price index that covers the top 50 listed companies on Stock Exchange of Thailand (SET) in terms of large market capitalization, high liquidity, and compliance with the requirements regarding distribution of shares to minor shareholders
Frontier markets		
Bangladesh	MSCI Bangladesh IMI Index	It measures the performance of the large-cap, mid-cap, and small-cap segments of the Bangladesh market. With 40 constituents, it covers approximately 99% of the free float-adjusted market capitalization in Bangladesh
Kazakhstan	KASE Index	It is the main index of Kazakhstan Stock Exchange (KASE). It reflects the change in the total market value of the most liquid shares of the KASE official list, issued by major financially stable companies-residents of the Republic of Kazakhstan. It currently comprises 8 constituents

(continued)

Table 7.4 (continued)

Country	Index	Description
Vietnam	MSCI Vietnam Index	It measures the performance of the large-cap and mid-cap segments of the Vietnamese market. With 17 constituents, it covers approximately 85% of the Vietnam equity universe

Source Own study

References

Balchunas, E. (2016). *The Institutional ETF Toolbox: How Institutions Can Understand and Utilize the Fast-Growing World of ETFs*. Hoboken: Wiley and Bloomberg Press.

Bioy, H., Garcia-Zarate, J., Lamont, K., Boyadzhiev, D., & Kang, H. (2019). *A Guided Tour of the European ETF Marketplace*. Morningstar. https://www.morningstar.com/lp/guided-tour-european-etf-marketplace. Accessed 10 Sept 2019.

BlackRock. (2011, April). ETF Landscape. *Latin America Industry Review*.

BlackRock. (2020). *BlackRock Global ETP Landscape*. Quarterly Highlights Q4 2019. https://cdn.prgloo.com/media/download/ac84a79c8d5b4b5eba637f4418602d01. Accessed 15 Mar 2020.

CETFA. (2020). *Canadian ETF Assets as of March 31, 2020*. http://www.cetfa.ca/files/1586909647_NEW-%20CETFA%20March%202020.pdf. Accessed 14 Apr 2020.

Choi, N., Fedenia, M., Skiba, H., & Sokolyk, T. (2017). Portfolio Concentration and Performance of Institutional Investors Worldwide. *Journal of Financial Economics, 123*(1), 189–208.

Deutsche Boerse. (2020). *20 Years ETF Trading on Xetra*. https://www.xetra.com/resource/blob/1866384/a822d6fdb9c3bacf095c8970b838da42/data/Factsheet-Zahlen-und-Fakten-2019_en.pdf. Accessed 15 Apr 2020.

Dimson, E., Marsh, P., & Staunton, M. (2015). *Credit Suisse Global Investment Returns Yearbook 2015*. Credit Suisse Research Institute. https://www.credit-suisse.com/media/assets/corporate/docs/about-us/research/publications/global-investment-returns-yearbook-2015.pdf. Accessed 5 Jan 2020.

Edwards, T., & Lazzara, C. J. (2019). *Sector Effects in the S&P 500: The Role of Sectors in Risk, Pricing, and Active Returns*. https://www.cboe.com/products/research-sector-effects-in-the-sp-500.pdf. Accessed 22 Feb 2020.

ETFGI. (2020). *Happy 20th Anniversary to the ETF Industry in Europe*. https://etfgi.com/news/press-releases/2020/04/happy-20th-anniversary-etf-industry-europe. Accessed 28 Apr 2020.

FTSE Russell. (2019). *Guide to Chinese Share Classes v. 1.5*. https://research.ftserussell.com/products/downloads/Guide_to_Chinese_Share_Classes.pdf. Accessed 2 Mar 2020.

Fuhr, D. (2015). The Global Footprint of ETFs and ETPs. In J. M. Hill, D. Nadig, & M. Hougan (Eds.), *A Comprehensive Guide to Exchange-Traded Funds (ETFs)*. Charlottesville: CFA Institute Research Foundation.

Glow, D. (2020, March). *Monday Morning Memo: Review of the European ETF Market*. https://lipperalpha.refinitiv.com/wp-content/uploads/2020/04/20-04-20-ETF-Market-Report-March-2020-FINAL.pdf. Accessed 21 Apr 2020.

Gupta, A., & Subramanian, M. (2014). *Economic Exposure in Global Investing: Tilting Portfolios Based on Macroeconomic Views*. https://www.msci.com/documents/10199/5caee365-79ba-44a4-8643-15b7dbea5999. Accessed 20 Feb 2020.

Irish Funds. (2018). *Ireland—Europe's Centre of Excellence for Exchange Traded Funds*. https://irishfunds-secure.s3.amazonaws.com/1520434523-Exchange-Trade-Funds_Web_March-2018.pdf. Accessed 27 Feb 2020.

Lovelace, R., & Polak, D. (2019). *Guide to International Investing: How to Go Global in an Uncertain World, Capital Group*. https://www.capitalgroup.com/content/dam/cgc/shared-content/documents/brochures/Capital-Group-Guide-to-International-Investing.pdf. Accessed 22 Dec 2019.

Marszk, A., & Lechman, E. (2019). *Exchange-Traded Funds in Europe*. Cambridge, MA: Academic Press/Elsevier.

Marszk, A., Lechman, E., & Kato, Y. (2019). *The Emergence of ETFs in Asia-Pacific*. Cham: Springer.

Mier, J. (2017). *Deep Concentration: A Review of Studies Discussing Concentrated Portfolios, Lazard Asset Management*. https://www.lazardassetmanagement.com/docs/-m0-/16054/deepconcentration-areviewofstudies_lazardresearch_en.pdf. Accessed 20 Feb 2020.

MSCI. (2019a). *Selected Geographical Issues in the Global Listed Equity Market*. Analysis for the Norwegian Ministry of Finance. https://www.regjeringen.no/globalassets/upload/fin/aff/2019-10-03-msci_report-for-the-norwegian-gpfg.pdf. Accessed 18 Dec 2019.

MSCI. (2019b). *MSCI Capped Indexes Methodology*. https://www.msci.com/eqb/methodology/meth_docs/MSCI_Capped_Indexes_Methodology_Aug2019.pdf. Accessed 23 Feb 2020.

OECD. (2016). Changing Business Models of Stock Exchanges and Stock Market Fragmentation. In *OECD Business and Finance Outlook 2016*. https://www.oecd.org/daf/ca/BFO-2016-Ch4-Stock-Exchanges.pdf. Accessed 25 Feb 2020.

Osaki, S. (2001). The Development of Exchange-Traded Funds (ETFs) in Japan. *Capital Research Journal, 4*(3), 45–51.

PwC. (2019). *European ETF Listing and Distribution*. PricewaterhouseCoopers. https://www.pwc.lu/en/asset-management/etfs/etf-poster.html. Accessed 20 Nov 2019.

S&P Dow Jones Indices. (2020). *S&P Dow Jones Indices Linked Products*. https://us.spindices.com/additional-reports/related-products/?indexId=340&sourceIdentifier=index-data-widget&parentIdentifier=index-data-widget. Accessed 10 Apr 2020.

S&P Global. (2019). *2019 Investor Fact Book*. http://investor.spglobal.com/file/4023623/Index?KeyFile=1500122176. Accessed 28 Feb 2020.

Silverblatt, H. (2019). *S&P 500 2018: Global Sales*. https://us.spindices.com/documents/research/sp-500-global-sales-2018.pdf?force_download=true. Accessed 18 Feb 2020.

Whitelaw, T., Lucas, A., Greengold, R., Boyadzhiev, D., & Malseed, M. (2019). *A New Perspective on Geographical Diversification*. Revenue Exposure by Region, Morningstar Manager Research. https://www.morningstar.com/lp/revenue-exposure. Accessed 14 Feb 2020.

Williams, S. (2020). *If You Do This, You'll Make Money Every Time*. https://www.fool.com/investing/2020/04/01/if-you-do-this-youll-make-money-every-time.aspx. Accessed 10 Apr 2020.

8

International Sector and Thematic Equity Exchange-Traded Funds

8.1 Introduction

Among many various manners of passive investing in international equity markets, sector and thematic exchange-traded funds are financial instruments that enable to achieve the most targeted exposure. Thanks to these ETFs, one can invest quickly, easily, and at a low cost in companies from various regions of the world representing either a specific sector of the economy or an investment theme. Unlike other forms of international equity ETFs presented in previous chapters, the selection of stocks for such investment portfolios is made not only on a geographical criterion, but it is also based on their sectoral affiliation or exploitation of a secular investment theme. Naturally, this concentrated investment approach is not risk-free, which may prove to be pernicious in unfavorable circumstances. Given that, one should particularly cautiously engage in these types of investments and closely monitor and navigate their risks. Still, it is worth considering the supplementation of an investment portfolio with those ETFs, as they can more than compensate for the risk taken. Owing to their nature, they seem to be best suited to investors with a longer-term investment horizon as well as those who are seeking exposure to an international equity market.

While sector investing across the largest, most developed economies has been known and well-established for years, a regional or global approach is relatively new.[1] Likewise, thematic investing has become increasingly popular

[1]Our attention in this chapter will be focused on international sector ETFs, i.e., those investing in the regional or global market. For portfolio diversification, sector funds with single-country exposure

T. Miziołek et al., *International Equity Exchange-Traded Funds*,
https://doi.org/10.1007/978-3-030-53864-4_8

only recently, when more and more international ETFs, focused on long-term civilization megatrends, have been entering the financial market. Investing in them not only can be a great investment opportunity, but it may also contribute to solving many serious problems facing modern societies—e.g., demographic, social, or environmental ones. In this chapter, we will look at the pros and cons of investing in sector and thematic ETFs with international exposure, and suggest how to avoid investment pitfalls and mitigate related risks.

8.2 Sector Investing

Sector investing offers targeted exposure to the stocks of companies in specific segments of economy. This selective approach can help diversify portfolio, manage risks, and elevate returns, although obviously it is not free from flaws. In general, this strategy exhibits potentially better performance in relation to other forms of international investments, though at the price of a higher investment risk. This is mainly due to the fact that sectors are burdened—to a varying degree—with individual risk factors. Both sector-specific or industry-specific risks and potential benefits are the result of macroeconomic sensitivity, as companies from particular sectors perform differently in various stages of the business cycle. It is possible to get prepared for this through overweighting or underweighting procyclical or countercyclical sectors, depending on the phase of the cycle. This is practically impossible, however, when unexpected events occur and they significantly affect the operating conditions at a given industry or sector. They are generally regional and relatively short-living (e.g., terrorist attack, earthquake, social tensions, volcanic eruption, tsunami). Still, there are also those—like wars or pandemics—that have supra-regional and even global nature and affect many sectors in the long term, though to a varying degree.[2]

Additionally, international sector equity indexes—regardless of whether they relate to a specific region or the whole world—are highly country-concentrated in many cases, sometimes also stocks-concentrated. To reduce

---

can be also employed, but due to the limited scope of the book, they will not be discussed (with a few exceptions).

[2]The latest example of such a global event is the Covid-19 pandemic. According to the S&P Global (2020) analysis, the industries that were most impacted by COVID-19 during March 2020 included airlines, casinos and gaming, leisure facilities, auto parts and equipment, and oil and gas drilling. On the other hand, streaming services, e-gaming, producers of co-working software, data storage services, online food ordering and delivery platforms, and child care services are among those that most benefited from coronavirus outbreak in the first stage of pandemic.

an excessive concentration risk of individual holdings, capped indexes[3] are employed to restrict the weight of the largest component(s) in the portfolio. Furthermore, the degree of risk is also dependent on the level of sector granularity. As a rule, the lower tier of sector classification (i.e., more narrowly defined sector/industry), the higher the potential risk is due to a lower degree of business activity diversity.

Sector equity ETFs offer a means of making active selection[4] decisions through passive vehicles and are becoming an increasingly popular tool for investors seeking to implement sector strategies (SPDR 2019). To make the most of these financial instruments, the potential merits and disadvantages of sectoral investing, its nuances, impact of the business cycle of investment performance of individual sectors, and sector classifications used by ETF providers should be thoroughly considered.

Sectors are clearly defined economic groupings that offer targeted investing within a larger index.[5] This approach has its good and bad sides. The most important argument in favor of sector investing seems to be the possibility of achieving attractive investment results by selecting—through macroeconomic analysis—those sectors that are most likely to outperform. However, this choice must be very well thought out because of the defining characteristic of sector investing—return dispersion. Generally, it refers to stocks and measures the degree according to which the components of a market index perform similarly. If component returns are grouped tightly around the index's return, dispersion will be low, but if the spread among component returns is wide, dispersion will be high (Bennett and Lazzara 2016).[6] From the sector investing perspective, dispersion measures the spread among the returns of various sectors (difference in sector indexes' returns within a broad index). Analogously to stock dispersion, sector dispersion points out to potential opportunities for adding value to investment portfolio through sector selection. The bigger the dispersion is, the higher the opportunity to add (or lose) value through active sector selection becomes. Conversely, the smaller the sector dispersion is, the lower investment opportunity is.

As various research indicates, the spread among returns of the top and bottom performing sectors can be striking. This applies mainly to the sector

[3]Capped indexes were described in detail in Chapter 7.

[4]Index-based products linked to sectors, including sector equity ETFs, often require an active approach to investing due to the changing attractiveness of individual sectors throughout the entire business cycle.

[5]These groups are defined by entities creating sector classifications of public companies. More about this later in the chapter.

[6]In practice, dispersion is the weighted standard deviation of returns. It tells us how far from the index's return a one-standard deviation return falls.

dispersion in single-country indexes, since they are more exposed to the country risk. For example, according to the Nasdaq Dorsey Wright analysis, the average annual dispersion of broad sector indexes across S&P 500 Index amounted to as high as 43.45 pp per year during study period (2007–2017), ranging between 21.97 pp (2010) and 84.21 pp (2009) (Jones 2018).[7] Even wider sector dispersion occurs in emerging markets—for example the average difference between sector returns in the Chinese stock market (MSCI China Index) reached 56.3 pp in the years 2012–2017, fluctuating between 34.9 pp and 93.2 pp (Rodstrom 2018). The selection of the right sector within domestic equity investments is therefore essential from the point of view of those who want to achieve additional benefits from international investments.[8] The problem associated with such a choice can be eliminated by investing in funds implementing the sector rotation strategy. This approach, by actively adapting the fund's portfolio composition to changing economic conditions, has the potential to exploit the returns from outperformed sectors while limiting exposure to underperformed sectors.[9]

Sector returns dispersion in broader equity indexes is generally lower than in single-country indexes, which is a consequence of wider portfolio diversification. However, the differentiation of sector returns in regional and global equity indexes can also be significant, which emphasizes importance of the decision to choose the appropriate sector fund.[10] According to our calculations, the average spread between the top-performed and bottom-performed sectors in developed markets equities, i.e., the difference between the best and the worst sector index return within MSCI World Index in 2006–2019, was 33.75 pp, ranging from 20.01 pp to 59.51 pp (Table 8.1). What is more, since sectors have different drivers, the combination of top and bottom performing sector changes every year, reflecting fluctuations in performance determinants—for example healthcare index was the best in 2014 and 2015, and the worst in 2016, while the energy index was the worst in 2014 and 2015, and the best in 2016. The average spread between the top and bottom

[7] Current analysis of sector dispersion of returns on the US equity market, carried out on a monthly basis, is available at: https://us.spindices.com/indexology/sectors/us-sector-dashboard.

[8] Incidentally, this choice is also important for US investors in the case of stock selection. According to S&P Dow Jones Indices research (Edwards and Lazzara 2019), the dispersion between sector returns accounts for roughly half of the dispersion between stock returns. This implies that half of the value added from picking stocks could be achieved by selecting the right sectors.

[9] There are sector ETFs available on the US market (e.g., First Trust Dorsey Wright Focus 5 ETF) that apply this strategy to sector investments on the domestic market. When investing in those funds, however, one should keep in mind that active sector allocation policy tends to generate greater portfolio turnover than purely buy-and-hold investment strategy, and thus leads to higher transaction costs. Furthermore, it may result in short-term capital gains that are less favorably taxed, in some countries, than long-term capital gains.

[10] For global investments, sector equity rotation ETFs are also available. More on this in Chapter 5.

Table 8.1 The average spread between top and bottom performing GICS sectors in global, developed and emerging markets' equities (pp)

	2006	2007	2008	2009	2010	2011	2012	2013	2014	2015	2016	2017	2018	2019
Global equities	27.72	44.11	32.58	59.89	24.72	30.77	26.36	38.25	31.65	28.42	34.97	34.63	17.85	33.75
Developed equities	31.59	41.54	32.99	59.51	29.11	30.01	31.59	35.81	29.72	29.26	33.89	32.41	20.01	35.07
Emerging equities	102.25	67.54	49.08	89.77	33.14	30.00	46.96	31.00	46.26	16.04	44.05	43.90	37.34	38.88

Source Own study based on factsheets of MSCI ACWI sector indexes, MSCI World sector indexes, and MSCI Emerging Markets sector indexes performing sectors in global equities (MSCI ACWI Index) was similar to developed equities (33.26 pp), since the portfolios of both overlap to a large extent. In contrast, emerging markets (MSCI EM Index) experienced much higher discrepancies—the average spread was 48.30 pp, oscillating between 102.25 pp and 16.04 pp[11]

Sector investing can be beneficial not only to returns, but also to risk, by capitalizing on varied intra- and inter-sector correlations. Understanding the correlation characteristics of each sector may facilitate diversification and thus help to manage risk. Firstly, the sector approach offers lower concentration risk than individual stocks and can help to mitigate the idiosyncratic risk associated with single-stock investing. Secondly, correlations between sectors and the overall market vary, thus investors can take advantage of these differences when aiming to reduce portfolio risk. According to the SPDR research, the lowest inter-correlations in the US equity market occur mostly between utilities and real estate sectors and the S&P 500 Index. In turn, the analysis of how the returns of stocks are correlated with each other within each S&P 500 sector demonstrated that consumer staples and health care are US sectors with the lowest intra-sector correlations. In their case, the preferred strategy seems to be choosing on a stock-by-stock basis rather than at a sector level. On the other hand, in sectors with the highest intra-correlations—namely utilities, financial, energy—macro-drivers can be more important to a stock's performance than any individual company's behavior (SPDR 2019).[12]

Sector dispersions and correlations also matter, since they provide an insight into the volatility of sector returns (market volatility is a function of both dispersion and correlation). If the index components are tightly bunched, dispersion will be low and, with other aspects equal, the index's volatility will be low as well. If the components tend to move together, correlation will be relatively high, and the volatility will rise. If the component moves tend to offset, correlation and volatility will be lower. The lowest dispersion and correlation values within the US sectors in the 1991–2014 were observed in consumer staples, and the highest in information technology (Lazzara 2015). However, while strongly positive historical correlations exist between volatility and dispersion, there are periods where they differ.[13] Thus,

[11]Detailed description of the MSCI ACWI Index is presented in Chapter 5, and of the MSCI World Index and MSCI Emerging Markets Index in Chapter 6.

[12]Correlations between sectors and S&P 500 Index were measured as an average correlation to S&P 500 for last three years (as of September 2019). Correlation of stocks within each sector was calculated from returns from the trailing 12 months (as of 30 September 2019).

[13]For instance, in the period of April 1999–January 2001, a marked increase in dispersion was observed, driven by the idiosyncratic behavior of the technology sector. However, index volatility did not rise, as other sectors performed more normally.

dispersion can better capture the periods when only a portion of the market either bubbles or crashes (Edwards and Lazzara 2013).

Since sectors comprise similar companies, they usually respond in a consistent way to economic conditions and risks. Within a given sector/industry, stocks have similar economic drivers and risks, hence typically they perform comparably during each period of the economic (business) cycle.[14] The cycle is a critical determinant of an individual sector's performance, especially over the intermediate term.[15] Sector performance is often driven largely by cyclical factors linked to the state of economy, such as corporate earnings, interest rates, and inflation. Thus, it seems essential to conduct a profound analysis of the business cycle, comprising cyclical fluctuations in an economy in the intermediate horizon—on a global scale, given a region or specific country (depending on the geographical exposure of our investment).

The business cycle focusing on an intermediate time horizon assumes that individual phases rotate, on average, from every few months to every few years.[16] Generally, four distinct phases of a typical business cycle can be distinguished (Fidelity 2019):

- Early-cycle phase—it is characterized by a sharp recovery from recession, marked by a rebound in economic activity (observed in, e.g., GDP, industrial production, unemployment), then an accelerating growth rate. Credit conditions cease to be tightened amid easy monetary policy, creating an environment for rapid margin expansion and profit growth. Business inventories are low, while sales growth improves considerably. Economically sensitive sectors (industrials, information technology) may tend to perform better, while more defensive sectors (communication services, utilities) rather underperform (cf. Table 8.2);
- Mid-cycle phase—it manifests itself by a positive but more moderate rate of growth than that experienced during earlier phase. Economic activity gathers momentum, credit growth becomes strong, and profitability is healthy against an accommodative, though increasingly neutral, monetary

[14]However, the more broadly defined the sector/industry, the larger the differences can be.

[15]According to the framework applied by Fidelity's Asset Allocation Research Team (AART), an analysis of cyclical factors and trends can be conducted during the following three temporal segments: tactical (1–12 months), business cycle (1–10 years), and secular (10–30 years). These timeframes may vary, depending on the subject making the analysis.

[16]Although an analysis of business cycle offers considerable potential for taking advantage of relative sector-performance opportunities, there are also other strategies that can be incorporated to complement this approach. They include: macro-fundamental analysis, bottom-up analysis, global business cycle analysis, inflation overlay, and secular overlay. More about these approaches in Fidelity (2019).

Table 8.2 Performance of sectors vs. the broad market during the typical business cycle

Sector	Early-cycle phase	Mid-cycle phase	Late-cycle phase	Recession phase
Financials	+			
Real estate	+ +			–
Consumer discretionary	+ +	–	–	
Information technology	+	+	–	–
Industrials	+ +			–
Materials	+	–	+ +	
Consumer staples			+ +	+ +
Health care	–		+ +	+ +
Energy	–		+ +	
Communication services		+		–
Utilities	–	–	+	+ +

Note The typical business cycle shown above is a hypothetical illustration. There is not always a chronological progression in this order
Source for sector performance during a business cycle: Fidelity's Asset Allocation Research Team (AART). Empty table cells suggest no clear pattern of over- or underperformance vs. broader market. Double +/– signs indicate that the sector is showing a consistent signal across all three metrics: full-phase average performance, median monthly difference, and cycle hit rate. A single +/– indicates a mixed or less consistent signal. Returns data from 1962 to 2016. Annualized returns are represented by the performance of the largest 3000 US stocks measured by market capitalization. Sectors are defined by the GICS (see Table A.4 in the Appendix)
Source Fidelity (2019)

policy backdrop. Inventories and sales grow, reaching equilibrium relative to each other. It is usually the longest phase of the business cycle. Making marginal portfolio allocation changes in order to manage drawdown risk with sectors may enhance risk-adjusted returns during this phase. Information technology is typically the best performer during this phase;

- Late-cycle phase—it often coincides with peak economic activity, implying that the rate of growth remains positive but slows down. It may be perceived as the overheating stage for an economy when its capacity becomes constrained, thus leading to rising inflationary pressures. Though inflation is not always high, inflationary pressures and tight labor market tend to crimp profit margins and lead to a tighter monetary policy. Defensive and inflation-resistant sectors (particularly health care, but also consumer staples and utilities) tend to outperform, while more cyclical sectors perform worse;

- Recession phase—economic activity decreases. Corporate profits decline and credit is scarce for all entities. Monetary policy becomes more accommodative and inventories gradually fall despite low sales levels, setting up for the next recovery. Since the performance is generally negative in this phase, investors should focus on the most defensive, historically stable sectors, while economically and interest-rate-sensitive sectors (industrials, information technology, and real estate) typically underperform the broader market.

Table 8.2 synthetically summarizes individual sectors' behavior during four business cycle phases. It employs historical analyses of the cycles conducted by Fidelity since 1962 and takes into account economic, fundamental, and quantitative research.

Sector equity investing is based on sector classifications developed mainly by the largest index providers, but also by some stock exchanges, and other entities. From the point of view of an investor aiming to internationally diversify portfolio with sector ETFs, in-depth knowledge of these classifications is essential, as the differences between them, occurring from time to time, translate into the composition of the indexes created on their basis, and consequently may affect the structure of ETFs they replicate and their investment results.[17] It may be useful to be aware of various nuances in classification methodologies, especially when comparing performance metrics across indexes, sectors, industries, and other sub-groupings.

There are two globally recognized sector classifications that are most frequently employed by financial institutions (including ETF providers): Global Industry Classification Standard (GICS) and Industry Classification Benchmark (ICB). The former is used mainly by the two leading index providers (MSCI and S&P Dow Jones Indices) and some stock exchanges,[18] while the latter was adopted by the three major index providers (FTSE Russell, CRSP, and STOXX), as well as many trading platforms.[19] Other important standards for categorizing companies within sectors are Thomson

[17]The airline companies provide a good example of how companies can be classified differently depending on the methodology used. It turned out to be extremely important in the early stages of the coronavirus pandemic. GICS classifies airlines as part of the industrials sector (at the highest level) and transportation industry group (at the second level), while the ICB taxonomy put these companies into consumer discretionary (at the first level) and travel and leisure (at the second level).

[18]For example, Australian Stock Exchange (ASX), Tadawul (Saudi Arabia), and Colombo Stock Exchange (CSE).

[19]For example, London Stock Exchange (LSE), Euronext, NASDAQ OMX, Borsa Italiana, SIX Swiss Exchange, Johannesburg Stock Exchange (JSE), Athens Exchange (Athex), Cyprus Stock Exchange (CSE), and Boursa Kuwait.

Reuters Business Classification (TRBC), Bloomberg Industry Classification Systems (BICS), and Revere Business Industry Classifications System (RBICS) (FactSet).

Global Industry Classification Standard is a four-tiered, hierarchical industry classification system. It was jointly developed in 1999 by MSCI in collaboration with S&P seeking to offer an efficient, detailed and flexible tool for use in the investment process, in particular regarding sector investments. Currently, it encompasses 11 sectors (described in Table A.4 in the Appendix), 24 industry groups, 69 industries, and 158 sub-industries. The GICS classification system comprises over 58,000 trading securities across 125 countries, covering approximately 95% of the world's equity market capitalization. Companies are classified quantitatively and qualitatively. Each company is assigned a single GICS classification at the sub-industry level, according to its principal business activity. MSCI and S&P Dow Jones Indices use revenues as a key factor in determining a firm's principal business activity.[20] Company classifications are regularly reviewed and maintained (MSCI 2020).[21]

MSCI calculates mostly international sector indexes with exposure to global equities (MSCI ACWI sector indexes covering both developed and emerging markets), developed markets' equities (MSCI World sector indexes) and emerging markets' equities (MSCI EM sector indexes). MSCI World sector indexes are the most commonly used in practice by ETF issuers—they are listed on many European exchanges and are described in detail in Table A.4 in the Appendix. Some companies bring to market international sector ETFs replicating the performance of other regional MSCI indexes—MSCI Europe (e.g., Amundi and SPDR).[22]

Industry Classification Benchmark is a globally utilized standard for the categorization and comparison of companies by industry and sector, operated and managed by FTSE Russell. It was launched by FTSE and Dow Jones

[20]Additionally, earnings and market perception are also recognized as important and relevant information for classification purposes and are taken into account during an annual review process.

[21]The review process includes daily monitoring of corporate actions that may change a company's classification and the annual review to capture changes in a company's business activity. Furthermore, consultations are held with market participants to ensure the capture of accurate and relevant changes in industry trends.

[22]Interestingly, in the USA, domestic-focused sector ETFs are much more popular than international sector ETFs. They include funds mirroring the performance of sector indexes based mainly on the following benchmarks: S&P 500 (managed by iShares, Lyxor, SPDR, Invesco), MSCI USA Index (Xtrackers), MSCI USA IMI Index (Fidelity), MSCI US IMI (Vanguard), and Dow Jones indexes (iShares, ProShares [short and leveraged ETFs], and Direxion [leveraged ETFs]). Furthermore, US investors have at their disposal, for example, ETFs with Chinese sector exposure based on MSCI China Index (Global X). Naturally, sector equity ETFs with single-country exposure are also listed on stock exchanges in other countries (predominantly developed ones). They are based on the main domestic broad index (e.g., S&P/TSX Composite in Canada, S&P/ASX 200 in Australia).

in 2005.[23] It provides four levels of classification: industry (11), supersector (20), sector (45) and subsector (173). The highest tier includes following industries: Technology, Telecommunications, Health Care, Financials, Real Estate, Consumer Discretionary, Consumer Staples, Industrials, Basic Materials, Energy, and Utilities. Each company in the ICB universe is allocated to the subsector that most closely represents the nature of its business. This allocation is determined by the company's primary source of revenue and other publicly available information (FTSE Russell 2019). Approximately 85,000 equity securities from over 80 countries and 150 exchanges are classified according to ICB's four-tiered structure (FTSE Russell 2020).

ICB is widely used, for instance, in STOXX international sector indexes. They are available for global and regional markets (Europe, the Eurozone, and Eastern Europe). STOXX Europe 600 sector indexes are most frequently employed by ETF providers. They track 20 supersectors of the relevant benchmark—STOXX 600 Index.[24] Their performance is mapped by the ETFs managed by, e.g., Invesco, iShares, Lyxor, ComStage, and Xtrackers.

Similarly to other forms of international equity ETFs, another important factor to consider, when investing in a particular sector ETF, is the concentration degree of the replicated index portfolio. Sector indexes differ significantly in this respect. Some of them are quite well-diversified, especially in terms of individual securities, while others are excessively concentrated, particularly in country terms. Given the most popular regional sector equity indexes among ETF providers, based on MSCI World Index, and using simple measures of concentration, one can roughly assess which benchmarks are, relatively, the most and which are the least diversified (Table 8.3). Among the former there are MSCI World Industrials Index (in terms of stocks and sub-industries), MSCI World Materials Index (in terms of countries and stocks), and MSCI World Financials Index (in terms of stocks and countries). Conversely, the least diversified, and thus the most exhibited to stock/country/subindustry-specific risks feature MSCI World Communication Services Index (in terms of stocks and countries), MSCI World Information Technology Index (in terms of countries and stocks), and MSCI World Energy Index (in terms of sub-industries and stocks).

[23]In 2011 FTSE became the sole owner of ICB. The classification was enhanced in 2019 by integration of the Russell Global Sectors (RGS) classification scheme and additional structural enhancements.

[24]It has a fixed number of 600 components and represents large, mid and small capitalization companies across 17 countries of the European region: Austria, Belgium, Denmark, Finland, France, Germany, Ireland, Italy, Luxembourg, the Netherlands, Norway, Poland, Portugal, Spain, Sweden, Switzerland, and the UK. It is derived from the STOXX Europe Total Market Index (TMI) and is a subset of the STOXX Global 1800 Index.

Table 8.3 Concentration measures of MSCI World sector indexes (as % of total market capitalization) (as of March 31, 2020)

	Top stock	Top 3 stocks	Top 10 stocks	Top country	Top 3 countries	Top sub-industry	Top 3 sub-industries
Consumer discretionary	23.00	32.55	49.94	63.58	85.28	28.29	50.51
Consumer staples	9.59	23.84	48.73	53.19	73.92	22.89	51.81
Energy	13.44	32.70	64.88	48.28	80.95	60.25	88.00
Financials	5.99	14.94	29.09	51.58	67.12	44.40	90.20
Health care	6.77	15.87	36.77	67.81	83.76	44.60	77.37
Industrials	2.72	7.77	21.67	51.87	75.25	16.32	39.03
Information technology	17.09	38.12	55.46	85.77	93.25	20.75	54.55
Materials	6.50	14.38	34.69	38.27	58.50	25.94	54.87
Real estate	8.67	19.40	39.24	65.61	84.56	31.24	53.83
Communication services	22.99	43.25	70.18	78.32	90.21	38.55	73.51
Utilities	8.95	18.09	42.48	60.10	72.30	59.97	94.63

Source Own study based on factsheets of MSCI World sector indexes

By far, the highest degree of portfolio concentration in the international MSCI World sector indexes relates to countries. The weight of the largest country—the USA—is 60.4% on average, ranging from 38.3% (Materials) to 85.8% (Information Technology); the average share of the three largest countries is 78.6%, fluctuating between 58.5% (Materials) to 93.3% (Information Technology). The above observations, showing that many industries and even sectors[25] are highly concentrated within particular countries, are confirmed by the ICB classification. According to it, the USA had the largest weighting in 33 out of 40 industries at the start of 2015.[26] In 22 sectors, either the US weighting accounted for over two-thirds of the world in total, or the weighting of the second largest country exceeded 20%.[27] In 35 industries, the two countries with the largest weights accounted for over half of their global capitalization, in 30 industries the top two countries accounted

[25]It is worth remembering that confusingly, GICS and ICB use different terminologies referring to the highest level of classification—in the former "sectors" are employed, and "industries" in the latter. In the ICB classification, "sectors" constitute the third level, after industries and supersectors.

[26]The seven sectors where the USA is not the largest player include automobiles, mobile telecoms, and electronics (Japan), real estate (Hong Kong), mining (UK), alternative energy (China), and leisure goods (South Korea).

[27]Among the latter group the UK is the major country in life insurance and tobacco, Japan in industrial engineering and leisure goods, Germany in chemicals, Australia in mining, Switzerland in food, and Denmark in alternative energy.

for more than 60%, in 18 industries for over 70%, and in seven industries for over 80% of total capitalization (Dimson et al. 2015). All this should be taken into consideration when investing internationally, as simultaneous investment in broad global, or regional, and sector equity ETFs may lead to the country overconcentration. This regards especially US stocks (in funds with global and DMs exposure) and Chinese stocks (in funds investing in emerging markets).[28]

Generally, in order to avoid exposure duplication, investors should select more diversified ETFs or funds tracking capped indexes, where the weight of a single entity (and sometimes a group of the largest stocks) is restricted at a certain level.

The largest international sector ETFs are presented in Table 8.5.

8.3 Thematic Investing

Thematic investing has been clearly gaining traction as well as capturing investors' imagination and interest worldwide in the recent years. There were as many as 923 investment funds with USD 195 bn assets under management (AUM) in thematic funds,[29] at the end of December 2019, compared to USD 75 bn only just three years earlier. This market segment is dominated by European-domiciled funds that represent 54% of the global thematic funds assets. Most assets invested in thematic funds globally are actively managed, including more than 90% of AUM in Europe, and over 80% in the rest of the world, excluding North America. The latter region is dominated by passive thematic funds, mostly ETFs, as their share equals to 80% (Johnson et al. 2020).[30]

There is a huge variety of definitions of thematic investments, provided by various entities—mainly asset managers and index providers offering thematic-based products (funds, indexes), as wells as research and consulting entities. Additionally, the approach to what can be considered "investment theme" has changed over time. MSCI defines thematic investing as a top-down investment approach that seeks to identify longer term, structural trends that are expected to be dominant and important explanatory

[28]The average weight of Chinese equities in MSCI EM sector equity indexes is 41.4%, but in some sectors it is about 70% (Real Estate, Consumer Discretionary, Communication Services) (as of March 31, 2020).

[29]Funds recognized by Morningstar as thematic ones.

[30]The largest providers of thematic funds in North America, in terms of assets, according to the Morningstar research are mainly ETF providers: FlexShares, iShares, Ark Financial, Global X, ETF Managers, and Robo Global (as of end 2019).

performance factors in a rapidly changing world. It is aimed at identifying emerging macroeconomic, geopolitical, and technological trends that are believed to be structural and transformative in nature and hence expected to influence society's behavior and needs over the long term (Kumar et al. 2019). According to Pictet Asset Management, the world's largest provider of thematic funds dominating within the European market, the primary purpose of a thematic equity strategy is to invest in assets whose returns are influenced by structural forces of change that evolve independently of the economic cycle. Thematic investing focuses on identifying long term, enduring sources of capital growth (Pictet 2016). As claimed by Global X—one of the largest providers of thematic ETFs in the USA—it refers to the process of identifying powerful macro-level trends and the underlying investments that stand to benefit from the materialization of those trends (Jacobs 2019). McKinsey notes that thematic investing requires not only recognition of long-term economic, political, and social trends, but also an understanding of their impact on regions and sectors that reveal investable opportunities (Bérubé et al. 2014). Towers Watson (2012) note that skillful capitalization on future trends is essential. It is necessary to identify and profit from the winners but, equally importantly, to avoid or underweight the losers, i.e., irrelevant or short-living trends.[31] Interestingly, forward-looking nature of thematic investing stands in contrast to a typically employed investing approach based on market capitalization, where it is implicitly assumed that past winners will continue to win out and therefore deserve more weight in the portfolio.

Adopting a thematic-investing approach may provide three kinds of benefits for investors. Firstly, it allows to generate alpha at scale by focusing on investment opportunities in hot spots where a significant amount of capital can be deployed. Secondly, a more systematic investment process and profound research required for thematic investing creates a deeper understanding of the basic drivers behind value creation and risk. Investors can employ this knowledge not just for thematic investing but also in other strategies, also international. Thirdly, it offers investors a dynamic and flexible way to validate and express their hunches by applying a forward-looking lens to investment decisions (Bérubé et al. 2014).

Thematic investing, however, also poses challenges. The most important involve the following: distinguishing real trends from fads or other short-term drivers, identifying the potential economic beneficiaries of a theme,

[31]A method of reducing the risk of choosing a wrong investment theme may be investing in a fund that combines numerous themes within a given category (e.g., Multiple Technology, Multiple Physical Themes [cf. Table 8.4]) or in the broad thematic fund.

identifying *investable* themes, defining the scope of a theme (more narrowly or more broadly focused[32]), assessing a thematic strategy, and determining the appropriate entry and exit moments (timing) (Kumar et al. 2019). The key challenge for investors seems to be the ability to separate a fad from a real theme. A huge number of thematic funds launched on the market in recent years were expected to be a great investment opportunity, but a large proportion of them did not meet these expectations, which led to their rapid closure. This is confirmed by a high mortality rate among thematic ETFs. For example, almost 80% of such funds launched in Europe prior to 2012 have since closed (Lamont and Bioy 2018). Therefore, to a much greater extent than other international equity ETFs, thematic funds are subject to three specific risks. The first two are the liquidation risk and delisting risk, when a fund provider, after analyzing the profitability of the functioning of this financial product, decides to close it, which results in its withdrawal from a stock exchange. The third one, occurring in similar circumstances, is the risk of changing the replicated index. This may alter investment policy and make it inadequate to an investor's expectations and needs, and thus expose them to a different from expected return-risk profile.[33]

In order to help navigate in thematic funds' market and avoid its pitfalls, it is necessary to know their taxonomy well. This is especially important for this category of funds due to their differentiation, complexity, and ambiguity. The situation is further aggravated by the fact that the line between sectors/industries and themes is often blurred. It hinders a transparent analysis of their functioning, but more importantly, poses an obstacle for investors who would like to take advantage of the new opportunities on the one hand, whereas on the other they are afraid of the risks they may face.

There is no single agreed standard taxonomy of investment themes and the funds employing them. Among various classifications, probably the most comprehensive and most granular is the one developed by Morningstar (Table 8.4). It distinguishes four main categories of investment topics: technology, physical world, social, and broad thematic. Technology is definitely the most popular broad theme, gathering half of assets in thematic funds globally (USD 97.3 bn) as of end 2019. Among the most popular themes

[32]If the investment topic is narrowly defined and includes only "pure play" companies, i.e., firms that are directly associated with the theme, the potential risk is higher.

[33]Those risks also apply to thematic funds listed in the US exchanges, as most of them have small asset bases. Morningstar research indicates that the median AUM among North American thematic funds stood at just USD 30.1 million as of December 2019 (Johnson et al. 2020).

Table 8.4 Morningstar's thematic funds' taxonomy

Technology	Connectivity	Digital Economy, Internet, Data Sharing, Mobile Internet, 5G, Telecoms Innovation, Wireless, Tech Platforms, Information Age, Internet of Things, Wearables, Smart Equipment, Smart Grid, Intelligent Cities, Smart Cities, web.x.0, Cloud Computing, Digitalization, Social Media, E-commerce, New Retail Cybersecurity
	Robotics + Automation	Smart Manufacturing, 3D Printing, Drone, Smart Industrial Tech, Mechatronics
	Artificial Intelligence + Big data	Deep Learning, Quant Computing, Machine Learning, Big Data, Information Revolution
	Battery tech	Battery Tech, Battery Value Chain, Secondary Battery Industry
	FinTech	Blockchain, ETF Industry, Pay Infrastructure, Crowd Funding
	Future mobility	Next-Gen Auto, Future Mobility, Automated Driving, Smart Car, Green Car, Hybrid Car
	Health tech	Innovative Healthcare, Medical Breakthroughs, Cancer, Genome, Digital Health, Generic Pharma, Pharma Breakthrough, Science Tech, Biotech Clinical Trials, Innovative BioPharma, Next-Gen Health, Immunology, Medical Innovation
	Electronics	Innovative Electronics, Integrated Circuits
	Digital media	Gaming + Esports, Multimedia

(continued)

Table 8.4 (continued)

	Multiple technology	New Economy, 4th Industrial Revolution, China's Silicon Valley, Disruptive Technologies, Transformative Innovation, Mega Tech, Future Innovations, Innovative Tech, Exponential Tech, Manufacturing Revolt, Frontier Tech, Future Economy, Disruptive Innovation
	Other	Nanotechnology, Space, Virtual Reality
Physical world	Agriculture	Fertilizers/Potash, Fishing, Agribusiness, Smart Food, Food, Nutrition, Paper and Forestry, Timber
	Resource management	Shale Revolution, Upstream Natural Resources, Rare Earth Resources, Resource Tech, Rare Resources, Clean Water, Water, Waste, Water Infrastructure, Air, Efficient Resources, New Resources
	Energy transition	Solar, Wind, Alternative Energy, Energy Transition, Environmental New Deal, Nuclear, Energy Innovation, Clean Tech, Clean Disruption, New Power, New Energy, Clean Tech, Green Energy, Smart Power
	Digital media	Shipping, Logistics
	Industrial	Ship Building, Global Jets
	MultiplePhysical themes	Multiple Physical Themes
Social	Consumer	EM Consumer, Luxury Consumer, Global Lifestyles, New Age Consumer, Alcohol, Classic Cars, Pets, Millennials, Baby Boomers, Kids, Cosmetics, Sports, Consumer Innovation, Entertainment
	Demographics	Aging Population, Demographic Trends

(continued)

Table 8.4 (continued)

	Security	National Defense, General Security, Safety
	Wellness	Healthy Lifestyle, Wellness, Alternative Health, Health and Fitness, Obesity, Organics, Education
	Political	Energy Independence, New Silk Road, Structural Reform, National/Regional Interest, Trade War, State-Owned Enterprise, Korean Unification, US Policy
	Other	Marijuana, Holding Companies, Gig Economy
Broad thematic	Broad thematic	Mega Trends, Smart Future, Global Themes, Future Trends, Smart Industries, Secular Trends, Thematic New Trends

Source Johnson et al. (2020)

(second column of Table 8.4) are: Robotics & Automation (USD 27.0 bn),[34] Resource Management (USD 25.2 bn), and Connectivity (USD 23.1 bn) (Johnson et al. 2020).

Investors interested in thematic investments via ETFs must, however, not only select the "winning" theme, but also choose a fund that is well-placed to harness that theme, and they should make an investment at the right time, i.e., before valuations indicate that the market has already priced-in the theme's potential. Selecting an ETF that allows to monetize a specific theme should not pose a particular challenge—compared to choosing, for example, single-country ETFs or developed market's funds—as one theme is usually covered by only a few funds. Competition on this market is relatively small, since thematic funds are still considered niche products, not offering too much potential to their providers; hence, they are launched by single companies.[35] However, it is important to invest—even having only a few funds to choose from—in the fund that not only best utilizes the potential

[34]Interestingly, European funds account for as much as 55% of total assets engaged in this theme, while North American funds account for just 6%. The two largest European thematic ETFs fall into this category: iShares Automation & Robotics UCITS ETF and L&G ROBO Global Robotics and Automation ETF.

[35]Additionally, the phenomenon of first-mover advantage is clearly visible in this market segment, which discourages the creation of such funds by followers.

of the theme, but also is low cost (typically, thematic ETFs are quite expensive comparing to their broad market counterparts), liquid enough, and has a well-diversified portfolio.

In the last respect, international thematic ETFs usually look slightly better than international sector ETFs as their strategies go beyond typical sector funds. The latter are habitually riskier since their performance depends on the fortunes of just one sector or industry, often quite narrowly defined. Meanwhile, thematic funds tend to be more diversified and their results are dependent on many sectors. They usually invest across various industries that are woven around a common theme and are often unconstrained by size groupings (although they are rather tilted toward the companies with relatively smaller market capitalization).

Still, international thematic ETFs can involve high concentration in a single country and/or region as a result of market-cap-weighting approach. Most of them exhibit excessive concentration on the USA and North American stocks, as the vast majority of leading public companies representing the most popular, among investors, technology themes, and other disruptive businesses, are domiciled in the USA. Only some thematic funds are more geographically diversified.[36] To avoid overconcentration, some thematic indexes apply single stock, sector, or geographic weighting caps and/or floors or equal weight of the holdings.[37] On the other hand, while most thematic ETFs are global in scope, their geographical footprints can be different from broad global or DMs benchmarks like MSCI ACWI and MSCI World. Furthermore, investors need to be on the lookout for overlap, especially when they already have an international exposure through other funds.

As for the issue of proper timing, the idiosyncratic nature of thematic ETFs causes that assessing their valuations and evaluating their performance can be tricky. They often have little or no performance history, and the theme, by its nature, is yet to play out. It should therefore be approached with caution to evaluate robustness of the strategy and to choose appropriate moment of transaction.

[36]For instance, First Trust Global Wind Energy ETF, First Trust NASDAQ Clean Edge Smart Grid Infrastructure Index Fund, and Invesco Global Water ETF are firmly tilted toward West European stocks, VanEck Vectors Rare Earth/Strategic Metals ETF, VanEck Vectors Coal ETF, and Global X Video Games & Esports ETF are heavily biased to APAC countries, VanEck Vectors Steel ETF and Global X Yield Co. & Renewable Energy Income ETF have a relatively large weight (ca. 20%) of Latam equities, VanEck Vectors Junior Gold Miners ETF and Global X Cybersecurity ETF have quite a significant exposure (over 10%) to Middle East and Africa regions, First Trust Indxx Global Natural Resources Income ETF and VanEck Vectors Oil Refiners ETF invest above 10% in East European stocks, and the portfolio of North Shore Global Uranium Mining ETF is relatively high concentrated (about 15%) on Central Asian equities.

[37]The latter approach, however, exposes investors to smaller, undervalued companies; it leads to higher turnover and lower liquidity, and may result in higher volatility.

Summarizing, owing to a narrow exposure and related biases (e.g., the majority of thematic funds globally have a growth bias and small-cap bias), most international thematic ETFs are typically recommended as satellite investments rather than the core portfolio holding. It is essential to carefully consider whether such products suit our investment strategy and risk profile, and if they are tailor-made to our expectations.

The largest international thematic ETFs are presented in Table 8.5.

Table 8.5 Largest sector and thematic international (global and regional) equity ETFs in the world

Fund (ticker)	Index	Exchange	Assets (USD m)	Expense ratio (%)
VanEck Vectors Gold Miners ETF (GDX US)	NYSE Arca Gold Miners Index	NYSE Arca	13,155.5	0.53
FlexShares Morningstar Global Upstream Natural Resources Index Fund (GUNR US)	Morningstar Global Upstream Natural Resources Index	NYSE Arca	5080.23	0.46
VanEck Vectors Junior Gold Miners ETF (GDXJ US)	MVIS Global Junior Gold Miners Index	NYSE Arca	5024.37	0.54
iShares Global Infrastructure ETF (IGF US)	S&P Global Infrastructure Index	NASDAQ	3755.55	0.46
iShares Global Tech ETF (IXN US)	S&P Global 1200 Information Technology Sector Index	NYSE Arca	3471.21	0.46
iShares Developed Markets Property Yield UCITS ETF (IDWP LN)	FTSE EPRA/NAREIT Developed Dividend + Index	London Stock Exchange*	3125.46	0.59
iShares Automation & Robotics UCITS ETF (RBOT LN)	iSTOXX FactSet Automation & Robotics Index	London Stock Exchange*	2599.16	0.40
iShares Exponential Technologies ETF (XT US)	Morningstar Exponential Technologies Index	NASDAQ	2535.10	0.47

(continued)

Table 8.5 (continued)

Fund (ticker)	Index	Exchange	Assets (USD m)	Expense ratio (%)
ARK Innovation ETF (ARKK US)	n.a.**	NYSE Arca	2384.72	0.75
SPDR Dow Jones Global Real Estate ETF (RWO US)	Dow Jones Global Select Real Estate Securities Index	NYSE Arca	2337.62	0.50

*—Primary exchange
**—Actively managed ETF
Note As of 19 February 2020. Single-country sector and thematic ETFs are excluded According to some sources (e.g., www.etfdb.com), the largest international sector equity ETF is Invesco QQQ Trust (one the most recognizable and most liquid ETFs in the USA) tracking the Nasdaq-100 Index. Although it includes 100 of the largest both domestic and international nonfinancial companies listed in the NASDAQ, the weight of non-US firms is negligible (below 3%)
Source Bloomberg

References

Bennett, C., & Lazzara, C. J. (2016). *Some Implications of Sector Dispersion, S&P Dow Jones Indices*. https://us.spindices.com/documents/research/research-some-implications-of-sector-dispersion.pdf. Accessed 4 Mar 2020.

Bérubé, V., Ghai, S., & Tétrault, J. (2014). *From Indexes to Insights: The Rise of Thematic Investing*. McKinsey & Company. https://www.mckinsey.com/industries/private-equity-and-principal-investors/our-insights/from-indexes-to-insights-the-rise-of-thematic-investing. Accessed 23 Mar 2020.

Dimson, E., Marsh, P., & Staunton, M. (2015). *Credit Suisse Global Investment Returns Yearbook 2015*. Credit Suisse Research Institute. https://www.credit-suisse.com/media/assets/corporate/docs/about-us/research/publications/global-investment-returns-yearbook-2015.pdf. Accessed 5 Jan 2020.

Edwards, T., & Lazzara, C. J. (2013). *Dispersion: Measuring Market Opportunity, S&P Dow Jones Indices*. https://us.spindices.com/documents/research/research-dispersion-measuring-market-opportunity.pdf. Accessed 6 Mar 2020.

Edwards, T., & Lazzara, C. J. (2019). *Sector Effects in the S&P 500: The Role of Sectors in Risk, Pricing, and Active Returns*. https://www.cboe.com/products/research-sector-effects-in-the-sp-500.pdf. Accessed 22 Feb 2020.

Fidelity. (2019). *Sector Investing Using the Business Cycle*. https://www.fidelity.com/viewpoints/investing-ideas/sector-investing-business-cycle. Accessed 10 Mar 2020.

FTSE Russell. (2019). *Industry Classification Benchmark (ICB) Reclassification*. Expanded and Improved. https://www.ftserussell.com/research/industry-classification-benchmark-icb-reclassification. Accessed 18 Mar 2020.

FTSE Russell. (2020). *Industry Classification Benchmark (ICB)*. https://www.ftserussell.com/files/support-document/icb-methodology-overview. Accessed 18 Mar 2020.

Jacobs, J. (2019). *Investing in Tomorrow: A Whitepaper on Thematic Investing*. https://www.globalxetfs.com/content/files/Investing_in_Tomorrow_White_Paper_2020-Final.pdf. Accessed 23 Mar 2020.

Johnson, B., Lamont, K., & Sotiroff, D. (2020). *Global Thematic Funds Landscape*. Morningstar. https://www.morningstar.com/lp/global-thematic-fund-landscape. Accessed 22 Mar 2020.

Jones, B. (2018). *Sector Dispersion & Correlation*. Providing Opportunity for Sector Rotation Strategies, NASDAQ Dorsey Wright. https://indexes.nasdaqomx.com/docs/DWANQFF%20Research.pdf. Accessed 4 Mar 2020.

Kumar, N., Doole, S., Garg, K., Bhalodia, V., & Ghate, D. (2019). *Indexing Change: Understanding MSCI Thematic Indexes*. https://www.msci.com/www/research-paper/indexing-change-understanding/01647260939. Accessed 23 Mar 2020.

Lamont, K., & Bioy, H. (2018). *Picking Your Dream Theme: Selecting the Right Thematic ETF*. Morningstar. Accessed 25 Mar 2020.

Lazzara, C. (2015). *Sector Dispersion and Active Management, S&P Dow Jones Indices*. https://www.indexologyblog.com/2015/04/13/sector-dispersion-and-active-management/. Accessed 6 Mar 2020.

MSCI. (2020). *Global Industry Classification Standard*. https://www.msci.com/documents/1296102/11185224/MSCI_GICS_Overview.pdf/cfdc73ec-9704-1685-7742-96bf2c3ec699. Accessed 15 Mar 2020.

Pictet. (2016). *Thematic Stocks—An Alternative to Mainstream Global Equities*. https://www.am.pictet/en/us/global-articles/2016/insights/equities/in-depth/thematicstocks-jun2016#overview. Accessed 23 Mar 2020.

Rodstrom, C. (2018). *Embracing China's Growth with a Sector-Based Approach, Global X*. https://www.globalxetfs.com/embracing-chinas-growth-with-a-sector-based-approach/. Accessed 4 Mar 2020.

S&P Global. (2020). *Industries Most and Least Impacted by COVID 19 from a Probability of Default Perspective March 2020 Update*. https://www.spglobal.com/marketintelligence/en/news-insights/blog/industries-most-and-least-impacted-by-covid-19-from-a-probability-of-default-perspective-march-2020-update. Accessed 12 Apr 2020.

SPDR. (2019). *Harness the Power of Sector Investing with ETFs, SPDR EMEA Strategy Team White Paper*. https://www.ssga.com/library-content/story/general/etf/emea/spdr-harness-power-sector-investing-etfs.pdf. Accessed 4 Mar 2020.

Towers Watson. (2012). *Thematic Investing: How to See the World*. https://www.thinkingaheadinstitute.org/-/media/TAI/Pdf/Research-Ideas/Thematic-Investing—How-we-see-the-world.pdf?modified=20151210195849. Accessed 23 Mar 2020.

Part IV

Exchange-Traded Funds Investing: Strategies for International Markets

9

Predicting Country Equity Returns: Data, Methods, and Empirical Evidence

9.1 Introduction

The last three decades brought an unprecedented growth of exchange-traded funds (ETFs) and index funds, which enable investors to quickly move their capital around the world. Currently, more easily than ever before, investors can relocate their equity allocation from Germany to Brazil or from Japan to South Africa. Not surprisingly, the ETF industry has been rising very rapidly. Already in 2017, the assets under management of ETFs exceeded five trillion US dollars, and the compound annual growth rate over the past four years amounted to almost 19% (Lord 2018). The growth of ETFs coincides with a structural change in the asset management and shift from active investing to passive investing. As of December 2017, passive fund accounted for 45% of the aggregate assets under management in the US equity funds, compared to less than 5% in 1995 (Anadu et al. 2018). This profound revolution requires a whole new set of tools for equity investors, who now focus much less on which stocks to choose than on which countries to allocate money in.

The asset pricing literature produced a preponderance of trading signals, which help to predict the cross-section of individual stock returns. Recent surveys documented literally hundreds of different equity anomalies (e.g., Harvey et al. 2016; Hou et al. 2020). Notably, many of these cross-sectional patterns, such as value, momentum, or seasonality, have their parallels at the

A modified version of this chapter has been previously published in Zaremba (2019b). Adam Zaremba acknowledges support from the National Science Centre of Poland. This paper is a part of project No. 2016/23/B/HS4/00731 of the National Science Centre of Poland.

T. Miziołek et al., *International Equity Exchange-Traded Funds*,
https://doi.org/10.1007/978-3-030-53864-4_9

inter-market level, and could be potentially used for country allocation. The last 30 years of asset pricing research produced mounting evidence regarding the cross-sectional predictability of country equity returns. The studies documenting numerous country-level equity anomalies not only provide new insights into international asset pricing but can also be translated into efficient country allocation strategies. Moreover, they are invaluable to practical investors.

The studies of cross-section of country equity returns not only examined different return patterns but also employed different methodologies and data sources. Issues such as choice of the index provider, return computation methodology, or portfolio formation can visibly influence the results. The diversity of empirical design and data sources and preparation methods calls for systematic review and for introducing a structure into the methodological choices in the field of country-level asset pricing.

The major objective of this chapter is to provide a comprehensive review of the current state of literature on the cross-section of country equity returns. In particular, our survey considers data sources and preparation, research methods, and, last but not least, the cross-sectional return patterns documented in the country-level equity returns. The cross-section of stock-level returns is summarized in many excellent surveys, concerning both the anomalies themselves (e.g., Nagel 2013; Harvey et al. 2016; Hou et al. 2020; Bali et al. 2016), as well as methodological and data choices (Jagannathan et al. 2010; Waszczuk 2014a, b). For the country-level cross-sectional asset pricing, such surveys are clearly missing. To the best of our knowledge, any such review has not been yet presented. This work aims at filling this gap. We not only review, but we also structure and introduce some order into the current state of country-level asset pricing literature.

The chapter reviews three aspects of the studies of cross-section of country equity returns. First, we focus on the choice of data and the underlying asset universe as well as on dataset preparation. At the same time, we review the approaches regarding the country coverage, study period, return measurement, currency unit, and asset universe. Second, we survey some common methodological choices in the asset pricing literature, such as the number of portfolios, return calculation, and portfolio weighting scheme. Finally, we examine the current state of knowledge on country-level cross-sectional return patterns. We review the most prominent of such patterns, such as momentum, value, long-run reversal, size, seasonality, and price and non-price risk, as well as a basket of minor anomalies. We also discuss several additional aspects of these return patterns, including their fundamental sources and implementation details. Finally, we also consider additional practical aspects of country-level return patterns: the role of trading costs and strategy timing.

9.2 Datasets and Sample Preparation

This section concentrates on the choice of dataset representing country equity returns and preparation of the sample. We survey the approaches to selection of country coverage, study period, return measurement period, currency unit, and asset universe.

9.2.1 Country Coverage

The datasets used in examinations of the cross-sectional patterns in country index returns are obviously smaller than in the stock-level studies, which often encompass several thousand companies. Naturally, the scope in this case is limited to the countries with operating stock markets. The early studies usually focused on less than 20 developed markets. For example, Keppler (1991a), Ferson and Harvey (1994a), Richards (1995) considered 18 developed markets. Modern studies usually concentrate on about 40 countries selected on the basis of classification into developed and emerging by one of the major index providers. For instance, Clare et al. (2016) investigate 40 markets, and Fisher et al. (2017) examine 37. The broadest studies take into account also less tradable frontier markets, and their sample size can exceed 70. The article by Avramov, Chordia, Jostova, and Philipov, investigating 75 equity markets, may serve as an example of such approach. Perhaps one of the broadest studies was conducted by Suleman et al. (2017), who took into consideration 83 countries.

In general, the larger sample size increases the power of statistical tests and allows additional insights on the examined return pattern. However, some studies may deliberately limit the sample of considered countries. One reason for that may be the focus put on some particular geographical region. For example, Grobys (2016) concentrates solely on the European Monetary Union. Another motivation to limit the number of countries in the sample may be alignment of the study with research practice. Since very liquid futures or ETFs cover only a small number of countries, the examinations may be reduced to just 10–20 most tradable markets. For example, the highly influential studies of Asness et al. (2013) or Keloharju et al. (2016) examined the samples of only 18 and 16 equity indices, respectively. Also, the studies utilizing early security data tend to be sometimes quite narrow due to data unavailability. For example, Hurst et al. (2017), who investigated more than a century of evidence of trend following profits, constrained their scope to only 11 countries.

9.2.2 Study Period

The study period is usually dictated by the index data availability. In consequence, numerous studies focusing on the most prominent cross-sectional patterns start in the years 1969 or 1970, when the coverage of many developed markets by MSCI begins (e.g., Balvers and Wu 2006; Bhojraj and Swaminathan 2006; Muller and Ward 2010; ap Gwilym et al. 2010). Consequently, the research period encompasses usually three to four decades. If the study period is shorter, this is usually due to inability to collect some sort of additional data for the 1970s or 1980s. For example, Berkman and Yang (2019), who focus on country-level analysts' recommendations, reduce their study period to the years 1994–2015. Also, Zaremba and Szczygielski (2019), who employ several more sophisticated valuation measures, such as EBITDA-to-EV ratio, limit the study period to the years 1996–2017. Finally, as an alternative to equity indices, some studies proxy the equity markets with respective ETFs. In such cases, the price availability is, naturally, shorter. Smith and Pantilei (2015), who test the "Dogs of the World" strategy in ETFs, examine their returns for the years 1997–2012.

A separate and rapidly growing field encompasses studies of early security data that allow insights into the long-run nature of the financial market phenomena. In asset pricing studies in particular, examinations of the close-to-century long datasets make it possible to check the true robustness of the return patterns and secure against the risk of false discoveries and data mining. Some data providers, like Global Financial Data, offer their own proprietary indices going back to the nineteenth century or even eighteenth century. A representative study of this type could be Geczy and Samonov (2017), who examine the momentum effect in the returns on major asset classes for the years 1800–2014. Baltussen, Swinkels et al. (2019) research several major anomalies for the years 1799–2016, and Zaremba, Kizys et al. (2020) explore long-term reversal for the period 1830–2019. Other studies researching similar long-run datasets include Ilmanen et al. (2019), Hurst et al. (2017), or Spierdijk et al. (2012).

9.2.3 Return Measurement Periods

The most common choice in individual stock studies is to use monthly returns. The motivation is that this choice forms a consensus that allows to accumulate large number of observations necessary for statistical tests and, at the same time, to mitigate the influence of microstructure effects (Waszczuk 2014a). Nearly all of country-level studies take a similar approach and utilize monthly returns (e.g., Richards 1997; Chan et al. 2000; Blitz and van Vliet 2008). This refers, in particular, to the studies of early security data (e.g., Geczy and Samonov 2017; Baltussen, Swinkels et al. 2019), where the more frequent observations are hardly available.

The use of different return intervals is rather infrequent and usually limited to examinations of alternative holding periods, as in Andreu et al. (2013) or Kasa (1992). On the other hand, Vu (2012) is one of the very few studies that rely on weekly returns to amass a bigger quantity of observations.

9.2.4 Currency Unit

Asset pricing studies of firm-level data frequently focus on single countries (e.g., Fama and French 2015) or replicate analyses in multiple individual markets (e.g., Chui et al. 2010). Therefore, the role of currency unit is of lesser importance and the calculations oftentimes rely on local currencies. On the other hand, in the cross-country analysis the volatile foreign exchange rates and inflation rates—especially in emerging and frontier markets—play significant role. Consequently, the majority of cross-country studies set a common currency as a unit of calculations, and the most obvious and common choice is the US dollar. Dobrynskaya (2015), Clare et al. (2016), Keppler and Encinosa (2011), Zaremba (2015), or Smith and Pantilei (2015) may serve as examples of papers that denominate all the prices in US dollars. This currency is also a default choice in the studies that utilize futures or ETFs as representation of the country exposure, as it directly expresses the perspective of a US investor (e.g., Andreu et al. 2013; Daniel and Moskowitz 2016; Moskowitz et al. 2012; Zaremba and Miziolek 2017; Zaremba and Andreu 2018; Smith and Pantilei 2015).

The use of returns calculated on the basis of local currency prices is rather rare. Usually, such framework is applied a sort of robustness check or is examined explicitly to evaluate the role of currencies in return predictability (Chan et al. 2000; Bhojraj and Swaminathan 2006). For example, Jordan et al. (2015) examine empirically the importance of the currency numeraire for the stock return predictability. They argue that, for instance, the presence (absence) of predictability for an American investor does not need to imply the existence (absence) of predictability for other international investors. Sometimes the local currency returns are also used in the studies of early security data to alleviate the problem of reliability of more than century-old foreign exchange rates (Geczy and Samonov 2017). Nonetheless, even for the early asset prices studies the US dollar is the very common choice (Zaremba, Kizys et al. 2020; Baltussen, Swinkels et al. 2019).

9.2.5 Asset Universe

Examination of cross-sectional patterns in country equity markets requires some representation of the market return. In country-level studies, the asset universe comprises usually one of two types of instruments: either equity indices, or some real investable instruments.

The major benefit of equity indices is that they provide a broad and accurate representation of the local equity markets. The articles investigating samples of international stock market indices, basically follow one option. Most commonly, the studies are based on indices from a single provider. Alternatively, a study can rely on an amalgamation of local indices computed by national stock exchanges or local companies.

The use of indices from a single provider certainly has some benefits. They include calculation transparency, result comparability, and consistency in index calculation across many countries. Indices provided by MSCI are the most popular choice in country-level asset pricing. MSCI indices represent value-weighted equity portfolios covering approximately 85% of the largest and most liquid companies in each country. They also form the basis for multiple investment products, including popular iShares ETFs. MSCI estimated that more than 7 trillion US dollars were benchmarked to MSCI indices as of June 2011 (Cenedese et al. 2016). Furthermore, importantly from a practitioner's perspective, MSCI usually does not apply any retroactive changes to the reported returns of its indices, so it reduces the risk of potential biases.

The current coverage encompasses 85 countries, including developed, emerging, frontier, and so-called standalone markets. The data period dates back to December 1969. The additional benefit of the MSCI indices is that they are calculated in several different ways, including different currencies, controlling for taxes, accounting for dividends, etc. For example, the MSCI indices were used by Dobrynskaya (2015), Clare et al. (2016), Zaremba (2015), Fisher et al. (2017), Keppler and Encinosa (2011), Richards (1997),

Balvers and Wu (2006), Keimling (2016), Keloharju et al. (2016), Malin and Bornholt (2013), Ferson and Harvey (1994b), and many others.

Datastream Global Equity Indices are the second most popular index choice. These cover currently 64 countries and go back in time to January 1973. Notably, the Datastream indices also assure a broad and consistent international representation, and at certain periods in the past their coverage may be better than in the case of MSCI. This index provider was selected, for example, by Bali and Cakici (2010), Umutlu (2015, 2019), and Zaremba (2019a).

The studies of more than century-long datasets usually take advantage of indices computed by Global Financial Data (GFD). This provides time series going back to the nineteenth century for numerous developed and emerging markets. Obviously, such long-run datasets are not free from different biases, omissions, and the index portfolios frequently contain very few securities, but certainly they provide a unique look into the past data. The GFD indices were employed by Geczy and Samonov (2017), Baltussen, Swinkels et al. (2019), and Zaremba, Kizys et al. (2020), among others.

One of the drawbacks of the indexes obtained from different providers is that their coverage may differ; some countries may be taken into account by one provider but not considered by others. Consequently, to maximize the size of the research sample, some of the studies merge indices from different sources. Erb et al. (1995) in one of the first studies of this type, represent the developed markets by the MSCI indices and the emerging ones by the portfolios calculated by International Finance Corporation (IFC). Avramov et al. (2012) use MSCI indices and supplement the coverage of missing countries with Datastream portfolios. Geczy and Samonov (2017) blend Bloomberg and GFD indices. Zaremba, Kizys et al. (2020) combine Datastream and GFD. Finally, Batltussen, Swinkels, et al. (2019) collect data from Bloomberg, with gaps filled in by Datastream data, spliced with index-level data, as in Baltussen, van Bekkum et al. (2019), and, eventually, backfilled data downloaded from Global Financial Data.

Besides using the indices from acknowledged providers, there are also several other options. Ellahie et al. (2019) use aggregated stock-level data from CRSP and Compustat. In other words, they calculate the country portfolios themselves instead of obtaining them from external sources. The final variant is to use national indices computed by local providers such as DAX, NIKKEI, or S&P. This approach is employed by Chan et al. (2000) and Vu (2012), among others. This approach has two major benefits. First, it may help to increase the dataset, because these local indices may have a longer history available than their counterparts offered by MSCI or Datastream. Second, the most liquid equity index futures are oftentimes linked with local indices rather than with international ones. For instance, in Poland the most liquid equity index future is based on the WIG20 index computed by the Warsaw Stock Exchange. Consequently, the use of local index may be more aligned with investment practice. Nevertheless, on the other hand, the major shortcoming in relying on the local indices is the lack of computational consistency. Different indexes rely on different selection and weighting methods, so the study outcomes may be potentially influenced by the index calculation methodology, resulting in misleading conclusions. For example, better performance of an index in a certain market may stem from its bigger exposure to small-cap companies rather than from a true factor examined by the researcher.

Instead of investigating "paper" equity indices some studies focus on actual investment instruments providing exposure to international markets. While this framework may potentially limit the size of the dataset, certainly it reflects most closely the investor's practical perspective. Following this reasoning, Daniel and Moskowitz (2016), Moskowitz et al. (2012), and Hurst et al. (2017) base their computations on futures markets. Alternatively, Andreu et al. (2013), Breloer et al. (2014), Smith and Pantilei (2015), and Zaremba and Andreu (2018) focus on single-country ETFs.

9.3 Methodological Choices

The country-level asset pricing studies strongly rely on econometric and statistical toolsets very similar to those used in the regular studies applied to the individual firms. The two most common approaches are cross-sectional (or panel) regressions and portfolio sorts. These two complementary approaches are frequently used jointly, as recommended by Fama (2015), and their benefits and shortcomings are discussed in details by Fama and French (2008).

In the most typical applications of the cross-sectional regressions following Fama and MacBeth (1973), the future returns are regressed against a number of return-predicting variables, i.e., characteristics. Cross-sectional regressions are used, for instance, by Bali and Cakici (2010), Fisher et al. (2017), and Stocker (2016). Sometimes this approach is supplemented with different types of panel regressions, as in Hjalmarsson (2010), Lawrenz and Zorn (2017), and Bali and Cakici (2010). Wisniewski and Jackson (2018) apply pooled ordinary least squares and two-way fixed-effects regressions.

Portfolio sorts are the second most popular tool. In this framework, all the considered assets—which are in this case country equity markets—are ranked based on certain empirical characteristics, such as past returns or valuation ratios. Subsequently, they are grouped into subsets and portfolios are formed. Finally, the performance of the cross-sectional portfolios is evaluated on the basis of mean returns, volatilities, Sharpe ratios, and with factor pricing models and monotonicity checks in the style of Patton and Timmerman (2010). The portfolio sorts reduce the cross-sectional dimension of the joint distribution of returns and also help to reduce the impact of measurement error (Waszczuk 2014a).

In the evaluation of the portfolios from one-way sorts, called also single-sorts, there is also a common practice to calculate the returns on a differential portfolio (or spread portfolio, long-short portfolio, zero-investment portfolio), which takes long and short positions in the two most extreme quantiles of assets from one-way sorts. The performance of such portfolios is then subsequently evaluated. Importantly, it should be noted that frequently this exercise serves as a quick check of monotonicity rather than a reflection of actual investment performance. Due to tradability and short-sale limitations, forming and rebalancing zero-investment portfolios across many countries is not always possible, unless they are made of liquid futures, as in Daniel and Moskowitz (2016) or Moskowitz et al. (2012). Some further discussion of the details of sorting methods in asset pricing studies is provided in Bali et al. (2016), Vaihekoski (2004), van Dijk (2011), and Waszczuk (2014a).

The outcomes of the cross-sectional analysis based on portfolio sorts are sensitive to several methodological choices made by the researcher. Importantly, some of the country-level practices may differ from stock-level studies due to different number of assets, data availability, liquidity considerations, etc. I will focus then on several most important methodological choices.

9.3.1 Number of Portfolios

The studies of the cross-section of returns on common stocks rely on datasets of hundreds or thousands of companies. Therefore, decile (e.g., Jegadeesh and Titman 1993, 2001; Lakonishok et al. 1994) or quintile (Banz 1981; Chan et al. 1998) groupings belong to the most common choices. At the country level, the number of assets is more limited, so this type of studies requires also a smaller number of portfolios. Otherwise, the grouping could result in portfolios containing only a few—or even one—markets, hence being susceptible to the noise in returns. The most popular choices include tertiles (e.g., Daniel and Moskowitz 2016; Geczy and Samonov 2017; Asness et al. 2013; Atilgan et al. 2019), quartiles (Richards 1997; Blitz and van Vliet 2008; Macedo 1995a, b, c; Malin and Bornholt 2013; Erb et al. 1995), or quintiles (Clare et al. 2016; Zaremba, Umutlu et al. 2019). Alternatively, some studies which assume different portfolio formation methodologies, consider only two portfolios—long and short (e.g., Moskowitz et al. 2012; Zaremba et al. 2018). Bali and Cakici (2010) consider portfolio groupings including 30, 40, and 30% of the markets, respectively.

Finally, a number of studies, instead of assuming a certain quantile cut-off point, focus only on the extreme portfolios from single-sorts and assume a fixed number of countries included. For instance, Kortas et al. (2005) include 11 most extreme countries in each portfolio. On the other hand, Keloharju et al. (2016) test the cross-sectional seasonality based on portfolios including the three equity indices with the highest or lowest average return in the past.

9.3.2 Portfolio Weighting Scheme

Once the portfolios are formed, the next important step is the selection of the weighting scheme. The most common choice is between the value-weighted portfolios and equal-weighted portfolios. In the first framework, the returns are weighted according to the market capitalization. On the other hand, in the equal-weighted approach, all the returns are assigned an equal-dollar value. At the stock level, the value-weighting approach is markedly more popular, and there are several reasons for that. The equal-weighted portfolios may tend to assume very large positions in small and micro-companies, which would be unrealistic in practice, due to liquidity or market capacity issues, for example. Also, the equal-weighted portfolios have a build-in rebalancing assumption, which may distort the results (Willenbrock 2011). Finally, value-weighting deemphasizes observations that are more likely to suffer from the data errors, thus reducing the variation in average returns. Nevertheless, at the country level the choice is not that obvious. Indeed, the equal-weighted portfolios may gravitate toward small and illiquid frontier markets, where any large exposure of frequent share purchases may be unrealistic. However, on the other hand, in the case of limited sample size of just 30–40 countries, the value-weighted portfolios may be strongly dominated by only a few largest countries. Furthermore, the aggregate market value may not always be available, or it may not have any intuitive equivalent, as is the case with the futures or ETFs. Consequently, the equal-weighted portfolios are much more common, or at least used along with the value-weighted portfolios. The equal-weighted portfolios are used, for example, by Geczy and Samonov (2017), Clare et al. (2016), Hurst et al. (2017), and Balvers and Wu (2006).

The value-weighted strategies, on the other hand, are analyzed by Chan et al. (2000), Rikala (2017), and Zaremba (2016a).

Besides the classical value- or equal-weighted portfolios, some articles pursue alternative frameworks. Clare et al. (2016) and Moskowitz et al. (2012) use so-called risk-parity, i.e., they weight the portfolio components on their inverse volatility. On the other hand, Ilmanen et al. (2019), Asness, Moskowitz, and Pedersen (2013), and Zaremba et al. (2018) link the weight with the value or rank of the underlying characteristic, so that the absolute weight increases when the sorting variables take more extreme values. Finally, Zaremba and Miziolek (2017) explore the country-level counterparts of enhanced indexing strategies.

9.3.3 Return Calculation: The Treatment of Dividends and Taxes

The index-level return calculations face two major methodological choices. The first issue refers to the treatment of dividends. Most of the studies are based on total return indices, that include reinvested dividends, regardless of the particular index provider (e.g., Richards 1997; Balvers and Wu 2006; Bali and Cakici 2010). Accounting for dividends reflects well the investor's perspective; nonetheless, sometimes the coverage and the length of the time series may be bigger for the price returns. Therefore, the price indices, which do not account for dividends, are employed by Keppler (1991a), for instance. On the other hand, ap Gwilym et al. (2010) and Geczy and Samonov (2017) use both price and return indices. Finally, some examinations use the two types of measures in combination as different inputs. For example, Clare et al. (2016) measure portfolio performance with the total return indices but compute return predictive signals based on price indices.

The total returns indices include dividends, which are taxed in various ways in the majority of countries. Importantly, the dividend tax rates may vary both across time and countries, affecting the net portfolio performance. Some groups of investors, like mutual funds, may be exempted from taxation on dividends in many countries. Nonetheless, this is not true for all the countries, at all times, and for all the groups of investors. Consequently, the taxes may still potentially affect the cross-section of country equity returns. The majority of the country-level asset pricing studies use gross returns, not accounting for taxation. On the other hand, Zaremba and Konieczka (2016) also use MSCI Net Return indices, which account for dividend tax rates within the particular countries.

9.4 Cross-Sectional Patterns in Country-Level Returns

We now turn to the review of patterns demonstrated in the cross-section of country equity returns. We begin by focusing on the most prominent and best-established ones, such as momentum, size, and value, and, subsequently, carry on with more minor return regularities. In addition, we consider different types of risk that influence future index-level returns. To introduce some order, we arbitrarily classify these risks into the ones that can be derived from prices (price based), and others, that is, non-price risks such as credit or political risks. Eventually, we survey the studies' treatment of some additional aspects of the country-level anomalies, such as factor timing and the role of trading costs.

9.4.1 Momentum

The momentum effect, which is the tendency of assets with high (low) past returns to continue to overperform (underperform) in the future, is one the most robust and pervasive asset pricing anomalies ever documented. It has been demonstrated in the USA and international stocks, including developed, emerging, and frontier, markets, commodities, bonds, currencies, and also in equity market indices.

Index-level evidence. The first empirical evidence for the momentum effect in country equity indices may be found in Ferson and Harvey (1994b), Macedo (1995a, b), Richards (1997), and Asness et al. (1997). Other researchers have continued the examinations of country-level momentum in the following years. Balvers and Wu (2006) investigate a Jegadeesh and Titman (1993)-style portfolio based on stock market indices from 18 developed equity markets within the years 1969–1999. They demonstrate strong momentum effects, which worked particularly well in combination with the mean-reversion patterns. In the same year, Bhojraj and Swaminathan (2006) published a paper which examined a broader sample of 38 country indices within the same periods. The authors document that the quintile of the best-performing countries over the past 6 months continued to significantly outperform the laggard indices during the next three quarters. The mean return on the long/short portfolio within a year after its formation amounted to 7.65%.

The following years saw further examinations of the momentum effect that extended the study sample both in terms of number of countries and the length of the study period. Muller and Ward (2010) investigated 70 countries and Zaremba (2015) researched 78. In terms of the sample length, several studies extended the time series back to the nineteenth century and researched approximately 200 years of returns (Geczy and Samonov 2017; Hurst et al. 2017; Baltussen, Swinkels et al. 2019). The momentum effect remains strong and robust, though it looks markedly weaker in certain situations, such as for the value-weighted portfolios (Zaremba 2015). The momentum effect is robust to many considerations and could be successfully implemented with the use of ETFs (Andreu et al. 2013). Angelidis and Tessaromatis (2018) argue that "country-based factor portfolios offer a viable alternative implementation of factor investing in a world of illiquidity, transaction costs, and capacity constraints." Some other studies that investigated the momentum effect at the country level are Chan et al. (2000), Daniel and Moskowitz (2016), Grobys (2016), Guilmin (2015), Ilmanen et al. (2019), Breloer et al. (2014), Nijman et al. (2004), L'Her et al. (2004), Vu (2012), Kortas et al. (2005), and Shen et al. (2005).

Formation and holding periods. The seminal study of Jegadeesh and Titman (1993) considered 3–12 month-long sorting and holding periods. Numerous country-level studies, including the early ones, take a similar approach (e.g., Balvers and Wu 2006; Andreu et al. 2013). Later studies frequently used the approach advertised by Fama and French (1996), i.e., 1-month holding period and 12-month sorting period with the most recent month skipped (e.g., Dobrynskaya 2015; Blitz and van Vliet 2008; Asness et al. 2013). The 1-month skip period is usually applied in order to disentangle the short-term reversal effect discovered by Rosenberg et al. (1985) Jegadeesh (1990), and Lehmann (1990). Nonetheless, at the country level no similar one-month reversal effect has been documented, and Zaremba, Karathanasopoulos et al. (2019) argue that the returns display rather a short-term continuation. Consequently, the country-level studies do not always assume the one-month skip period, and if they do, this is usually motivated by liquidity and implementation issues (Asness et al. 2013; Baltussen, Swinkels et al. 2019). For this reason, Geczy and Samonov (2017), who study early security data, decided to skip even two months in part of their tests.

Momentum improvements and alternative implementations. While the classical momentum assumes sorting the indices on raw past returns, a number of studies offer alternative, but closely related approaches. Notably, while some are conceptually very close to momentum, more detailed tests show that they provide incremental information about future returns. Moskowitz et al. (2012) and Hurst et al. (2017) evaluate so-called time-series momentum. This strategy assumes including markets into long or short portfolio depending on whether the excess return in the sorting period was positive or negative. ap Gwilym et al. (2010), Clare et al. (2017), Baltussen, Swinkels et al. (2019), Zaremba (2016a), test trends following strategies that focus on whether the most recent index value is above or below its moving average. Bornholt and Malin (2010, 2011) research the 52-week high strategy, whereby the return-predicting signal is the distance to 52-week maximum index value. Zaremba et al. (2018) and Zaremba, Umutlu et al. (2019) adjust the past return with volatility and sort the equity indices on past regression residuals and alphas, respectively. Avramov et al. (2018) concentrate on the distance between short- and long-run moving averages of prices. Zaremba, Szyszka et al. (2020) test the market breadth signal by comparing the number of rising and falling shares in a given country. Finally, several studies demonstrate that the momentum effect could be efficiently combined with long-run reversal to augment the performance of the strategy (Balvers and Wu 2006; Asness et al. 2013; Bornholt and Malin 2014).

Sources of the momentum effect. The stock-level momentum studies highlight a number of different explanations of the momentum effect, such as risk premium, behavioral underreaction or overreaction, herding, or confirmation bias (see Zaremba and Shemer 2018 for a comprehensive analysis). For example, Bhojraj and Swaminathan (2006) stress out potential overreaction to news about macroeconomic conditions. In addition, Cenedese et al. (2016) link the momentum effect with the tendency of investors to increase their holdings in markets that have recently outperformed (Froot et al. 1992; Bohn and Tesar 1996; Griffin et al. 2004; Chabot et al. 2014). On the other hand, Zaremba, Umutlu et al. (2019) focus on alpha momentum, which would be more consistent with underreaction hypothesis, and Zaremba, Szyszka et al. (2020) accentuate the role of herding. Other studies offer some alternative explanations. Balvers and Wu (2006) link the momentum effect with production-based asset pricing concepts. From the risk-based perspective, Asness et al. (2013) argue that global funding liquidity risk is a partial source of the momentum pattern. Cooper et al. (2019) demonstrate that the momentum returns are explained by the portfolio loadings on global macroeconomic risk factors. Eventually, Evans and Schmitz (2015) link the global momentum effect with data mining for anomalies, calling it a likely example of a selection bias.

9.4.2 Size Effect

The country-level size effect is a phenomenon parallel to the firm-level size effect discovered by Banz (1981). Keppler and Traub (1993) were the first to demonstrate that the low-capitalization equity markets outperform large equity markets. The authors found that the smaller national equity markets in the MSCI Developed Markets universe produced an average annual return of 19.19% within the years 1975–1992. This outcome compared favorably with the 12.67% total compound return on the MSCI World Index. Furthermore, the small markets displayed lower downside characteristics. The outperformance of the small firms was later confirmed also by Asness et al. (1997) and by Keppler and Encinosa (2011). The size, measured with market capitalization also belonged to the risk attributes examined by Harvey (2000).

The size effect was further demonstrated in several more recent studies. Fisher et al. (2017) show that stocks from small equity markets tend to have higher average returns than stocks from large countries. Notably, they accentuate that the country size effect is largely independent of the firm size effect and other country quantitative factors such as the momentum or value effects. Zaremba and Konieczka (2016) and Zaremba and Umutlu (2018a) also demonstrate the size effect in large international sample, and Li and Pritamani (2015) show that it drives the returns on emerging and frontier markets. Similarly, Pungulescu (2014) points out that the market size effects account for up to 1% per year in terms of expected returns in emerging countries. Finally, Rikala (2017) focuses solely on European markets and finds no consistent evidence that small countries outperform large ones.

Sources of the country size premium. The firm-level size effect is frequently linked to additional risk factors, such as liquidity, information risk (see Norges Bank 2012 for a comprehensive review of the sources of small firm effect). While Fisher et al. (2017) provide evidence that the country size effect is not simply a firm-size effect "in disguise" (the effect does not arise because smaller markets are populated by smaller firms), the potential explanations usually oscillate around the concept of risk. Rikala (2017) writes that "Intuitively, small countries producing higher returns is logical because of the widely acknowledged return profile of small stocks; investing in small firms produces higher returns in exchange for greater volatility and possibly even a return premium; a return in excess of the required compensation for additional risk." Fisher et al. (2017) conjecture that the small-country effect is due to home bias, but they provide mixed evidence in support of this conjecture. They also demonstrate that the country size effect does not simply stem from lower analysts' coverage. Zaremba (2016b) shows that accounting for country-specific risks (sovereign, political, etc.) can largely explain the abnormal returns on small markets. Finally, Pungulescu (2014), similarly to Zaremba (2016b), demonstrates that the size effect is more pronounced in emerging countries than in developed countries, and the size premium exists independently of the segmentation premium documented in the literature.

Finally, Zaremba and Umutlu (2018a) provide evidence that the country size premium is strongly concentrated in January, as in the case of the firm size effect (Keim 1983; Lamoureux and Sanger 1989; Daniel and Titman 1997). Last but not least, a white paper by Evans and Schmitz (2015) argues that the cross-sectional pattern related to the market capitalization may be simply a statistical artifact, which cannot be confirmed in the recent data.

9.4.3 Value Effect

The value effect refers to the tendency of stocks with low valuation ratios, such as price-to-earnings ratio or price-to-book ratio, to outperform stocks with high valuation ratios. For individual stocks, the phenomenon has been well known for about six decades now (Nicholson 1960; Basu 1975, 1977, 1983; Reinganum 1981), but in the equity indices it has been documented only in the 1990s (Keppler 1991a, b). In one of the earliest studies, Macedo (1995a, b, c) researches the performance of country portfolios based on 18 country equity indices. She forms quartile portfolios from sorts on three different indicators: the book-to-market ratio, dividend yield, and earnings yield, and test their performance within an almost 20-year period. She concludes that the "cheap" countries outperformed the "expensive" markets, and the differential annual return between the countries with the lowest and highest valuation ratios ranged from 1.25 to 8.54%, depending on the ratio selection, rebalancing frequency, and hedging approach.

The valuation effect was also confirmed in more recent studies that use broader data samples and longer time spans. For example, Angelidis and Tessaromatis (2018) investigated the performance of 23 developed markets within the 1980–2014 period. They found that the value portfolios vividly outperformed market portfolios, delivering information ratios ranging from 0.27 to 0.39, depending on the weighting scheme. Further evidence for the value effect across countries was provided by Faber (2012), Klement (2012), Angelini et al. (2012), Ellahie et al. (2019), Novotny and Gupta (2015), Keimling (2016), Kim (2012), Heckman et al. (1996), Ferson and Harvey (1994b, 1998), Kortas et al. (2005), Lawrenz and Zorn (2017), Ferreira and Santa-Clara (2011), Desrosiers et al. (2007), Zaremba (2015), Zaremba and Szczygielski (2019), Asness et al. (1997), and, finally, L'Her et al. (2004). Also Baltussen, Swinkels et al. (2019) included the value effect in their two-century study, confirming its pervasive and robust character. However, Kim (2012) and Zaremba (2016b) show that the effect is stronger among the emerging markets rather than in developed countries.

Valuation ratios. The value effect in country equity indices can be examined with different valuation rations. The majority of them are parallels of similar ratios or techniques used at the firm level. The most popular include price-to-earnings (P/E) ratio (e.g., Ellahie et al. 2019; Kim 2012; Keimling 2016), price-to-book (P/B) ratio (Ellahie et al. 2019; Angelidis and Tessaromatis 2018; Kortas, L'Her, and Roberge 2005), or dividend yield (Zaremba 2015; Keimling 2016; Hjalmarsson 2010; Keppler 1991a). Some articles focus also on modified versions of these valuation ratios. For instance, Kortas et al. (2005) use forward P/E ratios and Lawrenz and Zorn (2017) concentrate on conditional price-to-fundamental ratios. The other utilized ratios encompass price-to-cash flow ratio (e.g., Keppler 1991a; Keimling 2016). Desrosiers et al. (2007) offer an alternative framework based on residual income. Zaremba and Szczygielski (2019) review several popular valuation ratios to conclude that the EBITDA-to-EV signal seems to be the most effective predictor of future cross-sectional returns. Also, Ferreira and Santa-Clara (2011) show that several ratios can be combined to obtain superior performance.

Finally, there is one specific valuation ratio, which was designed purportedly for the country-level predictions: the cyclically adjusted price-to-earnings ratio, abbreviated CAPE. The technique could be traced back to the seminal work "Security Analysis" by Graham and Dodd (1940). The authors put forward an idea of smoothing earnings over the past few years in order to calculate valuation ratios. Nevertheless, the true father of the application of the CAPE to equity premium predictions is Robert Shiller, the Nobel laureate of 2013. In his 1988 study (Shiller and Campbell 1988, p. 675), he demonstrated that "a long moving average of real earnings helps to forecast future real dividends," and, consequently, might be also used to predict future returns. CAPE, called also Shiller P/E, is computed as an index value divided by the average of trailing 10-year earnings adjusted for inflation. Numerous studies demonstrate that CAPE could be also successfully applied to country selection. For example, Faber (2012) examines the role of CAPE in a sample of 30 country equity markets for the years 1980–2011. Faber (2012) provides evidence that an equal-weighted quarter portfolio of the countries with the lowest CAPE produces a mean yearly return of 13.5%, whereas the most expensive markets deliver only 4.3% per year. At the same time, the equal-weighted portfolio of all of the countries in the sample returned 9.4% per year. Klement (2012) demonstrates that CAPE can predict returns even within a five to ten-year horizon. The efficiency of CAPE as the predictor of future returns was later verified and confirmed also by Angelini et al. (2012), Novotny and Gupta (2015), Keimling (2016), and Ilmanen et al. (2019).

Sources of the value effect across countries. The common reasoning regarding the value effect is similar to the parallel effect at the firm level, linking it either to behavioral mispricing or to some risk factors not captured by the established asset pricing models. Nonetheless, the catalogue of risks may be slightly different due to differences in the nature of the asset class. Ellahie et al. (2019) find that low P/B countries face temporarily depressed current earnings and their recovery in future earnings growth is uncertain. Moreover, the markets with low P/B also exhibit greater downside sensitivity to global earnings growth. Ferson and Harvey (1998) argue, for instance, that the P/B ratio has cross-sectional explanatory power at the global level, mainly because it contains information about global market risk exposures. Zaremba (2016b) also shows that the country-specific risk explains a large part of the country-level value premium.

9.4.4 Seasonality

Cross-sectional seasonality is a relatively new phenomenon described by Heston and Sadka (2008) and later confirmed by several other authors in international markets (Heston and Sadka 2010; Keloharju et al. 2016). What Heston and Sadka (2008) found that the stocks with a high same-month average return in the past tend to outperform stocks with a low same-month return in the past. Notably, Keloharju et al. (2016) extend this evidence to country equity indices. They find that this seasonal return pattern is admittedly weaker than in other asset classes but still visible. The tertile of countries with the highest same-month return outperforms the tertile of the markets with the lowest same-month return by 0.48% (t-stat =2.20). Notably, the markets with the highest average return in the remaining months underperformed the markets with the lowest other-month return by −0.36% (−1.66). Consistent findings were also presented in a later paper by the same authors (Keloharju et al. 2019), but, again, the statistical significance was low. The phenomenon has also been verified in early data samples by Baltussen, Swinkels et al. (2019) and Zaremba, Kizys et al. (2020).[1]

[1]Note that this article focuses only on cross-sectional seasonality. Apart from this, there is some evidence that the equity indices demonstrate some monthly calendar patterns in the time series, for example, in Keppler and Xue (2003) or Bouman and Jacobsen (2002).

9.4.5 Long-Run Reversal

The long-term reversal at the firm level dates back to the seminal study of De Bondt and Thaler (1985), who provided convincing evidence that stocks with a poor (good) performance over the last 3–5 years tend to produce high (low) returns in the future. Further studies demonstrated that the effect is not only robust, but also pervasive, driving the returns on individual stocks globally (Baytas and Cakici 1999; Blackburn and Cakici 2017), futures (Lubnau and Todorova 2015), currencies (Chan 2013), and commodities (Bianchi, Drew and Fan 2015; Chaves and Viswanathan 2016). Notably, the effect is also present in country equity indices.

Index-level evidence. The first evidence of long-term reversal effect was provided by Kasa (1992), Richards (1995, 1997). These authors based their research usually on limited samples of developed markets and demonstrated that indices with low (high) long-term performance significantly outperform in the future. The results were later confirmed with larger and longer samples by Kortas et al. (2005), Balvers et al. (2000), Balvers and Wu (2006), and Shen et al. (2005). Gharaibeh (2015) corroborated the long-term reversal phenomenon in the Middle East market indices, and Spierdijk et al. (2012), and Zaremba, Kizys et al. (2020) confirmed the findings in study periods exceeding a century. The strategy works well for 36–60 month sorting periods, and Malin and Bornholt (2013), who develop so-called late stage contrarian strategies, experiment also with skipping the most recent 12-months as in Fama and French (1996). Finally, Smith and Pantilei (2015) develop a simple mean-reversion-based strategy, which they called "Dogs of the Word." The technique assumes buying five countries with the worst performance over the last year and holding it for five years. The strategy proves profitable both in indices and single-country ETFs. Smith and Pantilei (2015) argue that "assuming a five-year holding period, such a portfolio would have produced compounded annual returns of 10.39%," exceeding the profits on the global passive equity portfolios. In the years 1997–2012, their strategy implemented with the ETFs of worst-performing countries outperforms the MSCI All Country World Index (MSCI ACWI) by 246 bps, delivering a higher Sharpe ratio, net of ETF expenses.

Sources of long-run reversal. Although there is no consensus on the source of long-run reversals, the existing studies offered some potential explanations. Richards (1997) considers whether the contrarian profits may stem from risk-differentials but finds no support for this hypothesis. He argues that no evidence suggests that loser-index returns are riskier in terms of their volatility or exposure to the world equity market returns. Cooper et al. (2019)

link some similar patterns to global macroeconomic risks, but Zaremba, Kizys et al. (2020) find no evidence that the long-run reversal effect compensates for the exposure to macroeconomic risks.

The winner-loser reversals profits are larger among the smaller countries than in the larger markets, so there may be an element of a "small-country effect," but still this phenomenon does not fully explain the long-term reversal effect (Zaremba, Kizys et al. 2020; Zaremba and Umutlu 2018a).

Another option is that the long-run reversal is just a statistical artifact and that its returns were purely period specific. Indeed, the country-level long-term reversal tends to be very volatility and unstable over time (Zaremba 2016e), but its robustness over very long-periods casts doubt on such an explanation (Spierdijk et al. 2012; Zaremba, Kizys et al. 2020). Furthermore, Malin and Bornholt (2013), who employ longitudinal analysis, argue that the mean-reversion effect is present even in the post-1989 sample despite the absence of visible contrarian profits for the developed markets.

Further explanations point to behavioral mispricing that cannot be arbitraged away for many reasons, including cross-border flows limitations. The behavioral overreaction hypothesis is also consistent with the link to the momentum effect (Richards 1997; Balvers and Wu 2006; Malin and Bornholt 2013) and with the post-formation behavior of the global momentum portfolios (Zaremba et al. 2019).

9.4.6 Price Risk

The relationship between the risk measures calculated on the basis of prices and future returns on stocks is a controversial and intensively researched topic in recent years. On the one hand, early theoretical models suggest that systematic risk should positively correlate with future returns in the cross-section, and some early studies seem to produce consistent evidence (Sharpe 1964; Black et al. 1972; Fama and MacBeth 1973; Blume 1970; Miller and Scholes 1972; Blume and Friend 1973). Similarly, the stock-specific risk should be either also positively correlated or unrelated, depending on market integration (Levy 1978; Tinic and West 1986; Merton 1987; Malkiel and Xu 1997, 2004). However, the empirical evidence mounting over the past two decades documents a contrary phenomenon—the so-called low-risk anomaly. The high-risk firms tend to underperform the low-risk firms on the risk-adjusted basis, both when the risk is understood as a systematic risk or an idiosyncratic risk (Frazzini and Pedersen 2014; Ang et al. 2006, 2009). The effect is usually explained with the combination of behavioral biases and limits to arbitrage (for a comprehensive review, see Blitz et al. 2019). Notably, some other measures of price-based risk, such as value at risk, display a rather positive than negative relationship with future returns in the cross-section (Bali and Cakici 2004).

Market beta. The risk-return relationship at the country level is also far from obvious and depends strongly on risk measures. The first studies bring weak evidence on the pricing on systematic risks, especially in emerging markets (Harvey 1991, 1995; Harvey and Zhou 1993). In one of the first studies, Harvey (1995) finds no relationship between beta and future returns across 20 emerging markets. Also, more recent studies by Estrada (2000) and Bali and Cakici (2010) lead to similar conclusions. Nonetheless, the seminal study of Frazzini and Pedersen (2014) demonstrates that on risk-adjusted basis low-beta indices outperform high-beta indices, and the effect is confirmed by Berrada et al. (2015). Hedegaard (2018) also corroborates the low-beta effect in developed and emerging market indices, demonstrating additionally that it is partially predictable by past market returns.

Idiosyncratic risk. The country-level examinations display no evidence of the low-idiosyncratic risk anomaly, which is similar at the firm level. The majority of the studies find either a positive relationship or no significant relationship between idiosyncratic (or total) volatility and expected country returns in the cross-section. Bali and Cakici (2010) compute total and idiosyncratic volatility measures of different asset pricing models based on estimation periods ranging from one to six months and find a positive relationship. On the other hand, articles by Umutlu (2015, 2019), Zaremba (2016c), Liang and Wei (2019), and Hueng and Ruey (2013) show either very weak on unreliable links between idiosyncratic or total volatility and future returns in the cross-section. The pricing of similar measures of price risk has been also considered by Bekaert and Harvey (1995), and Hueng (2014).

Other definitions of risk. Several studies examined other definitions of price risk. Some of them documented significant relationships, while others were less successful. Hollstein et al. (2019) investigate the pricing of tail risk in international stock markets. They find that both local and our newly computed global tail risk strongly predict global equity index excess returns. Sorting equity markets countries into portfolios by their tail risk generates sizable excess returns across various holding periods. Arouri et al. (2019) examine the role of jump risk. Zaremba (2019a) evaluates a very simple measure of price range, calculated as the difference between maximum and minimum prices, and argues its strong positive relationship with the cross-section of returns. Umutlu and Bengitöz (2017) offer a similar metric based on return range. Finally, Atilgan et al. (2019) test the forecasting power of several measures of downside risk, i.e., downside beta, tail beta, value at risk, and expected shortfall, but find no consistent evidence of return predictability.

9.4.7 Non-price Risks

Besides the measures of risk derived from price behavior discussed in the previous section, numerous studies explore the role of alternative definitions and source of risk. The logic behind these studies is the following: if the country-specific risk matters for country-level asset pricing, what actually is this country-specific risk? Can it be conceptualized and captured more precisely with some alternative measures?

Examinations of the country-specific risks as determinants of future market-level performance are found in the earliest studies of cross-section of country returns and date back to the 1990s (Ferson and Harvey 1994a, b; Erb et al. 1995, 1996a; Bekaert et al. 1996). Some of these studies focus on just one type of risk, such as credit risk or political risk, while others examine several categories or exposures to them (Ferson and Harvey 1994a; Erb et al. 1996a, b; Harvey 2004; Zaremba 2016d, 2018a). The types of considered country-specific risks could be categorized into several broad classes.

Credit risk. Country credit risk (sovereign risk, default risk) belongs among the best-established predictors of future returns. Not only has it been extensively documented by practitioners, it is also widely employed by practitioners in models of cost of equity. A widely used database in Damodatan (2019) advocates using country risk premia based on local sovereign ratings. Erb et al. (1995) employ measures of credit risk calculated on the basis of the Institutional Investor Semiannual Survey of Bankers and demonstrate that the credit risk is priced in the country equity premium. In a later study, the same authors show how the credit risk could be used to estimate risk premia for 135 different countries—even those without developed stock markets (Erb et al. 1996b). More recent research confirms these early findings with different measures of credit risk. Avramov et al. (2012) use quantified credit ratings for 75 countries in the period 1989–2009. They show that the high credit risk tercile outperforms the stocks in the countries in the low credit risk tercile by 0.57% monthly. Zaremba (2018a) further corroborates these findings by using the Economist Intelligence Unit sovereign risk indicator calculated by its Country Risk Service. Having examined 75 countries for the years 1998–2015, Zaremba arrives at a qualitatively similar return on a tertile differential portfolio of 0.48% per month.

Political risk. The political risk is another category of risk that has been examined since the beginning of studies of cross-section of country returns (Erb et al. 1996; Diamonte et al. 1996). The political risk is most frequently measured with the Political Risk Index, which constitutes a component of the International Country Risk Guide calculated by the PRS Group.[2] In general, the studies find that the political risk is positively related to the expected returns in the cross-section (Erb et al. 1996; Dimic et al. 2015; Lehkonen and Heimonen 2015; Vortelinos and Saha 2016). Bilson, Brailsfort, and Hooper (2002) show that the political risk is more strongly priced in emerging markets rather than in developed ones. Consistently with this, Diamonte et al. (1996) concentrate on changes in political risk and demonstrate that average emerging market returns in countries experiencing declining political risk exceed those of emerging markets experiencing growing political risk by approximately 11% per quarter. In contrast, the analogous return for developed markets amounted to only 2.5%. Also Zaremba (2016b) show that country risk pricing is stronger in emerging and—in particular—frontier markets. Dimic et al. (2015) explore this difference further and show that while composite political risk is priced in all the types of stock markets (i.e., developed, emerging, and frontier), but the role of individual components vary across countries. For example, government action is a common source of risk in all market categories, but the impact of government stability is unique to frontier equities.

Recent studies offer some further insights into the effect of political risk. Pagliardi et al. (2019) propose an international capital asset pricing model that accounts for the political risk. The model explains up to 77% of cross-sectional returns, outperforms some other benchmark models, and has a good predictive power. Gala et al. (2019) offer two new politics and policy risk factors and demonstrate that markets with lower politics and policy rankings produce higher average returns. They also offer some long-short strategies, which are argued to produce returns exceeding 12% per year with a corresponding Sharpe ratio of 0.59.

Other non-price risks. While credit risk and political risk seem to be the most intensively researched categories, other studies consider also alternate types of risks, such as economic and financial risks (Erb et al. 1996a), currency and banking sector risks (Zaremba 2018a), macroeconomic and political risks and uncertainty (Chang et al. 2017; Rapach et al. 2005), or expropriation risk (Dahlquist and Bansal 2002). Lee (2011) empirically tests the liquidity-adjusted asset pricing model of Acharya and Pedersen (2005) at

[2] For details, see https://www.prsgroup.com/explore-our-products/international-country-risk-guide/.

the global level. The latter provide evidence that liquidity risk is priced internationally independently of other risks, and Zaremba and Andreu (2018) find some consistent evidence for this.

9.4.8 Other Predictors

In this section, we review an array of less known predictors, that have been discovered and examined in recent years.

Fund flows. Srimurthy et al. (2019) offer a new country asset allocation approach based on fund flows. The authors find reliable positive returns on a strategy that goes long in the countries that have attracted indirect investment via equity fund flows and short in the countries that have not. The effect is independent of some other well-established return predictors, such as size or momentum.

Economic freedom. Several studies explore the role of economic freedom for the future stock market returns. Stocker (2005) was, most probably, the first to try to examine this relationship. Having examined the returns on developed and emerging markets in the years 1975–2002, he demonstrates that the rate of increase in economic freedom is directly related to equity returns. He also develops an investment strategy based on this phenomenon, which earns attractive investment returns. Similar evidence is provided by Smimou and Karabegovic (2010) who concentrate on MENA markets. Finally, Stocker (2016) corroborates his own earlier results. He documents that the index of economic freedom provides incremental information about future returns that have low correlation with value, momentum, size factors. Stocker (2016) christens the abnormal returns from investing in low economic freedom countries "the price of freedom."

News. Calomiris and Mamaysky (2019) develop a new classification methodology for using the content and context of news to forecast the performance of 51 equity markets. They consider issues such as topic-specific sentiment, frequency, and unusualness (entropy) of word flow. They demonstrate significant predictive abilities of the news flow for returns, volatilities, and drawdowns, particularly, for longer (one-year) horizons. The effect is more pronounced in emerging markets.

Analyst recommendations. There are numerous studies of the predictive power of analysts' recommendations for individual stock returns (Kothari et al. 2016), but Berkman and Yang (2019) are the first to consider a country-level parallel. The authors digest analysts' reports from 30 countries for the years 1994–2015 to demonstrate that the aggregate recommendation score helps to predict international stock market returns. The country-level recommendations make it possible to predict future aggregate cash flow and returns. A country allocation strategy based on the insights of Berkman and Yang (2019) yields an approximate abnormal return of 1% per month.

Asset growth. The role of asset growth for future returns on individual stocks is well known since Cooper et al. (2010); it was even incorporated in some popular recent factor pricing models (Fama and French 2015; Hou et al. 2015). Wen (2019) checked whether any similar effect exists at the country level. The author provides convincing evidence that aggregate asset growth constructed from bottom-up data negatively predicts future market returns across the G7 countries. This information about future performance is not captured by other measures of investment growth and macroeconomic variables.

Growth of government debt. Using a set of 77 countries and data from World Development Indicators Wisniewski and Jackson (2018) document a negative association between increases in the central government debt-to-GDP ratio and stock index returns expressed in US dollars. The authors estimate that raising the debt ratio by one percentage point decreases the stock returns by between 39 and 95 basis points. Wisniewski and Jackson (2018) explain this phenomenon with an upward pressure on private interest rates, which appears to signal a greater tax burden in the future.

Democracy. Lei and Wisniewski (2018) explore the role of democracy, proxied with the Political Right Index calculated by the Freedom House. Having researched a sample of 74 countries for the years 1975–2015, they conclude that, compared with autocracies, democratic states are characterized by higher returns despite displaying lower volatility risk. Lei and Wisniewski (2018, p. 1) offer three potential explanations of this effect: "First, the strength of investor protection under authoritarian leaders is relatively weak, making capital holders more vulnerable to expropriation. Second, our findings appear to be partly attributable to investors' sentiment that is driven by media reports. Last but not least, autocracies appear to hinder the development of pension funds, suppressing thereby the demand for stocks."

Mergers and acquisitions. Zaremba and Grobelny (2017) develop a new measure based on intensity of mergers and acquisitions. The authors argue that across countries the mispricing theory of mergers by Shleifer and Vishny (2003) may imply that a large number of targets acquired in a given country is a sign of market-wide undervaluation. On the other hand, the intense acquisition activity in some country may indicate overvaluation. The measure of Zaremba and Grobelny (2017) compares the quantity of targets and acquirers in a given market and demonstrates that this "merger imbalance" helps to predict cross-sectional returns in a sample of 46 countries for the years 1999–2015.

Gravity. Bae (2017) documents an interesting linkage between performance of different countries, namely, large countries lead returns of small countries, and this predictability decreases with geographical distance of the two countries. The effect could be translated into a long-short strategy producing about 10% risk-adjusted return per annum, which is not explained by the well-established return predictors.

Initial public offerings. Initial public offerings (IPOs) are often considered by academics and practitioners a gauge of investors' sentiment and market valuation. Zaremba and Okoń (2016) research the cross-sectional relationship between past share issuance and future returns across 78 countries for the years 1995–2015. They exhibit convincing evidence that the share issuance is negatively correlated with future performance: the high (low) past share issuance predicts (low) high future returns. The effect is driven predominantly by small countries.

Interest rates. Hjalmarsson (2010) investigates several potential predictors of future stock returns. The empirical results demonstrate that short-term interest rate and the term spread are fairly robust predictors of stock returns in developed markets. In contrast, Hjalmarsson (2010) finds no robust and consistent evidence of predictability by earnings or dividend yields. Consistent evidence is provided by Charles et al. (2017).

Changes in bond and bill yields. The country equity indices tend to increase (decrease) following the decreases (increases) of government bond and bill yields. Zaremba, Bianchi et al. (2019), who investigate this effect, hypothesize that it may result from investors' underreaction to yield changes. Consistently with that, Neuhierl and Weber (2018) show that market participants underreact to Federa Open Market Committee decisions on interest rates. The effect echoes also the momentum spillover from bonds to equities displayed in one of the side analysis in Geczy and Samonov (2017), as well as the cross-asset time-series momentum documented by Pitkäjärvi et al. (2020).

9.4.9 Further Investment Considerations

Besides discovering, testing, and explaining different cross-sectional patterns, separate strains of literature examine different practical aspects of country allocation based on market-level cross-sectional patterns. From practitioners' perspective, two issues seem of particular importance: (1) the influence of trading costs, and (2) timing and selection of different country allocation strategies.

Transaction costs. At the individual stock level, Novy-Marx and Velikov (2016) and Chen and Velikov (2019) demonstrate that transaction costs may have a detrimental impact on the profitability of anomaly-based quantitative strategies, in particular in the case of high turnover anomalies. At the inter-market level, the effect could be potentially even worse due to the necessity to move capital across countries. The results may also strongly depend on the implementation method chosen. Nonetheless, several studies document that when implemented with the use of ETFs the most prominent country allocation strategies may remain profitable. Andreu et al. (2013) examine the momentum effect in single-country ETFs. They find that investors are potentially able to exploit the country momentum strategies with an excess return of about 5% per year. They note that the bid-ask spreads on ETFs are markedly below the implied break-even transaction costs levels, so the momentum effect could be profitable even after accounting for the trading costs. Blitz and van Vliet (2008) provide similar evidence extending the asset universe to additional asset classes, and Angelidis and Tessaromatis (2018) put forward analogous arguments also for value and size effects. Finally, Zaremba and Andreu (2018) test a large set of different country allocation strategies. Although they admit that the trading costs are very harmful for the performance of the strategies, the profitability of the most prominent anomalies—value, momentum, size and liquidity, or seasonality—could be regained through less frequent portfolio rebalancing.

Factor timing and selection. The large number of different potential factor strategies, that could be used to allocate money across countries raises the questions of factor timing and factor selection. In other words, which strategies could be selected at a given time and how can we predict their performance? Several studies demonstrate significant time-series variation in country-level strategy returns, that can be linked, for example, to macroeconomic variables, sentiment, or liquidity and arbitrage constraints (Zaremba 2016a; Asness et al. 2013; Cooper et al. 2019; Ilmanen et al. 2019). Indeed, some papers provide evidence that country-level strategies could be timed. Yara et al. (2018) and Zaremba and Umutlu (2018b) argue that values spreads, i.e., the differences in valuations of long and short sides of the spread portfolios, help to predict their performance. Zaremba (2018b) finds the momentum effect in country-level anomaly portfolios, as Avramov et al. (2017) do for the stock-level strategies. Finally, Ilmanen et al. (2019) compare several well-known anomaly selection strategies from the firm-level universe. In particular, they investigate 12 different timing signals. In general, they find weak and inconsistent evidence of factor timing. The strongest results are found for timing based on inverse volatility and valuation spreads.

Over the last 30 years, the asset pricing literature has accumulated remarkable evidence on the predictability of the country equity returns in the cross-section. The empirical findings demonstrate numerous cross-sectional patterns in country equity indices. Some of them resemble their stock-level counterparts, such as value, momentum, or seasonality. Others, such as fund flows or political risk, are strictly characteristic for country-level return patterns.

The studies of the cross-section of country equity returns use various datasets and differing methodologies. Such situation may lead to inconclusive results and inconsistencies across papers. This highlights the need, therefore, of further standardization of country-level asset pricing studies.

The current landscape of cross-section of market index returns is growing in sophistication. The number of documented patterns is increasing. Meanwhile, the sources of this massive mispricing remain still largely unknown or not commonly agreed upon. Most probably, the future will bring more pan-anomaly studies that will not only try to bring some order into the factor structure of the country equity returns, but also improve our understanding of the economic mechanisms behind these patterns.

Acknowledgment Adam Zaremba acknowledges support from the National Science Centre of Poland. This chapter is a part of the project no. 2016/23/B/HS4/00731 of the National Science Centre of Poland.

References

Acharya, V. V., & Pedersen, L. H. (2005, August). Asset Pricing with Liquidity Risk. *Journal of Financial Economics, 77*(2), 375–410.

Anadu, K., Kruttli, M. S., McCabe, P. E., Osambela, E., & Shin, C. (2018). The Shift from Active to Passive Investing: Potential Risks to Financial Stability? (FRB Boston Risk and Policy Analysis Unit Paper No. RPA 18–4). Available at SSRN: https://ssrn.com/abstract=3321604.

Andreu, L., Swinkels, L., & Tjong-A-Tjoe, L. (2013, June). Can Exchange Traded Funds Be Used to Exploit Industry and Country Momentum? *Financial Markets and Portfolio Management, 27*(2), 127–148.

Ang, A., Hodrick, R. J., Xing, Y., & Zhang, X. (2006). The Cross-Section of Volatility and Expected Returns. *Journal of Finance, 61,* 259–299.

Ang, A., Hodrick, R. J., Xing, Y., & Zhang, X. (2009, January). High Idiosyncratic Volatility and Low Returns: International and Further U.S. Evidence. *Journal of Financial Economics, 91*(1), 1–23.

Angelidis, T., & Tessaromatis, N. (2018). Global Equity Country Allocation: An Application of Factor Investing. *Financial Analysts Journal, 73*(4), 55–73.

Angelini, N., Bormetti, G., Marmi, S., & Nardini, F. (2012). *Value Matters: Predictability of Stock Index Returns.* Available at SSRN: https://ssrn.com/abstract=2031406 or http://dx.doi.org/10.2139/ssrn.2031406.

ap Gwilym, O., Clare, A., Seaton, J., & Thomas, S. (2010, April). Price and Momentum as Robust Tactical Approaches to Global Equity Investing. *Journal of Investing, 19*(3), 80–91.

Arouri, M., M'saddek, O., & Pukthuanthong, K. (2019). Jump Risk Premia Across Major International Equity Markets. *Journal of Empirical Finance, 52*(June), 1–21.

Asness, C. S., Liew, J. M., & Stevens, R. L. (1997). Parallels Between the Cross-Sectional Predictability of Stock and Country Returns. *Journal of Portfolio Management, 23*(3), 79–87.

Asness, C. S., Moskowitz, T. J., & Pedersen, L. H. (2013). Value and Momentum Everywhere. *Journal of Finance, 68*(3), 929–985.

Atilgan, Y., Bali, Y. G., Demirtas, K. O., & Gunaydin, A. D. (2019). Global Downside Risk and Equity Returns. *Journal of International Money and Finance, 98.* Article no. 102065.

Avramov, D., Cheng, S. M., Schreiber, A., & Shemer, J. (2017). Scaling Up Market Anomalies. *Journal of Investing, 26*(3, Fall), 89–105.

Avramov, D., Chordia, T., Jostova, G., & Philipov, A. (2012). The World Price of Credit Risk. *Review of Asset Pricing Studies, 2*(2), 112–152.

Avramov, D., Kaplanski, G., & Subrahmanyam, A. (2018). *Stock Return Predictability: New Evidence from Moving Averages of Prices and Firm Fundamentals.* Available at SSRN: https://ssrn.com/abstract=3111334 or http://dx.doi.org/10.2139/ssrn.3111334.

Bae, J. W. (2017). *Gravity in International Equity Markets.* Available at SSRN: https://ssrn.com/abstract=3312433 or http://dx.doi.org/10.2139/ssrn.3312433.

Bali, T. G., & Cakici, N. (2004). Value at Risk and Expected Stock Returns. *Financial Analysts Journal, 60*(2), 57–73.

Bali, T. G., & Cakici, N. (2010). World Market Risk, Country-Specific Risk and Expected Returns in International Stock Markets. *Journal of Banking & Finance, 34*(6), 1152–1165.

Bali, T. G., Engle, R. F., & Murray, S. (2016). *Empirical Asset Pricing: The Cross Section of Stock Returns.* Hoboken, NJ: Wiley.

Baltussen, G., Swinkels, L., & van Vliet, P. (2019). *Global Factor Premiums.* Available at SSRN: https://ssrn.com/abstract=3325720 or http://dx.doi.org/10.2139/ssrn.3325720.

Baltussen, G., van Bekkum, S., & Da, Z. (2019). Indexing and Stock Market Serial Dependence Around the World. *Journal of Financial Economics, 132*(1), 26–48.

Balvers, R. J., & Wu, Y. (2006). Momentum and Mean Reversion Across National Equity Markets. *Journal of Empirical Finance, 13,* 24–48.
Balvers, R., Wu, Y., & Gililand, E. (2000). Mean Reversion Across National Stock Markets and Parametric Contrarian Investment Strategies. *Journal of Finance, 55*(2), 745–772.
Banz, R. W. (1981). The Relationship Between Return and Market Value of Common Stocks. *Journal of Financial Economics, 9,* 3–18.
Basu, S. (1975). The Information Content of Price-Earnings Ratios. *Financial Management, 4*(2), 53–64.
Basu, S. (1977). Investment Performance of Common Stocks in Relation to Their Price-Earnings Ratios: A Test of the Efficient Market Hypothesis. *Journal of Finance, 32,* 663–682.
Basu, S. (1983). "The Relationship Between Earnings Yield, Market Value and Return for NYSE Common Stocks: Further Evidence. *Journal of Financial Economics, 12,* 129–156.
Baytas, A., & Cakici, N. (1999). Do Markets Overreact: International Evidence. *Journal of Banking & Finance, 23*(7), 1121–1144.
Bekaert G., Erb, C. B., Harvey, C. R., & Viskanta, T. E. (1996). *The Cross-Sectional Determinants of Emerging Equity Market Returns.* Retrieved from https://www0.gsb.columbia.edu/faculty/gbekaert/PDF_Papers/The_cross-sectional_determinants.pdf.
Bekaert, G., Erb, C. B., Harvey, C. R, & Viskanta, T. E. (1997). *The Cross-Sectional Determinants of Emerging Equity Market Returns* (Chapter 11, pp. 221–272). Chicago: Glenlake Publishing.
Bekaert, G., & Harvey, C. R. (1995). Time-Varying World Market Integration. *Journal of Finance, 50,* 403–444.
Berkman, H., & Yang, W. (2019). Country-Level Analyst Recommendations and International Stock Market Returns. *Journal of Banking & Finance, 103,* 1–17.
Berrada, T., Messikh, R. J., Oderda, G., & Pictet, O. V. (2015). Beta-Arbitrage Strategies: When Do They Work, and Why? *Quantitative Finance, 15*(2), 185–203.
Bhojraj, S., & Swaminathan, B. (2006). Macromomentum: Returns Predictability in International Equity Indices. *Journal of Business, 79*(1), 429–451.
Bianchi, R. J., Drew, M. E., & Fan, J. H. (2015). Combining Momentum with Reversal in Commodity Futures. *Journal of Banking & Finance, 59,* 423–444.
Bilson, C. M., Brailsfort, T. J., & Hooper, V. C. (2002). The Explanatory Power of Political Risk in Emerging Markets. *International Review of Financial Analysis, 11*(1), 1–27.
Black, F., Jensen, M., & Scholes, M. (1972). The Capital Asset Pricing Model: Some Empirical Tests. In M. C. Jensen (Ed.), *Studies in the Theory of Capital Markets* (pp. 79–124). New York: Praeger.
Blackburn, D. W., & Cakici, N. (2017). Overreaction and the Cross-Section of Returns: International Evidence. *Journal of Empirical Finance, 42,* 1–14.

Blitz, D. C., & van Vliet, P. (2008). Global Tactical Cross-Asset Allocation: Applying Value and Momentum Across Asset Classes. *Journal of Portfolio Management, 35*(1), 23–38.

Blitz, D., van Vliet, P., & Baltussen, G. (2019). *The Volatility Effect Revisited.* Available at SSRN: https://ssrn.com/abstract=3442749.

Blume, M. E. (1970). Portfolio Theory: A Step Towards its Practical Application. *Journal of Business, 43*(2), 152–174.

Blume, M. E., & Friend, I. (1973). A New Look at the Capital Asset Pricing Model. *Journal of Finance, 28*(1), 19–34.

Bohn, H., & Tesar, L. L. (1996). U.S. Equity Investment in Foreign Markets: Portfolio Rebalancing or Return Chasing? *American Economic Review, 86,* 77–81.

Bornholt, G., & Malin, M. (2010). Predictability of Future Index Returns Based on the 52-Week High Strategy. *Quarterly Review of Economics and Finance, 50*(4), 501–508.

Bornholt, G., & Malin, M. (2011). Is the 52-Week High Effect as Strong as Momentum? Evidence from Developed and Emerging Market Indices. *Applied Financial Economics, 21*(18), 1369–1379.

Bornholt, G., & Malin, M. (2014). Strong and Weak Momentum Components: Evidence from International Market Indices. *JASSA the Finsia Journal of Applied Finance, 2,* 11–16.

Bouman, S., & Jacobsen, B. (2002). The Halloween Indicator, "Sell in May and Go Away": Another Puzzle. *American Economic Review, 92*(5), 1618–1635.

Breloer, B., Scholz, H., & Wilkens, M. (2014). Performance of International and Global Equity Mutual Funds: Do Country Momentum and Sector Momentum Matter? *Journal of Banking & Finance, 43,* 58–77.

Calomiris, C. W., & Mamaysky, H. (2019). How News and Its Context Drive Risk and Returns Around the World. *Journal of Financial Economics, 133*(2), 299–336.

Campbell, J. Y., & Shiler, R. J. (1988). Stock Prices, Earnings, and Expected Dividends. *Journal of Finance, 43*(3), 661–676.

Cenedese, G., Payne, R., Sarno, L., & Valente, G. (2016). What Do Stock Markets Tell Us About Exchange Rates? *Review of Finance, 20*(3), 1045–1080.

Chabot, B. R., Ghysels, E., & Jagannathan, R. (2014). *Momentum Trading, Return Chasing and Predictable Crashes.* Available at SSRN: https://ssrn.com/abstract=2516796 or http://dx.doi.org/10.2139/ssrn.2516796.

Chan, E. P. (2013). Mean Reversion of Currencies and Futures. In *Algorithmic Trading: Winning Strategies and Their Rationale.* Hoboken, NJ: Wiley.

Chan, K., Hameed, A., & Tong, W. (2000). Profitability of Momentum Strategies in the International Equity Markets. *Journal of Financial and Quantitative Analysis, 35*(2), 153–172.

Chan, L., Karceski, J., & Lakonishok, J. (1998). The Risk and Return from Factors. *Journal of Financial and Quantitative Analysis, 33,* 159–188.

Chang, Y. Y., Jacobsen, B., & Zhu, L. (2017). *Macroeconomic and Political Uncertainty and Cross-Sectional Return Dispersion Around the World*. Available at SSRN: https://ssrn.com/abstract=3032191 or http://dx.doi.org/10.2139/ssrn.3032191.

Charles, A., Darne, O., & Kim, J. H. (2017). International Stock Return Predictability: Evidence from New Statistical Tests. *International Review of Financial Analysis, 54,* 97–113.

Chaves, D. B., & Viswanathan, V. (2016). Momentum and Mean-Reversion in Commodity Spot and Futures Markets. *Journal of Commodity Markets, 3*(1), 39–53.

Chen, A. Y., & M. Velikov. (2019). Accounting for the Anomaly Zoo: A Trading Cost Perspective. *Finance Down Under 2019 Building on the Best from the Cellars of Finance.* Available at SSRN: https://ssrn.com/abstract=3073681 or http://dx.doi.org/10.2139/ssrn.3073681.

Chui, A. C. W., Titman, S., & Wei, K. C. J. (2010). Individualism and Momentum Around the World. *Journal of Finance, 65*(1), 361–392.

Clare, A., Seaton, J., Smith, P. N., & Thomas, S. (2016). The Trend Is Our Friend: Risk Parity, Momentum and Trend Following in Global Asset Allocation. *Journal of Behavioral and Experimental Finance, 9,* 63–80.

Clare, A., Seaton, J., Smith, P. N., & Thomas, S. (2017). Size Matters: Tail Risk, Momentum and Trend Following in International Equity Portfolios. *Journal of Investing, 26* (3), 53–64.

Cooper, I., Mitrache, A., & Priestley, R. (2019). *A Global Macroeconomic Risk Model for Value, Momentum, and Other Asset Classes*. Available at SSRN: https://ssrn.com/abstract=2768040 or http://dx.doi.org/10.2139/ssrn.2768040.

Cooper, M. J., Gulen, H., & Schill, M. J. (2010). Asset Growth and the Cross-Section of Stock Returns. *Journal of Finance, 63*(4), 1609–1651.

Dahlquist, M., & Bansal, R. (2002). *Expropriation Risk and Return in Global Equity*. EFA 2002 Berlin Meetings Presented Paper. Available at SSRN: https://ssrn.com/abstract=298180 or http://dx.doi.org/10.2139/ssrn.298180.

Damodatan, A. (2019). *Country Default Spreads and Risk Premiums*. Damodaran Online. Available at http://pages.stern.nyu.edu/~adamodar/New_Home_Page/datafile/ctryprem.html. Accessed 1 Sept 2019.

Daniel, K., & Moskowitz, T. J. (2016). Momentum Crashes. *Journal of Financial Economics, 122*(2), 221–247.

Daniel, K., & Titman, S. (1997). Evidence on the Characteristics of Cross Sectional Variation in Stock Returns. *Journal of Finance, 52,* 1–33.

De Bondt, W. F. M., & Thaler, R. (1985). Does the Stock Market Overreact? *Journal of Finance, 40*(3), 793–805.

Desrosiers, S., Lemaire, N., & L'Her, J.-F. (2007). Residual Income Approach to Equity Country Selection. *Financial Analyst Journal, 63*(2), 76–89.

Diamonte, R. L., Liew, J. M., & Stevens, R. L. (1996). Political Risk in Emerging and Developed Markets. *Financial Analysts Journal, 52*(3), 71–76.

Dimic, N., Orlov, V., & Piljak, V. (2015). The Political Risk Factor in Emerging, Frontier, and Developed Stock Markets. *Finance Research Letters, 15,* 239–245.

Dobrynskaya, V. (2015). *Upside and Downside Risks in Momentum Returns* (Higher School of Economics Research Paper No. WP BRP 50/FE/2015). Available at SSRN: https://ssrn.com/abstract=2695001 or http://dx.doi.org/10.2139/ssrn.2695001.

Ellahie, A., Katz, M., & Richardson, S. A. (2019). *Risky Value*. Available at SSRN: https://ssrn.com/abstract=2325524 or http://dx.doi.org/10.2139/ssrn.2325524.

Erb, C. B., Harvey, C. R., & Viskanta, T. E. (1995). Country Credit Risk and Global Equity Selection. *Journal of Portfolio Management, 21*(2), 74–83.

Erb, C. B., Harvey, C. R., & Viskanta, T. E. (1996a). Political Risk, Economic Risk, and Financial Risk. *Financial Analyst Journal, 52*(6), 29–46.

Erb, C. B., Harvey, C. R., & Viskanta, T. E. (1996b). Expected Returns and Volatilities in 135 Countries. *Journal of Portfolio Management, 22*(3), 46–58.

Estrada, J. (2000). *The Cost of Equity in Emerging Markets: A Downside Risk Approach*. EFMA 2000 Athens, EFA 2000 London, FMA 2000 Edinburgh. Available at SSRN: https://ssrn.com/abstract=170748 or http://dx.doi.org/10.2139/ssrn.170748.

Evans, A., & Schmitz, C. (2015). *Value, Size and Momentum on Equity Indices: A Likely Example of Selection Bias*. WINTON Global Investment Management Working Paper available at https://www.winton.com/research/value-size-and-momentum-a-likely-example-of-selection-bias.

Faber, M. (2012, August). *Global Value: Building Trading Models with the 10 Year CAPE*. Cambria Quantitative Research, No. 5. Available at SSRN: https://ssrn.com/abstract=2129474.

Fama, E. F. (2015). *Cross-Section Versus Time-Series Tests of Asset Pricing Models* (Fama-Miller Working Paper). Available at SSRN: https://ssrn.com/abstract=2685317.

Fama, E. F., & French, K. R. (1996). Multifactor Explanations of Asset Pricing Anomalies. *Journal of Finance, 51*(1), 55–84.

Fama, E. F., & French, K. R. (2008). Dissecting anomalies. *Journal of Finance, 63*, 1653–1678.

Fama, E. F., & French, K. R. (2015). A Five-Factor Asset Pricing Model. *Journal of Financial Economics, 116*(1), 1–22.

Fama, E. F., & MacBeth, J. D. (1973, May–June). Risk, Return and Equilibrium: Empirical Tests. *Journal of Political Economy, 81*(3), 607–636.

Ferreira, M. A., & Santa-Clara, P. (2011). Forecasting Stock Market Returns: The Sum of the Parts is More Than the Whole. *Journal of Financial Economics, 3*, 514–537.

Ferson, W. E., & Harvey, C. R. 1994a. Sources of Risk and Expected Returns in Global Equity Markets. *Journal of Banking and Finance, 18*, 775–803.

Ferson, W. E., & Harvey, C. R. 1994b. An Exploratory Investigation of the Fundamental Determinants of National Equity Market Returns. In J. A. Frankel (Ed.), *The Internationalization of Equity Markets* (pp. 59–147). Chicago: NBER/University of Chicago Press.

Ferson, W. E., & Harvey, C. R. (1998). Fundamental Determinants of National Equity Market Returns: A Perspective on Conditional Asset Pricing. *Journal of Banking & Finance, 21,* 1625–1665.

Fisher, G. S., Shah, R., & Titman, S. (2017). Should You Tilt Your Equity Portfolio to Smaller Countries? *Journal of Portfolio Management, 44*(1), 127–141.

Frazzini, A., & Pedersen, L. H. (2014). Betting Against Beta. *Journal of Financial Economics, 111,* 1–25.

Froot, K. A., Scharfstein, D. S., & Stein, J. C. (1992). Herd on the Street: Informational Inefficiencies in a Market with Short-Term Speculation. *Journal of Finance, 47,* 1461–1484.

Gala, V., Pagliardi, G., & Zenios, S. A. (2019). *International Politics and Policy Risk Factors*. Available at SSRN: https://ssrn.com/abstract=3242300 or http://dx.doi.org/10.2139/ssrn.3242300.

Geczy, C. C., & Samonov, M. (2017). *Two Centuries of Multi-Asset Momentum (Equities, Bonds, Currencies, Commodities, Sectors and Stocks)*. Available at SSRN https://ssrn.com/abstract=2607730 or http://dx.doi.org/10.2139/ssrn.2607730.

Gharaibeh, O. (2015). Long-Term Contrarian Profits in the Middle East Market Indices. *Research Journal of Finance and Accounting, 6*(16), 77–85.

Graham, B., & Dodd, D. (1940). *Security Analysis: Principles and Techniques*. New York: McGraw-Hill Book Company.

Griffin, J. M., Nardari, F., & Stulz, R. M. (2004). Are Daily Cross-Border Equity Flows Pushed or Pulled? *Review of Economics and Statistics, 86,* 641–657.

Grobys, K. (2016). Another Look at Momentum Crashes: Momentum in the European Monetary Union. *Applied Economics, 48*(19), 1759–1766.

Guilmin, F. (2015). *The Effective Combination of Risk-Based Strategies with Momentum and Trend Following*. Available at SSRN: https://ssrn.com/abstract=2556747 or http://dx.doi.org/10.2139/ssrn.2556747.

Harvey, C. R. (1991). The World Price of Covariance Risk. *Journal of Finance, 46*(1), 111–157.

Harvey, C. R. (1995). Predictable Risk and Returns in Emerging Markets. *Review of Financial Studies, 8*(3), 773–816.

Harvey, C. R. (2000). The Drivers of Expected Returns in International Markets. *Emerging Markets Quarterly, 3,* 32–49.

Harvey, C. R. (2004). Country Risk Components, the Cost of Capital, and Returns in Emerging Markets. In S. Wilkin (Ed.), *Country and Political Risk: Practical Insights for Global Finance* (71–102). London: Risk Books. Available at SSRN: http://dx.doi.org/10.2139/ssrn.620710.

Harvey, C. R., Liu, Y., & Zhu, H. (2016). … and the Cross-Section of Expected Returns. *Review of Financial Studies, 29*(1), 5–68.

Harvey, C. R., & Zhou, G. (1993). International Asset Pricing with Alternative Distributional Assumptions. *Journal of Empirical Finance, 1,* 107–131.

Heckman, L., Mullin, J. J., & Sze, H. (1996). Valuation Ratios and Cross-Country Equity Allocation. *Journal of Investing, 5*(2), 54–63.

Hedegaard, E. (2018). *Time-Varying Leverage Demand and Predictability of Betting-Against-Beta*. Available at SSRN: https://ssrn.com/abstract=3194626 or http://dx.doi.org/10.2139/ssrn.3194626.

Heston, S. L., & Sadka, R. (2008). Seasonality in the Cross-Section of Stock Returns. *Journal of Financial Economics, 87*(2), 418–445.

Heston, S. L., & Sadka, R. (2010). Seasonality in the Cross-Section of Stock Returns: The International Evidence. *Journal of Financial and Quantitative Analysis, 45*(5), 1133–1160.

Hjalmarsson, E. (2010). Predicting Global Stock Returns. *Journal of Financial and Quantitative Analysis, 45*(1), 49–80.

Hollstein, F., Nguyen, D. B. B., Prokopczuk, M., & Simen, C. W. (2019). International Tail Risk and World Fear. *Journal of International Money and Finance, 93,* 244–259.

Hou, K., Xue, C., & Zhang, L. (2015). Digesting Anomalies: An Investment Approach. *Review of Financial Studies, 28*(3), 650–705.

Hou, K., Xue, C., & Zhang, L. (2020). Replicating Anomalies. *Review of Financial Studies, 33*(5), 2019–2133.

Hueng, C. J. (2014). Are Global Systematic Risk and Country-Specific Idiosyncratic Risk Priced in the Integrated World Markets? *International Review of Economics and Finance, 33,* 28–38.

Hueng, C. J., & Ruey, Y. (2013). Country-Specific Idiosyncratic Risk and Global Equity Index Returns. *International Review of Economics and Finance, 25,* 326–337.

Hurst, B., Ooi, Y. H., & Pedersen, L. H. (2017). A Century of Evidence on Trend-Following Investing. *Journal of Portfolio Management, 44*(1), 15–29.

Ilmanen, A. S., Israel, R., Moskowitz, T. J., Thapar, A. K., & Wang, F. (2019). *Do Factor Premia Vary Over Time? A Century of Evidence*. Available at SSRN: https://ssrn.com/abstract=3400998 or http://dx.doi.org/10.2139/ssrn.3400998.

Jagannathan, R., Schaumburg, E., & Zhou, G. (2010). Cross-Sectional Asset Pricing Tests. *Annual Review of Financial Economics, 2,* 49–74.

Jegadeesh, N. (1990). Evidence of Predictable Behavior of Security Returns. *Journal of Finance, 45*(3), 881–898.

Jegadeesh, N., & Titman, S. (1993). Returns to Buying Winners and Selling Losers: Implications for Stock Market Efficiency. *Journal of Finance, 48,* 65–91.

Jegadeesh, N., & Titman, S. (2001). Profitability of Momentum Strategies: An Evaluation of Alternative Explanations. *Journal of Finance, 56,* 699–720.

Jordan, S. J., Vivian, A., & Wohar, M. E. (2015). Location, Location, Location: Currency Effects and Return Predictability? *Applied Economics, 47*(18), 1883–1898.

Kasa, K. (1992). Common Stochastic Trends in International Stock Markets. *Journal of Monetary Economics, 29*(1), 95–124.

Keim, D. (1983). Size-Related Anomalies and Stock Return Seasonality. *Journal of Financial Economics, 12,* 13–32.

Keimling, N. (2016). *Predicting Stock Market Returns Using the Shiller CAPE: An Improvement Towards Traditional Value Indicators?* Available at SSRN: https://ssrn.com/abstract=2736423 or http://dx.doi.org/10.2139/ssrn.2736423.

Keloharju, M., Linnainmma, J. T., & Nyberg, P. (2016). Return Seasonalities. *Journal of Finance, 71*(4), 1557–1590.

Keloharju, M., Linnainmma, J. T., & Nyberg, P. (2019). *Are Return Seasonalities Due to Risk or Mispricing? Evidence from Seasonal Reversals.* Available at SSRN: https://ssrn.com/abstract=3276334 or http://dx.doi.org/10.2139/ssrn.3276334.

Keppler, A. M., & Traub, H. D. (1993). The Small-Country Effect: Small Markets Beat Large Markets". *Journal of Investing, 2*(3), 17–24.

Keppler, A. M. (1991a). The Importance of Dividend Yields in Country Selection. *Journal of Portfolio Management, 17,* 24–29.

Keppler, A. M. (1991b). Further Evidence on the Predictability of International Equity Returns. *Journal of Portfolio Management, 18*(1), 48–53.

Keppler, A. M., & Encinosa, P. (2011). The Small-Country Effect Revisited. *Journal of Investing, 20*(4), 99–103.

Keppler, A. M., & Xue, X. H. (2003). The Seasonal Price Behavior of Global Equity Markets. *Journal of Investing, 12*(4), 49–53.

Kim, D. (2012). Value Premium Across Countries. *Journal of Portfolio Management, 38*(4), 75–86.

Klement, J. (2012). *Does the Shiller-PE Work in Emerging Markets?.* Available at SSRN: https://ssrn.com/abstract=2088140 or http://dx.doi.org/10.2139/ssrn.2088140.

Kortas, M., L'Her, J.-F., & Roberge, M. (2005). Country Selection of Emerging Equity Markets: Benefits from Country Attribute Diversification. *Emerging Markets Review, 6*(1), 1–19.

Kothari, S. P., So, E., & Verdi, R. (2016). Analysts' Forecasts and Asset Pricing: A Survey. *Annual Review of Financial Economics, 8,* 197–219.

Lakonishok, J., Shleifer, A., & Vishny, R. (1994). Contrarian Investment, Extrapolation, and Risk. *Journal of Finance, 49,* 1541–1578.

Lamoureux, C., & Sanger, G. (1989). Firm Size and Turn-Of-The-Year Effects in the OTC/Nasdaq Market. *Journal of Finance, 44,* 1219–1245.

Lawrenz, J., & Zorn, J. (2017). Predicting International Stock Returns with Conditional Price-To-Fundamental Ratios. *Journal of Empirical Finance, 43,* 159–184.

Lee, K.-H. (2011). The World Price of Liquidity Risk. *Journal of Financial Economics, 99*(1), 136–161.

Lehkonen, H., & Heimonen, K. (2015). Democracy, Political Risks, and Stock Market Performance. *Journal of International Money and Finance, 59,* 77–99.

Lehmann, B. N. (1990). Fads, Martingales, and Market Efficiency. *Quarterly Journal of Economics, 105*(1), 1–28.

Lei, X., & Wisniewski, T. P. (2018). *Democracy and Stock Market Returns.* Available at SSRN: https://ssrn.com/abstract=3198561 or http://dx.doi.org/10.2139/ssrn.3198561.

Levy, H. (1978). Equilibrium in an Imperfect Market: A Constraint on the Number of Securities in the Portfolio. *American Economic Review, 68,* 643–658.

L'Her, J.-F., Desrosiers, S., & Plante, J.-F. (2004). Style Management in Equity Country Allocation. *Financial Analysts Journal, 60*(6), 40–54.

Li, T., & Pritamani, M. (2015). Country Size and Country Momentum Effects in Emerging and Frontier Markets. *Journal of Investing, 24*(1), 102–108.

Lord, J. (2018, February 9). *ETF Industry Celebrates $5 Trillion AUM Milestone.* ETF Strategy. Available at https://www.etfstrategy.com/etf-industry-celebrates-5-trillion-aum-milestone-29633/.

Liang, S. X., & Wei, J. K. C. (2019/in press). Market Volatility Risk and Stock Returns Around the World: Implication for Multinational Corporations. *International Review of Finance.*

Lubnau, T., & Todorova, N. (2015). Trading on Mean-Reversion in Energy Futures Markets. *Energy Economics, 51,* 312–319.

Macedo, R. (1995a). Country-Selection Style. In R. A. Klein & J. Lenderman (Eds.), *Equity Style Management* (pp. 333–355). Chicago: Irwin Professional Publishing.

Macedo, R. (1995b). Value, Relative Strength, and Volatility in Global Equity Country Selection. *Financial Analysts Journal, 51*(2), 70–78.

Macedo, R. (1995c). Style-Based Country-Selection Strategies. In P. Carman (Ed.), *Quantitative Investing for the Global Markets: Strategies, Tactics, Advanced Analytical Techniques* (pp. 145–167). New York: Routledge.

Malin, M., & Bornholt, G. (2013). Long-Term Return Reversal: Evidence from International Market Indices. *Journal of International Financial Markets, Institutions, and Money, 25,* 1–17.

Malkiel, B., & Xu, Y. (1997). Risk and Return Revisited. *Journal of Portfolio Management, 23*(3), 9–14.

Merton, R. (1987). A Simple Model of Capital Market Equilibrium with Incomplete Information. *Journal of Finance, 42,* 483–510.

Miller, M. H., & Scholes, M. (1972). Rates of Return in Relation to Risk: A Reexamination of some Recent Findings. In M. C. Jensen (Ed.), *Studies in the Theory of Capital Markets.* New York: Praeger.

Moskowitz, T. J., Ooi, Y. H., & Pedersen, L. H. (2012). Time Series Momentum. *Journal of Financial Economics, 104*(2), 228–250.

Muller, C., & Ward, M. (2010). Momentum Effects in Country Equity Indices. *Studies in Economics and Econometrics, 34*(1), 111–127.

Nagel, S. (2013). Empirical Cross-Sectional Asset Pricing. *Annual Review of Financial Economics, 5,* 167–199.

Neuhierl, A., & Weber, M. (2018). *Monetary Momentum.* Available at SSRN: https://ssrn.com/abstract=3030126 or http://dx.doi.org/10.2139/ssrn.3030126.

Nicholson, F. (1960). Equilibrium in Capital Asset Market. *Econometrica, 34,* 768–783.

Nijman, T., Swinkels, L., & Verbeek, M. (2004). Do Countries or Industries Explain Momentum in Europe? *Journal of Empirical Finance, 11*(4), 461–481.

Norges Bank. (2012). *A Survey of the Small-Firm Effect*. NBIM Discussion Note #12-2012. Available at https://www.nbim.no/en/publications/discussion-notes/2012/a-survey-of-the-small-firm-effect/.

Novotny, J., & Gupta, M. (2015). *The Dynamics of Value Across Global Equity Markets: The Risk Contagion*. Available at SSRN: https://ssrn.com/abstract=2589026 or http://dx.doi.org/10.2139/ssrn.2589026.

Novy-Marx, R., & Velikov, M. (2016). A Taxonomy of Anomalies and their Trading Costs. *Review of Financial Studies, 29*(1), 104–147.

Pagliardi, G., Poncet, P., & Zenios, S. A. (2019). *A Political Capital Asset Pricing Model*. Available at SSRN: https://ssrn.com/abstract=3351403 or http://dx.doi.org/10.2139/ssrn.3351403.

Patton, A., & Timmermann, A. (2010). Monotonicity in Asset Returns: New Tests with Applications to the Term Structure, the CAPM, and Portfolio Sorts. *Journal of Financial Economics, 98*(3), 605–625.

Pitkäjärvi, A., Suominen, M., & Vaittinen, L. (2020). Cross-Asset Signals and Time-Series Momentum. *Journal of Financial Economics, 136*(1), 63–85.

Pungulescu, C. (2014). *Market Size Effects and Financial Integration*. Available at SSRN: https://ssrn.com/abstract=991704 or http://dx.doi.org/10.2139/ssrn.991704.

Rapach, D. E., Wohar, M., & Rangvid, J. (2005). Macro Variables and International Stock Return Predictability. *International Journal of Forecasting, 21*(1), 137–166.

Reinganum, M. R. (1981). Misspecification of Asset Pricing: Empirical Anomalies Based on Earnings' Yields and Market Values. *Journal of Financial Economics, 9*, 19–46.

Richards, A. J. (1995). Comovements in National Stock Market Returns: Evidence of Predictability, but Not Cointegration. *Journal of Monetary Economics, 36*(3), 631–654.

Richards, A. J. (1997). Winner-Loser Reversals in National Stock Market Indices: Can They Be Explained? *Journal of Finance, 52*(5), 2129–2144.

Rikala, N. (2017). *Small-Country Effect Within Europe: Liquidity Risk, Small-Firm Effect or Other Factors?* Aalto University School of Business. Available at https://pdfs.semanticscholar.org/2990/c4ec2ea696f1ce5690e1ae4b2faaa6034d2d.pdf.

Rosenberg, B., Reid, K., & Lanstein, R. (1985). Persuasive Evidence of Market Inefficiency. *Journal of Portfolio Management, 11*, 9–17.

Sharpe, W. F. (1964). Capital Asset Prices: A Theory of Market Equilibrium Under Conditions of Risk. *Journal of Finance, 19*(3), 425–442.

Shen, Q., Szakmary, A. C., & Sharma, S. C. (2005). Momentum and Contrarian Strategies in International Stock Markets: Further Evidence. *Journal of Multinational Financial Management, 15*, 235–255.

Shleifer, A., & Vishny, R. W. (2003). Stock Market Driven Acquisitions. *Journal of Financial Economics, 70*(3), 295–311.

Smimou, K., & Karabegovic, A. (2010). On the Relationship Between Economic Freedom and Equity Returns in the Emerging Markets: Evidence from the

Middle East and North Africa (MENA) Stock Markets. *Emerging Markets Review, 11*(2), 119–151.

Smith, D. M., & Pantilei, V. S. (2015). Do 'Dogs of the World' Bark or Bite? Evidence from Single-Country ETFs. *Journal of Investing, 24*(1), 7–15.

Spierdijk, Laura, Bikker, Jacob A., & van den Hoek, Pieter. (2012). Mean Reversion in International Stock Markets: An Empirical Analysis of the 20th Century. *Journal of International Money and Finance, 31*(2), 228–249.

Srimurthy, V. K., Shen, S., & Smalbach, M. (2019). Fund Flows as Country Allocator. *Journal of Alternative Investments, 21*(3), 87–95.

Stocker, M. L. (2005). Equity Returns and Economic Freedom. *Cato Journal, 25*(3), 583–594.

Stocker, M. L. (2016). The Price of Freedom: A Fama-French Freedom Factor. *Emerging Markets Review, 26,* 1–19.

Suleman, T., Gupta, R., & Balcilar, M. (2017). Does Country Risks Predict Stock Returns and Volatility? Evidence from a Nonparametric Approach. *Research in International Business and Finance, 42,* 1173–1195.

Tinic, S. M., & West, R. R. (1986). Risk, Return and Equilibrium: A Revisit. *Journal of Political Economy, 94,* 126–147.

Umutlu, M. (2015). Idiosyncratic Volatility and Expected Returns at the Global Level. *Financial Analyst Journal, 71*(6), 58–71.

Umutlu, M. (2019). Does Idiosyncratic Volatility Matter at the Global Level? *The North American Journal of Economics and Finance, 47*(C), 252–268.

Umutlu, M., & Bengitöz, P. (2017). *The Cross-Section of Expected Index Returns in International Stock Markets* (Working paper presented at the 2017 Infiniti Conference in Valencia, Spain).

Vaihekoski, M. (2004). Portfolio Construction for Tests of Asset Pricing Models. *Financial Markets, Institutions and Instruments, 13,* 1–30.

van Dijk, M. (2011). Is Size Dead? A Review of the Size Effect in Equity Returns. *Journal of Banking & Finance, 12,* 3263–3274.

Vortelinos, D. I., & Saha, S. (2016). The Impact of Political Risk on Return, Volatility and Discontinuity: Evidence from the International Stock and Foreign Exchange Markets. *Finance Research Letters, 17,* 222–226.

Vu, J. D. (2012). Do Momentum Strategies Generate Profits in Emerging Stock Markets? *Problems and Perspectives in Management, 10*(3), 9–22.

Waszczuk, A. (2014a). *Diversity of Empirical Design: Review of Studies on the Cross-Section of Common Stocks.* Available at SSRN: https://ssrn.com/abstract=2428054 or http://dx.doi.org/10.2139/ssrn.2428054.

Waszczuk, A. (2014b). *Assembling International Equity Datasets: Review of Studies on the Cross-Section of Common Stocks.* Available at SSRN: https://ssrn.com/abstract=2427622 or http://dx.doi.org/10.2139/ssrn.2427622.

Wen, Q. (2019). Asset Growth and Stock Market Returns: A Time-Series Analysis. *Review of Finance, 23*(3), 599–628.

Willenbrock, S. (2011). Diversification Return, Portfolio Rebalancing, and the Commodity Return Puzzle. *Financial Analysts Journal, 67*(4), 42–49.

Wisniewski, T. P., & Jackson, P. M. (2018). *Government Debt Expansion and Stock*. Available at SSRN: https://ssrn.com/abstract=3237393 or http://dx.doi.org/10.2139/ssrn.3237393.

Yara, F. B., Boons, M., & Tamoni, A. (2018). *Value Timing: Risk and Return Across Asset Classes*. Available at SSRN: https://www.ssrn.com/abstract=3054017.

Zaremba, A. (2015). Country Selection Strategies Based on Value, Size and Momentum. *Investment Analysts Journal, 44*(3), 171–198.

Zaremba, A. (2016a). Investor Sentiment, Limits on Arbitrage, and the Performance of Cross-Country Stock Market Anomalies. *Journal of Behavioral and Experimental Finance, 9*, 136–163.

Zaremba, A. (2016b). Risk-Based Explanation for the Country-Level Size and Value Effects. *Finance Research Letters, 18*, 226–233.

Zaremba, A. (2016c). Is There a Low-Risk Anomaly Across Countries? *Eurasian Economic Review, 6*(1), 45–65.

Zaremba, A. (2016d). Country Selection Strategies Based on Quality. *Managerial Finance, 41*(12), 1336–1356.

Zaremba, A. (2016e). Has the Long-Term Reversal Reversed? Evidence from Country Equity Indices. *Romanian Journal of Economic Forecasting, 19*(1), 88–103.

Zaremba, A. (2018a). Country Risk and Expected Returns Across Global Equity Markets. *Czech Journal of Economics and Finance, 68*(4), 374–398.

Zaremba, A. (2018b). The Momentum Effect in Country-Level Stock Market Anomalies. *Economic Research, 31*(1), 703–721.

Zaremba, A. (2019a). Price Range and the Cross-Section of Expected Country and Industry Returns. *International Review of Financial Analysis, 64*, 174–189.

Zaremba, A. (2019b). The Cross Section of Country Equity Returns: A Review of Empirical Literature. *Journal of Risk and Financial Management, 12*, 165.

Zaremba, A., & Andreu, L. (2018). Paper Profits or Real Money? Trading Costs and Stock Market Anomalies in Country ETFs. *International Review of Financial Analysis, 56*, 181–192.

Zaremba, A., Bianchi, R., & Long, H. (2019). *Momentum Spillover from Bonds to Equity Markets* (SSRN Working Paper).

Zaremba, A., & Grobelny, P. (2017). Merger Imbalance and Returns in International Equity Markets. *Investment Analysts Journal, 46*(2), 117–131.

Zaremba, A., Karathanasopoulos, A., & Long, H. (2019). Short-Term Momentum (Almost) Everywhere. *Journal of International Financial Markets, Institutions & Money, 63*, 101140.

Zaremba, A., Kizys, R., & Raza, M. W. (2020). "The Long-Run Reversal in the Long Run: Insights from Two Centuries of International Equity Returns." *Journal of Empirical Finance, 55*, 177–199.

Zaremba, A., & Konieczka, P. (2016). Do Quantitative Country Selection Strategies Really Work? *Journal of Investment Strategies, 5*(2), 1–33.

Zaremba, A., & Miziołek, T. (2017). Nothing Lasts Forever (and Everywhere): Fundamental Indexation at the Global Level. *Journal of Index Investing, 8*(3), 6–20.

Zaremba, A., & Okoń, S. (2016). Share Issuance and Expected Returns Around the World. *Journal of Investing, 25*(4), 97–107.

Zaremba, A., & Shemer, J. (2018). The Trend Is Your Friend: Momentum Investing. In *Price-Based Investment Strategies*. Cham: Palgrave Macmillan.

Zaremba, A., & Szczygielski, J. J. (2019). And the Winner Is... A Comparison of Valuation Measures for Country Asset Allocation. *Journal of Portfolio Management, 45*(5), 84–98.

Zaremba, A., Szyszka, A. Karathanasopoulos, A., & Mikutowski, M. (2020). Herding for Profits: Market Breadth and the Cross-Section of Global Equity Returns. *Economic Modelling*.

Zaremba, A., & Umutlu, M. (2018a). Size Matters Everywhere: Decomposing the Small Country and Small Industry Premia. *The North American Journal of Economics and Finance, 43,* 1–18.

Zaremba, A., & Umutlu, M. (2018b). Strategies Can Be Expensive Too! The Value Spread and Asset Allocation in Global Equity Markets. *Applied Economics, 50*(60), 6529–6546.

Zaremba, A., Umutlu, M., & Karathanasopoulos, A. (2019). Alpha Momentum and Alpha Reversal in Country and Industry Equity Indexes. *Journal of Empirical Finance, 53,* 144–161.

Zaremba, A., Umutlu, M., & Maydybura, A. (2018). Less Pain, More Gain: Volatility-Adjusted Residual Momentum in International Equity Markets. *Investment Analysts Journal, 47*(2), 165–191.

Appendix

Table A.1 Selected single-country equity exchange-traded funds with developed markets exposure (as of June 30, 2019)

Country	Exchange-traded fund	Replicated index	Listed on[a]		
			Americas exchanges	EMEA exchanges	Asia-Pacific exchanges
Panel A. Americas					
Canada	BMO S&P/TSX Capped Composite Index ETF	S&P/TSX Capped Composite Index	Toronto Stock Exchange		
	iShares Core S&P/TSX Capped Composite Index ETF	S&P/TSX Capped Composite Index	Toronto Stock Exchange		
	iShares MSCI Canada ETF[b]	MSCI Canada Custom Capped Index	NYSE Arca		
	iShares MSCI Canada UCITS ETF	MSCI Canada Index		SIX Swiss Exchange	
	JP Morgan BetaBuilders Canada ETF	Morningstar Canada Target Market Exposure Index	EXN-CGM		
	UBS ETF MSCI Canada UCITS ETF	MSCI Canada Index		SIX Swiss Exchange	

(continued)

T. Miziołek et al., *International Equity Exchange-Traded Funds*, https://doi.org/10.1007/978-3-030-53864-4

Table A.1 (continued)

Country	Exchange-traded fund	Replicated index	Listed on[a]		
			Americas exchanges	EMEA exchanges	Asia-Pacific exchanges
USA	BMO S&P 500 Index ETF	S&P 500 Index	Toronto Stock Exchange		
	iShares Core S&P 500 ETF	S&P 500 Index	NYSE Arca		
	iShares Core S&P 500 UCITS ETF	S&P 500 Index		London Stock Exchange	
	SPDR S&P 500 ETF Trust	S&P 500 Index	NYSE Arca		
	Vanguard S&P 500 ETF	S&P 500 Index	NYSE Arca		
	Vanguard S&P 500 UCITS ETF	S&P 500 Index		London Stock Exchange	
Panel B. Europe and Middle East					
Austria	ComStage ATX UCITS ETF	ATX Index		Xetra (Deutsche Boerse)	
	iShares ATX UCITS ETF	ATX Index		Xetra (Deutsche Boerse)	
	iShares MSCI Austria ETF[b]	MSCI Austria IMI 25/50 Index	NYSE Arca		
	Xtrackers ATX UCITS ETF	ATX Index		Xetra (Deutsche Boerse)	
Belgium	iShares MSCI Belgium ETF[b]	MSCI Belgium IMI 25/50 Index	NYSE Arca		
	Lyxor BEL 20 UCITS ETF	BEL20 Index		Euronext Brussels	
Denmark	iShares MSCI Denmark ETF	MSCI Denmark IMI 25/50 Index	CBOE BZX		
	XACT OMXC25 UCITS ETF	OMX Copenhagen 25 Index		Nasdaq Copenhagen	
Finland	iShares MSCI Finland ETF	MSCI Finland IMI 25/50 Index	CBOE BZX		
	Seligson & Co OMX Helsinki 25 UCITS ETF	OMX Helsinki 25 Index		Nasdaq Helsinki	
France	Amundi CAC 40 UCITS ETF DR	CAC 40 Index		Euronext Paris	
	Franklin FTSE France ETF	FTSE France Capped Index	NYSE Arca		
	iShares MSCI France ETF[b]	MSCI France Index	NYSE Arca		

(continued)

Table A.1 (continued)

Country	Exchange-traded fund	Replicated index	Listed on[a]		
			Americas exchanges	EMEA exchanges	Asia-Pacific exchanges
	iShares MSCI France UCITS ETF	MSCI France Index		London Stock Exchange	
	Lyxor CAC 40 (DR) UCITS ETF	CAC 40 Index		Euronext Paris	
	Xtrackers CAC 40 UCITS ETF	CAC 40 Index		Xetra (Deutsche Boerse)	
Germany	ComStage DAX UCITS ETF	DAX 30 Index		Xetra (Deutsche Boerse)	
	Deka DAX UCITS ETF	DAX 30 Index		Xetra (Deutsche Boerse)	
	Franklin FTSE Germany ETF	FTSE Germany Capped Index	NYSE Arca		
	iShares MSCI Germany ETF[b]	MSCI Germany Index	NYSE Arca		
	Lyxor DAX (DR) UCITS ETF	DAX 30 Index		Xetra (Deutsche Boerse)	
	Xtrackers DAX UCITS ETF	DAX 30 Index		Xetra (Deutsche Boerse)	
Ireland	iShares MSCI Ireland ETF	MSCI All Ireland Capped Index	NYSE Arca		
	WisdomTree ISEQ 20 UCITS ETF	ISEQ 20 Index		Euronext Dublin	
Israel	ARK Israel Innovative Technology ETF	ARK Israeli Innovation Index	CBOE Global Markets		
	BlueStar Israel Technology ETF	BlueStar Israel Global Technology Index	NYSE Arca		
	iShares MSCI Israel ETF	MSCI Israel Capped Investable Market Index	NYSE Arca		
	iShares TA-35 Israel UCITS ETF	TA-35 Index		London Stock Exchange	
	KSM ETF (4A) TA-35	TA-35 Index		Tel Aviv Stock Exchange	

(continued)

Table A.1 (continued)

Country	Exchange-traded fund	Replicated index	Listed on[a]		
			Americas exchanges	EMEA exchanges	Asia-Pacific exchanges
	VanEck Vectors Israel ETF	BlueStar Israel Global Index	NYSE Arca		
Italy	Amundi FTSE MIB UCITS ETF	FTSE MIB Index		Euronext Paris	
	Franklin FTSE Italy ETF	FTSE Italy Capped Index	NYSE Arca		
	iShares FTSE MIB UCITS ETF	FTSE MIB Index		London Stock Exchange	
	iShares MSCI Italy ETF[b]	MSCI Italy 25/50 Index	NYSE Arca		
	Lyxor FTSE MIB UCITS ETF	FTSE MIB Index		Borsa Italiana	
	Xtrackers FTSE MIB UCITS ETF	FTSE MIB Index		Xetra (Deutsche Boerse)	
Netherlands	Amundi MSCI Netherlands UCITS ETF	MSCI Netherlands Index		Euronext Paris	
	iShares AEX UCITS ETF	AEX Index		London Stock Exchange	
	iShares MSCI Netherlands ETF[b]	MSCI Netherlands IMI 25/50 Index	NYSE Arca		
	Think AEX UCITS ETF	AEX Index		Euronext Amsterdam	
Norway	DNB OBX ETF	OBX Index		Oslo Børs	
	Global X MSCI Norway ETF	MSCI Norway IMI 25/50 Index	NYSE Arca		
	iShares MSCI Norway ETF	MSCI Norway IMI 25/50 Index	CBOE BZX		
	Xact OBX UCITS ETF	OBX Index		Oslo Børs	
Portugal	ComStage PSI 20 UCITS ETF	PSI 20 Index		Xetra (Deutsche Boerse)	
	Global X MSCI Portugal ETF	MSCI All Portugal Plus 25/50 Index	NYSE Arca		
Spain	Amundi ETF MSCI Spain UCITS ETF	MSCI Spain Index		Euronext Paris	
	BBVA Acción IBEX 35 ETF	IBEX 35 Index		Bolsa de Valores de Madrid	

(continued)

Table A.1 (continued)

Country	Exchange-traded fund	Replicated index	Listed on[a]		
			Americas exchanges	EMEA exchanges	Asia-Pacific exchanges
	ComStage MSCI Spain UCITS ETF	MSCI Spain Index		Xetra (Deutsche Boerse)	
	iShares MSCI Spain ETF[b]	MSCI Spain 25/50 Index	NYSE Arca		
	Lyxor IBEX 35 (DR) UCITS ETF	IBEX 35		Bolsa de Valores de Madrid	
	Xtrackers Spain UCITS ETF	Solactive Spain 40 Index		Xetra (Deutsche Boerse)	
Sweden	iShares MSCI Sweden ETF[b]	MSCI Sweden 25/50 Index	NYSE Arca		
	iShares OMX Stockholm Capped UCITS ETF	OMX Stockholm Benchmark Cap Index		London Stock Exchange	
	Xact OMXS30 UCITS ETF	OMXS30 Index		Nasdaq Stockholm	
Switzerland	Amundi MSCI Switzerland UCITS ETF	MSCI Switzerland Index		Euronext Paris	
	Franklin FTSE Switzerland ETF	FTSE Switzerland Capped Index	NYSE Arca		
	iShares MSCI Switzerland ETF[b]	MSCI Switzerland 25/50 Index	NYSE Arca		
	iShares SMI ETF (CH)	Swiss Market Index (SMI)		SIX Swiss Exchange	
	UBS ETF (CH)—SMI	Swiss Market Index (SMI)		SIX Swiss Exchange	
	Xtrackers Switzerland UCITS ETF	Solactive Swiss LargeCap Index		Xetra (Deutsche Boerse)	
UK	Franklin FTSE United Kingdom ETF	FTSE UK Capped Index	NYSE Arca		
	iShares Core FTSE 100 UCITS ETF	FTSE 100 Index		London Stock Exchange	
	iShares MSCI United Kingdom ETF[b]	MSCI United Kingdom Index	NYSE Arca		
	Lyxor FTSE 100 UCITS ETF	FTSE 100 Index		Borsa Italiana	
	SPDR Solactive United Kingdom ETF	Solactive GBS United Kingdom Large & MidCap USD Index	NYSE Arca		

(continued)

Table A.1 (continued)

Country	Exchange-traded fund	Replicated index	Listed on[a]		
			Americas exchanges	EMEA exchanges	Asia-Pacific exchanges
	Vanguard FTSE 100 UCITS ETF	FTSE 100 Index		London Stock Exchange	
Panel C. Asia-Pacific					
Australia	BetaShares Australia 200 ETF	Solactive Australia 200 Index			ASX
	Franklin FTSE Australia ETF	FTSE Australia Capped Index	NYSE Arca		
	iShares MSCI Australia ETF[b]	MSCI Australia Index	NYSE Arca		
	iShares MSCI Australia UCITS ETF	MSCI Australia Index		London Stock Exchange	
	SPDR S&P/ASX 200 Fund	S&P/ASX 200 Index			ASX
	Vanguard Australian Shares Index ETF	S&P/ASX 300 Index			ASX
Hong Kong	Franklin FTSE Hong Kong ETF	FTSE Hong Kong Capped Index	NYSE Arca		
	Hang Seng Index ETF	Hang Seng Index			Hong Kong Stock Exchange
	iShares Core Hang Seng Index ETF	Hang Seng Index			Hong Kong Stock Exchange
	iShares MSCI Hong Kong ETF[b]	MSCI Hong Kong Index	NYSE Arca		
	Lyxor Hong Kong (HSI) UCITS ETF	Hang Seng Index		Borsa Italiana	
	Tracker Fund of Hong Kong	Hang Seng Index			Hong Kong Stock Exchange
Japan	Daiwa ETF TOPIX	TOPIX Index			Tokyo Stock Exchange
	iShares Core MSCI Japan IMI UCITS ETF	MSCI Japan Investable Market Index		London Stock Exchange	
	iShares MSCI Japan ETF[b]	MSCI Japan Index	NYSE Arca		

(continued)

Table A.1 (continued)

Country	Exchange-traded fund	Replicated index	Listed on[a]		
			Americas exchanges	EMEA exchanges	Asia-Pacific exchanges
	JP Morgan BetaBuilders Japan ETF	Morningstar Japan Target Market Exposure Index	EXN-CGM		
	Nikkei 225 ETF	Nikkei 225 Index			Tokyo Stock Exchange
	TOPIX ETF	TOPIX Index			Tokyo Stock Exchange
New Zealand	iShares MSCI New Zealand ETF[b]	MSCI New Zealand IMI 25/50 Index	NASDAQ		
	Smartshares NZ TOP 10 ETF	S&P/NZX 10 Index			NZX
	Smartshares NZ TOP 50 ETF	S&P/NZX 50 Portfolio Index			NZX
Singapore	iShares MSCI Singapore ETF[b]	MSCI Singapore 25/50 Index	NYSE Arca		
	Nikko AM Singapore STI ETF	Straits Times Index			Singapore Exchange
	SPDR Straits Times Index ETF	Straits Times Index			Singapore Exchange
	UBS ETF MSCI Singapore UCITS ETF	MSCI Singapore Index		SIX Swiss Exchange	
	Xtrackers MSCI Singapore UCITS ETF	MSCI Singapore IM Index			Hong Kong Stock Exchange

[a]Primary exchange or first place of listing (primary listing usually corresponds to the first listing). European ETFs are often cross-listed on European exchanges and sometimes on Asian and South American exchanges. American ETFs are often cross-listed on South American exchanges and sometimes on Asia-Pacific exchanges
[b]Options available as of end of 2018
Note Table presents a maximum 6 selected equity ETFs with exposure to a given country. Table includes only ETFs replicating large-cap and/or mid-cap indexes, and excludes small-cap indexes, sector indexes, smart-beta indexes, leveraged indexes, and short indexes. In situation, where there are more than 6 ETFs with exposure to a given market, the table presents funds with both relatively large exposure and large AUM, but their final choice is discretionary. List of exchange-traded funds is presented in alphabetical order
Classification of countries in the table is based on "MSCI Country Classification Standard" (as the end of June 2019). The list of developed markets consists of all countries belonging to MSCI World Index (MSCI World Index is a broad global equity index that represents large and mid-cap equity performance across 23 developed market countries and covers approximately 85% of the free float-adjusted market capitalization in each country). List of countries is presented in alphabetical order
Source Own elaboration

Table A.2 Selected single-country equity exchange-traded funds with emerging markets exposure (as of June 30, 2019)

Country	Exchange-traded fund	Replicated index	Listed on[a]		
			Americas exchanges	EMEA exchanges	Asia-Pacific exchanges
Panel A. Americas					
Argentina	Global X MSCI Argentina ETF	MSCI All Argentina 25/50 Index	NYSE Arca		
	iShares MSCI Argentina and Global Exposure ETF	MSCI All Argentina 25/50 Index	Cboe BZX		
Brazil	Franklin FTSE Brazil ETF	FTSE Brazil Capped Index	NYSE Arca		
	iShares Ibovespa Fundo de Índice	Ibovespa Index	B3 (Bovespa)		
	iShares MSCI Brazil ETF[b]	MSCI Brazil 25/50 Index	NYSE Arca		
	iShares MSCI Brazil UCITS ETF	MSCI Brazil Index		London Stock Exchange	
	Lyxor MSCI Brazil UCITS ETF	MSCI Brazil Index		Borsa Italiana	
	Xtrackers MSCI Brazil UCITS ETF	MSCI Brazil Index		Xetra (Deutsche Boerse)	
Chile	ETF It Now S&P IPSA	S&P IPSA Index	Bolsa de Santiago		
	iShares MSCI Chile ETF[b]	MSCI Chile IMI 25/50 Index	Cboe BZX		
Colombia	Fondo Bursátil iShares COLCAP	COLCAP Index	Bolsa De Valores De Colombia		
	Global X Colombia Select ETF	S&P Colombia Select Index	Bolsa de Valores de Colombia		
	Global X MSCI Colombia ETF	MSCI All Colombia Select 25/50 Index	NYSE Arca		
	iShares MSCI Colombia ETF	MSCI All Colombia Capped Index	NYSE Arca		
Mexico	Franklin FTSE Mexico ETF	FTSE Mexico Capped Index	NYSE Arca		
	iShares IPC LargeCap Total Return TRAC	S&P/BMV IPC LargeCap Index	Bolsa Mexicana de Valores (BMV)		

(continued)

Table A.2 (continued)

Country	Exchange-traded fund	Replicated index	Listed on[a]		
			Americas exchanges	EMEA exchanges	Asia-Pacific exchanges
	iShares MSCI Mexico Capped UCITS ETF	MSCI Mexico Capped Index		SIX Swiss Exchange	
	iShares MSCI Mexico ETF[b]	MSCI Mexico IMI 25/50 Index	NYSE Arca		
	iShares NAFTRAC	S&P/BMV IPC Index	Bolsa Mexicana de Valores (BMV)		
	Xtrackers MSCI Mexico UCITS ETF	MSCI Mexico Index		Xetra (Deutsche Boerse)	
Peru	iShares MSCI Peru ETF	MSCI All Peru Capped Index	NYSE Arca		
Panel B. Europe, Middle East and Africa (EMEA)					
Czechia	Expat Czech PX UCITS ETF	PX Index		Bulgarian Stock Exchange	
Egypt	EGX30 ETF	EGX30 Index		Egyptian Stock Exchange (EGX)	
	VanEck Vectors Egypt Index ETF	MVIS Egypt Index	NYSE Arca		
Greece	ALPHA ETF FTSE Athex LargeCap Equity UCITS	FTSE/Athex LargeCap Index		Athens Exchange	
	Expat Greece ASE UCITS ETF	Athex Composite Index		Bulgarian Stock Exchange	
	Global X MSCI Greece ETF	MSCI All Greece Select 25/50 Index	NYSE Arca		
	Lyxor MSCI Greece UCITS ETF	MSCI Greece IMI + Coca-Cola 20/35 Index		Euronext Paris	
Hungary	BUX ETF Fund	BUX Index		Budapest Stock Exchange	
	Expat Hungary BUX UCITS ETF	BUX Index		Bulgarian Stock Exchange	
Poland	Beta ETF WIG20TR	WIG20TR Index		Warsaw Stock Exchange	

(continued)

Table A.2 (continued)

Country	Exchange-traded fund	Replicated index	Listed on[a]		
			Americas exchanges	EMEA exchanges	Asia-Pacific exchanges
	Expat Poland WIG20 UCITS ETF	WIG20 Index		Bulgarian Stock Exchange	
	iShares MSCI Poland ETF[b]	MSCI Poland IMI 25/50 Index	NYSE Arca		
	iShares MSCI Poland UCITS ETF	MSCI Poland Index		London Stock Exchange	
	Lyxor WIG 20 UCITS ETF	WIG20TR Index		Warsaw Stock Exchange	
Qatar	Al Rayan Qatar ETF	QE Al Rayan Islamic Index		Qatar Exchange	
	iShares MSCI Qatar ETF	MSCI All Qatar Capped Index	NASDAQ		
	QE Index ETF	Qatar Stock Exchange Price Index		Qatar Exchange	
Russia	FinEx Russian RTS Equity UCITS ETF	RTS Index		Moscow Exchange	
	iShares MSCI Russia ADR/GDR UCITS ETF	MSCI Russia ADR/GDR Index		SIX Swiss Exchange	
	iShares MSCI Russia ETF[b]	MSCI Russia 25/50 Index	NYSE Arca		
	ITI Funds RTS Equity UCITS ETF	RTS Index		Moscow Exchange	
	Lyxor MSCI Russia UCITS ETF	MSCI Russia IMI Select GDR Index		Xetra (Deutsche Boerse)	
	VanEck Vectors Russia ETF	MVIS Russia Index	NYSE Arca		
Saudi Arabia	Falcom Saudi Equity ETF	F30 Falcom Saudi Equity Index		Saudi Stock Exchange Tadawul	
	Franklin FTSE Saudi Arabia ETF	FTSE Saudi Arabia Capped Index	NYSE Arca		
	HSBC MSCI Tadawul 30 Saudi ETF	MSCI Tadawul 30 Index		Saudi Stock Exchange Tadawul	
	Invesco MSCI Saudi Arabia UCITS ETF	MSCI Saudi Arabia 20/35 Capped Index		London Stock Exchange	

(continued)

Table A.2 (continued)

Country	Exchange-traded fund	Replicated index	Listed on[a] Americas exchanges	EMEA exchanges	Asia-Pacific exchanges
	iShares MSCI Saudi Arabia Capped UCITS ETF	MSCI Saudi Arabia 20/35 Index		London Stock Exchange	
	iShares MSCI Saudi Arabia ETF	MSCI Saudi Arabia IMI 25/50 Index	NYSE Arca		
South Africa	Franklin FTSE South Africa ETF	FTSE/JSE South Africa Capped Index	NYSE Arca		
	iShares MSCI South Africa ETF[b]	MSCI South Africa 25/50 Index	NYSE Arca		
	iShares MSCI South Africa UCITS ETF	MSCI South Africa Index		London Stock Exchange	
	Lyxor MSCI South Africa UCITS ETF	MSCI South Africa Index		Euronext Paris	
	Satrix 40 ETF	FTSE/JSE Top 40 Index		Johannesburg Stock Exchange (JSE)	
	Sygnia Itrix Top 40 ETF	FTSE/JSE Top 40 Index		Johannesburg Stock Exchange (JSE)	
Turkey	BIST30 ETF	BIST 30 Index		Borsa Istanbul	
	Dow Jones Istanbul 20 ETF	Dow Jones Turkey Titans 20 Index		Borsa Istanbul	
	HSBC MSCI Turkey UCITS ETF	MSCI Turkey Index		London Stock Exchange	
	iShares MSCI Turkey ETF[b]	MSCI Turkey IMI 25/50 Index	NASDAQ		
	iShares MSCI Turkey UCITS ETF	MSCI Turkey Index		London Stock Exchange	
	Lyxor MSCI Turkey UCITS ETF			Xetra (Deutsche Boerse)	
United Arab Emirates (UAE)	iShares MSCI UAE ETF	MSCI All UAE Capped Index	NASDAQ		

(continued)

Table A.2 (continued)

Country	Exchange-traded fund	Replicated index	Listed on[a]		
			Americas exchanges	EMEA exchanges	Asia-Pacific exchanges
Panel C. Asia					
China	ChinaAMC China 50 ETF	SSE 50 Index			Shanghai Stock Exchange
	Huatai-Pinebridge CSI 300 ETF	CSI 300 Index			Shanghai Stock Exchange
	iShares China LargeCap ETF[b]	FTSE China 50 Index	NYSE Arca		
	iShares FTSE A50 China Index ETF	FTSE China A50 Index			Hong Kong Stock Exchange
	iShares MSCI China ETF[b]	MSCI China Index	NASDAQ		
	Xtrackers MSCI China UCITS ETF	MSCI China Index		Xetra (Deutsche Boerse)	
India	iShares India 50 ETF[b]	Nifty 50 Index	NASDAQ		
	iShares MSCI India ETF[b]	MSCI India Index	Cboe BZX		
	Lyxor MSCI India UCITS ETF	MSCI Emerging Markets India (USD) Index		Euronext Paris	
	Reliance ETF Nifty BeES	Nifty 50 Index			National Stock Exchange (NSE)
	SBI—ETF Nifty 50	Nifty 50 Index			National Stock Exchange (NSE)
	UTI Nifty ETF	Nifty 50 Index			National Stock Exchange (NSE)
Indonesia	HSBC MSCI Indonesia UCITS ETF	MSCI Indonesia Index		London Stock Exchange	
	iShares MSCI Indonesia ETF[b]	MSCI Indonesia IMI 25/50 Index	NYSE Arca		
	Reksa Dana Premier ETF IDX30	IDX30 Index			Indonesia Stock Exchange (IDX)
	Reksa Dana Premier ETF LQ-45	LQ-45 Index			Indonesia Stock Exchange (IDX)

(continued)

Table A.2 (continued)

Country	Exchange-traded fund	Replicated index	Listed on[a]		
			Americas exchanges	EMEA exchanges	Asia-Pacific exchanges
	VanEck Vectors Indonesia Index ETF	MVIS Indonesia Index	NYSE Arca		
	Xtrackers MSCI Indonesia Swap UCITS ETF	MSCI Indonesia Index		London Stock Exchange	
Malaysia	FTSE Bursa Malaysia KLCI ETF	FTSE Bursa Malaysia KLCI Index			Bursa Malaysia
	iShares MSCI Malaysia ETF[b]	MSCI Malaysia Index	NYSE Arca		
	Lyxor MSCI Malaysia UCITS ETF	MSCI Malaysia Index		Xetra (Deutsche Boerse)	
	MyETF Dow Jones Islamic Market Malaysia Titans 25	Dow Jones Islamic Market Malaysia Titans 25 Index			Bursa Malaysia
	Next Funds FTSE Bursa Malaysia KLCI ETF	FTSE Bursa Malaysia KLCI Index			Tokyo Stock Exchange
	Xtrackers MSCI Malaysia UCITS ETF	MSCI Malaysia Index		Xetra (Deutsche Boerse)	
Pakistan	Global X MSCI Pakistan ETF	MSCI All Pakistan Select 25/50 Index	NYSE Arca		
	Xtrackers MSCI Pakistan Swap UCITS ETF	MSCI Pakistan Index		Xetra (Deutsche Boerse)	
Philippines	Fist Metro Philippine Equity ETF	Philippine Stock Exchange Index			Philippine Stock Exchange (PSE)
	iShares MSCI Philippines ETF[b]	MSCI Philippines Investable Market Index	NYSE Arca		
	KINDEX MSCI Philippines (Synth) ETF	MSCI Philippines Investable Market Index			Korea Stock Exchange (KRX)
	Xtrackers MSCI Philippines UCITS ETF	MSCI Philippines Investable Market Index		Xetra (Deutsche Boerse)	

(continued)

Table A.2 (continued)

Country	Exchange-traded fund	Replicated index	Listed on[a]		
			Americas exchanges	EMEA exchanges	Asia-Pacific exchanges
South Korea	Franklin FTSE South Korea ETF	FTSE South Korea Capped Index	NYSE Arca		
	iShares MSCI Korea UCITS ETF USD (Dist)	MSCI Korea Index		London Stock Exchange	
	iShares MSCI South Korea ETF[b]	MSCI Korea 25/50 Index	NYSE Arca		
	KB KBSTAR 200 Securities ETF	KOSPI 200 Index			Korea Stock Exchange (KRX)
	Mirae Asset TIGER 200 ETF	KOSPI 200 Index			Korea Stock Exchange (KRX)
	Samsung KODEX 200 ETF	KOSPI 200 Index			Korea Stock Exchange (KRX)
Taiwan	Franklin FTSE Taiwan ETF	FTSE Taiwan Capped Index	NYSE Arca		
	Fubon FTSE TWSE Taiwan 50 ETF	FTSE TWSE Taiwan 50 Index			Taiwan Stock Exchange (TWSE)
	iShares MSCI Taiwan UCITS ETF	MSCI Taiwan Index		London Stock Exchange	
	iShares MSCI Taiwan ETF[b]	MSCI Taiwan 25/50 Index	NYSE Arca		
	Xtrackers MSCI Taiwan UCITS ETF	MSCI Taiwan Index		Xetra (Deutsche Boerse)	
	Yuanta/P-shares Taiwan Top 50 ETF	FTSE TWSE Taiwan 50 Index			Taiwan Stock Exchange (TWSE)
Thailand	BCAP MSCI Thailand ETF	MSCI Thailand ex Foreign Board Index			Stock Exchange of Thailand (SET)
	BCAP SET100 ETF	SET100 Index			Stock Exchange of Thailand (SET)

(continued)

Table A.2 (continued)

Country	Exchange-traded fund	Replicated index	Listed on[a]		
			Americas exchanges	EMEA exchanges	Asia-Pacific exchanges
	iShares MSCI Thailand ETF[b]	MSCI Thailand IMI 25/50 Index	NYSE Arca		
	Lyxor MSCI Thailand UCITS ETF	MSCI Thailand Index		Xetra (Deutsche Boerse)	
	ThaiDex SET50 ETF	SET50 Index			Stock Exchange of Thailand (SET)
	Xtrackers MSCI Thailand UCITS ETF	MSCI Thailand Index		Xetra (Deutsche Boerse)	

[a]Primary exchange or first place of listing (primary listing usually corresponds to the first listing). European ETFs are often cross-listed on European exchanges and sometimes on Asian and South American exchanges. American ETFs are often cross-listed on South American exchanges and sometimes on Asia-Pacific exchanges
[b]Options available as of end of 2018
Note Table presents a maximum 6 selected equity ETFs with exposure to a given country. Table includes only ETFs replicating large-cap and/or mid-cap indexes, and excludes small-cap indexes, sector indexes, smart-beta indexes, leveraged indexes, and short indexes. In situation, where there are more than 6 ETFs with exposure to a given market, the table presents funds with both relatively large exposure and large AUM, but their final choice is discretionary. List of exchange-traded funds is presented in alphabetical order
Classification of countries in the table is based on "MSCI Country Classification Standard" (as the end of June 2019). The list of emerging markets consists of all countries belonging to MSCI Emerging Markets Index (MSCI Emerging Markets global equity index that represents large and mid-cap equity performance across 26 emerging market countries and covers approximately 85% of the free float-adjusted market capitalization in each country). List of countries is presented in alphabetical order
Source Own elaboration

Table A.3 Selected single-country equity exchange-traded funds with exposure on frontier markets and other markets (including countries belonging to MSCI Standalone Market Indexes) (as of August 31, 2019)

Country	Exchange-traded fund	Replicated index	Listed on[a] Americas exchanges	EMEA exchanges	Asia-Pacific exchanges
Panel A. Americas					
Jamaica	Sagicor Financial Select Fund	JSE Financial Index	Jamaica Stock Exchange		
Trinidad & Tobago	Calypso Macro Index Fund[b]	All T&T Index	Trinidad and Tobago Stock Exchange		
Panel B. Europe and CIS					
Bulgaria	Expat Bulgaria SOFIX UCITS ETF	SOFIX Index		Bulgarian Stock Exchange	
Croatia	Expat Croatia CROBEX UCITS ETF	CROBEX Index		Bulgarian Stock Exchange	
Iceland	Landsbréf—LEQ UCITS ETF	OMX Iceland 10 Cap Index		Nasdaq OMX Iceland	
Kazakhstan	FinEx FFIN Kazakhstan Equity ETF	KASE Index		Moscow Exchange	
North Macedonia	Expat Macedonia MBI10 UCITS ETF	MBI10 Index		Bulgarian Stock Exchange	
Romania	ETF BET Tradeville	BET Index		Bucharest Stock Exchange	
	Expat Romania BET UCITS ETF	BET Index		Bulgarian Stock Exchange	
Serbia	Expat Serbia BELEX15 UCITS ETF	BELEX15 Index		Bulgarian Stock Exchange	
Slovakia	Expat Slovakia SAX UCITS ETF	SAX Index		Bulgarian Stock Exchange	
Slovenia	Expat Slovenia SBI TOP UCITS ETF	SBI TOP Index		Bulgarian Stock Exchange	
Panel C. Africa					
Nigeria	Global X MSCI Nigeria ETF	MSCI All Nigeria Select 25/50 Index	NYSE Arca		
	Greenwich Alpha ETF	NSE 30 Index		Nigerian Stock Exchange	
	Lotus Halal Equity ETF	NSE Lotus Islamic Index		Nigerian Stock Exchange	

(continued)

Table A.3 (continued)

Country	Exchange-traded fund	Replicated index	Listed on[a]		
			Americas exchanges	EMEA exchanges	Asia-Pacific exchanges
	Stanbic IBTC ETF 30	NSE 30 Index		Nigerian Stock Exchange	
	The Siaml Pension ETF 40	Pension Index		Nigerian Stock Exchange	
	Vetiva Griffin 30 ETF	NSE 30 Index		Nigerian Stock Exchange	
Panel D. Middle East					
Kuwait	KMEFIC FTSE Kuwait Equity UCITS ETF	FTSE Kuwait All Cap 15% Capped Index		London Stock Exchange	
Panel E. Asia					
Bangladesh	Xtrackers MSCI Bangladesh Swap UCITS ETF	MSCI Bangladesh IMI		Xetra (Deutsche Boerse)	
Vietnam	Premia MSCI Vietnam ETF	MSCI Vietnam Index			Hong Kong Stock Exchange
	VanEck Vectors Vietnam ETF	MVIS Vietnam Index	Cboe		

[a]Primary exchange or first place of listing (primary listing usually corresponds to the first listing). European ETFs are often cross-listed on European exchanges and sometimes on Asian and South American exchanges. American ETFs are often cross-listed on South American exchanges and sometimes on Asia-Pacific exchanges
[b]Fund invests part of its assets in All T&T Index constituents, the remaining are invested mostly in ETF shares with exposure to global energy sector
Note Table presents a maximum 6 selected equity ETFs with exposure to a given country. Table includes only ETFs replicating large-cap and/or mid-cap indexes, and excludes small-cap indexes, sector indexes, smart-beta indexes, leveraged indexes, and short indexes. In situation, where there are more than 6 ETFs with exposure to a given market, the table presents funds with both relatively large exposure and large AUM, but their final choice is discretionary. List of exchange-traded funds is presented in alphabetical order
Classification of countries in the table is based on "MSCI Country Classification Standard" (as the end of June 2019). The list of frontier markets consists of all countries belonging to MSCI Frontier Markets Index (MSCI Frontier Markets Index is a broad global equity index that represents large and mid-cap equity performance across 28 frontier market countries and covers approximately 85% of the free float-adjusted market capitalization in each country). List of countries is presented in alphabetical order
Source Own elaboration

Table A.4 Description of GICS sectors, MSCI World sectors indexes, and providers of sector equity ETFs tracking MSCI World sectors indexes

Sector Number of industry groups/industries/ sub-industries	Description	Index (number of constituents[a])	Top 5 constituents[a]	Providers of sector ETFs[a]
Energy 1/2/7	It comprises companies engaged in exploration & production, refining & marketing, and storage & transportation of oil & gas and coal & consumable fuels. It also includes companies that offer oil & gas equipment and services	MSCI World Index (67)	Exxon Mobil (US), Royal Dutch Shell (GB), Chevron (US), Total (FR), BP (GB)	Amundi, Xtrackers, iShares, Lyxor, SPDR
Materials 1/5/17	It includes companies that manufacture chemicals, construction materials, glass, paper, forest products and related packaging products, and metals, minerals and mining companies, including producers of steel	MSCI World Materials Index (127)	Linde (New) (US), Air Liquide (FR), BHP Group (AU), Rio Tinto (GB), Air Products & Chemicals (US)	Xtrackers, Lyxor, SPDR
Industrials 3/14/25	It includes manufacturers and distributors of capital goods such as aerospace & defense, building products, electrical equipment and machinery and companies that offer construction & engineering services. It also includes providers of commercial & professional services including printing, environmental and facilities services, office services & supplies, security & alarm services, human resource & employment services, research & consulting services. It also includes companies that provide transportation services	MSCI World Industrials Index (271)	Union Pacific (US), Honeywell International (US), Lockheed Martin (US), Boeing (US), 3M (US)	Xtrackers, Lyxor, SPDR
Consumer Discretionary 4/11/29	It encompasses those businesses that tend to be the most sensitive to economic cycles. Its manufacturing segment includes automotive, household durable goods, leisure equipment, and textiles & apparel. The services segment includes hotels, restaurants and other leisure facilities, media production and services, and consumer retailing and services	MSCI World Consumer Discretionary Index (202)	Amazon.com (US), Home Depot (US), Toyota Motor (JP), McDonald's (US), LVMH Moet Hennessy (FR)	Xtrackers, iShares, Lyxor, SPDR

Sector Number of industry groups/industries/ sub-industries	Description	Index (number of constituents[a])	Top 5 constituents[a]	Providers of sector ETFs[a]
Consumer Staples 3/6/12	It comprises companies whose businesses are less sensitive to economic cycles. It includes manufacturers and distributors of food, beverages and tobacco, and producers of non-durable household goods and personal products. It also includes food & drug retailing companies as well as hypermarkets and consumer super centers	MSCI World Consumer Staples Index (121)	Nestle (CH), Procter & Gamble (US), Coca-Cola (US), Pepsico (US), Walmart (US)	Xtrackers, iShares, Lyxor, SPDR
Health Care 2/6/10	It includes healthcare providers & services, companies that manufacture and distribute healthcare equipment & supplies, and healthcare technology companies. It also includes companies involved in the research, development, production, and marketing of pharmaceuticals and biotechnology products	MSCI World Health Care Index (145)	Johnson & Johnson (US), UnitedHealth Group (US), Roche Holding Genuss (CH), Merck & Co (US), Pfizer (US)	Xtrackers, iShares, Lyxor, SPDR
Financials 3/7/17	It contains companies involved in banking, thrifts & mortgage finance, specialized finance, consumer finance, asset management and custody banks, investment banking and brokerage and insurance. It also includes Financial Exchanges & Data and Mortgage REITs	MSCI World Financials Index (248)	JPMorgan Chase & Co (US), Berkshire Hathaway (US), Bank of America (US), Wells Fargo & Co (US), HSBC Holdings (GB)	Amundi, Xtrackers, Lyxor, SPDR
Information Technology 3/6/13	It comprises companies that offer software and information technology services, manufacturers and distributors of technology hardware & equipment such as communications equipment, cellular phones, computers & peripherals, electronic equipment and related instruments, and semiconductors	MSCI World Information Technology Index (169)	Microsoft (US), Apple (US), Visa (US), Intel (US), Mastercard (US)	Xtrackers, iShares, Lyxor, SPDR

(continued)

Table A.4 (continued)

Sector Number of industry groups/industries/ sub-industries	Description	Index (number of constituents[a])	Top 5 constituents[a]	Providers of sector ETFs[a]
Communication Services 2/5/10	It includes companies that facilitate communication and offer related content and information through various mediums. It includes telecom and media & entertainment companies including producers of interactive gaming products and companies engaged in content and information creation or distribution through proprietary platforms	MSCI World Communication Services Index (104)	Alphabet (US), Facebook (US), Verizon Communications (US), AT&T (US), Disney (US)	Xtrackers, Lyxor, SPDR
Utilities 1/5/6	It comprises utility companies such as electric, gas, and water utilities. It also includes independent power producers & energy traders and companies that engage in generation and distribution of electricity using renewable sources	MSCI World Utilities Index (83)	NextEra Energy (US), Iberdrola (ES), Dominion Energy (US), Duke Energy (US), Southern Company (US)	Xtrackers, Lyxor, SPDR
Real Estate Sector 1/2/12	It contains companies engaged in real estate development and operation. It also includes companies offering real estate-related services and Equity Real Estate Investment Trusts (REITs)	MSCI World Real Estate Index (106)	American Tower (US), Crown Castle International (US), Prologis (US), Equinix (US), Digital Realty Trust (US)	-

[a]As of March 31, 2020

Note MSCI World sector indexes capture large- and mid-cap representation across 23 developed market countries

Source Own elaboration based on: MSCI (2020a), MSCI & S&P Global (2018), factsheets of MSCI sector indexes, MSCI (2020b)

References

MSCI. (2020a, January). *Global Industry Classification Standard (GICS) Methodology*. Guiding Principles and Methodology for GICS. https://www.msci.com/documents/1296102/11185224/GICS+Methodology+2020.pdf/9caadd09-790d-3d60-455b-2a1ed5d1e48c?t=1578405935658. Accessed 15 Mar 2020.

MSCI. (2020b). *Exchange Traded Products Based on MSCI Indexes*. ETFs, ETNs, Futures, Options. Q1 2020. https://www.msci.com/documents/1296102/15496518/msci-GLOBAL-ETFB-cbr-en.pdf/558414e6-3c6e-4763-6937-93171d849069. Accessed 13 Apr 2020.

MSCI & S&P Global. (2018). *Global Industry Classification Standard (GICS)*. https://www.msci.com/documents/1296102/11185224/GICS+Sector+definitions+Sept+2018.pdf/afc87e7b-bbfe-c492-82af-69400ee19e4f. Accessed 15 Mar 2020.

Index

T. Miziołek et al., *International Equity Exchange-Traded Funds*,
https://doi.org/10.1007/978-3-030-53864-4